The Manager
and the Modern
Internal Auditor

The Manager and the Modern Internal Auditor

A Problem-Solving Partnership

Lawrence B. Sawyer

amacom

A Division of American Management Associations

Library of Congress Cataloging in Publication Data

Sawyer, Lawrence B
  The manager and the modern internal auditor.

  Includes index.
  1. Management. 2. Auditing, Internal. I. Title.
HD38.S3188   658.4   79-656
ISBN 0-8144-5515-8

First Printing

To my Esther,
wife and friend

Preface

Modern internal auditors and managers have the same objective: the well-being and effectiveness of their organizations. To help achieve their objective, a special relationship must be created and maintained between them: a professional relationship. It must be one that is no different from that which exists between a lawyer and his client.

The lawyer evaluates his client's problems, provides guidance and instruction, and recommends a course of action, but he does not make decisions for his client. The modern internal auditor functions in the same way. He must carry out his responsibilities so that the manager will look upon him as a counselor and a problem-solving partner, not as an adversary or an object of fear and distrust. And he must maintain that relationship despite the fact that, as an internal auditor, he may ultimately report what he finds to levels above the manager.

The lawyer who is not thoroughly acquainted with his client's business and its goals, functions, and operations cannot provide an able, professional service. And modern internal auditors who do not understand the functions, responsibilities, theories, and practices of management cannot ably assist and counsel managers.

One of the purposes of this book, therefore, is to explore the profession of management so as to show internal auditors how to enlarge their service to their organizations by expanding their own approach to internal auditing. The internal auditor will find that his understanding of management principles and good business practice will help him further his highest aspiration: to be a part of executive management much as the organization's legal counsel is.

Identifying unsatisfactory conditions and making recommendations for improvement represent only two aspects of modern internal auditing. There are others. They include counseling those whose activities the auditors evaluate. And to carry out that responsibility, internal auditors must have thorough indoctrination in what modern management is all about. They must therefore have a working knowledge of the nature of management, the skills of management, and the process of management.

Both modern internal auditing and modern management are relatively young professions. Their flowering emerged in this century, which puts them in the budding stage, as professions go. And they are parallel functions. Indeed, I see them as symbiotic—as relying on each other for life support and effectiveness. It is time that they understand each other.

And so this book also seeks to acquaint modern managers with modern internal auditors and to cement a partnership that can become an effective, productive working relationship in all kinds of organizations. There is a need to broadcast the essential nature of that relationship; for when it flourishes in an organization, both the individual managers and their people stand to gain.

Managers can gain through objective analyses of operations of all kinds, through professional appraisals of control systems and performance, through recommendations that are designed to improve operations and enhance profits, and through suggestions for establishing policies, installing procedures, or tightening controls to reduce the possibility of errors, deviations from instructions, or intentional wrongdoing. Chiefly, they stand to gain through counsel on good business practices and the adherence to proven principles of management.

Moreover, there is useful information here for managers of small departments or small companies. The precepts directed toward internal auditors apply equally to such managers, who should be able to do for themselves what the internal auditor does for the managers of larger organizations.

This book brings together material on the principles of management that has been developed by respected writers and researchers. My focus has been on the relations between managers and internal auditors. But I have also sought to construct this book as a simply stated summary of management growth and principles for the following readers:

□ All people concerned with management, as a brief indoctrination to or refresher course in the principles of management.

- Executive managers, to show what a topflight internal audit team can do for them and for subordinate managers.
- Audit committees of boards of directors, to show how objective information can be obtained about internal and operating controls and how those controls are functioning.
- Operating managers, to show that internal auditors can be a help and not a carping hindrance.
- Working internal auditors, to show how the principles of management can be applied to their day-to-day jobs and to lay out a new dimension to their approach to internal auditing.
- Students of business administration, to show the inviting potentialities of the new and rewarding profession of internal auditing.
- Teachers of business administration, to point out hitherto little-known aspects of what many of them have regarded as merely a verification process.
- Candidates for the Certified Internal Auditing examination. Part 3 of that examination is devoted entirely to the principles of management.

The book is divided into three parts.

The first deals with the nature of internal auditing and of management. It is concerned with the development of internal auditing from the early beginnings, when internal auditors were employed chiefly to detect errors and fraud, up to the present management-oriented approach. It looks into the growth of modern management and at some of the people who developed the science of management. Finally, it explores management and management theories and shows how internal auditors deal with the various models of managers.

The second part deals with the skills of management. It speaks of how managers and internal auditors deal with people and emphasizes the patterns of behavior that occur at all levels of an enterprise. It is concerned with decision making and problem solving; how managers make decisions and how internal auditors can help them by making sure they are supplied with the information they need for rational decision making. It deals with communications and the results of poor communication. It has to do with measuring and evaluating performance and the forms of measurement available to managers and internal auditors. Finally, it explores the scientific methods available to both managers and internal auditors to carry out their jobs with greater precision.

The third and last part deals with the process of management: planning, organizing, directing, and controlling. It relates the process to both management and internal auditing. In Chapter 12, Controlling, it explores a new relationship which is now forming: that between the internal auditor and the board of directors.

With the exception of Chapter 1, which discusses the development of modern internal auditing, each chapter is divided into two parts. The first part deals with principles of management. The second part deals with the internal auditor's involvement with those principles—how he is now providing assistance to management in those fields and the opportunities awaiting him to expand that assistance.

I received help from a number of people in preparing this book. I should put Peter Drucker first. Although we did not communicate personally, his book *Management: Tasks, Responsibilities, Practices* gave me the inspiration for this one. I am especially indebted to Paul E. Heeschen and Rodney A. White, both Certified Internal Auditors and fellow teachers of my course in operations auditing, for their meticulous reviews of my drafts and their wise counsel.

I deeply appreciate the overall review by Dr. Victor Z. Brink, Professor Emeritus, Graduate School of Business, Columbia University. His background as a working internal auditor and a teacher of management principles made his critique especially valued and useful.

I am, as ever, hopelessly in debt to my wife, Esther, for her patience as I struggled with the manuscript, her perceptive reviews of the draft, and her help in typing my scribbled pages.

Lawrence B. Sawyer

Contents

PART I

Trends in Modern Internal Auditing and Professional Management

Management started in the beginning from the need to get things done. Modern internal auditing grew from management's need for help to do its job.

1

The Development
of Modern
Internal Auditing

The problem-solving partnership. Auditing rooted in antiquity. Growth during the Industrial Revolution. Internal auditing as a new profession. Analyzing operations. The definition of modern internal auditing. The difference between the auditor's and the manager's responsibilities. The internal auditor as a career professional. New behavioral patterns. The benefits of modern internal auditing. The teacher-counselor. Auditing and the functions of management. The auditor-investigator and custom-made frauds. The risk areas. The delicate appraisal of individuals.

The Partnership

The modern internal auditor and the professional manager are partners. Their roles in the partnership are different, but their goals are the same: to solve problems for the benefit of the organization, to prevent difficulties from happening, and to correct those that do

3

occur. The modern manager sees to it that things get done, come violence, strikes, floods, or disaster. The modern internal auditor helps the manager do his job effectively, efficiently, and economically.*

That is the basis for the manager–internal auditor problem-solving partnership. Each needs the other. Each helps the other. Each brings to the partnership a store of background, expertise, and professionalism. And the two can work together for the greater good of the organization because each fully understands the function and the potential of the other—the principles that guide him and the methods that smooth the way.

Unfortunately, the partnership is today a desideratum, not an accomplishment. The literature of modern internal auditing depicts wide scope and broad-gauged evaluations of all operations in both private and public organizations—the so-called operational audits— as a service to management. But that is only a hope in many organizations throughout the country in which managers have not yet learned to use the internal auditor's professional talents.

In speaking of working managers, as contrasted with textbook managers, Henry Mintzberg refers to the application of modern management techniques as folklore rather than fact.[1] His extensive surveys and studies of the work of people in management, from foremen to chief executives, showed that few managers had the time to either learn or use accepted management functions and principles. He found that half of the activities engaged in by five chief executives whose work he studied lasted less than nine minutes. Only 10 percent exceeded an hour. The 56 foremen in the United States whom he studied averaged 583 activities per 8-hour shift, an average of one activity every 48 seconds.

Mintzberg cites a study of the diaries of 160 British middle and top managers in which it was found that the managers worked for half an hour or more without interruption only about once every two days. He says that no study has found important patterns in the way managers schedule their time. They seem to jump from issue to issue, continually responding to the needs of the moment. None of the studies found the reflective planner and organizer; instead, the picture that emerged was of a frantic fire fighter.

Mintzberg does not deny that accepted management principles should be put to use. It is just that the harried, harassed manager

---

* In this book such words as "his" and "man" should be read as general terms, without any connotation of sex. The English language is unfortunately lacking in neutral substitutes.

does not have the time to learn and apply them during his daily combat in the arena. But that is an excuse, not a valid reason. The need for the principles is still there because, in my own experience in the field of internal auditing in both government and business, deficiencies in control and performance were invariably traceable to violations of accepted management principles and disregard of administrative techniques.

The expensive correction of defective conditions might often have been avoided had the basic principles been observed and the proper techniques been used. Indeed, the corrective action almost always invoked the application of proven management methodology.

This, then, brings compelling force to the concept of the problem-solving partnership. It underscores the need for the internal auditor to do more than compare one piece of paper with another for the sole purpose of bringing to light some random deviation from procedures or some violation of the rules of arithmetic. The time has come for the internal auditor to equip himself to be more than an after-the-fact critic and to become at last a counselor and adviser to the treadmilling problem-beset manager.

The world has taken a few spins since the first entrepreneur sought to gain a profit and the first tribal chieftain directed his people in their fight for survival. And the years are long past since the first slave tallied up his master's store of grain. Much of what was done then may still need doing. But a great deal more is necessary in today's complex environment if the manager and the internal auditor are to hold their heads above the underbrush and understand the terrain in which they function.

Both managers and internal auditors are members of relatively new professions. But the manager has the advantage of being known and accepted as a necessary part of every functioning entity. The word "manager" has an admirable and respected ring. The internal auditor is not so fortunate. He has long had a poor press. His title denotes, in many minds, a complete absorption in amounts and accounts. Only recently, with painful slowness, has he begun to emerge from his cocoon to take his place at the side of managers. It is important, then, in understanding the new partnership, to consider where the internal auditor has been, what he's doing now, and where he's headed in his partnership with management.

Internal Auditing—The Beginnings

Auditing has its roots in antiquity. In about 3600 B.C., according to records of an early Mesopotamian civilization, scribes used to prepare summaries of financial transactions.[2] The summaries were separate from the lists of amounts handled which others had prepared. Tiny marks, dots, and circles indicated the painstaking comparison of one record with another—marks that have survived the centuries and that auditors still use to tick off their verification of records. Here, perhaps, were born two control devices still used around the world: Divide duties. Provide for the review of another's work.

The Greeks, and the Romans after them, had an abiding regard for firm control over finances. There is evidence in their records of control devices such as the authorization of transactions and the auditing of records. The suspicious Greeks preferred slaves to freemen as accountants, however. Their reasons were logical, although their means may be deplored. They reckoned that a slave under torture could be considered more trustworthy than a freeman under oath.

With the development of paper and pen, transactions became easier to record and review. During the Roman empire, officials known as *quaestors* were assigned to examine the accounts of provincial governors. Toward the end of the Dark Ages, rulers wanted assurance that they would receive the revenues due them. So they provided for records and for audits of amounts due and received. The audits were first made by barons and justices. Later they were made by specially appointed officials.

The auditing function, as we know it now, started during the Industrial Revolution. Many commercial and industrial organizations employed expert accountants to examine and certify the validity of their accounts. Auditing spread. Even Columbus, in 1492, was accompanied to America by an auditor representing Queen Isabella.

In the United States the Comptroller General, head of the General Accounting Office, audits federal accounts and operations. He is responsible to the Congress and is independent of the executive branches he reviews. Most states conduct audits through comptrollers' offices. Many others, and municipalities as well, make use of independent accounting firms.

The General Accounting Office auditors have long performed so-called comprehensive audits in which they examine government operations for efficiency and economy and review program results to determine whether desired benefits have been achieved. A number of city and state audit teams have begun to follow their lead.

In practically all European countries there are government branches responsible for the review and appraisal of public accounts. In France it is the *cour des comptes*. In Germany it is the *Rechnungshof des deutschen Reiches*. In the British Isles the Exchequer and Audit Act of 1866 gave authority to the Crown to appoint a comptroller and an auditor general to examine the accounts that the various government departments prepare.

But the concern throughout the ages, still widespread today, has been with matters financial. The term "internal auditor" has been equated with "accountant." And although as an accountant the internal auditor is a strong and important adjunct to management, he does not reach his true potential in that role. He has other and more significant things to do in order to serve managers fully. That is because managers have other needs to fill, and those needs gave rise to the modern internal auditor.

Modern Internal Auditing—The New Profession

Modern internal auditing in the United States began to emerge in 1941. At that time the Institute of Internal Auditors was organized and internal auditing began to be regarded as a separate discipline. In that year, Victor Z. Brink wrote the first text on the subject, entitled *Internal Auditing*.[3] But the establishment of the institute heralded the birth of a hope, not a new profession. The profession still had a long way before it, yet the mileposts along the way describe a steady progress.

The first Statement of Responsibilities of Internal Auditors, published in 1947, said that internal auditing "deals primarily with accounting and financial matters but may also properly deal with matters of an operating nature." The umbilical cord tying the auditor to the books of account had not yet been cut. Accounting and financial matters still supplied the infant's primary sustenance. The first nick of the scalpel appeared 10 years later when the 1957 Statement, reflecting new approaches in some companies, said: "Internal auditing is an independent appraisal activity within an organization for the review of accounting, financial, and other operations."

Operational auditing was beginning to see the light of day, but it was still a part, and the lesser part, of accounting and financial auditing. The emergence of internal auditing as an overview of all operations in an organization and the tying off of the cord were signaled, finally, in the 1971 Statement, which said: "Internal auditing is an independent appraisal activity within an organization for the review of operations as a service to management." (See Appendix A at the end of this book.)

The words "accounting" and "financial" were dropped. The new Statement symbolized the internal auditor's equal concern with every aspect of his organization's functions. It regarded "operations" as embracing both the financial and the nonfinancial activities of the entity. The internal auditor's services were as applicable to the manager of the marketing branch as they were to the manager of the accounting branch.

Internal auditing was growing and expanding, but it still was not a profession. That came within reach with the development of a common body of knowledge, a code of ethics, standards, a growing body of literature, courses in the universities, a board of regents, an examination, and certification. The number of internal auditors in the United States and Canada who sat for the first four-part examination in August 1974 was 647, and 122 of them became certified internal auditors—harbingers of a new profession.[4]

Internal auditing has a scope and breadth that make it comparable with the other learned professions. Scope is hinted at by the subjects covered in the examination:

Principles of internal auditing
Internal auditing techniques
Principles of management
Disciplines relating to internal auditing
   Accounting
   Economics
   Law
   Finance
   Computer systems
   Quantitative methods

The knowledge required of the certified internal auditor must parallel that required of the modern manager. Each must bring to the partnership equal and complementary assets. Each must speak the other's language. Each must be prepared to pull his considerable weight in helping the enterprise meet its objectives.

Many companies make use of the modern internal auditor's skills in analyzing and appraising operations. And the results can be eye-opening. An actual example offers an illustration that is not unusual in the profession:

> The president of an airframe manufacturing firm was concerned about the costs being experienced in the production of a new model. He asked his internal auditors to organize a team that would follow an airplane through the assembly line. He wanted the team to live with that plane from the time it was only pieces of sheet metal, nuts, bolts, and wires until

the moment it flew over the fence. For six months the auditors studied blueprints, planning documents, production methods, quality control, and all the other diverse operations that go into making an airplane.

They came to know managers, supervisors, and production people. They proposed improvements. They suggested more efficient methods. They pointed out wasteful practices. They became accepted as a part of the working team because their reports were current, candid, and open to all who had an interest in what they were doing and accomplishing. They became accepted into a problem-solving partnership.

At the end of the production cycle, their hard dollar savings totaled $4,000,000. The value of improved coordination and cooperation, not to speak of enhanced safety in the production areas, was incalculable but significant. A specific example will indicate the operational audit approach.

One of the internal auditors noted that certain bolts and screws were tightened with torque wrenches. Such wrenches have gauges that show the twisting force applied in tightening a bolt, nut, or screw. He also noted that, when a torque wrench was used, an inspector was called to witness the torquing, or tightening, operation. There were about 2,200 bolts and 6,000 screws that had to be torque-wrench-tightened in the aircraft.

By making a swift mental calculation, the internal auditor could see an astronomical number of man-hours spent by inspectors in witnessing torquing operations. And that did not take into account the man-hours production workers spent in waiting when an inspector was not right on the spot.

So he discussed the matter with production, inspection, and engineering personnel and asked the classic audit question, Why? They told him that basic specifications called for torquing inspection if the required torque value—degree of tightness—exceeded 25 inch-pounds. The auditor did some more work and found that most of the bolts and screws he was interested in did not need any more than 20–25 inch-pounds of torque.

Then he called a conference of all concerned. He set forth his findings; he made his recommendations; and the evidence was compelling. The conferees looked into the matter and issued new torquing instructions. The saving in labor totaled $1,016,000.

Modern Internal Auditing Defined

Improvements such as those just discussed could not result from the thinking of an auditor whose mind was shackled to the books of account. The new kind of auditing is variously called operational auditing, management auditing, performance auditing, and comprehensive auditing. I like to refer to it as *modern internal auditing,* since it is a part of the entity and is as new as tomorrow. It is more than a discipline. It is also a state of mind; for it is doing what the president of the company or the head of the agency would do if he had the time and knew how.

My definition of this new brand of auditing is this: *Independent appraisals of the diverse operations and controls within an organization to determine whether acceptable policies and procedures are followed, established standards are met, resources are used efficiently and economically, planned missions are accomplished effectively, and the organization's objectives are being achieved.*

That definition addresses the modern internal auditor's opportunities as well as his responsibilities. It underscores, also, the management view, the view from the top.

- □ "Independent appraisals" suggests complete objectivity and a position within an organization that assures adequate consideration of and action on the auditor's findings and recommendations.
- □ "Diverse operations and controls" implies the access to all records, properties, and personnel relevant to the subject the auditor is reviewing.
- □ "Acceptable policies and procedures" indicates the auditor's responsibility for seeing that prescribed rules are workable and are in accord with organizational objectives; in short, that they make sense under current conditions and in the light of the entity's objectives.
- □ "Established standards are met" connotes reviewing for compliance with laws and regulations and encompasses the determination whether operations are properly conducted and reports are fairly presented.
- □ "Resources are used efficiently and economically" embraces the appraisal of the management of men, money, and materials and stresses the search for causes of any inefficiencies or uneconomical practices so that managers may correct them.
- □ "Planned missions" aims at the evaluation of program results— finding whether desired benefits are being obtained.
- □ "Objectives are being achieved" raises the auditor's sights to those of the managers at all levels of the organization; for the achievement of organizational objectives is the lodestar for all those who direct the destinies of the enterprise.

The Internal Auditor's and the Manager's Responsibilities

Responsibilities Compared

The internal auditor's responsibilities are, fundamentally, to review and appraise. The auditor has collateral responsibilities as well, and they will be touched on later. But his authority is limited to the responsibility granted him, and that authority does not reach to the functions of management. There is nothing in the Statement of Responsibility of Internal Auditors and nothing in the definition of modern internal auditing that implies or permits the auditor to usurp managerial authority. Indeed, the Statement says:

> In performing their functions, internal auditors have no direct responsibilities for nor authority over any of the activities reviewed. Therefore, the internal audit review and appraisal do not in any way relieve other persons in the organizations of the responsibilities assigned to them.

The functions over which managers are delegated authority and for which they are charged with both responsibility and accountability are as follows:

- □ *Planning.* To decide what should be done and how, when, where, and by whom it should be done, to establish organizational objectives and goals, and to prescribe policies, procedures, and rules.
- □ *Organizing.* To set up human relations and deploy resources within the organization so that objectives, goals, and plans can be met or carried out effectively and efficiently.
- □ *Directing.* To govern, lead, and motivate people within the organization to move in accordance with established plans toward the organization's objectives.
- □ *Controlling.* To provide the means needed to see that directed action is performed or planned so that desired objectives will be achieved.

Those are the tasks and responsibilities of the manager, not of the internal auditor. But the internal auditor has a duty to know the functions of management as thoroughly as the manager does. He is not responsible for carrying them out, but he is responsible for understanding them so that he can complement the work of the manager.

The Internal Auditor's Functional Authority

As we indicated earlier, the internal auditor has responsibilities that are collateral to his basic responsibility for review and appraisal. The higher he moves in his profession and the greater his acceptance in his organization, the more significant those responsibilities become. The added responsibilities include counsel and guidance.

The internal auditor is a member of staff, not line. He is relieved of line decisions; but not of staff responsibilities. Those responsibilities are a natural attribute of what Peter Drucker calls the "career professional."[5] The career professional produces ideas and information, and he has as much authority and responsibility for his product as the engineer has for blueprints. His task is to counsel and guide managers, improve standards, and search for new horizons. He receives the functional authority to carry out his task directly from the chief executive officer. And when he properly exercises his authority, he is in effect speaking for the chief executive.

Within the purview of his functional authority, as monitor of the organization's controls, the internal auditor may inform managers that controls are inadequate or ineffective and then make sure that the control system is improved. He should not prescribe the precise controls to be installed; for then he would have to stand as sponsor for them. But he should be authorized to pass upon their adequacy.

That is nothing new. Functional authority has been recognized and carried out for years in every large organization. In technical and professional areas, the organization could not operate effectively if that authority did not exist. For example, as Peter Drucker points out:[6]

The quality control engineer in a machine tool company has no command authority over production people; he does decide the design and structure of the manufacturing process. The manufacturing manager makes the decision, but the quality control man can veto it within the orbit of his professional scope and competence.

The tax accountant gives no orders, but his opinion on the tax consequences of a course of action often sets the pattern for what a company can do and how it must do it.

The industry specialist in a large commercial bank does not make loans; in other words, he does not make the "line decisions." But he is personally responsible for deciding whether the bank should expand or contract its lending to retail stores. He makes the decisions on what the criteria for loans to stores should be. And he can pick up the phone and tell the lending officer—who may outrank him—that a loan should be called or cut back. The lending officer, without feeling that his authority is being undercut, will follow the specialist's recommendations.

The attorney in the general counsel's office has no authority over the director of purchasing. Yet the director would be very upset if his buyers failed to send a contract to the attorney for approval of its terms and compliance with organization policy before it was signed.

Each of these people has a particular professional product to sell to managers: quality, tax advice, special information on loans, and legal counsel. The modern internal auditor, in his expanding role, has several products to sell to managers. There is the traditional one of control. As the voice of the chief executive, he has the broader responsibility of offering counsel on the practices and techniques of management when he sees that violations of basic management principles are causing difficulties. Obviously, some managers will resent the internal auditor's assuming a mantle of omniscience in their special preserves. And if that is the mantle the internal auditor assumes, the resentment he encounters will be deserved. But for years the internal auditor has had to sell his products. He should have no difficulty selling a new one if it is of value to the consumer.

He should know by now that it is better to counsel than to direct; it is better to explain than to order; it is better to teach than to serve ultimatums; it is more productive to sell than to tell. If his facts are right, if his vision is high, if his product is needed, and if he carries the bearing of a knowledgeable, professional counselor, managers will buy his product.

The New Face of Internal Auditing

In 1922, Elbert Hubbard wrote a brief essay called "The Buyer." It appeared in Volume VIII of *Selected Writings of Elbert Hubbard,* published in 1922 by Roycrofter's Press. The terms used to describe a buyer have over the years been adapted to define an auditor. The definition that evolved is as follows:

> The typical auditor is a man past middle age, spare and wrinkled, intelligent, cold, passive, noncommittal, with eyes like codfish, polite in contact, but at the same time unresponsive, calm and as damnably composed as a concrete post or plaster-of-paris cast; a human petrification with heart of feldspar and without charm, minus bowels, passion, or a sense of humor. Happily, they never reproduce, and all of them finally go to hell.

And this, the aspect of the dour faultfinder, has constantly haunted the internal auditor. The growth of modern internal auditing and its stress on cooperation between auditor and auditee prompted the Institute of Internal Auditors to commission a research study on the subject to be carried out by Frederic E. Mints.[7]

The study was concerned with the patterns of behavior that affect auditors, those whose work they audit, and the audit product. Carried out in both the laboratory and the field, the study gave substance to what was previously intuitive conjecture. It showed that the brilliant but antagonistic auditor could unerringly put his finger on waste and inefficiency—within the areas of his competence—but that his methods sharply reduced the chances for improving conditions. The faultfinder had a technically excellent product, but not everybody wanted to buy it.

The modern internal auditor, with the charm, compassion, and sense of humor lacking in the definition of "the typical auditor," performed a more effective audit. He received cooperation. His path was cleared. His product was bought. He may not have exceeded his dour counterpart in cold, hard, analytical ability, but his willingness to cooperate and consider the auditee's point of view made his work more productive.

One part of the research study called for field audits made by separate teams of auditors. The teams made roughly similar audits, but their styles varied with their personalities and training. Some used a participative approach; others used the traditional adversary approach. Audit teams from four large companies—the Monsanto Company, Agway, Inc., Honeywell, Inc., and the B. F. Goodrich Company—participated in the research studies.

The audit results were later evaluated and reported on by the directors of internal auditing for the several teams. In addition, questionnaires evoked the auditees' views on the styles of audits. The participative approach won hands down in terms of auditor-auditee relations and audit results. One internal audit director reported that a competent adversary-minded auditor had made some excellent, cost-saving recommendations but that the auditor's attitude had been so antagonistic that the operating manager absolutely refused to listen to his recommendations. The manager's antagonism toward the auditor counterbalanced his desire to improve his own operation.

Some of the views of the auditees, as reported in the research study, are indicative of the results of the different audit approaches. Here are several excerpts:[8]

Traditional Approach

The group being audited does not fully trust auditors. Past experience has shown that if they [the group] talk too much they may talk themselves into a "grave." The group [of auditors] that visited this plant was of this type. If it were somehow possible to have more trust in each other, the audit would be most beneficial. But when a group of auditors swarms down upon a department the natural inclination seems to be: "Don't tell them anything because it may come back to haunt you."

My peers informed me that Auditor B was devious and obviously trying to "brainwash." He was given only the barest information after this became apparent.

I think we had the unfortunate experience of having one of the most obnoxious, theoretical clods I have ever met, on the team. He was a dominant factor to the other members.

Could be a valuable service if the personnel involved were more knowledgeable, mature, and objective.

The big problem is that they really don't know the business—the job has to be more than a bean-counting function . . . the type of person is the key to making this a positive, not a negative.

Participative Approach

There was no doubt in our minds that they were sincere in their objective to assist us and the general impression is that this has been a very beneficial exercise for all concerned.

I was very impressed that this group was only interested in helping and did not get the impression that their jobs depended on making a damaging analysis.

The team used here was a very positive, helpful group. I consider them professional in every way. Armed with very little knowledge of this product on the way in, they gained [it] to an extent that, with very few exceptions, all interim recommendations were accepted.

I wish I could use this group more often . . . that they had additional time to spend with me.

Their thoroughness is helpful in giving us an overall opinion on how we are operating. They take time to do surveys which we in management never find the time to do.

There has been a noticeable shift over the past three years towards the audits being more helpful, and away from the policing, prosecuting atmosphere that previously had been my experience.

As these comments indicate, the internal auditor must place more and more stress on human relations, participative auditing, and the problem-solving partnership. He must recognize, as he leaves the security blanket of accounting functions, that he needs help in understanding esoteric operations—esoteric to him, not to the operating personnel. He knows he will have to learn new terms and new concepts and that he will have to speak new languages.

Time does not permit him to equip himself on his own for those jobs. He'll go much farther and faster if he has help. And he is beginning to learn that there may be a hand to grasp if he reaches for it first.

Many internal auditors look with suspicion on the cooperative approach. They see their role as protecting company assets, and the executives in their companies see it that way too. Within certain risk areas in an organization there is much to be said for the hypercritical review. Cash, securities, and inventories offer many temptations. And they must be guarded and audited carefully. But that is another subject, and it will be discussed more fully later in this chapter.

The Benefits of Modern Internal Auditing

Modern internal auditing, of nonaccounting functions especially, is more efficient than the classic compliance approach. It tends to get to the heart of an operation without waiting for the tedious testing of numerous transactions. The understanding of management principles and related administrative controls offers an open sesame that parts the stone doors more effectively than blasting through the rock.

The traditional audit approach is to review procedures and instructions and then check whether the rules were followed. The modern internal audit approach is to survey the entire operation by identifying objectives, determining standards, discussing operations with people, applying a knowledge of management techniques, and then zeroing in on the problem areas.

The second approach is obviously more effective. And it can work. The story of an actual audit of a sales promotion department provides an illustration of first the traditional approach and then the modern internal audit approach.

The sales promotion department was responsible for programs to bring the company's products to the public's attention. It conceived sales promotion projects, purchased promotional materials, procured sales aids, and distributed samples.

An experienced internal auditor, accustomed to obtaining audit results solely by the test of transactions, was assigned to the audit. He made detailed tests of the inventories of promotional materials: pens, knives, desk sets, radios, and the like, all of superior quality. He made extensive reviews of the orders for such products. He tested large quantities of the receipts and the inventory records. Here were two of his findings:

1. There were wide differences between the quantities of promotional materials shown by the inventory records and the actual stock on hand. The differences indicated extensive losses. During his tests of transactions, the auditor learned that one employee had complete control over ordering, receiving, storing, issuing, and recording materials. He also learned that a number of people had keys to the storeroom.
2. Most of the models and products used in sales promotion projects were ordered by the manager of the department directly from suppliers. No competition was engaged in, and no purchase orders were issued for the purchases. The supplier's invoices were paid under a system known as executive approvals. The manager signed the invoices, and the accounts payable department, which had a copy of his signature on hand for comparison, then authorized payment.

The internal auditor, by dint of his testing, had done an adequate audit job. But he had difficulty convincing the manager and the manager's manager that corrective action was needed; he had not been able to explain cause and effect in language they could understand. His methods were inefficient and unproductive.

In contrast, here is how an experienced modern internal auditor would have approached the same job.

1. He would have surveyed the system and the controls over promotional materials before embarking on extensive tests of transactions. He would have been concerned immediately with the violation of two management principles:
   a. No one person should have complete control over a significant operation. The employee handling the promotional stock should not have been permitted both to order and to receive—both to disburse and to record the disbursements. Such a violation permits undetected peculations and invariably leads to trouble.
   b. Whoever is charged with responsibility must have concomitant authority. If the employee is charged with safeguarding the assets—

the promotional materials—he should have the authority and the means for carrying out his responsibilities: control over access to the storeroom. Other employees should not have duplicate keys.

2. The executive approval system would have immediately alerted him to the risks. The purchasing organization had abdicated its responsibility for being the sole source for commitment of company funds. Permitting that responsibility to be taken over by an operating department asks for kickbacks and for unsavory relations with suppliers.

3. The internal auditor would have had an immediate meeting with all concerned in which he would have pointed out the risks, the causes, and the probable effect in language his audience could understand. Corrective action would most likely have been instituted promptly, and the audit would have been carried out more economically.

But beyond the review of sales promotion "housekeeping" functions, the modern internal auditor would have included in his audit program the search for answers to questions such as these:

- Are all sales promotion projects reviewed and approved at the appropriate management levels?
- Are budgets and estimates for all projects prepared and approved?
- Is there an adequate system for reporting actual costs and scheduled milestones?
- Are price-reduction deals reviewed for compliance with controlling statutes?
- Are promotional goods shipped to dealers in proper proportion to purchased goods?
- Is there a proper relation between quantities of sales promotion coupons redeemed and related sales?
- Are house-to-house distributions of free samples properly supervised?
- Are free samples properly marked?
- What means are employed to make sure that promotions are actually accomplished?

The Internal Auditor as a Teacher

The Need

The internal auditor's role as teacher is little known, insufficiently practiced, and generally not believed or accepted. Mints, during his research study on behavioral patterns, asked a representative group of operating managers how they regarded the internal auditor: as teacher, policeman, prosecuting attorney, or in some other light.[9] Only 11 percent regarded the internal auditor as teacher. The blame must be laid at the door of the internal auditor himself. Clearly, if a customer won't buy a seller's wares—his ability to teach and counsel— it is not the customer who can be faulted. Somehow the seller has not conveyed the value of his product, what needs it will fill, and how it will benefit the customer. It does not matter that the customer has lost out by refusing to buy a useful product. A sale has not been consummated. And probably at the bottom of the difficulty is the fact that the seller has not sold himself.

The internal auditor of today has a long road to trudge before his 11 percent rating as a teacher creeps up to a passing grade. He must change his attitude. He must equip himself properly. He must show a new aspect and demeanor. He must learn the operating people's language. And he must sell himself and his expertise. Above all, he must desperately want to do all those things.

Becoming a teacher, practicing teaching, and obtaining results do wonders for the operating manager, the internal auditor, and the organization in which they both work. All stand to gain. The middle manager, usually an elevated technician rather than a master of business administration, needs the internal auditor's tutoring most. At that level he is usually beset, harried, and harassed by day-to-day problems of production, schedules, costs, safety, union grievances, and ecology and the hundreds of other vexing annoyances that sit at the foot of his bed when he goes to sleep and await him when he arises. He has little time to study or contemplate management principles—principles that could save him administrative headaches and that could help him set and meet meaningful goals.

A Solution

It is at that level that the internal auditor, after finding defective conditions, could say to him:

"Mr. Manager, despite all the good intentions in the world, things don't always go according to plan, no matter what the operation is. In addition, the technical expert, such as you are, may not have experience in dealing with administrative details. Yet such details are central to a smooth-running organization. Some managers wait for the internal auditor to pick up deviations from procedures, ineffective controls, and the like. But the internal auditor comes around only at intervals—sometimes long intervals. And, in the meantime, tiny cracks can appear and may develop into wide fissures by the time the internal auditor shows up. That really doesn't have to happen.

"Please let me show you how you yourself, with the aid of your people, can periodically evaluate your own operations, detect the little problems, and keep them from becoming big ones. Then the internal auditor, when he visits you and sees the results of your regular program of appraisal, can reduce the time he spends in your shop.

And believe me, if it is properly done, such a program isn't burdensome or time-consuming. In fact it is a time-saver, because it substitutes fire prevention for fire fighting. And fire fighting is a costly process."

An illustration, based on an actual audit, will show the benefits of such an approach.

> The tool control department in a manufacturing company was subject to periodic audit. People in the department maintained records of all "project tools"—that is, all the tools other than small hand tools used to build parts and assemblies. The department stocked the tools, disbursed them on request, maintained them, and safeguarded them.

> The tools and their records ran into the thousands. The procedures and job instruction were adequate, but they weren't being followed in a great number of instances. The internal auditor came up with dozens of deficiency findings. Each one of the findings was significant in terms of safeguarding important company assets, because if project tools weren't available, or if the records of their location were not accurate, the results could be either stoppage of a production line or duplicate purchases of some expensive tools.

> When the auditor presented his findings at an exit conference, following the end of the audit, the department manager was aghast at the number and seriousness of the defects. Any doubts were brushed aside by the abundant evidence presented. The manager had not been aware of the difficulties because his people had been working like Trojans to keep production going despite inadequate records.

> The manager must have had an inkling, but it was not until he was shown chapter and verse that he awoke to the enormity of his problem. And so he was ready for counsel. He was prepared to accept the auditor as a teacher. The auditor suggested that the manager incorporate the more significant instructions in a checklist, give a copy of the checklist to each of his three supervisors, and instruct them as follows:

> □ Take random samples every three months of records or tools or both and verify compliance with procedures.
> □ Show the results of their tests and any needed corrective action on copies of the checklists.
> □ Sign and date the completed checklists and give them to the department manager.

> The department manager would review the checklists and make sure that everything that should have been done was done. Then he would initial and date the completed checklists as evidence of his review. Finally, he would file the lists for subsequent review and for analysis of trends to see whether operations were improving or deteriorating.

With all the defects he had just seen, the manager was ripe for counsel and accepted it. He asked for assistance in developing the checklist, and the auditor gladly gave it. The system was put into effect and was followed formally and regularly.

A year later the auditor returned for a follow-up review. He found the operation running as smooth as silk. The records were accurate and up to date. The tools were stored where they were supposed to be stored. There was adequate evidence of tool inspection and of prompt repairs when needed. And there was one strange coincidence that proved the case for self-conducted evaluations.

When the internal auditor reviewed the checklist for completeness, he observed that, for some reason, a significant procedure had not been incorporated. It was an apparent oversight. The internal auditor, of course, made a fairly intensive test of compliance with that particular procedure and, sure enough, he found a number of deviations. When the internal auditor brought the matter to the manager's attention, the manager promptly revised his checklist.

The audit report downplayed those deviations and included well-deserved praise for the good job of management the manager was performing. But the most heartwarming result was the manager's new attitude toward the internal auditors. He accepted them as counselors and teachers. He became the internal auditor's staunchest champion in the production division.

Opportunities for Improved Service

Some skeptics may feel that, by recommending self-conducted evaluations, the internal auditor might work himself out of a job. But that is just not true. He would become able to reserve his talents for the more challenging tasks that he is capable of performing. It is much better from the organization's standpoint for the operating manager to check his own system of control regularly, knowledgeably, and formally. Then the control system would work well *all* the time; not only when the internal auditor showed up to point out defects.

Here is another example. Time was when all internal auditors reconciled bank account balances with the books of account. But that's an administrative detail—an essential one, of course—best done by the people in the general accounting department. The internal auditor is still responsible for seeing that the reconciliations are done regularly and completely, but he does not have to do them himself. More and more internal auditors are taking that approach, and everybody benefits. The internal auditor has not run out of a job because of it. He has merely lifted his sights and is able to devote his time, energy, imagination, and considerable skills to more serious and significant problems.

Instead of checking the accuracy of filing, he can spend his time figuring out whether the filing systems will best carry out the objectives of the department using them. Instead of checking one piece of paper against another, he can try to figure out whether all that paper is necessary. In the case of the tool control department, the auditor was able to devote his time to such matters as the manager's relations with the production organization, the tooling organization, and the purchasing organization. That was where the auditor was able to find some serious roadblocks that could not have been detected by concentrating on administrative details.

A Career Professional

By raising his own standards and by equipping himself to become an expert on the principles of management, the internal auditor can feel comfortable in his role as teacher and counselor. He can stand with assurance on the same level as his problem-solving partner, the manager. Indeed, some students of management feel that the term "manager" should not be reserved exclusively for those who direct the output of workers.[10] They believe that it may also be applied to anyone who has a responsibility for contributing to organizational objectives and producing results. Function, rather than power, has to be the distinctive criterion of who is a manager. And under the broad umbrella of "manager" may come both the leaders of others and such "career professionals" as modern internal auditors.

The Internal Auditor as a Problem-Solving Partner

The role of the teacher and counselor is many steps up the ladder that will take the modern internal auditor to his rightful position in the councils of management. The role is usually played in fields where the internal auditor has sufficient background to make his own appraisals and offer constructive, knowledgeable recommendations. But there are other fields, equally in need of the internal auditor's services, that are highly professional and are beyond his technical proficiency.

Here there must be an amalgam of professional ability and internal audit methodology, technical competence and managerial competence, teamwork involving the manager-technician and the management-oriented internal auditor. In such an environment the self-appraisal technique is desirable, but it must be closely guided by the internal auditor to achieve credibility, objectivity, and independence. It calls for a combination of mutual respect, a willingness to work together, and complementary objectives. It functions best when the relation between auditor and auditee is founded on openness, candor, and a clear understanding of the responsibilities of each of the partners to the undertaking. It makes use of the preliminary survey—a powerful internal audit tool used to obtain an overview of an operation. But under the problem-solving partnership it calls upon the auditee to provide the information, not for the internal auditor to dig it up. The results are self-analysis, the best form of analysis, and self-control, the best form of control.

That use of the preliminary survey has been tried in a number of organizations, including government agencies, with considerable success. One example, in which the author was involved, was of particular interest because the author was the only professional auditor on the audit team. The other team members were engineers who carried out the audit under the general guidance of the professional internal auditor.

Three engineers in a large manufacturing company had been assigned by the company's chief executive officer to answer some questions about a research and development function within the company. And these were hard questions:

□ Is the R&D division staffed for and capable of doing research and development work?
□ Is the work essential?
□ Is the work productive?
□ Are the people technically competent?
□ Is the division husbanding and deploying its resources prudently?
□ Is anything of value coming out of expenditures for R&D work?

Those were not easy questions to answer, and the three engineers, competent enough in their own field, saw the need for an understanding of modern internal audit methodology. So the author was engaged to provide a crash course in that methodology and to advise on the audit approach.

It was made clear to the audit team that evaluations call for measurements and that measurements demand standards; those are basic internal audit rules. So the first step was to devise a set of standards of excellence for the development activity. The standards were compiled by combing available literature and interrogating engineers and scientists in other research organizations.

The results were some 40 to 50 standards by which the R&D division's work would be measured. The standards were closely related to management principles, and they included matters such as these:

◻ The objectives and goals for the development organization should be reduced to writing and should be clearly understood by those doing the work.

◻ The technological requirements for the research and development work should be identified, and the personnel responsible for the work should have the requisite knowledge and skills in their technologies.

◻ The work should contribute to cost reductions and profit enhancement.

◻ R&D managers should be provided with adequate systems of financial control that would assist them in accomplishing their goals and missions within allocated budgets.

Having established their standards, the audit team met with the director of R&D and asked for his views on the list of criteria they had developed. The list was accepted as satisfactory. Then the director was asked to engage in a partnership with the audit team whereby both auditors and R&D managers would constitute themselves as a sort of committee of the whole to carry out the audit objectives. The director agreed.

The auditors then developed a questionnaire, based on the standards, which would be answered by the R&D managers. In developing the questionnaire, the auditors had two concerns: They wanted the questionnaire to be raised to the management level. They wanted to be sure that the answers to the questions would be responsive, accurate, and capable of being verified. They found the answers to those concerns in these approaches:

◻ The questions would be listed under the generally accepted management functions of planning, organizing, directing, and controlling.

◻ While there might always be a question whether an item was being categorized with strict accuracy, that was less important than demonstrating the management view.

◻ Under each question there would be a sample answer—not necessarily the correct answer—which would guide the respondent along the path the auditors wished and which would provide for documentation of the answer, the sort of documentation that would add validity to the answer and that could be verified.

The questions looked something like this:

Planning. What are the objectives and goals of the R&D division?

Example

Our objectives are to design new products, to develop new uses for existing products, and to improve products in use. Our goal for 1976 is to design two new, patentable products.

Organizing. What are the basic technologies required for development work within the R&D division? What special skills and knowledge should an individual have if he is assigned to R&D work in each of these technologies?

Example

See the attached job descriptions for the positions in the development group.

Directing. What action is taken to encourage open and frank exchanges of information and to motivate creative thinking?

Example

"Rap" sessions are held on development projects, and in them each person is encouraged to participate and contribute ideas. See copy of minutes for session held 2/13/75. See also agenda for next session.

Controlling. What forms of feedback are used to help managers see that goals are accomplished within allocated budgets? Who is responsible for deciding on the size of the budget, and what input is used to help in making the decisions?

Example

Status reports at key milestones. Recommendations for specific action to recover from unfavorable trends. See copy of report dated 2/27/76. Executive committee sets budget based on proposals identifying budget elements. See copy of budget proposal for 1976.

The audit team set a schedule for the review of the questions and the development of the answers. The questionnaire would be given to the director for his review; the audit team wanted to be sure that the director would be involved in the survey. Having approved the questionnaire, the director would parcel copies out to the appropriate managers, who would complete them within a week and return them. The director would review the responses and pass them on to the auditors.

On the appointed day the director gave the audit team the answers to the questionnaires. The results exceeded the most optimistic expectations. All the questions were answered with specificity. Documents supported and validated many of the responses. The participation was complete and wholehearted. Subsequent questions of the operating managers gave evidence that the managers had welcomed the opportunity for a structured, well-planned, self-analysis of their operations; that the audit has had a cleansing, fine-tuning effect.

The remainder of the audit moved with dispatch. Many of the questions that would have required exhaustive work on the part of the auditors had been answered, documented, and rendered easy to verify. When responses hinted at problems, the audit proceeded to those areas without fumbling or backing and filling.

There were further benefits from the problem-solving partnership. The audit disclosed a number of areas in which improvement was needed.

And the auditee became as concerned with prompt effective action as the auditors were.

This form of auditing, by reason of its efficiency and effectiveness, must become a part of the audit inventory. It has much to recommend it and little to deplore. But, as we shall now discuss, there may be areas within an organization that do not lend themselves to participative auditing.

The Other Face of Internal Auditing: Detection and Investigation

The concept of a problem-solving partnership does not imply that the modern internal auditor must be a perennial "nice guy" who is all sweetness and light no matter what the circumstances. The partnership should extend upward beyond the operating people and the operating managers. Executives bear a solemn responsibility for the stewardship of the organization's resources. And the Statement of Responsibilities of Internal Auditors holds the auditor responsible for "Ascertaining the extent to which the company assets are accounted for and safeguarded from losses of all kinds."

The internal auditor should employ openness and candor in his regular assignments. That approach is beneficial for his clients, his audit objectives, and himself. But, as the lawyers say, "Fraud vitiates everything," and to engage in a problem-solving partnership with a villain is ludicrous on its face. Hence, to carry out his responsibility for safeguarding and accounting for entity assets—which include the resources of men, money, and materials—the auditor may have to engage in some investigative activities. We shall discuss those phases of the internal auditor's work under the heads of fraud investigations and evaluations of people.

Fraud Investigations

It must be made abundantly clear that the internal auditor does not bear and cannot be charged with the unlimited responsibility for the prevention and detection of fraud in his organization. There is the notion in some quarters that the internal auditor should be regarded as the scapegoat for all the evils of fraud, embezzlement, and peculation that can befall an organization.[11]

That is a completely unwarranted notion. Illegal and improper actions are infinite in their variety: conflicts of interest involving members of the board of directors and suppliers of services, embezzlement in the treasurer's office, kickbacks to buyers, thefts from inventories, hands in the petty cash box, under-the-table agreements with scrap dealers, collusion between suppliers and inspectors, mutually beneficial arrangements between public relations people and advertising agencies, truck drivers who drop off products to their associates in crime, company officials holding financial interests in supplier organizations, branch managers manipulating inventories to make their records look good to the home office, and wizards in the data processing department who can make the computer jump through hoops for their own gain. The possibilities of such improprieties are omnipresent, and the internal auditor is not omniscient. To be held responsible for guarding the company's assets from all forms of chicanery, he would need the faces of Janus and the eyes of Argus, together with a staff whose size would bankrupt the organization.

Also, the notion of total responsibility runs counter to good administration—to the appropriate division of responsibility among those best capable of carrying it out. The Internal Auditor's Statement recognizes that division when it points out that "the internal audit review and appraisal does not in any way relieve other persons in the organization of the responsibilities assigned to them."

The ultimate responsibility for the control of internal fraud rests with management.[12] The internal auditor cannot be regarded as an insurer or guarantor against the existence of fraud, embezzlement, or employee theft. On the other hand, he can and should be regarded as the monitor of the organization's control system. He should be charged with identifying the known risk areas within his company and with seeing to it that reasonable, workable controls are in force over those areas.

The internal auditor should have a constantly updated list of the diverse risk areas and activities within his organization.[13] He should see that appropriate control systems assist managers in protecting and safeguarding the organization's assets. And he should make periodic reviews to satisfy himself that the systems are working as intended. But he should make those reviews as an appraiser of controls, not as an insurer against improprieties. He is responsible for due professional care and ordinary prudence, and not for extraordinary prudence and all-knowingness.

At the same time, the internal auditor has the responsibility for carrying through to a conclusion and tracking down any serious problem or potential problem that is brought to his attention and that is within the purview of his responsibility. Some internal auditing departments, in banks, for example, have trained investigators on their staffs. In those cases the department takes full responsibility for investigations and interrogations of suspects. In other organizations, and they are probably in the majority, the security department is separate from the internal auditing department. In those organizations, when he is made aware of illegal activities, the internal auditor should promptly bring the matter to the attention of the trained security investigators.

Thereafter, the internal auditor may work together with the investigators to develop whatever evidence and information may be needed to bring the case to a conclusion. He has a special ability to analyze accounting records and other documents. He can become an invaluable problem-solving partner to the security investigator. But he is well advised, unless he is trained in investigation and interrogation, to leave the face-to-face dealing with suspects to the professionals. There is great risk in carrying out interrogations without understanding the attendant dangers. By investigating or interrogating ineptly, the internal auditor may lay himself and his organization open to charges of defamation of character, false arrest, false imprisonment, libel, slander, or malicious prosecution.[14]

The commission of fraud is usually found when there is an intent to steal, the opportunity to steal, and the ability to carry it off. So what an organization must do is reduce temptation and opportunity and increase the certainty of detection. The internal auditor best carries out his responsibility if he recommends controls designed to achieve those ends, and executive management must provide him with the authority to pass on the control systems. A further discussion of fraud, focusing on management deceit, will be found in Chapter 12, Controlling.

Controlled Errors

Although the internal auditor cannot be held responsible for detecting fraud as a part of his regular audit program, he can test a system's ability to detect and reject errors or improprieties by using a technique variously referred to as "created," "planted," or "controlled" errors or as "custom-made frauds." The technique provides for the introduction of false or fictitious transactions into a manual system to determine whether the system or the people running it will detect and reject the spurious transactions. Such a technique is used regularly in testing computer systems. Test decks containing fictitious transactions are used as input to test the computer's ability to flash "Tilt" when the erroneous transaction is encountered.

Few people object to that method of testing computer systems. But there is considerable opposition to using the technique when people are involved. The objections can be summed up as follows:[15]

1. The organization may lay itself open to charges of entrapment.
2. Some managers or supervisors may take it upon themselves to use the practice surreptitiously to their own advantage. If detected, they can declare innocently that they were only "testing the system."
3. It would be impossible to keep the practice secret, and honest personnel might be alienated.
4. The internal auditor's reputation for fairness would be damaged.

On the other hand, there are those who support the technique and give the following arguments.[16]

1. The doctrine of entrapment does not apply. Entrapment is neither a crime nor a civil wrong; it is a defense that a defendant can raise in a criminal trial. The defense must prove that government officers or agents (not, it will be noted, private individuals) conceived the entire crime and then *persuaded the defendant to commit it.* The defense would not apply when the purpose of the test was to evaluate a system's ability to detect and reject erroneous transactions with no intent to criminally prosecute.

2. Properly administered, the controlled testing program could not be used with impunity by unscrupulous operating managers. The rules for the program would have to be strict. Each test would have to be approved in writing by at least three members of top management. Any controlled test not so approved would be as improper as any other deviation from prescribed policies and procedures.

3. There is no more chance of alienating honest employees by controlled errors than by the techniques of surprise cash counts. Other restraints and controls have long been used: time clocks, inspections of lunch pails of employees leaving a plant, surveillance systems whereby investigators observe personnel in the conduct of their duties, and searching security questionnaires. Usually, it is the guilty, not the innocent, who flee from such controls.

4. The internal auditor's image should be and most likely is based on his methods during his regular audits, when he is completely open with his clients. It is doubtful that his responsibility for taking all reasonable means to safeguard the organization's assets will affect that image. Besides, desperate diseases call for desperate remedies, and the current welter of frauds and embezzlements demands rigorous cures.

In organizations in which controlled tests are considered appropriate and are applied under strict rules of conduct, here are some applications:

□ Send improperly authorized requests to purchase to the purchasing department to see whether they will be accepted and acted upon.

□ Place substandard items or an insufficient number of acceptable items in an incoming shipment or in a production batch to see whether they will be passed by inspectors.

□ When designated signatures are required on documents, use poor forgeries.

□ Send improper paperwork to payroll accounting to see if fictitious employees can be placed on the payroll.

□ Send to accounts payable such improper documents as:
Invoices marked paid.
Carbon copies instead of original invoices.
Invoices on typed instead of printed billheads.
Invoices for materials that are not or will not be received.

In each organization a decision must be made on whether the advantages of controlled testing outweigh the disadvantages. The ultimate decision rests with top management. The internal auditor may personally regard the technique as repugnant; but when the organization is facing serious problems of system breakdown, it would seem that he owes a duty to his problem-solving partners in top management to submit the proposition for high-level consideration before he takes it upon himself to reject the concept.

Evaluations of People

Ordinarily the modern internal auditor resists evaluating people as distinguished from systems and transactions. He has a great reluctance to mention names. In his audit reports he may refer, say, to the manager of the accounts receivable department and rarely identify the manager by name. Also, if the work of a manager or an employee is less than satisfactory, that intelligence emerges from the description of the defects found through tests rather than from a direct reference to an individual. In that way, the internal auditor maintains a reputation for objectivity and avoids the imputation of headhunting.

But there are times when executive management has a serious and understandable need to know whether its employees are competent and capable, whether they have the capacity for turning out the kind of work that will keep the organization competitive with other organizations in the same field. That may be particularly true in the professional activities of the organization: law, medicine, training, engineering, science, and research.

Being asked to evaluate persons can present the auditor with a serious dilemma. On the one hand, as the problem-solving partner of managers, he can perceive the need to assist management in obtaining vital information about the organization's manpower resources. On the other hand, he can see such evaluations as eroding the reputation he is trying to build within the organization.

But there are ways and means by which the internal auditor can carry out such an assignment.[17] In one audit of a research organization, the internal auditor asked scientists "How do you judge performance of your peers?" The answer he received was: "By the frequency of publication of papers." The internal auditor analyzed publications over a period of several years and turned over his findings—which disclosed some deplorable gaps—to the director of research for appropriate action.

In other instances the academic approach may be used. It is not unusual in academe for peer groups to evaluate the quality of a teaching department. Such an evaluation is accepted as a matter of course; for who can better review the ability of a professional than his professional peers? The results of such reviews can be put together by the internal auditor in a report to management; they will express not his opinions, but those of the experts qualified to make them. Such reports, understandably, should not be given the wide distribution accorded regular audit reports; the studies, after all, are not regular audits. And while the professionals whose ability is being reviewed may accept the reviews with good grace, it would be wise to consider their personal feelings by not broadcasting the results of evaluations based on subjective rather than objective data.

Other approaches to the evaluation of professional personnel— from the standpoint of how the personnel are regarded by their peers —could include questions on:

Hiring practices and the follow-up of references.
The professional organizations they belong to.
The offices they hold or have held in the organizations.
How other professionals within the organizations regard them.
The degrees and awards they have received.
The reports and papers they have prepared.
How and to what extent they have continued their education.
The formal ratings given them by their superiors.

As to the last question, it would be important for the internal auditor to determine whether a satisfactory, objective rating system is in effect, whether appropriate rating standards have been established, whether timely, consistent measurements and evaluations are being made, whether the people evaluated are regularly informed of their evaluations, and whether the evaluations are discussed with them.

CONCLUSION

The early internal auditors were concerned chiefly with financial and accounting matters. In effect, they were "shackled to the books." They were aids to the chief accountants, and usually good ones. But they had little concern with the vast area of operations in which inefficiencies and mismanagement could have an adverse effect on profits far more serious than peculations and embezzlement of cash. The modern internal auditors raise their sights to encompass not only control over cash and securities but also the myriad operations within the organization that concern top management.

With that ability to see the organization's objectives and operations through the eyes of top management, the modern internal auditor is preparing himself to take his place as the counselor of managers at all levels of the enterprise.

References

1. Henry Mintzberg, "The Manager's Job: Folklore and Fact," *Harvard Business Review,* July-August 1975, p. 49.
2. Gordon McIntyre, "Auditing for Management Control," *The Internal Auditor,* May-June 1975, p. 37.
3. Victor Z. Brink, *Internal Auditing* (New York: Ronald Press, 1941).
4. Duane E. Wilson, "Highlights of the First Certified Internal Auditor Examination," *The Internal Auditor,* March-April 1975, p. 15.
5. Peter F. Drucker, *Management: Tasks, Responsibilities, Practices* (New York: Harper & Row, 1974), p. 395.
6. Ibid., p. 449.
7. Frederic E. Mints, "Behavioral Patterns in Internal Audit Relationships," *Research Committee Report 17* (New York: The Institute of Internal Auditors, 1972).
8. Ibid., pp. 111–114.
9. Ibid., p. 10.
10. Drucker, op. cit., p. 394.
11. Lawrence B. Sawyer, "What's the Internal Auditor's Responsibility for Preventing and Detecting Fraud, Grandfather?" *The Internal Auditor,* May-June 1974, p. 69.
12. Orion A. Hill, Jr., "The Role of the Internal Auditor with Respect to Internal Control and Fraud," *The Internal Auditor,* May-June 1968, p. 37.

13. Lawrence B. Sawyer, *The Practice of Modern Internal Auditing* (Orlando, Fla.: The Institute of Internal Auditors, 1973), pp. 88–91.
14. Thomas R. Igleski, "Legal Considerations When Employee Fraud Is Evident," *The Internal Auditor,* January-February 1969, p. 37.
15. "Readers' Problem Clinic," *The Internal Auditor,* Spring 1961, pp. 69–76.
16. "Readers' Problem Clinic," *The Internal Auditor,* Fall 1961, pp. 66–69.
17. John T. Reeve, "Auditing a Research Division," *The Internal Auditor,* January-February 1975, p. 27.

2

Modern Management—
Links with Modern
Internal Auditing

The divine right of the owner-manager. Management principles in antiquity. Government, the origin of management. Robert Owen, the first flesh-and-blood manager. Georg Siemens and top management. Shibusawa: business and the national purpose. Du Pont and modern big business. Sloan and the professional management team. Rosenwald of Sears: determining what the business is. Taylor: father of scientific management. Fayol and the 14 principles of management. Urwick and principles of administration. Davis and accountability. Gilbreths and Therbligs: measuring work. Gantt: scheduling work. Follett and administration. Barnard: decision making and the functioning executive. Mayo and Roethlisberger: discovering human relations in Hawthorne. Putting management principles to work in the practice of modern internal auditing.

THE DEVELOPMENT OF MODERN MANAGEMENT

Early History

Management, in one sense, is as old as mankind itself. It reaches back to the earliest days when one man led and controlled others. Its seeds were planted in the soil from which governments sprang. But it did not approach fruition until the twentieth century.

Before 1900 there were, of course, private businesses, but they were run by their owners. The people we now call managers were merely assistants to the owners, and the owners ruled as by the divine right of kings. Some kings rule badly, but they rule nevertheless. So too the owners of businesses; they ruled their companies not because they ruled well but simply because they were the owners. Ownership was the controlling factor, not performance, innovation, or vision.

The divine right of ownership died hard. Henry Ford is a case in point: By the early 1920s he had built one of the world's most profitable companies and almost monopolized the automobile market in the United States. By 1927, however, his business was crumbling. He lost millions, year after year. Hindsight now tells us that his difficulties stemmed largely from the fact that he had no managers working for him—only assistants.[1] Any assistant who tried to act like a manager, take on management authority, make management decisions, and take management risks was fired. It was the present-day version of "off with his head."

But then, in 1944, Ford's 26-year-old grandson took over the company. The young man, short on experience and training but long on vision and managerial instinct, had other ideas. He got rid of the assistants, replaced them with managers who could perform, and brought the company back to its place of preeminence.

Like the modern internal auditor, the professional manager is a relatively new breed. He follows principles that have but recently been enunciated by the teachers of management theory. But the principles seem to follow natural laws, since they are rooted in early history.

The oft-told tale of Moses and Jethro illustrates some of the management principles. The Book of Exodus, chapter 18, tells us that Jethro saw Moses, his son-in-law, sitting from morning until night judging all his people. And Jethro said to him, "The thing that thou doest is not good. Thou wilt surely wear away, both thou, and this people that is with thee: for this thing is so heavy for thee; thou art not able to perform it thyself alone."

And then Jethro, the archetype of the internal auditor-teacher-counselor, having analyzed the problem and determined the causes, recommended that Moses "provide out of all the people able men . . . to be rulers of thousands, and rulers of hundreds, rulers of fifties, and rulers of tens. And let them judge the people at all seasons: and it shall be that every great matter they shall bring unto thee, but every small matter they shall judge."

And in that wise counsel, so simply and succinctly stated, lay a clutch of "modern" principles of management:

- □ *Span of control.* There is a limit to the number of people a manager can personally supervise effectively.
- □ *The scalar principle.* There should be a direct chain of authority from supervisor to subordinate throughout the organization.
- □ *Management by exception.* Only significant deviations should be brought to the manager's attention.

Other sages in history also spoke in terms of modern principles of management. Here are some of them.[2]

Confucius, in the sixth century B.C., said, "Require of others only what you first taught them." It is fundamental to the tasks of management that the manager set standards and explain them to his subordinates before he can expect the subordinates to meet the levels of excellence he has in his mind. To achieve understanding, there must be adequate communication between the manager and his people.

Lao-tzu, a contemporary of Confucius, said, "As for the leader at the very top, it is best if people barely know he exists. . . . The people are pleased because they think they did it all themselves." That statement is a precursor of what modern teachers of management propound: The worker must organize his own work with the advice and counsel of supervisors and professionals. The supervisors should be available for guidance, and not for organizing the work for the worker. Only then does the worker feel involvement and only then does he feel that he is master of his job. No longer need he feel that the work is master over him. And with him as the designer of his own job, the organization can hope to get from him the best that he can give.

Mencius, or Meng-tzu (379–289 B.C.) said, "The man whose sole pursuit is Profit-and-Advantage can be ruined by a bad harvest. But the man whose sole pursuit is excellence cannot be confused by evil times." Today the teachers of management theory say the same thing when they talk about goal setting, management by objectives, and determining what one's business really is. And as the teachers now write, profit-maximization is not the ultimate goal of the business.

Hau-fei-tzu (282–233 B.C.) pronounced that "Leaders should never be exempt from blame or punishment for their failures." Here are seen the principles of responsibility and accountability. Whoever is given the authority for carrying out assigned tasks must be held accountable for performance.

More recently, the oft-maligned but truly brilliant management theorist Machiavelli suggested "examining problems in a practical way in the light of the experience of others who have faced a similar problem in the past." His simple statement would seem to encapsulate the rules of problem solving and decision making.

The principles of management started with the need to govern wisely, and the modern principles of management are, in effect, a continuation of the old art of government. But it took managers to apply the principles to current business problems. They put the principles to work. They thought the problems through. They showed how management as a science can be used by the professional manager to build a business and make it productive.

The Professional Managers

Robert Owen

The early professional managers are of relatively recent origin. Perhaps the first manager worthy of the title was Robert Owen (1771– 1858), and it was a long, long time before he had a successor. In him the flesh-and-blood manager first emerged from the abstractions of earlier theorists.

Robert Owen ran a textile mill in New Lanark, Scotland. In that mill, in 1820, he was the first to deal with productivity and motivation, with the worker and his work, with the worker's relation to the company, and with the worker's relation with his supervisor.

Most important, his business was a commercial success. He was able to prove that a profitable enterprise and concern for people can go hand in hand. According to the unanimous testimony of all who visited New Lanark, results were excellent. Children were happy and well brought up. There was health and plenty for the workers. Owen's methods were a demonstrated success. Yet it was a long while before another true manager came along.

Georg Siemens

The next individual to have an impact on the science of management, to start the schism between owner and manager, was Georg Siemens (1839–1901). As a young man of 30, he took over the management of the then puny Deutsche Bank in Germany. And from 1870 to 1880, he built the bank into Germany's leading financial institution.

The Deutsche Bank's rise stemmed not from financial brilliance or baronial ruthlessness, but from managers. Not assistants; managers. Siemens built a top-management team. He analyzed the bank's activities. He assigned responsibilities and granted authority to each member of the team. He saw to it that the job fit the man. And yet, through the delegation of responsibility over all of the bank's functions, every operation was in one way or another covered by a manager. That was a sharp break with the divine-right approach to running a business.

It is a sad commentary that Siemens' successful venture into modern management was not adopted by others, and sadder still that many a promising business was lost through the failure to follow Siemens' methods. The story was there for all to see, but few saw it. The past is prologue; the fruition of the future lies in the seeds of the past. The busy manager may not have the time to study it, but business history should be a part of the internal auditor's store of knowledge ready to be tapped in his counsel to managers.

Ei-ichi Shibusawa

Another management pioneer was Ei-ichi Shibusawa (1840–1931). He was a statesman who became a business leader. He raised some fundamental questions about the relation between business enterprise and national purpose, between business needs and individual ethics. He was perhaps the first to envision the professional manager. In fact, Japan's rise to economic leadership can be traced to Shibusawa's thought and work.[3]

Shibusawa's professional manager was ahead of his time. But then, many strokes of brilliance are, and the internal auditor should be alert to them. He must study the principles and translate them into practical rules for practical men. He must show those men how to apply the rules in their day-to-day tasks and how such an application will help managers reach their objectives. He has a signal opportunity to carry out his mission; for it is he who detects deficiencies, inefficiencies, and ineffectiveness. And as he points out unsatisfactory conditions and identifies their causes, he can reach into his store of knowledge and show the practical effect of violating sound management principles.

Pierre S. du Pont

In more recent years, giants in the United States took long strides in advancing our knowledge of the practice of modern management.

Pierre S. du Pont (1870–1954) first developed the principle of decentralization and helped create the modern "big business." He transformed his family-dominated company into modern business by giving it a management structure. Du Pont worked out the system of organization known as "federal decentralization," later perfected by Sloan.[4] Federal decentralization is the organization of a company into a number of autonomous businesses. Each unit has its own management and runs its own business; each is responsible for its own performance and results; each makes a contribution to the entire company and is held accountable for that contribution.

Federal decentralization can be applied to institutions other than business. In a hospital, for example, the entire hospital function can be arranged into units of activity: One unit can take care of intensive-care patients; another unit can take care of short-term and ambulatory patients; another mental patients; still another convalescents; and so on. Common service units, such as laboratories, kitchens, case workers, and physical therapists, can be shared by the decentralized units.

Similarly, certain service units can aid decentralized businesses. For example, a central purchasing department can develop master purchase agreements for suppliers of common items, such as stationery and maintenance supplies, which would be available to the decentralized companies.

The involvement of the du Pont family in the company would seem to be a reversion to the old owner-manager concept, but in the du Pont organization only the family members who can qualify as true managers stay on. Obviously, family has the inside track. But in the case of the du Ponts, as it was of Georg Siemens, being a family member may get you in but only contribution to the business permits you to stay.

Alfred P. Sloan, Jr.

Alfred P. Sloan, Jr. (1875–1966) followed Pierre S. du Pont and improved on what du Pont had done. Sloan developed systematic approaches to business objectives and to strategic planning. After the du Ponts acquired the then floundering General Motors in the early 1920s and put Sloan in as president, Sloan developed the "professional management team" which raised GM to heights of greatness.[5]

Julius Rosenwald

Julius Rosenwald (1862–1932) built the first business based on the marketing approach. Richard Sears founded the business, and it escalated because he was a shrewd speculator. But as the company grew and Sears' reach exceeded his scope, he was forced to take

Rosenwald in. Rosenwald was truly a manager. He built an organization in which managers were given maximum authority and full responsibility for results. Most important, he determined early on just what his business was.

And that determination heralded Sears, Roebuck's future. Rosenwald thought through the business and decided that its essence was to be the farmer's friend. Simply that. But that simple-sounding concept was central to the success of the business. For the company to be the farmer's friend, Rosenwald had to determine where his customers were and what they needed. He had to develop the mail order catalog as a marketing instrument; the customer had to get what he wanted at a low price and with assurance of regular supply.

Most important, Rosenwald had to give a warranty of reliability and honesty, because the remote locations he served—this was before the company went into retail sales—made it impossible for the customer to inspect his purchase in advance of delivery. So Rosenwald changed the concept of "buyer beware" to "seller beware." And he made stick the famous Sears policy of "your money back and no questions asked." Rosenwald was the father of the marketing-and-distribution revolution.[6]

The Advance Guard of the Modern Theorists

In recent years there has been an enormous boom in management texts. Before World War II, the books on management could have fit on an office bookshelf. Since then, hundreds of management titles have been appearing each year. Some of them have been written by brilliant theorists who have had a profound effect on our understanding of management.

In this chapter we will speak of some of the theorists who began to formulate management principles and blaze the trail for others to follow. No attempt is made to be all-encompassing. The writers are legion and the field is too broad. We have selected theorists whose ideas seem to mesh with the work of the internal auditor, ideas that evoke examples of the relation between management theory and modern internal auditing. The examples, described later in this chapter, underscore the feasibility of the problem-solving partnership.

The numerous schools of management theory are reserved for discussion in Chapter 3. And a number of the modern management theorists, particularly those concerned with behavioralism, are identified in Chapter 4.

Frederick W. Taylor

Frederick W. Taylor (1856–1915) laid the foundation for scientific industrial management. In 1880 or 1881, while employed as a gang boss at the Midvale Steel Company, he became convinced that a standard day's work in any operation could be measured and that scientific methods could be applied to work in the shop. He concluded that a large percentage of labor and material was wasted through inefficiencies both in organizing and in supervising work.

In 1911 he wrote *The Principles of Scientific Management*. His intention was to provide principles of general applicability for managers, but his application was particular. It emphasized time-and-motion studies. Nevertheless, in terms of management theory, he made an important contribution by showing that scientific methods could be applied to management problems.

The very importance of Taylor's contributions emphasized the drawbacks. The great interest in Taylor's scientific methods drew attention away from general management and focused it on shop management.[7] Although born in the shop, however, many of Taylor's principles have equal applicability today in other environments. Some of the principles that have stood the test of time and changing occupations are:

- Replacing intuition and guesswork with the analysis of each element of a worker's tasks.
- Scientifically selecting and training workers.
- Promoting the cooperation of management and labor so as to better accomplish work through scientific method.
- Establishing a more equal division of responsibility between managers and workers.

Some of Taylor's ideas, on the other hand, are becoming less relevant. Taylor advocated systems of incentive pay for labor, but the decline of piecework and the growing strength of unions has made such systems much less important in the field of compensation and motivation for workers. Nevertheless, it should be noted that Taylor's own motivation was not to be a cold and calculating stopwatch artist; instead, it was to free the nineteenth-century worker from the burden of heavy, destructive toil and break the wage barriers that condemned workers to unremitting poverty. He was responsible for making it possible to increase wages by increasing productivity.

Henri Fayol

If Taylor was the father of scientific management, then Henri Fayol (1841–1925) can be considered to be the father of modern management theory. His was the first rational approach to organizing an enterprise along functional lines. He considered the business function as a "bundle of related skills." It was his answer to the organizational question of which activities belong together.

Fayol's approach may have applied admirably to the relatively small—by present standards—coal-mining company that he ran. Today it may be more important to bring together the contributions that groups make to the enterprise than to bundle the skills. Nevertheless, many of the principles Fayol propounded with brilliant insight are largely valid to this day.[8]

Fayol developed 14 principles from his own experience in managing an organization.[9] They apply primarily to the manager, but, as we shall demonstrate later in this chapter, they are of vital interest to the internal auditor as well. They are summarized as follows:

1. *Division of work.* The division of work involves the principle of specialization: each to his ability. Fayol first discovered the principle in connection with his study of shop work, but he saw its applicability to all kinds of work, both administrative and technical.

2. *Authority and responsibility.* Whenever authority is delegated, responsibility for the actions taken and the decisions made must be exacted. Authority has two aspects. One is rooted in the manager's official designation of his position; the other is rooted in his own ability, experience, intelligence, and moral worth.

3. *Discipline.* Discipline implies conformity to the organization's rules. Fayol said that this principle requires clear and fair agreements and good superiors at all levels.

4. *Unity of command.* An employee should not be required to serve two masters within the organization. He should receive his orders from one superior only.

5. *Unity of direction.* Each group of activities that has the same objective should have the same plan and the same direction. Fayol saw unity of direction as related to the organization as a whole and unity of command as related to personnel and their superiors.

6. *Subordination of individual interest.* The interest of the group should always transcend the interest of the individual. It is the job of the manager to reconcile conflicting interests.

7. *Remuneration of personnel.* Payment to people should be fair

and consistent and should give maximum satisfaction to employee and employer.

8. *Centralization.* The centralization principle refers to the degree to which authority within an organization is concentrated or dispersed so as to be cost-effective.

9. *Scalar chain.* The scalar chain denotes the line of authority from the highest to the lowest ranks. It derives from the Latin for "ladder." And although it depicts an upward-and-downward movement, with the implication that subordinates should comply strictly with protocol, the horizontal rungs permit a sidewise movement when strict adherence to protocol would be inefficient or ineffective.

10. *Order.* Order involves the organization of people and functions: a place for everyone and everything, and everyone and everything in their places.

11. *Equity.* The equity principle deals with human relations. It calls for fair dealing between supervisor and worker.

12. *Stability of personnel tenure.* Fayol was concerned with unnecessary employee turnover, and he saw it as both the cause and effect of bad management.

13. *Initiative.* Fayol regarded initiative as thinking through problems and devising and executing plans. He looked to managers to stimulate initiative in subordinates, since he saw initiative as one of the "keenest satisfactions for an intelligent man to experience."

14. *Esprit de corps.* The final principle has to do with teamwork and morale; to achieve them is heavily dependent on good communication.

Fayol's genius lies in his ability to foresee what will remain valid through the years, but even geniuses can have their blind spots. Fayol said that "long experience has taught me that the use of *higher* mathematics counts for nothing in management businesses."[10] Fayol might have retracted that statement if he were to observe the present use of probability theory, regression analysis, simulations, and the like. Certainly, the early operations research craze, during which it was said that mathematics would replace managers, has not realized the predictions made for it. Yet higher mathematics can be an important aid to management decision making.

Lyndall Urwick

Lyndall F. Urwick (b. 1891) was one of the first management consultants and a leading advocate of Henri Fayol. Like Fayol, he believed in using principles of management to provide criteria for good administration. Among the principles he propounded were:[11]

□ *Uniformity.* All reports and figures used to control activities should be the same throughout the organization.

□ *Objectives.* Contributions by individuals in the organization will be effective to the extent that they are in gear with the organization's aims and goals.

□ *Span of control.* There is a limit to the number of subordinates a manager can supervise effectively.

Ralph C. Davis

Ralph Currier Davis (b. 1894), who taught management at Ohio State University, helped develop a unified theory of management. He was a proponent of the concept of accountability as an addition to the concepts of authority and responsibility. Accountability is the charge laid upon a subordinate to account for the proper discharge of his duties.[12]

The Gilbreths

A man and his wife, Frank and Lillian Gilbreth (1868–1924 and 1878–1972), powered the work that is referred to as motion study. They classified work according to motions, such as moving, lifting, and putting down. Their Therbligs (an anagram of Gilbreth) encompass the entire range of manual operations.[13] The Gilbreths sought to develop "the one best way" for each operation. Each of the Therbligs, which look something like Chinese ideographs, depicts the information needed to engineer a motion.

The Gilbreths' purpose was work simplification, not work speedup. For example, they found that, if working conditions were merely held constant so that employees became familiar with the operations of the work, there would be a significant increase in output.[14] Essentially, work simplification is merely applying common sense to find easier, better, more economical ways of doing things. Briefly stated, the steps are as follows:[15]

1. Identify the work that could use simplification.
2. Analyze the job. Break it down into its component parts.
3. Question each component part of the work.
4. Try to improve existing processes or methods by eliminating, combining, rearranging, simplifying, and substituting mechanical for manual means.
5. Put the improved methods into effect and monitor them. All the analysis and creativity in the world go for naught without action, follow-up, and feedback.

One of the weaknesses of that form of analysis is that the analysis may be starting at the wrong end. It usually starts by analyzing the work being done while accepting without question the need for the end product.

Henry Gantt

Henry L. Gantt (1861–1919), another great pioneer in work analysis, fully understood the necessity of determining "what do we want to produce?" His charts started out with the end product and then detailed each step, in proper sequence, needed to attain it; they provided for scheduling work so that the entire process spread before the eye like a road map.[16] In brief, each Gantt chart shows on the left the producing department, the number of operators, and the department's weekly capacity. Each job proceeding through a department is scheduled, day by day. The chart shows which jobs are on schedule and which are not meeting their schedules.

Mary Follett

Mary Parker Follett (1868–1933) did some significant work in the field of administration and the relation between management and the worker and between members of the organization. She pointed out, in the 1920s and 1930s, that effective managership was more than a function of official position within the organization. The senior manager appoints the operating manager and puts him in the job. But the subordinates must accept the manager before he can function effectively. Follett could see that assigned authority is like a wave breaking on the rocks if the subordinates are not willing to obey. She proposed the "law of the situation," which states that people will be moved not by divine right or domination, but rather by how they regard the manager's ability to interpret the situation in which the group finds itself. She conceived coordination involving direct contacts among people as being the essence of management. She saw coordination as a continuing process that must be introduced at the outset of a function and pursued to the end.

Coordination is conditional to communication, and communication is conditional to how the communicating parties perceive the situation. That perception, in turn, is conditional to the backgrounds, experiences, and prejudices of the parties. What one sees clearly the other sees not at all. Both, according to Follett, are likely to see "reality," but their inner eyes may capture entirely different pictures of reality.[17]

Chester Barnard

Chester I. Barnard (1886–1961), a corporation executive, was one of the first to study the management process of decision making in the functions of the executive and to explore the formal and informal organizations within a business entity.[18] Barnard searched for the universal fundamentals to explain the executive's job and to help the executive improve his ability as a manager.

In decision making, Barnard stressed the need to identify the strategic factor that, when recognized and properly weighed, lies at the heart of wise decisions. All systems, conditions, or sets of circumstances consist of elements or factors. When regarded from the viewpoint of the purpose to be achieved, the factors fall into two classes: those which, if absent or changed, would accomplish the desired purpose (provided all the other factors remain unchanged) and the other, unchanged factors.[19]

For example, if an otherwise properly functioning automobile runs out of fuel, the fuel is the strategic, or limiting, factor. In a business seeking to expand, the availability of capital may be the strategic factor. Strategic factors for a particular set of circumstances may vary with different organizations and with points in time within the same organization.[20] Strategic factors may be extremely difficult to identify and isolate, and that is the challenge to the decision-making executive.

Barnard spoke also of formal and informal organizations.[21] The formal organization is represented by the activities of two or more people who consciously coordinate their efforts toward mutual goals. The informal organization comprises the sum total of relations among people who may not have common purposes but from which arise joint results. There need not be a conflict between formal and informal organizations. The informal organization permits the individual to maintain his personality against the effect of the formal organization, which, through its impersonality and coldness, may tend to disintegrate his personality. Indeed, informal organizations may be important to the enterprise because they foster a feeling of belonging, status, and self-respect.

Elton Mayo

Elton Mayo (1880–1949), an Australian working at Harvard, developed the concept of "human relations," the study of people working together in an enterprise. He perceived the dominance of the interpersonal relations within the work group and the fact that the human character of business organizations had been largely ignored.[22]

The project that had the most to do with the concept that human relations was an integral part of business was the Hawthorne experiment, 1927–1932, of the Western Electric Company. The researchers sought to prove the validity of accepted management principles by observing employees at their tasks. Different variables were introduced into the work group, and the results in terms of production were measured. For example, a rest period was introduced where there previously had been no rest period, and increased production was noted and measured. Additional benefits to the workers were introduced, and each brought about an increase in production. That the researchers had expected. What they had not expected was that, when the amenities were gradually withdrawn, there was no decrease in production. Evidently there were uncontrolled and unknown factors in the experiment.

To find the uncontrolled factors, Mayo, along with F. J. Roethlisberger, followed up the experiments with an intensive counseling program and learned that the way managers perceived workers was not the way the workers perceived themselves. The workers saw themselves as members of a group, and they regarded interpersonal values as superior to individual or managerial values. The interpersonal relations brought about by the experiment itself carried on despite the removal of amenities. Some questions have been raised about the validity of the methods used in the Hawthorne experiments and whether those methods would stand up under modern scientific scrutiny. Be that as it may, the experiments brought about new thinking about manager-worker relations and have had a lasting effect on the study of scientific management.

Mayo showed that, unless the manager understands the values of the group and gives them full consideration, he will not get much enthusiasm out of the workers. Instead of trying to get across what management wants, the manager should try to find out what his subordinates want, need, and have to know. That includes making the worker responsible for his own work and giving him the authority to structure his own job—with the advice of experienced supervisors, of course. When that condition obtains, the manager can expect to see commitment and involvement on the part of the worker. But workers structuring their own jobs is not a practice often seen. Usually, the manager or the supervisor or the industrial engineer structures the job and expects the worker to follow the dictated operations blindly.

Yet the concept of involvement is being used in other areas. For example, it has become general practice in many organizations to have those who are subject to budgets and schedules be party to establishing them. The budgets and schedules are then *their* budgets and schedules and there is less resentment in trying to achieve them.

LINKS WITH INTERNAL AUDITING

The writings about management evoke a sharp echo from the work of modern internal auditors. There is a link between the two: in the way professional management and modern internal auditing developed, in the application of management principles to internal auditing practice, and in the dealings between managers and internal auditors. In this section, several of those links will be examined in relation to the work of the theorists just discussed.

Taylor: The Focus on Manufacturing

Taylor's work was criticized for being focused on shop management. Similar criticism is leveled at writers on modern internal auditing on the ground that much of the literature is focused on manufacturing. But in the growth of a profession, that is a fault to be expected. It was in the large manufacturing companies that internal auditing made its first great strides. The principles developed there are now in use in financial institutions, hospitals, and government.

Fayol: Principles of Management

Fayol's principles can be seen to be operative in many of the conditions the internal auditor finds in his examinations. For that reason we shall discuss at some length a number of actual conditions found by internal auditors and key them to many of Fayol's principles.

Authority and Responsibility

Fayol saw responsibility as a corollary of authority; the internal auditor may see the emphasis reversed. For example, the procurement department has the responsibility for purchasing materials and services for the organization. It should have the commensurate authority to be the only group in the enterprise to make commitments of that kind. And because of its responsibilities, it develops strict rules to make sure that buyers place orders without favoritism and in the best interests of the organization.

In one case an internal auditor found that the purchasing department's authority was not being fully exercised or protected. The manager of the transportation department was buying automotive equipment and supplies directly from suppliers; he was making commitments and consummating purchase agreements. All that was done without the strict controls imposed on buyers.

When the internal auditor observed the conditions and the dangers inherent in them, he counseled senior management to issue directives to all department heads that the authority to commit the company's funds was vested exclusively in the purchasing organization. Authority was thus made commensurate with responsibility.

Done without finesse, such an audit action would not sit well with the transportation manager, since it implies doubt as to that manager's objectivity. But the internal auditor pointed out the dangers the manager was facing in the event a purchase, made with all the good intentions in the world, turned out to reek of favoritism. The manager was convinced that the new rules were designed to protect him as much as they were to protect the organization.

Discipline

The internal auditor has a responsibility for seeing that the rules are followed as intended. He also has a responsibility for seeing that the rules are reasonable and are in accordance with organizational objectives. In some companies internal auditors were instrumental in having formal conflict-of-interest programs developed. Under such programs each employee answers an annual questionnaire designed to disclose potential conflicts. Everyone is informed of the rules and of the penalties for disobeying them. The rules apply to everyone in the company from members of the board of directors to junior buyers within the purchasing department.

Conflicts may include ownership in a company supplying goods or services to the organization, acceptance of gifts from suppliers, and kickbacks from suppliers. The internal auditor in a company will be concerned with learning whether the rules are reasonable, will protect the company, and are not unnecessarily onerous to employees Then he will see to it that all questionnaires are executed completely and that any deviations are appropriately dealt with. And as a part of his responsibility for determining that the rules are followed as intended, he will be sure to review questionnaires executed by senior management, including the board of directors.

Division of Work

The concept of specialists working together toward the common good is high on the internal auditor's list of audit priorities. For example:

□ When he audits purchase orders, the internal auditor wants to be sure that representatives from the traffic department have checked and approved routings and that representatives from the accounting department have approved the accounts or contracts shown as being charged.

□ When he audits contracts, he wants to be sure that reviews and approvals were obtained from the general counsel's office, the tax department, and the insurance department.

□ When rules and regulations that affect employees' rights, such as charges for lost equipment, are issued, he wants to make sure that specialists within the personnel department agree that no union agreements are being violated.

Unity of Command

In one company, the manager of quality control was organizationally responsible to the director of manufacturing. The manager prescribed rules under which his inspectors were to operate, and the rules were in agreement with contract specifications governing the quality of delivered products. But the director of manufacturing and the managers working for him bowed more deeply to the gods of cost and schedule than to the god of quality, and inspectors were constantly being pressured to accept nonstandard products. The inspectors, working for two masters, were confused and resentful. They were not sure which was the last authority—the rules written by their manager or the oral demands of manufacturing managers to bend those rules.

The internal auditors recommended autonomy for quality control —a level in the organization that was equal to the level of the director of manufacturing. The difficulties of the inspectors' jobs were not eased, but the frustration and confusion on the part of the inspectors were eliminated. Now there was no question which manager was their superior.

Unity of Direction

One internal auditor encountered a violation of unity of direction in the audit of scrap generation and sale. The scrap sales department was trying to receive the most dollars from scrap no matter how much it cost the manufacturing department, where the scrap was generated, to sort and segregate the scrap.

Now, scrap *should* be segregated into types, because when different types of metals are mixed together, the value of the total will not exceed the value of the cheapest ingredient. If, for example, aluminum were mixed with titanium, an extremely expensive metal, the whole batch would command only the lower price offered for aluminum. So segregation is important, but segregation can also be expensive, particularly if the metals are already mixed.

Unity of direction would require the departments in the company to work together for the highest *net* return. And if the cost of segregating the materials exceeded the return that could be obtained, it would make no economic sense to insist on high-cost segregation.

The answer was to seek segregation at the source of the scrap. If initial segregation was impossible, then the expensive chore of assigning production workers to sort the scrap was to be avoided. At the same time, the manufacturing managers were to be given monthly reports of the cost of different types of metals on the scrap market to alert them to the benefits of segregation. Also, their superiors were to be given reports of unnecessary contamination of expensive metals with cheaper types of metals. Unity of direction resulted in lower costs to the enterprise.

Subordination of Interest

Internal auditors should have an abiding interest in whether supervisors and managers know what their people are doing. During a defense contract audit, the government auditors made floor checks to determine the probable extent of idleness. The auditors observed that employees in the second and third shifts were spending time in places other than their assigned working areas; their individual interests took them there. The foremen should have known where their employees were, and so 33 of them were asked to name the employees assigned to them, state the employees' job assignments, and locate the individual employees. Over half of the foremen quizzed did not have lists of the people assigned to their supervision. Five of the foremen had to admit that they did not know the whereabouts of one or more of their assigned workers.

When the matter was reported to management, the system was promptly improved. Each foreman was required to have in his possession at all times an up-to-date crew list annotated to show absences, loans, and transfers. Managers were to make periodic observations to be sure the foremen were following the new rules. It was estimated, by the management people themselves, that about $1 million was saved through the institution of the improved controls.[23]

Centralization

In one company, the electronic data processing department was under the control of the chief accountant. All requests for data processing work by the chief accountant were complied with promptly. Other requests, sometimes of greater significance to the company as a whole, were given lower priorities. The internal auditor analyzed the requests and presented his findings to senior management. The result was an organizational change. The head of data processing was elevated to a level equal to that of the department managers for whom he performed services.

Order

Internal auditors are beginning to get involved in the appraisal of organizational structure. A research study by the Institute of Internal Auditors examined the internal auditor's involvement with organizational control.[24] The report explores the basic concepts of organization, the nature and scope of organizational control, and the auditor's relation to such control. In addition, it provides audit guides for evaluating organization control.

The study cites a number of examples of the results of organizational audits. One of them describes a food company's thrift store operation in which a number of factors contributed to inefficiency, many of them organizational. For example, the central director lacked adequate authority over the field units. As a result there were no uniform policies for pricing, staffing, or store hours. Also, the field units lacked coordination with other company operations. Once the internal auditor identified the reasons for the inefficiencies, he made recommendations for changes in the organizational structure and increased authority for the central director.[25]

Equity

Equity is a nebulous field and one in which the internal auditor's application of objective evaluation and the quantification of results may not be appropriate or possible. Nevertheless, the human resource is valuable and poor morale reduces productivity and the value of that resource. Senior managers are, or should be, concerned with employee morale, yet they cannot always be close enough to the workers to assess the level of morale.

Internal auditors are close to people as they do their audit jobs. They are, or should be, sensitive to feelings and attitudes, so they can obtain impressions that can be objective even if they are not quantifiable. Such judgments can be of considerable importance to managers. In some internal audit organizations, the auditors present an informal report to senior management that sets out impressions and judgments on such matters as working conditions, employee attitudes, availability and experience of supervisors, and employee morale.

Those reports, judiciously presented, can be very helpful to senior management and beneficial to the employees themselves. Management interest is heightened when observed conditions can be traced to morale and working conditions.[26]

Stability of Tenure

In audits of a personnel department, the internal auditor will usually want to know if, in exit interviews, an effort is made to find why departing employees are leaving. He will try to determine whether turnover rates are reasonable or excessive and how those rates compare among departments or among major divisions of the organization. High turnover is costly, and the internal auditor will want to know whether managers at appropriate levels receive information on reasons for excessive turnover and what they are doing about the causes.

Initiative

Innovation is the key to growth. A climate that restricts initiative inhibits growth, but initiative is hardly a simple thing to audit. It does, however, come within the purview of the internal auditor's impressions about an organization. When the auditor visits a department and finds that there is no provision for self-appraisal, for seeking to do new things or to do the old things in new ways, he has a responsibility to discuss the matter with management people.

Certainly, the discussion calls for tact and delicacy, but even the asking of a pertinent question may get the manager thinking. "To what extent and how, Mr. Manager, do you stimulate initiative and innovativeness?" The internal auditor may receive an offhand response, but the manager may have started thinking about a program to tap the innovative wellsprings of his people. Also, the informal report to senior management may insure the continuance of his thinking.

Urwick: Principles of Administration

Urwick's principles, like Fayol's, find echoes in the work of the modern internal auditor. Illustrations, as they relate to two of the principles previously mentioned, follow:

Uniformity

The internal auditor usually reviews policies on employee wage and salary rates when he makes audits of the personnel department.

He is particularly concerned with consistent treatment. If one employee of a group receives a certain salary and a co-worker in the same wage classification receives even a minor amount more, the lower-paid worker will conceive the difference as a reflection on his standing in the company. He will feel justified in producing less than his co-worker.

That applies to travel allowances as well as to pay checks. In multidivisional organizations, each relatively autonomous, there are often a good many transfers between divisions. The internal auditor will pay particular attention to reasonable consistency among the divisions to prevent employee dissatisfaction.

Objectives

The first rule of modern internal auditing is to know the objective of the activity under review. This does not necessarily mean the published statements or policies. They may be just window dressing. It means understanding the true, the real objective and how it relates to organizational objectives.

The basic objective of accounts payable is not merely to process payments to suppliers. That's the ostensible objective. The real objective must be much broader if it is to carry out the mission of the activity. A much better audit is made if the internal auditor sees the objective of accounts payable as approving payments to creditors when due, for what is done, while achieving the maximum conservation of cash. When the internal auditor views the accounts payable activities in that light, he can perform an audit that is management-oriented, not merely a clerical verification.

Span of Control

There is an old proverb that says the best fertilizer for the soil is the shadow of the owner. To the internal auditor that means that the best form of control is knowledgeable, available, respected supervision. Hence, the internal auditor must be concerned, as he performs his audits throughout the organization, about the supervision of employees:

□ Do supervisors appear to know their jobs, and do they have the respect of their employees?
□ Do supervisors seem to be exercising control and providing direction to employees?

When supervision is inadequate because there are not enough supervisors to go around, or when, on the other hand, the ratio of supervisors to employees is higher than necessary to perform an adequate job, the matter of span of control becomes significant to the internal auditor, who should report his conclusions to management.

Davis: The Concept of Accountability

Davis was responsible for many important concepts and principles of management theory. We have singled out his concept of accountability because it has particular meaning for the internal auditor.

In large organizations, accountability is evidenced in reports to superiors. Such reports are usually the means by which top management learns what has been accomplished and how performance measures up to the goals that have been set. Also, they provide data on which decisions are based. The reports must therefore be accurate, timely, and meaningful. Most internal auditing organizations maintain a list of the key operating reports and see to it that the reports are reviewed periodically during the audits of related activities.

The managers who receive the reports must rely upon report integrity, yet operating managers may have a tendency to put the best face on things and gloss over unsatisfactory conditions or accomplishments. The internal auditor, as the partner of senior management, must insure the integrity of the reports. As partner to operating management, he should point out defects and recommend improvements. Moreover, when the internal auditor perceives the need for accountability and an absence of reports, he has a responsibility to report the need for preparing the reports.

The Gilbreths: Simplifying the Work

The Gilbreths were concerned with work simplification, and so is the internal auditor. He need not be an industrial engineer, but he must know enough about work methods to be able to tell when an industrial engineer should be called upon to help simplify work. And if he knows the steps of work simplification, he could probably suggest improved methods himself. Some of the questions he can ask himself, as he approaches any ongoing process, are:[27]

How can this process be improved?
How can this form be combined with another?
How can this flow of work be rerouted for greater efficiency?
How can this step be eliminated completely?
How can this amount of copying be done away with?

And as he addresses himself to the simplification of the work, he will start with determining whether the means justify the ends. He does not begin his analysis of an operation until he has determined the objective of the activity he will review. He will want to know precisely what end product is desired and needed.

There is a big difference between efficiency and effectiveness. Efficiency implies doing a job expeditiously and well. Effectiveness implies doing the right job. What profits it a man or an organization if the wrong job is done with the utmost precision and dispatch? The internal auditor, before he analyzes the operation, will always ask:

Is this operation needed?
Does it accord with the organization's objectives?
Will it further the organization's goals?

Gantt: Scheduling the Work

Many variations of the Gantt charts are now in use, but all emphasize the significance of time values in planning work. In industrial companies, the internal auditors concern themselves with production schedules, and they regularly audit the Gantt charts or the modern-day counterparts. The internal auditor is interested in the premises on which schedules are based. He wants to know if there is coordination between the company's master schedules and its detailed schedules, between the sales organization and the manufacturing organization, between scheduling and both man loading and machine loading.

He is particularly concerned with whether off-schedule jobs are highlighted and brought to the attention of higher management and whether appropriate steps are taken to recover from off-schedule work. One of the most important services the internal auditor can perform for higher management is to make sure that the reports it receives on schedule accomplishment are supported by the facts.

Follett: Perception and Communication

The internal auditor can be the catalyst to obtain congruence of perception among interfacing groups within the organization. Traditionally, accounts payable is at odds with purchasing, engineering is at odds with production, sales is at odds with production scheduling, and budgeting is at odds with just about everyone. The mutual objectives are the same—the good of the enterprise, but perception of those objectives and how to achieve the objectives may vary widely. In specific situations in which conflicts abort goals, the internal auditor can bring the parties together to reconcile divergencies and meet mutual objectives.

The internal auditor endorses Mary Parker Follett's preachments that good communications are absolutely essential. Many of the problems that the internal auditor runs into have their causes in faulty communications. For example, inspectors might be evaluating products against outdated specifications because new specifications were not promptly and properly communicated to them. In one audit, an internal auditor observed that new specifications were posted on a bulletin board for a week and then taken down. The inspectors were supposed to read and study those specifications, but the auditor found that many of them paid no attention to the bulletin board. Also, he was able to trace a number of customers' rejections of inspected parts to the problems of communication.

At the internal auditor's urging, the chief inspector took these steps:

□ Inspectors were instructed to initial and date a master copy of all new specifications, and the master copy was then filed in a binder available to all.
□ Supervisors were required to hold weekly meetings with their people to discuss all new and revised specifications.

Barnard: Decision Making and the Executive

The internal auditor can play an important role in the decision-making process of the executive. His role is not that of the decision maker; that would be an unwarranted usurpation of authority and responsibility assigned to the manager. Instead, his role is to make sure that the executive is provided with the proper information and factors needed for a knowledgeable decision. Information submitted to executives by subordinates may be incorrect, incomplete, not meaningful, or not timely. As we pointed out previously, one of the most important services the internal auditor can provide is to carry out a continuing review of management reports, the reports on which executive decisions are based. And the internal auditor's knowledge of the theory of strategic or limiting factors can improve the effectiveness of that service. Decision making will be discussed more fully in Chapter 5.

The internal auditor must be aware that informal organizations exist and are important to the workers within the enterprise. Then his own findings, conclusions, and recommendations become related to the "real world" and not the plastic world of organization charts and procedures. The auditor is more readily accepted by worker and manager alike when his audit program is geared to activity objectives rather than sterile rules. He may find those objectives are being met by bending the rules, and then he will fault the rules instead of the performance.

Mayo: The Human Resource

The internal auditor must be concerned with the feelings of the individuals and the group. Coldly logical recommendations for improvement of a process or a system must be examined for their impact on the individual. And in many internal auditing organizations, such recommendations are fully discussed with members of the personnel department to guard against unfortunate repercussions.

Also, as he conducts his audits, the internal auditor most be careful of the feelings of the manager. He must not, of course, suppress deficiency findings, but he can be candid, open, and fair. He can keep the manager informed, as the audit progresses, about what he is finding. He can provide ample opportunity for corrective action. And he can give credit for steps taken to improve conditions.

CONCLUSION

Books and articles on the principles of management are rapidly inundating the management community. Many of the principles set forth have stood the harsh test of time. Field studies and surveys have pointed to business downfalls when those principles have been violated. But the busy manager, beset on all sides by the problems he faces each working day and pressed to make the decisions needed to overcome those problems, has little time to study or research those principles and put them into effect.

Yet the modern internal auditor, in his day-to-day encounters with operational difficulties, can trace most of the difficulties to violations of management principles or good administrative techniques, and so he must understand and keep abreast of the studies in management. He is the one who must be counselor and teacher to the end that he can aid the busy manager in putting the principles and practices to practical use—to help him make decisions that not only solve a problem but keep it from recurring.

References

1. Peter F. Drucker, *Management: Tasks, Responsibilities, Practices* (New York: Harper & Row, 1974), pp. 380, 381.

2. Albert Newgarden, "The Tao of Management," *The Arthur Young Journal,* Autumn 1967, pp. 31–34.

3. Drucker, op. cit., p. 23.

4. A. D. Chandler, Jr., and Stephen Salisbury, *Pierre S. du Pont and the Making of the Modern Corporation* (New York: Harper & Row, 1971).

5. A. P. Sloan, Jr., *My Years with General Motors* (Garden City, N.Y.: Doubleday, 1964).

6. Drucker, op. cit., pp. 50–57.

7. Harold Koontz and Cyril O'Donnell, *Principles of Management* (New York: McGraw-Hill, 1955), pp. 21, 22.

8. Henri Fayol, *General and Industrial Administration* (London: Pitman, 1949), trans. from the French, originally published in 1916.

9. Ibid, chap. 4.

10. Ibid., p. 84.

11. Lyndall F. Urwick, *The Elements of Administration* (New York: Harper & Brothers, 1943).

12. Ralph C. Davis, *The Fundamentals of Top Administration* (New York: Harper & Brothers, 1951).

13. Drucker, op. cit., p. 200.

14. E. B. Flippo and G. M. Munsinger, *Management,* 3rd ed. (Boston: Allyn & Bacon, 1975), p. 96.

15. G. R. Terry, *Principles of Management,* 6th ed. (Homewood, Ill.: Irwin, 1972), p. 236.

16. Ibid., pp. 194, 195.

17. H. C. Metcalf and L. F. Urwick, eds., *Dynamic Administration: The Collected Papers of Mary Parker Follett* (New York: Harper Brothers, 1941).

18. C. I. Barnard, *The Function of the Executive* (Cambridge, Mass.: Harvard University Press, 1938).

19. Ibid., pp. 202, 203.

20. Koontz and O'Donnell, op. cit., pp. 508, 509.

21. Barnard, op. cit., chap. 9.

22. Elton Mayo, *The Human Problem of an Industrial Civilization* (Cambridge, Mass.: Harvard University Press, 1933).

23. H. J. Mintern, ed., *How to Save $14,500,000 Through Internal Auditing* (Orlando, Fla.: The Institute of Internal Auditors, 1955), p. 174.

24. V. Z. Brink, "The Internal Auditor's Review of Organizational Control," *Research Committee Report 18* (Orlando, Fla.: The Institute of Internal Auditors, 1972).

25. Ibid., p. 44.

26. Lawrence B. Sawyer, *The Practice of Modern Internal Auditing,* (Orlando, Fla.: The Institute of Internal Auditors, 1973), pp. 118, 119.

27. Ibid., p. 115.

3

Management, Managers, and Internal Auditors

Management—an American term. Art or science? Management defined. What is a manager? The management theories: classical, behavioral, decision-making, systems, quantitative, communications center, social system. The integrationists: fusion process, modified theory, organization overlay. The models of managers: autocratic, custodial, supportive, and collegial. Models of internal auditing: the classical, the operational, and the counselor, teacher, problem solver. The internal auditor and the models of management. The internal auditor's dealings with the four models of managers. Partnership. Acceptance by management. What management expects from the internal auditor.

THE NATURE OF MANAGEMENT AND MANAGERS

The Field of Management

There are as many theories of management as there are theorists. The boom in management theory since World War II let loose a Niagara of thoughts, ideas, and theories about management into the libraries of the world. To dissect the anatomy of management, hundreds of scalpels busily probed the core of the growing profession.

Not all the words were in English, and not all the scalpels were made in America. Yet it is an interesting fact that the word "management" is completely American.[1] It is not a very precise word, because it is used to describe both a function and the people who carry it out. It is considered both a position and a field of study.

The function is universal, but the significance of the word varies. In hospitals, universities, and government, administrators manage. In the armed services, commanders manage. In businesses managers manage. And in many organizations, executives are the counterparts of top managers.

Managers are professionals. Their function is now generally independent of the function of ownership. Although they use the tools of many disciplines—economics, quantification, and behavioral science—they practice a separate discipline called management. Managers may be indifferent technicians; but if they have absorbed the skills and techniques of management, they may be superb in evoking and putting to use the best from the skilled technicians.

Some theorists call management a science; some call it an art; some call it a practice; some call it a discipline. Perhaps it is an amalgam of all four. It has a body of systematized knowledge, predicated on persuasive principles. It seeks to bring about desired results through the application of skill. It calls for intensive, disciplined training and application to meld together a multitude of efforts and activities to reach desired goals.

On the quality of managers hinges the success or failure of business, government, churches, universities, and other organizations. It is becoming an aphorism that what goes well or what goes badly within an enterprise depends on how well managers innovate, function, and produce. And so the search for the ingredients of this phenomenon on the human scene has been feverish.

Management and Manager Defined

Each student of management and managers has his favorite definition of the terms and his own philosophy of the functions. Here are a few from among a myriad:

Koontz and O'Donnell say that the function of managers is to "create and maintain an environment in which individuals can work together to accomplish group goals."[2] More succinctly, they see it as "getting things done through and with people."[3] Flippo and Munsinger, using the systems concept, see management as one of the subsystems—the regulatory element.[4] Terry says simply that management deals with establishing and achieving objectives.[5]

Drucker views management through the functions of defining the specific purpose and mission of the enterprise, making work productive and the worker achieving, and managing social impacts and social responsibilities.[6] Along with his broad view of management, he sees the manager in a different light than most other writers. He sees as managers not only the leaders of others but also those whose actions and decisions are intended to have a significant impact on the business and its ability to perform and the direction it will take. In that context, the internal auditor, as one of those whom Drucker calls the "knowledge professionals," has a place on the management team.

Drucker spins a provocative little tale that illuminates his view of what a manager is:[7] "Three stonecutters, busy at their jobs, were asked what they were doing. The first said he was making a living. The second said he was doing the best job of stonecutting in the entire country. The third, with a look upward, said 'I am building a cathedral.'"

The first stonecutter knows what he wants out of the job, and being a manager is not a part of it. The second may think he's a manager, but his view is too narrow. The third is the true manager. He is a craftsman and not a leader of others, but he identifies with the enterprise and its goals. His contribution transcends his personal needs or his competence as a craftsman; it is identified with the prime purpose of the job and not his parochial concerns.

Internal auditors may see parallels in the work of the stonecutters. One may perform an audit in strict compliance with the established audit program. Another, following the same program, may apply imagination and innovation in detecting deficient conditions that require special skills to unearth and develop and to bring articulately and persuasively to management's attention.

The third goes a step further: He learns the underlying causes of the defects, and he counsels managers on why the difficulties occurred and how recurrence may be prevented. Then he seeks out other activities within the enterprise in which like defects might exist and other managers might need similar counsel. He is more than a craftsman; he is a "knowledge professional." He is a member of the management team.

The Management Theories

Each theorist who examines management sees it as the blind men "saw" an elephant: a rope, a tree, or a wall depending on what they touched. The varied views have become a tangle of strands each seen by someone as the sole line to the truth. Indeed, one author called the tangled skein "the management theory jungle."[8] A host of theories and combinations of theories seek to explain the management function. Here is a brief explanation of some of them.

Classical

Together with the classical[9] school can be considered the school of scientific management, management by custom,[10] and the operational and empirical schools of management theory.[11] The classical school is also referred to as traditional, universalist, and the management process.

The classical school started as a system of management in the eighteenth century when handcraft at home with personally owned tools gave way to factory systems. People were brought together. They worked for someone else with someone else's equipment. Formal organizations were developed. Rules and regulations were imposed. The owners ruled chiefly by reason of ownership and by instilling feelings of fear.

Then, with the advent of Taylor, Fayol, Gantt, and the Gilbreths, some order was imposed on the haphazard organizational structures that had been built at the whims of individuals. In the late nineteenth and early twentieth centuries, management began to emerge as a science as Taylor and others concentrated on the study of processes and on systematic planning.

Taylor's classic pig iron experiment is an illustration. Laborers, relying on brute force and ignorance, could load only 12½ tons of iron per man-day onto a railroad car from a storage yard. By using Taylor's improved methods, which were based on studies of motion, time, and fatigue, along with incentive wages, they boosted daily output from 12½ to 48 tons. The daily pay rose 60 percent to $1.85 a day—minuscule by today's standards, but much higher than the average rate being paid in the community.[12]

The school of scientific management developed methods of confirming or disproving business propositions. It sought to discover causal relations to business phenomena, and it contributed tremendous knowledge through a structured rather than a catch-as-catch-can approach to problems. The school made use of investigation, experimentation, and the careful interpretation of results. Method replaced intuition.

Management by custom is similar to the law of precedents followed by lawyers and judges. It is guided by traditions: "What was good enough for Sloan is good enough for me." It makes use of biographical studies of pioneers in business. It employs case studies to present and solve propositions as others have solved them in the past. To a considerable extent it maintains the status quo, relying on what has been done rather than on what new approaches might be better.

There can be little looking ahead when the eyes are fixed on the past, yet the custom school can be productive. It is difficult to quarrel with success, and it is hard to fault a manager who uses an old technique effectively to solve a current problem.

The operational approach was fashioned by Fayol. It made use of a universal body of knowledge, theory, and principles and applied them to all types of enterprises. Fayol viewed management as a process that can be understood by analyzing the functions of the manager. Past experience can be the source from which basic principles can be distilled. The principles can serve as standards for managers and, with time, be either refined or disproved. The proven principles remain valid whether the manager uses them or elects to ignore them. But the operational approach is encapsulated; it is isolated from other fields we now know to have a profound effect on the enterprise: economics, sociology, psychology, and other sciences. Therein lies its weakness.

The empirical view is similar to management by custom and, as its name suggests, relies on experience. The premise is that a study of how other managers solved specific problems will reveal helpful techniques that have universal applicability. That may often be true, but it may just as often be misleading. It is rare indeed that today's problem is precisely the same as yesterday's. And management is not so exact a science that precedent will be completely applicable in all cases.

One thread runs through the fabric of all five schools of management theory: The approach is relatively mechanistic; it leaves little room for the human being who is subject to the decisions, rules, and principles. The single beam of the spotlight illuminates the manager. He is the unquestioned authority. The law flows down. Those beneath may not question; they may not disobey; they may not even debate or suggest.

Yet that approach is most prevalent today; indeed, in some organizations, suborganizations, or environments, no other is appropriate. Still, different schools of management thought are making themselves felt, as we shall point out.

Behavioral

Starting with the 1920s, observers of the management scene began finding some blind spots in the scientific view of management.[13] The discovery began with the work of Mayo and Roethlisberger, who carried out organized research into the subject of humanities in business. The school is variously called "human relations," "behavioral science," and "leadership." It focuses on the human side of management and the worker. It seeks to obtain greater understanding to accomplish group objectives. The research has been able to buttress the proposition that, if the needs and desires of people are satisfied, the organization's output will increase.[14]

The followers of the behavioral approach see the manager not as a doer but as an accomplisher through others.[15] And there have been significant contributions in the use of participation and in dealing with organizational conflicts. Besides, new understandings have been reached about the motivations of people, the effect of authority, the place of irrationality in behavior, and the all-important informal relations within an organization.

On the other hand, some proponents have sought to elevate the behavioral approach to unattainable heights. They see it as the core of management. They equate human behavior with the entire field of management, whereas, at most, it is only a tool of management and one of the many tools the manager must master if he is to do his job.[16]

If the worker is to be productive, the manager must understand not only the work but also the physiological, psychological, social and community, and economic dimensions of working.[17]

The physiological dimension. The worker is a human being and not a machine. He lacks the strength and stamina of a machine, but he exceeds the machine in coordination and imagination. The machine works best at a steady speed, but the worker performs at varying speeds and so his work is best organized to provide diversity.

The psychological dimension. People are conditioned to work; unemployment creates severe psychological disturbances. As an extension of his personality, work gives the individual a feeling of worth and accomplishment. The Western work ethic gives respect and dignity to working.

The social and community dimension. Belonging to a work group satisfies an individual's need. Outside his family, the person's job is his one great bond with others.

The economic dimension. Work is the basis for the individual's economic existence. It creates power relations between management and labor.

Those four dimensions are important to the manager in dealing with people; the manager cannot avoid them or will them away. He must be concerned with the behavioral and human relations approach to his job. There are several reasons why.[18] First, human relations can contribute to greater productivity. Second, if the manager does not concern himself with human relations, something else, like the labor union, will step in to force that concern. Third, the government may intervene, as witness Fair Employment Practice laws. Finally, every organization must meet certain moral objectives, and concern for the human being is a paramount objective.

That the manager may not always have the time for concern with people is irrelevant. Mintzberg's analysis of the manager's work—racing through the day just to stay even—underscores the difficulty: The manager does not erase the problems; he accentuates them. So long as management is required to accomplish results through people, managers will have to be concerned with the findings of sociology, anthropology, and psychology.

Decision Making

Proponents of one school of management contend that decision making is the pivotal job of the manager.[19] Whatever the manager does involves selecting a course of action from among different choices. Whatever he plans to do can be a legitimate reason for a decision-making study. The theorists have studied decisions for improving communication, incentives, reactions of workers, and human values in terms of enterprise objectives. Thus the decision theory school has expanded its concepts. It has gone beyond evaluating alternatives. It has reached into the entire bag of the entity's functions, including value considerations about the enterprise goals.

As in many schools of thought, adherents seek to use the decision-making umbrella to cover every conceivable enterprise activity. But there may be a question whether decision making is the center of the management universe or just one of the spheres within the totality. There is more to managing than making decisions; there is also implementation, evaluation, and feedback. Nevertheless, decision making as a key function of management cannot be underestimated.

Systems

The systems management school sees every organization as a complex system made up of integrated subsystems. The manager functions through systems; he can grapple with a huge system by dealing with the many smaller systems that constitute the whole.[20] Each system has the elements of input, processing, output, and feedback, and all are governed by some means of control. The input is received from an upstream system's output. The output is passed on to a downstream system.

The systems concept simplifies dealing with the numerous and varied activities within a large organization. Also, it brings about a coalescence of disciplines usually considered isolated: economics, engineering, psychology, sociology, and anthropology. It crosses organizational lines. It penetrates the departmental capsule.

In similar fashion, the internal auditor, as occasion warrants, may depart from the review of a single department or group—the organizational audit—and cross organizational lines to trace a function from headwater to delta—the functional audit.[21] In a functional audit of purchased products, he might trace the various interlocking subsystems that begin with preliminary design and drafting—where the purchased products needed are identified—through production planning, purchasing, receiving, and storing and the incorporation of the procured products into a final assembly. To the internal auditor, as to the manager, the functional or systems approach leads to a completely different view of the organization's operations.

The multitudinous interrelations among subsystems call for the assimilation of masses of data. Thus the advent of the computer added muscle to the management system concept by permitting new, complex control devices to function.

Quantitative

The quantitative, or mathematical, school traces its heritage to Taylor's scientific management and its birth to World War II.[22] In the 1940s what is now known as operations research was developed in England to solve war-related problems. Professor P. M. S. Blackett of the University of Manchester gathered a team of physiologists, mathematical physicists, mathematicians, astrophysicists, and other specialists to study combat and logistical systems. That group, as well as others like it set up in the United States, had excellent results from using mathematical models to solve difficult problems. They determined the best size for war convoys and the depth at which charges should explode in an attack on submarines.

The results were so good that the approach was adopted by business enterprises. The development of the computer simplified handling great amounts of statistical data dealing with numerous variables and solving complex problems. Calculus can be used to determine the extent of change in one factor with respect to another factor. The businessman is given answers to "what if" questions:

How are overhead rates affected by changes in the labor base, or productivity, or greater sales? What is the best geographical location of warehouses? What is the proper size of salesmen's territories? What will be the effect of lowered or raised prices?

Models can be developed to represent systems and to assist in decision making. The techniques used include probability theory, regression analysis, linear programming, Monte Carlo simulation, inventory theory, queuing theory, sensitivity analysis, game theory, dynamic programming, and exponential smoothing.[23]

Nevertheless, the quantitative approach is no more the whole story of management than accounting is. It offers assistance in decision making and even in evaluating risks. It contributes to orderly thinking. It forces managers to identify and think through problems thoroughly, establish goals, and measure effectiveness. It fosters the development of logical systems of management. But it is less a school of management than a tool of management.

The early promise of substituting operations research for management thought and the computer for the manager has not been and cannot be realized. Management in many ways is still an art. The quantitative approach places emphasis on techniques, not on principles.[24]

Communications Center

In the communications center approach, the manager is a walking information center. He is the focal point for receiving, storing, and processing information and then disseminating it as he directs people and controls activities.[25] The approach gained greater popularity with the advent of the computer and management information systems, and it is akin to the decision-making theory of management. But the reliance on computers overshadows a simple fact of life: Managers have always been communications centers. By being privy to bits and pieces of information not available to their subordinates, they emerge as the nerve centers of their organizational units. By contacts with peers, their own superiors, and their own people, they become depositories of information that goes beyond anything known by their people. And that information puts them in the position of being able to make more knowledgeable decisions than their people can make.[26] Like other schools, however, communication is not the whole story. Important, yes. All-embracing, no.

Social System

The social system school is related to the behavioral approach. It conceives of the organization as a series of cultural interrelations within the organization.   It seeks to integrate those relations into a system.[27]   The emphasis is on cooperation to solve the organization's problems and assist in making decisions.   It looks toward the balanced interests of the entity and rejects courses of action that benefit one group alone.

The social system school pays particular attention to ethics, to what is seen as right and moral.   Hence it is concerned with the relations among the organization, the internal and external environment, and the forces for change.[28]   The ethics of the manager is brought into sharper focus; the manager is not an island, and what he does in his personal life affects the organization and the organisms within it.

The concepts of the social system school are significant, but are they really the entire structure of management or merely some of its bearing members?

Integration

The manager is a practical man.   He does not see himself as a chameleon who must change his management colors with each new task or problem.   He wants some unified theory that selects the best from all theories and leads to increased productivity while preventing or reducing employee alienation.

Many attempts have been made to integrate the varying approaches that we have just identified.   Some theorists see valuable lessons in all the concepts propounded by each of the schools of management and have sought to extract and meld the best from each. The attempts at amalgamation go by many names.   They include but are not limited to the fusion process, the modified theory, and the organization overlay.   Here are brief explanations of the three.[29]

Advocates of *the fusion process* declare that, so long as the individual and the organization are in contact, they must in time coalesce and integrate their needs and desires.[30]   The individual, while he remains in the organization, must somehow change his behavior to meet the needs of the organization.   The organization must also change; its plans and structure must not be so rigid that they fail to accommodate the individual's needs.   If both parties satisfy their needs in that accommodation, then there is a successful fusion.   Perfect fusion is hardly ever possible because of basic differences in goals; indeed, may not be desirable, because progress is born in the crucible, not in the easy chair.

According to *the modified theory of management,* the classical approach succeeds only through the liquidation or erosion of human assets.   Drives for short-run productivity increases are bound to result in employee alienation. In the participative approach, an effort is made to obtain cooperation between employee and employer to the end that production increases and alienation is dissipated. Studies by Rensis Likert have indicated the practical benefits from the approach.[31]

The organization overlay school suggests that the formal structures of the organization, as depicted by the familiar organization charts, are too rigid; they exclude the human element and are out of touch with reality. Additional relations are vital and essential.[32] Those relations include the employee and his group, influences of intellectual leaders, decision-making centers, the power residing within groups and individuals, and the flow of informal communication.

Such patterns, guides, and networks can be laid over the official organization chart and hence display the "real world" organization. The resulting picture is extremely complex and serves to demonstrate, if nothing else, that the true organization chart is not as clean and crisp as it appears to be. The intelligent manager must take the human relations into account.

Models of Managers

Models of management have certain counterparts in models of managers. The schools of management theory produce echoes from the people who perform management functions. The correlation is not precise, but it is close enough to deserve attention.

The affluent society depicted by John Kenneth Galbraith owes its growth to many factors, including improved education, innovation, and an expanding technology, but central to all those factors are management and managers. Managers have responded to the needs of society and to the opportunities for improved productivity. Many shifts in the way managers function have occurred in response to the changes in society, the outlook of workers, and the findings of researchers who have probed management theory. As a result, new models of organizational behavior have evolved, and many are still evolving. The models are not merely catchwords or labels. The concepts that give rise to the models influence the managers: their thinking, the way they see the world around them, and their attitude toward the people they deal with.

When a manager, influenced by a new school of behavior thinks in new ways, he begins to act differently. On his actions depend the productivity of his organizational unit. If he follows outmoded or inappropriate models, he may be jeopardizing his job or his organization.

Four distinct models of organizational behavior have evolved during the last 100 years or so; they are the autocratic, custodial, supportive, and collegial.[33] The autocratic model, the traditional bull of the woods, held sway 75 years ago. Then, with the proliferation of studies on organizational behavior during the 1920s and the 1930s and with the growth of the unions, the more successful custodial model emerged. More organizations, however, are now beginning to turn to the supportive model, particularly among white collar workers. And just beginning to make itself felt in some advance organizations is the collegial model—the group of colleagues. Actually, no one organization follows a single model, nor does any manager use one model exclusively. Yet one model will tend to be dominant and will guide the methods of the organization and the thinking of the manager.

Within the organization's suborganizations, different models may be appropriate. The security department may use the autocratic approach; the production department the custodial approach; the internal auditing department the supportive approach; and the research department the collegial approach. The four models will now be analyzed in terms of the manager, the employee, and performance.

Autocratic Model

The autocratic model is rooted in history; it prevailed during the Industrial Revolution. It is based on power pure and simple. It uses threats, and motivation is negative. It sees people as passive, resistant, and lazy. Managers assume that employees have to be pushed into doing their jobs, and so they develop formal, structured organizations interwoven with detailed rules that are violated at the employees' peril. The manager gives the orders; the worker obeys "or else."

Employees bow to the authority of the boss, who *is* a boss rather than a leader. The worker has a psychological dependency on his boss, who holds the power of his job's life or death. He may like his boss, as a respected individual, and he may perform because of basic drives within him. But all that is attributable to the worker and not to the managerial model.

Modern observers tend to condemn it, but the autocratic model had its measure of success in building empires during the 1800s: the railroad systems, the steel mills, and an industrial society. Yet questions arise: Is there a better way? Can the same or better performance be achieved with enthusiasm instead of passive resistance? Can needs other than basic subsistence be filled in the employee and result in improved productivity? Those questions turned attention to other models of managerial behavior.

Custodial Model

The custodial model took form in the 1930s when interest started turning from the despotic organization to the "happy shop." Psychologists, industrial relations specialists, and economists pointed out that a satisfied employee could be a more productive worker. Under the autocrat, the compliant worker might be afraid to speak, but he couldn't be stopped from thinking. And somehow or other he would take his seething frustrations and suppressed aggressions out on productivity, the family, and the community.

And so began the development of the custodial model, with its fringe benefits, social security, and numerous programs to cater to what were seen as the needs and wants of the employee. Generally, the programs depended on the economic resources available to carry them out, and managerial orientation was toward material rewards for the worker. The employee saw security in the model. Morale improved; the employee tended to transfer dependence from his boss to the organization that provided him with his security blanket.

But the roseate picture that had been painted for the custodial model began to fade. People may have been happy, but they were not being fulfilled. A warm bath is relaxing, not invigorating. Security and happiness are important, but they are not the whole answer to work. People need to be motivated beyond what they think they are capable of doing in order to be achieving and in order to be fulfilled. As Ray E. Brown pointed out,[34]

> Men grow stronger on workouts than on handouts. It is the nature of people to wrestle with a challenge and rest with a crutch. . . . The great desire of man is to stand on his own, and his life is one great fight against dependency. Making the individual a ward of the organization will likely make him bitter, not better.

Observers began to see that neither the custodial nor the autocratic model provided the ultimate truth. Clearly, there may be some jobs and some people—insecure, timid, weak, not needing or desiring self-fulfillment—who function best in a custodial atmosphere. They see the job as a source of income and a necessary evil. If the evil can be made tolerable through pleasant relationships, there is nothing further to demand—at least they will not be alienated. But for others there is more to work than a relaxed way to earn a living.

Supportive Model

The supportive model found adherents when researchers, particularly in the Hawthorne experiments, showed that the happy employee was not necessarily the most productive employee. The supportive model moves away from the economic support of the custodial model to the psychological support provided by a leader-manager.

The supportive model depends on leadership and a climate that helps the employee grow vigorously, not langorously. The manager has positive feelings about his people: They *do* want to work. They *do* want to grow. They *do* want to be productive. They *do* want to take responsibility. They *do* want to achieve.

Since what is being supported is performance—rather than happiness—the employee is oriented toward that goal instead of obedience or security. Psychologically, he has a feeling of participation and involvement. He and his organization become "we" instead of "me and them." The model awakens drives that the worker may never have been aware he had.

The supportive model is a rung that is high in the ladder that reaches toward employee motivation and progress. But it is not the top rung of the ladder. That may well be the fourth model.

Collegial Model

The fourth and latest model is still beginning to take shape. It developed from recent research, especially by Likert[35] and Herzberg.[36] It depends on management building a feeling of mutual contribution. The manager and the employee are joint contributors; they are not boss and worker. Since much is expected, much is given. Each contributor—worker, co-worker, manager, and executive—is respected for what he can offer to meet organizational goals.

The manager is oriented toward teamwork instead of toward superior and subordinate. Performance is improved because there is an inner need to perform at maximum effectiveness, not to please the boss or the inspector, but to please the inner monitor that rejects everything but the best.

The result from the employee's standpoint can be self-discipline, responsibility, self-fulfillment, and enthusiasm.

Summary

Models are evolutionary. They grew out of the needs of organizations and of people. They are not static, and none as yet answers the needs of all situations. But managers must be aware of the models that exist. They must realize that no one model is the full-spectrum cure to organizational maladies. Low-skilled routine work and the people content with that kind of work may respond best to security and motivational rewards, that is, to the autocratic and custodial models. Other jobs, more professional in nature, may be made most productive in a climate of teamwork and self-motivation, that is, the climate of the supportive and collegial models.

As time goes by, as employees strive for more than a 9:00-to-5:00 existence, and as greater premiums are placed on innovation and commitment, the trends for all kinds of workers can be toward the supportive and collegial models and whatever lies beyond.

THE NATURE OF MODERN INTERNAL AUDITING

Models of Internal Auditing

Evolving models of management have counterparts in evolving models of internal auditing. There too the classical and autocratic beginnings are giving way to more enlightened schools of thought. The classical internal auditor was an adjunct of the autocrat. The autocrat made the rules; the internal auditor accepted them and checked to see whether they were being followed. The primary function of the classical auditor was to examine financial transactions, accounts, and reports and to evaluate compliance with applicable rules and regulations. To that end he needed a basic knowledge of accounting theory and practice and a facility for applying auditing techniques and procedures. The numbers came first; people came afterward if at all. A deviation was a deviation whether it was merely a smudge on the pillars of the organization or an earthquake that rocked the pillars.

The classical internal auditor performed, and still performs, a needed function, but that function is restricted and is sometimes warped. Besides, it looks to the past, not to the future. The classical auditor belongs to the "protective" school that concentrates on the conservation of resources and the detection of deviations. The high point in his auditing career would be to find fraudulent transactions and see to it that the thief or embezzler was put behind bars. It should be emphasized that being on the alert for fraudulent transactions is still a necessary function of internal auditing, but it is not the whole function.

Concepts and theories of internal auditing have advanced in many organizations in both the public and the private sectors. They have marched forward with the development of innovative and imaginative auditing organizations, with the establishment of The Institute of Internal Auditors and its motto "Progress Through Sharing," and with the writings of the modern thinkers in the profession.

The scope of internal auditing expanded to a review of efficiency and economy in the use of resources. "Resources" came to embrace more than what was recorded in the books of account; they now mean men, materials, and money. The range of the internal auditor has widened. The internal auditor no longer remains bound to the books of account; he roams at will through every activity in the organization where he can be of service to management. His preoccupation is no longer solely with assets and numbers; he now feels a responsibility for all resources and operations. He is now a member of the "constructive school"; his purpose is to evaluate all relevant and significant operations and make appropriate recommendations for improvement.

A third school of internal auditing is now forming. It is taking shape as the internal auditor takes on a new responsibility: to determine whether desired results are being achieved effectively. That is a quantum jump, but it is more than an increase in the scope of internal auditing. It is a change in thinking and a change in the levels of people with whom the auditor primarily deals.

To examine transactions calls for dealing with workers and supervisors. To review operations calls for adding operating managers to the clientele. To evaluate program results requires bringing executive management into the auditor's compass of concern.

Evaluating desired results and the effectiveness with which they are achieved calls for determining more than whether activities are being carried out with due concern for cost, quality, and schedule. It calls for determining whether the right activities were carried out to begin with, whether those activities mesh with the organization's objectives and goals, whether people are employing appropriate management and administrative techniques, whether people know what they should be achieving and are using their resources wisely to achieve, and whether people need counsel and guidance to do the right thing in the best way.

That is the newest school of modern internal auditing theory: the school of the counselor, teacher, and problem-solving partner.

Understanding Models of Management

The schools of management theory are not merely textbook caricatures. Research has identified and delineated them. Different managers follow different philosophies of management. If the internal auditor were to deal with a classical environment as if it were a collegial one, the certain results would be conflict and misunderstanding. Also, he would be prevented from achieving his own audit goals.

In a classical environment the internal auditor emphasizes transactions and deviations. That the classical manager understands: he makes the rules; he wants them followed. Once he is convinced that deviations have occurred—and he alone must be convinced—he will take the steps to correct them and to see that they do not recur. The auditor is not debarred from evaluating effectiveness and results, but he treads softly and recognizes that he has a selling job on his hands.

In the behavioral school environment the internal auditor must take a different tack. He must speak of goals and objectives, of values and needs. When people of the behavioral school are made aware that they are not achieving what was intended, both they and the auditor may not only assess production but reassess the goals themselves.

In the environment of the decision-making school the internal auditor's orientation will be toward the elements of the decision. Has the problem been formulated precisely in terms of goals? Does the decision tree take into account the controllable factors and those beyond control—the fixed factors and the variable factors? Have the possible solutions been tested? Have the solutions been put into effect? Have feedback systems been established to help determine whether objectives are being met?

The internal auditor should be careful not to become a second-guesser of management decisions; 20-20 hindsight is easy to develop and difficult to appreciate. But he can evaluate the *methods* used in making decisions, and he can make sure that managers are receiving the kind of prompt, accurate, meaningful information they need for their decision-making process.

In the systems school environment the internal auditor might describe problem areas in terms of input, processing, output, feedback, and control and point out how breakdowns in any of those elements result in difficulties that need correction.

In the environment of the quantitative or mathematical school the internal auditor can use his analytical ability to assure senior management that appropriate quantitative approaches and techniques were used, that the input is relevant, accurate, and complete, and that the methods employed can be tested objectively. There may be a tendency to place overreliance on numbers; it is easy to forget, in the passion for mathematics, that the end result must pass the test of reason and must make good sense.

In the communication school environment the internal auditor can provide a service in seeing that the communications received are relevant, current, complete, and usable. He can also perform a service by looking at the economies of the communication received. Is the flood of information necessary? Is it all raw data that are useless to the recipient? Can it be synthesized to have more meaning and be made more readily usable?

In the social system school environment the internal auditor should keep abreast of new legislation on safety, the environment, and social impacts. Managers are not always kept informed or new laws that have an immediate effect on their work. When government inspectors come around to check on compliance, it may be too late. Hence, as counselor to management, the internal auditor should be alert to new laws that will affect systems and controls. He should bring them to the attention of managers and point out the steps needed to bring activities into compliance.

The schools of management theory proliferate. There is no unanimity; no one seems to have the whole answer. Yet each school, in its way, has some effect on management thinking, so the internal auditor should have more than a nodding acquaintance with the schools to keep attuned with the managers he must deal with.

Dealing with Models of Managers

Each manager the internal auditor deals with has his unique style. Some managers may be exclusively autocratic, custodial, supportive, or collegial. Others may be amalgams of two or more of the model styles, although usually one model style will predominate. The internal auditor should be aware of the individual styles, which may affect his audit approach. They may have a bearing on how he "gets through" to the manager to present his findings, make his recommendations, and decide how he must proceed to be sure that corrective action is taken and is effective.

The autocratic style should signal to the internal auditor that workers and subordinate managers lack independence. They will be fearful of taking any action that might conflict with the autocrat's views—or with their views of the autocrat's views. To aid the autocrat, the auditor should look for clear instructions, tight controls, and a rigid system of review and approval. And if the auditor encounters defects or proposes improvements, he will find it necessary to clear them with the autocrat, for nobody else within the group has authority to approve changes. But if defects are traceable to an environment of repression, the auditor may have to counsel the autocrat or his superior on the benefits that may flow from other management styles.

The custodial style calls for the internal auditor who encounters unsatisfactory conditions to point out how much easier matters will be if defects are corrected and recommendations are adopted. At the same time, the auditor should be aware of the faults inherent in the custodial style. The relaxed atmosphere is not always the climate in which productivity grows. Perhaps realistic goals and measurements need to be established—with the cooperation of those who will be measured.

The supportive style gives the internal auditor the opportunity to take both managers and employees into his confidence from the time the audit starts until it is completed. His recommendations gain readier acceptance when he can show how they will improve production and better achieve goals and objectives.

The collegial style beckons the auditor to be a contributor to the group and offer his recommendations and contributions to the greater good of the organization.

Acceptance into the Partnership

In law, a partnership is an association of two or more persons to carry on, as co-owners, a business for profit. Although the manager and the internal auditor are not co-owners, they can carry out their responsibilities only if they act as though the business were theirs and its profits depended on their working together to meet its objectives. Indeed, it has been said that before an internal auditor makes a recommendation for improvement, he should ask himself, "What would I do if I owned the enterprise?"

But another definition of partnership more precisely describes the hoped-for affiliation between management and internal auditing: A relationship involving close cooperation between parties who have specified and joint rights and responsibilities. A partnership is a delicate relationship. It is founded on mutual trust. It should combine complementary skills and assets that each partner brings to the undertaking. It calls for mutual respect and for agreement on what each partner demands of the other.

One of the most serious and recurring complaints from many internal auditors is the lack of acceptance of the internal auditing function by managers within the organization. Internal auditors, hearing of the high regard in which many of their colleagues are held in some organizations, become frustrated and bitter when their own managements fail to provide them with the status and support they feel they must have to carry out a topnotch audit job.

No one formula will provide the key to management acceptance, much less the hoped-for problem-solving partnership. Not all managements are the same, and certainly not all internal auditors are the same. Many have not stopped and thought through what their role and function within their organization is and how it fits into the particular management style or management needs. Clearly, the needs in a bank or insurance company vary widely from the needs in a government agency or a university.

Many more internal auditors have not equipped themselves with the skills, techniques, and know-how that bring respect and acceptance. And still others have not mounted the right campaign within their organization to parade their wares before management and determine what management really wants and what it really needs.

But some hints of what management expects from the internal auditor can be gleaned from the words of high-placed managers themselves. And what better source for such intelligence than the people who pay the bills? I have gathered a sampling of those thoughts, and the same theme seems to recur: Enlightened managers see the respected internal auditor as more than a verifier and a checker, more than a chronicler of things past, and more than a faultfinder. They see such an internal auditor as more of a counselor, more of a teacher, and more of a problem-solving partner. And so we have grouped these thoughts under the more respected heads.

Counselor

Ward Burns, controller for J. P. Stevens Company, Inc., lays down ten commandments for the internal auditor. Here are some extracts:[37]

1. Are the company's systems being properly controlled? Can management be sure, for example, that cash is protected by proper internal controls from receipt to disbursement, that excess cash is invested advantageously, that cash is borrowed at competitive rates for the shortest possible time, that "goodwill" bank accounts are minimized, and that foreign currencies are promptly exchanged at the best rates?

2. Be familiar with the organization and its controls. Be sure of the facts. Be expert in the methods of evaluation, the techniques of control, and the development of practical recommendations.

3. Be able to prepare clear, concise reports. Avoid trivia. Include matters that top management can do something about and also matters that were resolved but about which top management should be informed.

4. Inform management immediately about any significant deviations that need correction; do not wait for the final written report.

5. Resolve all disputes before the report reaches top management. Review draft reports up the management ladder. Report irreconcilable differences and give both sides.

6. Review data processing operations as top management would review them if it had the time and knew how.

7. Be available for consultation on matters and techniques of control. (Burns says, "Happy is the internal auditor who has so conducted himself over a period of time that he is invited to participate in establishing procedures and concepts at the start of a new venture of operation. It is the ultimate proof that the internal auditor is wanted and needed and that his skills are, at long last, clearly recognized.")

8. Have guts. Once he is sure of his facts, is certain of the relevance and significance of his recommendations, and perceives a clear and present danger if his recommendations are not followed, the internal auditor must have the fortitude to stand up and make himself heard, even if that takes going to the very top.

9. Be ethical. Be competent. Be professional.

10. Be interested in every aspect of the enterprise. Be concerned with the impact of accelerating technological, economic, regulatory, or social changes.

Burns concludes by saying that perhaps the most important thing top management should expect from internal auditing is the ability to welcome, evaluate, and assimilate change. The thrust of the internal auditor's work may have to be the evaluation of activities, transactions, and probabilities of the future rather than the present or past and counseling management on the findings and conclusions.

William O. Beers, president of Kraftco Corporation, writes:[38]

> The prime goal of business will not change. That goal is profit. But to obtain that profit, more than ever it will be necessary to plan accurately— plan with the help of the latest available information [while] considering the dynamics of our society, our environment, and our economy.
>
> In this endeavor, the internal audit function will be crucial . . . "the uninspected inevitably deteriorates."

Stephen F. Keating, president of Honeywell, Inc., expects the internal auditor (or operations analyst as he is called at Honeywell):[39]

> To know the total business.
> To think like the managers.

To develop, communicate, and sell ideas.
To keep evaluating his own function.
To be sensitive and diplomatic.
To be objective.
To be a coordinator of good business practice.

In connection with the coordination function, Keating says: "Because analysts study so many parts of the company, they are in a perfect position to perform this cross-pollenating function. So we look upon them to some extent as operating a consulting service."

Stuart D. Watson, president, chief executive officer, and a director of Heublein, Inc., sees internal auditing as follows:[40]

1. It must aid the chief executive in the planning process by ensuring the integrity of the information systems. Those are the systems the executive must rely upon in devising effective plans.
   □ Have all the risks been identified?
   □ Has there been adequate research on markets and on competition?
   □ Are sales forecasts, pricing strategies, and projected costs sound?
   □ How good are the budgeting methods for establishing goals and monitoring performance?
2. It must alert the chief executive in the organizing process when it encounters problems traceable to the organization structure: duties, responsibilities, and personnel policies.
3. The audit function should help head off and resolve business problems. The more exposure to company operations it has the better equipped it will be to identify and work on the more significant problems.
4. It is important to know how management thinks: its plans, its objectives, and its operating concepts; in short, its management model.

Teacher

Raymond Plank, president of Apache Corporation, which is involved in oil and gas exploration, uses his internal auditors to advise him on company acquisitions, on whether there is compatibility of interests and policies.[41] Then, when a company is acquired, the internal auditor helps advise management on making necessary transitions to bring the new company into gear with Apache in terms of policies, procedures, and systems.

Plank also asks his internal auditors to help owner-managers of subsidiary companies find ways to improve profits, ways to balance long-term and short-term profits. Above all, he wants the internal auditor "to get through to people" if they are to get results.

Dudley Stewart, vice president and comptroller for the Industrial Acceptance Corporation Group of Companies, in speaking about the internal auditor of the future, said:[42]

> The internal auditor must . . . function as an integral part of the management team. . . .

> The chief internal auditor will become more and more a creative executive. The more effective he becomes, the more he will find that a great deal of his time is spent on teaching those who report to him and teaching very subtly those on whose work he is reporting.

Problem-Solving Partner

Charles R. Gollihar, Jr., vice president, finance and treasurer for Douglas Aircraft Company of Canada Limited, concludes a detailed exposition on how he expects his internal auditors to provide assistance to management, by stating:[43]

> Overall, I recommend to you the principle and belief that the audit report should settle each question in the mind of management, not raise questions to which an answer must then be found.

> The message I most wish to convey is that I feel strongly that in the area of management audits, the auditor can and should be an integral part of the final *problem-solving* team. [Emphasis mine.] I do not feel his role is to stand apart and say "I warned you!", but rather [he] should roll up his sleeves and jointly with other managers report to top management: "we fixed it."

Kenneth W. Bahler, assistant to the president, Union Carbide Corporation, includes in his catalog of what management expects from the internal auditor:[44]

☐ Act and perform like a professional.
☐ Serve as an extension of management in doing the type of verification the manager would do personally if he could.
☐ Participate as a member of the management team to find better ways of doing the job.

William G. Phillips, president and chief executive officer of International Multifoods Corporation, draws these conclusions about internal auditing:[45]

> Now let me sum up by saying that the internal auditing profession has a tremendous opportunity to expand the service it provides to companies. In our company, for example, we have changed the name of the internal audit function to audit services so as to communicate an expanded concept of the function throughout the organization.
>
> An area of increasing importance to American business is the planning process. Within our company and many others, planning has been improved, and added emphasis placed on more and better attention to implementation, by defining proper action steps.
>
> Why shouldn't auditors be asked to become working partners in reviewing the basic assumptions and inputs which result in operating plans? This is one of the many new and exciting areas in which the profession can make a contribution.
>
> In today's vigorous and expanding business climate, you either move forward or you regress. If you rise to the occasion, the sky is truly the limit for today's internal auditor.
>
> With this change in the role of the internal auditor, his definition, of course, would have to be revised to read something like this:
>
>> The typical auditor is a beautiful man, intelligent, warm and considerate with an ability to put himself in the other man's shoes and understand his problems; polite in contact and helpful, but at the same time objective, calm and as composed in crisis as Stravinsky on opening night; a human person with a heart of gold and with the charm of a friendly poodle, plus brains, business foresight and a sense of humor. Happily they train others in their image and all of them finally go to Heaven.

Management acceptance of the modern internal audit function takes work. It must be founded on demonstrated professional competence and on the communication of the benefits of the function to managers through comprehensive long-range audit programs, through professional audits, through crisp, incisive audit reports, and through periodic summary reports to management on the accomplishments the internal auditor has made. There are no shortcuts or easy ways, but the benefits both to the auditor and to the organization are worth the effort.

CONCLUSION

The classic authoritarian form of management is being challenged by a host of new schools—new theories of how best to run an enterprise and motivate people. And it would seem that, as more theorists address themselves to the subject, additional schools will blossom in the jungle of management theories. Yet each has something to commend it, and both managers and internal auditors should be aware of what current research is bringing to the management table.

Certainly the internal auditor should know the nature of the manager he is dealing with and how best to deal with each type of manager, whether autocratic, custodial, supportive, or collegial. Also, if he is to gain acceptance in a problem-solving partnership, he should know how thoughtful executives regard the internal audit function and thereby bring to the partnership complementary assets needed to help the organization thrive.

References

1. Peter F. Drucker, *Management: Tasks, Responsibilities, Practices* (New York: Harper & Row, 1974), p. 5.
2. Harold Koontz and Cyril O'Donnell, *The Essentials of Management* (New York: McGraw-Hill, 1974), p. 5.
3. Ibid., p. 3.
4. E. B. Flippo and G. M. Munsinger, *Management*, 3rd ed. (Boston: Allyn & Bacon, 1975), p. 23.
5. G. R. Terry, *Principles of Management*, 6th ed. (Homewood, Ill.: Irwin, 1972), p. 3.
6. Drucker, op. cit., pp. 40, 449.
7. Ibid., p. 431.
8. Harold Koontz, "The Management Theory Jungle," *Journal of the Academy of Management*, December 1965.
9. Flippo and Munsinger, op. cit., p. 14.
10. Terry, op. cit., pp. 61, 65.
11. Koontz and O'Donnell, op. cit., pp. 17, 19.
12. Frederick W. Taylor, *The Principles of Scientific Management* (New York: Harper & Brothers, 1947), pp. 41–47.
13. Koontz and O'Donnell, op. cit., p. 19.
14. Flippo and Munsinger, op. cit., p. 17.
15. Terry, op. cit., p. 65.
16. Koontz and O'Donnell, op. cit., p. 20.
17. Drucker, op. cit., p. 183.
18. Flippo and Munsinger, op. cit., p. 17.

19. Terry, op. cit., p. 71.
20. Ibid., p. 68.
21. Lawrence B. Sawyer, *The Practice of Modern Internal Auditing* (Orlando, Fla.: The Institute of Internal Auditors, 1973), p. 291.
22. Florence N. Trefethen, "A History of Operations Research," in Joseph F. McCloskey and Florence F. Trefethen, eds., *Operations Research for Management* (Baltimore: The Johns Hopkins Press, 1954). p. 6.
23. Sawyer, op. cit., p. 63.
24. Drucker, op. cit., p. 509.
25. Koontz and O'Donnell, op. cit., p. 21.
26. Henry Mintzberg, "The Manager's Job: Folklore and Fact," *Harvard Business Review,* July-August 1975, p. 49.
27. Koontz and O'Donnell, op. cit., p. 20.
28. Terry, op. cit., pp. 66, 67.
29. Flippo and Munsinger, op. cit., pp. 667, 668.
30. E. W. Bakke, *The Fusion Process* (New Haven: Yale University Labor and Management Center, 1955).
31. Rensis Likert, *New Patterns of Management* (New York: McGraw-Hill, 1961) and *The Human Organization* (New York: McGraw-Hill, 1967).
32. J. M. Pfiffner and F. P. Sherwood, *Administrative Organization* (Englewood Cliffs, N.J.: Prentice-Hall, 1960).
33. Keith Davis, *Human Relations at Work: The Dynamics of Organizational Behavior,* 3rd ed. (New York: McGraw-Hill, 1967).
34. R. E. Brown, *Judgment in Administration* (New York: McGraw-Hill, 1966), p. 75.
35. Likert, *The Human Organization,* pp. 3–11.
36. Frederick Herzberg, Bernard Mausner, and Barbara B. Snyderman, *The Motivation to Work* (New York: Wiley, 1959).
37. Ward Burns, "What Top Management Expects of Internal Audit Now!" *The Internal Auditor,* May-June 1975, pp. 20–23.
38. W. O. Beers, "Profit Potentials in the Current Economic Environment," *The Internal Auditor,* May-June 1975, pp. 20–23.
39. S. F. Keating, "How Honeywell Management Views Operational Auditing," *The Internal Auditor,* September-October 1969, pp. 43–51.
40. S. D. Watson, "Internal Auditing Viewed from the Top," *The Internal Auditor,* November-December 1973, pp. 24–31.
41. Raymond Plank, "What I Expect of My Internal Auditors," *The Internal Auditor,* September-October 1972, pp. 40–45.
42. Dudley Stewart, "The Internal Auditor of the Future," *The Internal Auditor,* March-April 1970, p. 55.
43. C. R. Gollihar, Jr., "What Management Expects from a Management Audit," *The Internal Auditor,* May-June 1972, p. 38.
44. K. W. Bahler, "What Management Expects of the Auditor," *The Internal Auditor,* July-August 1971, p. 67.
45. W. G. Phillips, "The Internal Auditor and the Changing Needs of Management," *The Internal Auditor,* May-June 1970, pp. 55, 56.

4

Patterns of Behavior

Work and the worker. Herzberg's satisfiers and dissatisfiers. Job enlargement and enrichment. The knowledge worker. Maslow's hierarchy of needs. Chris Argyris and levels of maturity. Vroom's preference-expectation. Morale. Douglas McGregor's Theory X and Theory Y. Likert and participative management. Employee appraisals. The group culture. Task leaders and group leaders. Sensitivity training. Creativity and the creative worker. QC circles. The internal auditor's work—its enlargement and enrichment. The search for impoverished jobs. Auditing the organization's hiring practices. Evaluating morale. Appraising the appraiser. Auditing performance reviews. Reviewing group and committee functions. The creative auditor. Creativity in auditing.

THE WORKER AND THE MANAGER

Work

Nature of Work

The origins of work are veiled in the mists of antiquity. The scriptures told man to till the ground from whence he was taken because of his fall from grace. He was told also that if any would not work, neither should he eat.[1]

Two giants of Greek poetry wrote about work. Hesiod, in his *Work and Days,* says, "Before success the immortal gods have placed the sweat of our brows." First came work, then came the rewards. But Homer, in the *Iliad* and the *Odyssey,* wrote of glorious ideals, of epic deeds, and of gods and demigods whose work flashed like comets across the skies of mythology. Homer's heroes were fulfilled in their very work. Hesiod's man worked for his bread, not for fulfillment, and because work is man's estate. Homer dealt with myths; Hesiod dealt with reality.

But today's worker is beginning to reach for more than bread alone. He is beginning to see fulfillment in his work as more than a myth. Too, the enlightened manager is learning that fulfillment for the worker and profit for the company are not mutually exclusive. And, of course, whatever concerns the manager concerns the internal auditor.

Work has been examined and tested in myriad research studies. Conclusions have been drawn and pronouncements have been made, each professing to be the ultimate truth. Some have been tested by time and still stand firm; others may bow to the counterthrust of studies leading to opposing conclusions. As a result, managers may be reluctant to put their trust in the pontifications of any particular pundit. But among the profusion there may be some principles that will retain fast colors even in the harsh sunlight of reality. They can be extremely useful to manager and internal auditor alike, both of whom should therefore be aware of what is being done and said about work and the worker—the two factors that are so critical to the success of the organization. We will present some of the principal views here. They may be adopted or rejected in the light of the law of the situation and the bent of the reader, but they should be considered.

He who sweats on the road to success and he who runs only to stay even need more than the exercise to be a fulfilled person. The fact that a person has a job and receives a pay check is no guarantee of satisfaction. Every job has its constraints. Every job implies in some degree rules, deadlines, standards, measurement of results, and accountability that may conflict with the employee's ideas of what he needs and wants.

Satisfiers and Dissatisfiers

Work is seen differently by the worker's manager and by the worker himself. The traditional manager sees the worker as coming on the job to further the organization's goals and objectives. The worker, however, may march to the beat of a different drummer and see work as a means of satisfying many of his basic needs.[2]

Herzberg regards work as providing two separate and distinct factors: the hygienic factors and the motivators.[3] And the research that led to his conclusions was based on face-to-face interviews with workers, not anonymous answers to cut-and-dried questionnaires. Each of many subjects was asked to tell when he felt very bad on the job and when he felt very good.

The hygienic factors—pay, interpersonal relations, supervision, company policy, working conditions, status, and job security—surfaced when the worker spoke of feeling very bad. The motivators—recognition, achievement, and the potentials for growth and advancement—were cited when the worker spoke of feeling very good. From that Herzberg deduced that the hygienic factors form a continuum from *dissatisfaction* to *no dissatisfaction*. Those factors are negative. Their absence makes the worker feel bad. But their presence does not awaken *good* feelings, just as one does not pay attention to the temperature in a room that is completely comfortable.

On the other hand, the motivators form a continuum from *no job satisfaction* to *job satisfaction*. If the job is routine, there is no satisfaction. If the job is exciting, challenging, and fulfilling, there is full satisfaction. The motivators concern the work; the hygienic factors concern the environment. The motivators relate to productivity; the hygienic factors relate to employee turnover.[4]

Job Enlargement and Enrichment

The worker generally has no personal control over his environment—over matters like pay, supervision, and organization policies. He can achieve no gratification from them. But an interesting and absorbing job can provide personal satisfaction, and the degree of satisfaction is under the worker's control. The more the worker does in a job that stimulates him, the more satisfaction he can obtain.[5]

Many jobs that are routine and repetitive provide no satisfaction or gratification to the worker. True, many workers want no job gratification. They just want a pay check; they see their jobs as the penalty they must pay for the wages they receive. Yet many others live their lives of quiet desperation in jobs that give them no fulfillment.

Some managers are becoming aware of the adverse effects of undemanding jobs. The phenomenon is being brought to their attention by the new breed of workers with higher education and changing attitudes toward authority. The trend is therefore toward job enlargement, job rotation, and job enrichment. Mass production's demands for more routine and simpler jobs is being given a hard look. Efficiency may be destroying effectiveness.

Job enlargement implies adding more steps to the routine job. *Job rotation* implies switching workers, and managers as well, from one job assignment to another at horizontal levels to reduce boredom and display a more comprehensive panorama of the organization to the employee.

Job enrichment tends to relieve the poverty of job satisfaction by providing greater responsibility and more opportunity to exercise independent judgment. Job enrichment is not new. At least one company, IBM, has been practicing it with considerable success for a long time.[6]

It is said that IBM's founder and then president once saw a woman sitting idly at her machine. When he asked her why, she said that she was waiting for the setup man to change the tool setting for the new run. He then asked her if she could do the setup work herself. She replied, "Of course, but I'm not supposed to." It was found that a great deal of time was wasted in that manner and that only a few days of additional training would qualify workers to set up their own machines.

The success of that simple enlargement and enrichment of a job sparked a systematic program at IBM to engineer employee interest in the job. The operations themselves are kept simple, but a number of them are put together into one job and always the job is designed to require some skill or judgment. In addition, the variety of operations permits the worker to vary the rhythm of the work. Satisfactory experience with job enlargement and enrichment is put to use in the introduction of each new product or product change at IBM. Production supervisors and workers participate in production layout and job planning.[7]

IBM is not unique. During World War II, workers had to take on added responsibilities because of the shortage of industrial engineers and skilled supervisors. In one aircraft company, entire engines were assembled from start to finish by separate teams. The teams organized their jobs differently, and different men did different jobs at different times. Each had been trained for the enlarged job, and each had continuing learning through weekly meetings with the foremen and the engineering staff to discuss problems and improvement. In each case the teams exceeded the output norms that the engineers had suggested.[8]

Similarly, in Sweden, under pressure of labor shortages, teams are set up to build entire automobiles. The plant sets the output and quality standards, but the men themselves work out the structure and organization of the jobs with the help of industrial engineers. The industrial engineers assist rather than prescribe.[9]

Job enrichment is being found outside the assembly line. Experts define the elements of the operation; then the worker puts them together to design his own job. In that way the job becomes "my job," truly "my job." The results are reduced turnover and increased productivity.[10]

Enriching jobs is neither a simple matter nor a panacea. Nothing is simple when people are concerned. Studies show that job complexity is related to job enrichment, and what is complex for one individual may be simple for another. The worker's *perception* of the job's complexity becomes central to job enrichment; hence, that perception should be examined before the job enrichment program is carried out.[11] What generates interest in worker A may frustrate worker B.

Some researchers feel that job enrichment may not be the whole answer to productivity. They doubt the causal relation of job satisfaction to high performance. They feel the relation may be in reverse: High performance results from job satisfaction. The researchers suggest "positive reinforcement" of the worker: applauding and rewarding the good while promptly criticizing the bad. They believe in focusing on actual behavior rather than on measures of effectiveness.[12] Such opposing views by researchers make managers long for the days before behaviorists started proclaiming the new truths.

Clearly, people respond to attention and interest; the Hawthorne experiments proved that. (See Chapter 2.) But a challenging job should prompt and maintain more employee interest and response then a pat on the head. The new breed of worker is more concerned with essentials than with supervisory soothing, particularly if the positive reinforcement is contrived and manipulative rather than sincere. And the strain may be more than the suprvisor could bear for long. Certainly positive reinforcement will have its benefits for the people who need it, but it too is not the whole answer.

Workers

Work and the Workers

The relation between the worker and work, the way the employee perceives his job, what rewards he expects, and how he and his job relate to the community around him are complex, mysterious phenomena that are largely unexplored. Yet dealing with a problem calls for an understanding of the problem elements; and although the theorists explore and research, neither the worker nor the manager can stand around while they dredge up the answers.

Managers generally understand, as the old saw has it, that one does not hire a hand—the whole man goes along with it. Experienced managers are also well aware that there is no such thing as the average worker. How much easier the manager would find life if he could deal with all people alike. Unfortunately, his job is not that simple. He must apply a single set of his organization's rules and procedures to a diversity of human beings. Within those imposed bounds, he must somehow take the opportunity to make adjustments for the individual.

Although rules tend to be standardized, human beings are not standardized units.[13] They are not standardized in their reactions or in their goals. It would be naive to think that all employees work to their full potential and that all people rise to a challenge. The reasons to the contrary are various: work restrictions by employees, tenure and protected job security, poor discipline, or belief in the propaganda of exploitation.

The behavioralists tend to downplay employee reluctance; the classicists underscore it; but it remains a fact of life. So if the manager is to provide a challenge, he should have a decent chance of having the challenge accepted. And that must start with hiring workers for their potential. Management should give more than passing consideration to hiring practices and interviewing techniques within the constraints imposed by law and union contracts.

Managers are observing the change that is taking place in the worker himself. A hundred years ago work for the majority of people centered around the home. People performed largely manual work by and for themselves or in small groups. The rise of large companies brought people together, but the work still was chiefly manual. Being a manual worker carried no social stigma. The worker accepted the rigid, structured rules under which he worked. The human factor was often mishandled until the passage of the Wagner Act in the 1930s provided the muscle needed to develop a strong labor organization. Union strength leaped from 2.5 million in 1933 to about 20 million in 1975.[14]

The Knowledge Workers

Other changes in the workforce are now taking place. Larger and larger percentages of the labor force in the developed countries do not work with their hands; instead they work with ideas, concepts, and theories. They perform what Peter Drucker calls "knowledge work."[15] And that form of work need not be restricted to the college graduate. File clerks, after all, deal with a high level of abstraction: the alphabet.

The knowledge worker is a new breed to the classical manager, and the new breed has an elevated level of what is to be expected of life and work. He is highly educated compared with his counterpart of a century ago. He challenges traditional management with questions that managers are hard put to answer. He wants more from work than the economics of the job. He wants work to be fulfilling; he wants more than material rewards. As Drucker puts it, he wants more than a living out of work; he wants work to make a life as well.[16]

The knowledge worker needs careful treatment by management. He is moved more by self-motivation and self-direction than by fear. And that tends to frustrate the traditional manager. The knowledge worker's jobs are complex. Owing to the variables within his tasks, his productivity is hard to define or measure. And his achievement is still more difficult to appraise.

What managers will have to accept is that, for the knowledge worker especially, the worker and his work are tied together. If the job is to be dealt with effectively, it needs to be analyzed into its component parts, it needs to be synthesized into a process, and it needs to be provided with feedback so that the knowledge worker himself can control his own work. And managers will have to understand also that the job cannot be designed *for* the knowledge worker. It must be designed *by* the knowledge worker.[17]

The Manual Worker

In the meantime the manual worker, the hard hat, is entering a period of crisis. Since the majority of workers in developed countries are knowledge workers, his social position is diminishing and he does not respect himself. Drucker gloomily sees the new class war as between the hard hats and the knowledge workers, with the hard hats becoming more and more militant.[18] Drucker believes that the new breed of blue collar workers regard labor leaders as part of the establishment. As a result, union leaders are losing their control and unions are becoming weaker. Drucker questions the effectiveness of the important role the unions play as their slender grip on their members is held by their being against everything rather than for something positive. That lobs the ball into the court of management, which will have to develop new policies in industrial relations and think through the future of the unions. Management will have to face up to its business and social responsibilities toward the worker.

Management will also have to think through its personnel policies, according to Drucker. Instead of a single policy for all employees, there may have to be segmentation. Separate policies may have to be set for the manual worker, the knowledge worker, and the knowledge professional.[19] And if the manager must understand those changes, so also must the modern internal auditor.

The Needs of the Worker

The Hierarchy of Needs

All human beings have certain needs. The needs may vary with ethnic background, levels of skill and professionalism, social position, and family upbringing. And the urgency of the needs may also vary with the needs that are filled and those that remain unfulfilled. Such needs have been identified, and the following hierarchy, suggested by Abraham Maslow, is widely accepted:[20]

1. *Basic physiological needs.* The basic physiological needs constitute what the human being requires at the barest subsistence level: air, water, and food. Until those needs are satisfied, the higher needs have little meaning. On the other hand, once those needs are satisfied, offering to fulfill them has no power to move the employee to greater productivity.

2. *Safety and security.* The safety and security needs ask for assurance that the basic physiological requirements will be met. That calls for job security and the ability to continue working in a risk-free environment. The two needs are physical, and both need to be satisfied to an acceptable degree before the worker feels the stirrings of other needs.

3. *Love and acceptance.* From the need for love and acceptance arises the need to be part of a family, a gang, a club, a political organization, or a work group. It is a social need that is due to man's being gregarious by heredity and needing the comfort of being wanted.

4. *Esteem and status.* When physical and social needs are satisfied, the individual can become concerned with psychic needs. The psychic needs call for recognition of his work, his achievements, his status in the organization, and his standing among his peers. Under the first basic psychological need, the bread to fill his belly may occupy his full attention. Under the fourth need, for esteem and status, sustenance means nothing since he already has it. The thickness of the pile of the carpet in his office or the achievement of acceptable quality and

schedule within budgeted costs may become uppermost in his mind.

5. *Self-realization and fulfillment.* Meeting the need for self-realization and fulfillment provides the highest psychic or ego satisfaction. The satisfaction arises from self-actuating, from setting goals for oneself and achieving them.

The higher-priority needs—basic physiological needs and the need for safety and security—must be satisfied before the lower-level needs cry for satisfaction. Indeed, not all needs will be fully satisfied, and Maslow suggests as a hypothetical example the worker who is 85 percent satisfied in his physiological needs, 70 percent in his safety needs, 50 percent in his love and acceptance needs, 40 percent in his self-esteem needs, and 10 percent in his need for self-realization and fulfillment.

The needs are not followed in a rigid pattern, and under some circumstances a lower-priority (psychic) need may block out a higher-priority (physiological) need. For example, a research scientist may disregard his physiological needs and go without food and sleep while spurred by his own creativity. It is suggested that the hygienic factors of Herzberg, discussed earlier in this chapter, correspond to Maslow's physiological, safety, and security needs. Also, the motivators correspond to Maslow's needs for esteem and self-realization. But Maslow's proposed needs suggest a continuous sequencing, and Herzberg does not stipulate the satisfaction of hygienic needs before the motivators are felt. Yet one study found that a challenging job in a poor environment will not necessarily result in greater worker satisfaction than a routine job in a good environment.[21] That simply proves what the experienced manager and the modern internal auditor have known for some time: Principles are useful, but the law of the situation as observed by the perceptive manager still obtains, and the ability to read the individual worker's capacity and maturity is still significant.

Maturity

Behavioralists regard human nature, to some extent at least, as a function of maturity in the human being. Chris Argyris has suggested a series of continuums in a person's maturation from infant to adult. Some grown people, of course, may never mature in some or many of the dimensions presented by Argyris. Others may mature in all or most of the dimensions. In any case, perceiving the degree of maturation is important to the manager who deals with the individual. Argyris's dimensions are as follows:[22]

From (infant)	To (adult)
Passivity	Increasing activity
Dependence	Relative independence
Limited behavior patterns	Complex behavior patterns
Shallow interests	Deeper interests
Short-time perspective	Long-time perspective
Subordinate position	Superordinate (superior) position
Lack of self-awareness	Self-awareness and self-control

Wants and Expectations

In addition, a person's personality, wants, and needs are affected by what he prefers or expects. Vroom's preference-expectation theory, therefore, warrants consideration by the manager. His theory is based on two premises:[23]

1. As a person considers the expected outcomes of different courses of action, he will assign subjective values to them and thereby have certain preferences for them.
2. How the person reacts to situations will depend on two factors: (a) What he hopes to accomplish and (b) the extent to which he believes his own action will affect the outcome.

If a worker can be convinced by a manager that an outcome is desirable to him and that his action can affect the outcome, he will be more prone to act. But there are some behavioralists who contend that people can and will adjust to the structures and strictures of the organization. Where Argyris sees subordination to the entity as a sign of immaturity in the individual, Dubin thinks that most people will adjust to tight regimentation. Also, he cannot see everybody having a high degree of interest in every activity every day. He regards some indifference as a normal characteristic and believes that a certain amount of self-actualization will come from work outside the job.[24]

Yet one cannot lose sight of the fact that the human being is a wanting creature. Not all the wants are the same for either the individual or for classes of individuals. Tests have shown, for example, that the white collar (knowledge) worker is more concerned with work content, whereas the blue collar worker is more concerned with such environmental factors as security and pay.[25] Other researchers support that schism of wants and point out that technological, economic, and educational advances have emphasized the wants and needs of the knowledge worker.[26]   As a result they find a movement among managers toward self-determination, wider participation in decision making, and application of the worker's judgment in the performance of his job.   On that point, a vice president of the General Electric Company foresees increased emphasis upon "quality over mere quantity, the individual over the organization, equity and justice over economic efficiency, pluralism and diversity over uniformity and centralism, participation over authority, and personal conviction over dogma."[27]

In addition to the needs of the manual worker and the knowledge worker, there are the needs of the knowledge professional.   Improved technology calls for more professionals in business.   The professionals are of crucial importance to the organization, because they are the fount from which pour the ideas and innovations without which the entity cannot grow.   Yet the professional is bound more to his profession than he is to the organization for which he happens to be working.   Newly hired scientists and engineers are usually committed to their professional rather than to the organization's values.[28]

With all those conflicting wants, orientations, and levels of maturity, the manager has the unenviable job of supplying what the worker needs within the bounds that the organization has set while still fostering the kind of morale that knits people together for the common good and evokes voluntary cooperation.   His job is complicated further by the variety of subcultures within the organization, each with its varying needs and affiliations.

However, the difficulty of the problem does not excuse the failure to seek solutions.   The success of any organization lies in the ability to provide values to the members as compensation for the burdens imposed.[29]   Management, therefore, in laying its plans, must do so in the light of an understanding of the workers' needs.   When the needs will frustrate the meeting of the organization's goals, constraints must be placed on the worker.   But when personalization of tasks to satisfy needs will bring a *net* gain to the organization after the cost of personalization is considered, the plans should provide for acceding to the needs and raising employee morale.   Autocratic adherence to structured, restrictive plans must take into account that, as a result, the worker:[30]

Has reduced independence and self-control.
Is subject to boredom and apathy.
Loses valued participation in forming goals and objectives.
Does not relate to the organization.

Engages in a running conflict between his own needs and the organization's demands.

The Manager and the Worker

Self-esteem

The worker, according to Skinner, is a malleable instrument who is conditioned by his managers and can be shaped as a sculptor shapes clay. The process is gradual; but if the shaping has been through positive reinforcement by rewarding desired behavior, the worker develops a feeling of freedom. If it has been through negative, punitive reinforcement, the worker is left feeling controlled and coerced.[31]

So the way managers regard workers has a powerful effect on how workers will see themselves, their organization, and the people around them. Douglas McGregor, observing managers in operation, saw a duality in how they saw workers. The duality, which McGregor labeled Theory X and Theory Y, paralleled Argyris's view of worker maturity. Theory X paints a picture of infantilism; Theory Y paints a picture of maturity.[32] The Theory X manager, the classical, traditional Bull of the Woods, regards workers as follows:

1. The average person dislikes work and will avoid it if he can.
2. Because of that characteristic, workers must be controlled, directed, and threatened with punishment to obtain from them the effort needed to achieve organizational goals.
3. The average worker really wants to be directed, avoids responsibility, has little ambition, and more than anything else wants the security blanket of strong, autocratic leadership.

In contrast, the Theory Y manager, a behavioralist who believes in the innate goodness of people, gives the following assessment of workers:

1. Work is as natural to people as play or rest.
2. If the worker is committed to an objective, he will direct himself and control himself.
3. Commitment to goals is a function of the rewards associated with achievement.
4. The average worker, if given the opportunity, will seek and accept responsibility.
5. A majority rather than a minority of the population can and want to exercise imagination, ingenuity, and creativity in their work.

McGregor maintains that how the manager treats his people and how they react to him depend on his philosophy and the way he regards people. Accordingly, a manager who is predominantly X presents a climate that is coercive and restrictive. Also, managerial philosophy about the worker—X or Y, mature or immature, the seekers of hygiene or the thirsters for motivation—will affect how management designs its organization, establishes its personnel policies, and develops its rules and regulations.

Participation

The relation between manager and worker was also studied by Rensis Likert.[33] Likert sees the most effective manager as the one who practices participative management, is strongly oriented toward the worker, and engenders a mutual and genuine interest in the goals of both the organization and the worker. In an experiment reported by Likert, data were collected from 31 different departments doing substantially the same kind of work. To develop participation, group meetings were held in some departments but not in others:

- □ Group A, ten departments. Both the men and the supervisors thought the meetings were useful.
- □ Group B, seven departments. Group meetings were not held at all.
- □ Group C, fourteen departments. Group meetings were held; the men thought them a waste of time even though the attending supervisors thought they were useful.

Production was then measured and, on a scale of 0 to 100, group A measured 64, group C measured 32, and group B, with no meetings at all, measured 54. It appears that no meetings at all are better than meetings from which the participants feel they are gaining nothing—indeed, in which they may feel that they are being manipulated.[34]

Indifference and apathy on the part of the worker are a constant concern of the manager. Some writers, like Likert and Argyris, feel they can be countered with participation and job enlargement.[35] Others say they must be accepted as a fact of our structured lives and that the worker must satisfy his psychological needs off the job.[36] Drucker, taking another tack, feels that we just have not given enough attention to the totality of the worker's universe: task and job, perception and personality, work community, and rewards and power relations. And he concedes the universe may be so complex that it may never be truly understood.[37]

Despite the lack in some quarters of enthusiasm for participation, real-life studies and examples have shown definite improvements in productivity as a result of the participative approach. The first is from Coch and French.[38]

> In a textile factory changes were to be made in work methods and piece rates. Four groups were established. Group 1, the control group, was told about the change in the classic autocratic manner. From group 2, representatives were selected to be told of the change and to instruct their fellow workers in the revised methods. Groups 3 and 4 were accorded total participation.
>
> Previously, production had been 60 units per hour. A month after the changes were made, the production rates were as follows:

Group	Units per hour
1. Control	48
2. Representation	68
3. Participation	74
4. Participation	72

> In the control group, not only did production decrease, but 17 percent of the employees quit and conflicts arose among workers, method engineers, and supervisors. In the other groups, the cooperation was high.

The following study is from Fleishman.[39]

> A dress manufacturing firm's operations were subject to major style changes during the year. Each change brought reduced productivity. A participative approach was used on 30 sewing machine operators. The operators were asked to do what the managers used to do: prescribe the sequence of operations, bundling methods, and pricing the individual operations. Based on past experience, management figured that the 750-dress lot would be run in eight days. The participative group did it in three days. After that run, the old autocratic approach was reinstalled. On the next run, performance levels *ran even higher*. But with the continuation of the autocratic approach, the productivity eventually declined to former levels.

The third study is from Likert.[40]

> A pajama manufacturing company, A, which had long used the participative approach, took over a competitor, B, which used autocratic methods and which had been having unprofitable years. B's managers were retained, but their philosophy was changed to that of A. The change was accompanied by a 30 percent increase in earnings of piece-rate workers, a

20 percent decrease in labor turnover, and a change in profit on investment from minus 17 percent to plus 15 percent.

Performance Appraisals

A point of potential conflict between manager and worker, one which has a serious effect on relations, is the appraisal of employee performance. There is no easy or perfect way to appraise people, to tell the people the truth as the supervisor sees it, and to satisfy equally the needs of the job and the wants of the employee. Yet people want to know how they are doing and how they can improve, so long as the appraisal process is not abrasive to them. Patz provides some guidelines for a system of appraisal.[41]

- ☐ Keep it simple. Develop a cutoff point between above- and below-average performance and concentrate on the extremes.
- ☐ Keep it separate. Do not tie it into other systems, such as promotions and raises.
- ☐ Keep it contained. Restrict the collection of data. Be chiefly concerned with the appraisal of performance and potential, not with peripheral character evaluations.
- ☐ Keep it participative. Solicit the subordinate's point of view; ask the subordinate to appraise himself.

Groups

Group Dynamics

Most workers spend more time with their work groups than with any other groups; hence, work groups and group behavior demand the attention of the manager. Most people enjoy a social environment, and their work group becomes extremely important to them. It can be another family for them, so managers should cater to the group idea if it does not interfere with productivity. Certainly it is the height of optimism for any manager to think he can control every relationship within his unit. He may therefore have to deal with the group instead of the individuals within it.[42]

Groups may be formal or informal. They can be assembled for a specific task, or they may form naturally because of mutual attraction. Personal attraction in both formal and informal groups can be extremely important in meeting group goals. Research shows that people tend to agree with those they like and reject ideas of those they don't like—the very same ideas they would accept from someone they liked.[43]

Kurt Lewin popularized the term "group dynamics" in the 1930s and helped establish an organization devoted exclusively to the study of group phenomena: The Research Center for Group Dynamics.[44] A group is defined as two or more people who are interacting and interdependent and who have the ability to behave in a unified manner with shared purposes and objectives. Lewin's work confirmed the importance of the control that groups can have over productivity and output.[45]

Groups have personalities of their own—composites of the personalities of the members. The personality of the group can overpower that of the individual member. As for structured groups, those brought together by management, research has shown that a group of five members is best and seven is a maximum.[46] In groups of those sizes, members feel more comfortable and are willing to participate. Also, the odd number prevents deadlocks. Anything larger leads to the formation of cliques within the group and loss of participation.

Participative leadership promotes involvement of the members in the group objectives, whereas authoritarian leadership prevents it. Through constructive participation the group members display an interest in informing, clarifying, orienting, mediating, and encouraging. The leader has to watch for and control the orators, needlers, and fence-sitters.

Cohesiveness within the group is important if the members are to constitute a working entity. If the goals of a cohesive group are aligned with those of the organization, then the group is a powerful force for good. The other side of that coin is that if the goals of a cohesive group run counter to those of the organization, the group represents a major threat and needs to be dissolved.

In forming a potentially useful group, the manager must do more than merely assign people to it. He should:[47]

□ Demonstrate to the group the interdependency of group needs and organizational goals.

□ Enhance the status of the group and thereby give the group importance and the members self-esteem.

□ Stimulate participation by promoting democratic techniques of leadership.

□ Promote the maintenance of the group as a productive force.

□ Reduce perceived threats from the environment and management that might tend to foment group rebellion.

Managers and task leaders must understand the dynamics of the group and how to deal with it. The task leader may at times not be the same person as the group leader. The task leader must seek and the manager must promote harmony between the two. The task leader promotes the task goals. The group leader promotes congeniality and unanimity. When they agree, tasks get accomplished. When they are at odds, the task goals may never be reached.

The task goals are derivatives of organizational goals, and their achievement should help meet the organization's goals. For the task leader to push toward task goals unremittingly may disrupt the cohesiveness of the group, so chit-chatting and some relaxation may be useful in releasing frustrations and hostility. Also, trust is engendered, and that opens up the creative forces within the group and promotes originality and exchanges of ideas.

Formal organizations have their policies and procedures; social groups, those brought together by common interests, have their standards of behavior: how hard to work, the degree of commitment to the organization, and how much to cooperate with the establishment. The formal task goals may impinge on group norms, so the formal group leader should promote openness, cooperation, reduction of criticism, support for novel ideas, and participative leadership. Otherwise, he may find that informal group pressures can be stronger than official regulations.

Group Behavior

The individual in the group will not normally change his behavior from that which the group finds acceptable. Reeducating a group member individually and returning him to the group to disseminate his newfound knowledge can spell trouble for him and the group. It is far better to have a group member propose group changes. The group will listen to him more readily than to an outsider. When someone works with a group, he must identify with it.

Indoctrination in group behavior is provided by various methods. Currently, the most popular method is sensitivity training, also known as T-group and laboratory training. The goal is to improve the individual's understanding of himself and how he affects others. It seeks group participation under controlled laboratory conditions, and its expected outcomes are openness with others, greater concern for the needs and more tolerance for the differences of others, improved listening skills, and more realistic standards of behavior. Positive changes in behavior as a result of sensitivity training have been reported.

Yet sensitivity training has some disadvantages. It is difficult to administer, and participants have had breakdowns under the stress of the sessions. Also, although there may be an enhancement in personal relations, there is no perceived correlation between T-group training and performance. Moreover, as has been pointed out in connection with groups, training one group member and returning him to the group usually has little effect; the entire group needs the training. Under proper supervision, however, sensitivity training can open people's eyes to the importance of tolerance for others and the need to try to understand them.[48]

Further aspects of informal organizations will be discussed in Chapter 10, Organizing.

Creativity

The worker will produce under the lash of the disciplinarian, even though the output may not be all that is desired. He will satisfy certain of his basic needs even under a domineering, authoritarian manager. He will find certain satisfying relationships in sharing the security blanket of a group. But in a cold, repressive climate, he cannot hope to harvest the fruits of creativity.

And an organization must have creativity and innovation if it is to have growth. Some forms of creativity can take place under the classical manager: creativity that is based on logic, science, planning, and the calculated research for new combinations of existing ideas. That approach evokes artificial creativity through such structured techniques as brainstorming. But primary creativity, which draws upon the wellsprings of inspiration, insight, incubation, and seeing things from within, needs a mild and unrepressive climate.[49]

Primary creativity may be stifled by an organization that insists on tight controls and demands blind adherence to procedures. As a result, the creative flame may go out or the creative individual may leave the organization. Large organizations, therefore, have a smaller chance of nurturing the creative spark. Although the laboratories of AT&T developed the transistor, it took the smaller, new Texas Instruments to conceive its use in something other than the telephone.[50]

Hence, in larger companies especially, managers should be able to identify the creative worker and give him the special kind of freedom he needs. A summary of several studies shows that such a person has certain characteristics:

□ He is not necessarily more intelligent than the less creative. He must be intelligent, but intelligence does not insure creativity.

□ His view of authority is that it is not absolute; thus authority does not inhibit him.

□ He is less dogmatic, because he looks for the various sides of a situation—not just one. Hence, he tends to make fewer black-and-white distinctions.

□ He is not inhibited from expressing impulses the less creative might think irrational.

□ His sense of humor is generally better than that of the less creative.[51]

As one would expect intuitively, the creative person's patterns of behavior exhibit greater freedom and greater tendency to reject rigorous control by others.

Tapping the Worker's Creativity

Japanese products, in the first half of this century, were often characterized by shoddiness and inferior quality. After World War II, the Japanese government made better quality a national priority. It solicited a number of Americans to help instill the concept of and desire for superior quality in Japanese managers and workers alike. The excellence of modern Japanese products testifies to the success of the program.

Two Americans in particular, W. E. Deming and J. N. Juran, influenced Japanese thinking about quality. Deming taught the statistical aspects of problem identification and correction. Juran advanced the proposition that quality is everyone's responsibility and must be everyone's commitment. The combination of quantitative analysis and individual striving for excellence led to management support and worker training in what became known as QC circles.[52]

The QC circles made their appearance in Japan in 1962. Each circle is a group of about eight to ten workers and a supervisor. The objective of a circle is to identify and solve quality problems and thereby improve quality, reduce the costs generated by rejections, repairs, and rework, and stem the flood of customer dissatisfaction.

In 1972 Japan boasted about a half million circles with some six million members. The use of circles expanded enormously as the circle concept proved its worth and fired the enthusiasm of its participants. The circles build people, not use them. The ordinary worker is trained in such applications as brainstorming, data gathering, cause-and-effect diagrams, sampling techniques, Pareto curves (curves that identify the vital few from the trivial many; for example, 20 percent of the problems are responsible for 80 percent of the costs), check sheets, graphs, histograms, frequency tables, correlation analysis, basic quality cost analysis, and Ishikawa diagrams (mapping out variables that might cause problems).

Participation is voluntary. People receive no additional pay for their QC circle work. The rewards are a feeling of self-actualization and the recognition received when the group presents proposals and status reports to a higher management that listens respectfully to the workers' recommendations. All projects are carried out in teams that have a collegial orientation in which each learns from the others. The circles are project-, not individual-, oriented. They are synergistic in effect, since the united effort exceeds the total of the individual part.

Training is provided both to workers and to managers. Top management supports the effort and encourages creativity. In circle operation, no idea is stupid and no proposal is ridiculed. Since each project relates to the members' work, it becomes personal to the worker. Two hours of regular working time each week is allotted to circle deliberations, but many employees continue working on projects on their own time.

What Americans taught the Japanese has returned to America to create QC circles in American industry with gratifying success. Wayne S. Reiker, Lockheed's manufacturing manager in its Missiles and Space Division at Sunnyvale, California, learned about QC circles from a group of visiting Japanese. He then started the most encompassing in-depth study of QC circles ever undertaken by an American company. After their installation at Lockheed, the QC circles not only expanded workers' horizons and generated increased quality consciousness but also saved $3 million in two years.[53]

Thus, through innovative management that taps the sources of creativity in people, the Japanese made a startling turnaround in product quality by successfully integrating the findings and teachings of behavioral scientists with the application of quantitative problem-solving techniques. And the bread cast upon Japanese waters by American experts floated back across the Atlantic to help American companies improve quality and reduce costs.

THE WORKER AND THE INTERNAL AUDITOR

Work

The internal auditor, himself a worker, has a dual concern with the behavioral patterns of workers. First there is his concern with himself either as a subordinate or as a supervisor. Second, there is his concern with the people whose work he reviews. And often the role he has scripted for himself will influence the way he will work as an appraiser of the work of others.

The tasks of the internal auditor call for the talents of an architect, a pick-and-shovel worker, and a builder. When they are all put together, the audit assignment can lead to a complete structure of job satisfaction, because the job is then "my job." As an architect, the internal auditor develops the program. As a pick-and-shovel worker, he delves into the details and gathers information. And as a builder, he constructs conclusions and recommendations to assist management.

Of course, each professional needs a period of apprenticeship and training in which to learn the principles, techniques, and methodology of his calling. He must learn to differentiate between significant findings and nit-picking. He must learn to deal with people professionally and with empathy. He must learn the difference between a significant and relevant line of inquiry and one that merely satisfies idle curiosity. He must know when to hang on doggedly and when to let go.

But after the novice has learned the fundamentals, he should not be kept exclusively on pick-and-shovel work; the continued, routine listing and checking of transactions can be stultifying. He should be given a "piece of the action." He should be shown the overall audit program for the entire internal audit project. He should be told what the thrust or "theory" of the job is. And he should be given a part of the job to carry through to conclusion.

Assume, for example, that he is assisting in an audit of the marketing organization, which encompasses the activities of marketing research, advertising, sales promotion, credit, customer service, and budgets and costs. The assistant internal auditor who has been indoctrinated and taught the basics could be assigned one of the elements, such as advertising, or one of the subelements, such as advertising budgets, agency agreements, department purchases, or agency charges.

It would be up to him to carry out the assignment to conclusion under the watchful eye of the auditor-in-charge. He would:

□ Study the literature on audits of advertising and records of any prior audits.
□ Learn the objectives and the systems of control for the activity he is reviewing.
□ Prepare the audit purpose for the subject of his audit.

- Determine the total population of the activities and transactions he will be concerned with.
- Propose to the auditor-in-charge the extent of his tests, the size of the sample, and the sampling plan and technique he will use.
- Examine the transactions selected in the sample.
- Discuss any deviations with the people responsible.
- Record the results of his tests in a structured form that will facilitate the final report writing.
- Accompany the auditor-in-charge when the latter discusses any serious deficiencies with the department manager and division chief.
- Review corrective action proposed or taken and offer suggestions to the auditor-in-charge on whether the action is designed to cure the defects.

That is job enlargement and enrichment. It brings the novice internal auditor into the mainstream of the audit project, gives him responsibility, and, if the job is carried out properly, gives him job satisfaction.

The modern internal auditor, as we have said, has a dual concern: he is concerned with not only his own job enrichment but also that of the workers within the organization. Accordingly, he should be on the lookout for circumstances that tend to create encapsulated, impoverished jobs. Here are some indicators he can look for:[54]

- Communications units. An example is the telephone units that handle the flow of requests and perform narrow, routine functions.
- "Checking" functions, which may remove responsibility for quality.
- Troubleshooting jobs, which take coordinating, expediting, and control away from the line.
- "Super gurus"—consultants and analysts who can erode the completeness of others' jobs.
- Job title elephantiasis. Overspecialization can unnecessarily narrow the job.
- One-on-one relationships:

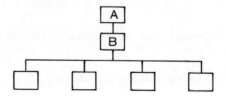

If A is strong, B has nothing more than paper-shuffling to do.

▫ Dual-reporting relationships:

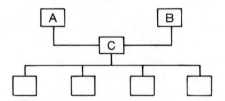

This organization tends to erode C's job, because if A and B are strong, C is merely a conduit between them and their subordinates.

▫ Unclear division of responsibility. Uncertainty as to its nature may result in shunning responsibility.
▫ Overly complicated work flow. Jobs may be poorly delineated; nobody feels complete responsibility for the full job.
▫ Duplication of functions. Staff groups may overlap.
▫ Labor pools. These may destroy "ownership of work."

Workers

To grow a good crop, the farmer needs good seed. To build a good organization, management must hire people with potential. Yet many personnel hiring policies are archaic and many hiring practices involve the hurried search for and adoption of the first warm body that comes along.

The internal auditor can perform a signal service to management by including a review of the hiring practices in his long-range audit program. His review should be concerned not only with practices that search for potential but also with practices that prevent the hiring of villains and misfits.

It is an unfortunate fact of life that many companies shun the publicity that attends the prosecution of an embezzler or a thief. When they detect the wrongdoer, they will usually walk him to the gate and let him be hired by another, unsuspecting company. The hiring organization must therefore protect itself by paying close attention to reasonable hiring practices.

Before employees are hired, attention should be given to the careful screening of applicants. Not only should prior employers be questioned but applicants should be queried and investigated about past histories of gambling, unusual expenses, and high living—conditions which may force people to steal. Psychological tests have been designed to point up a tendency toward dishonesty. Organizations that are hiring employees for sensitive positions such as purchasing agent should consider full-scale background investigations by reliable investigators.[55]

The polygraph, or lie detector, is being used more and more by commercial organizations for preemployment testing. The questions that are asked relate to thefts from former employers, lies on the application form, use of narcotics, length of time the applicant intends to stay with the organization, and whether female applicants are pregnant. Internal auditors who recommend polygraph tests in place of the more expensive background investigations should, however, be aware of the strong opposition to such tests by many unions and legislators. Also, some states have passed legislation forbidding employers to require polygraph tests.[56]

The internal auditor's tests in audits of personnel records should include these steps:

□ Review applications of employees in sensitive positions.
□ Find out whether adequate explanations were obtained for time gaps on the application forms.
□ Make sure all employment and school references have been verified.
□ If reference replies are unfavorable, make sure that the personnel people inquired of the prior employer whether the applicant was discharged for dishonesty.[57]

The audit program used by one company lists the following questions that are pertinent to hiring and to other personnel practices within the organization:

□ Is the company's application form laid out in a well-organized manner?
□ Is the application form designed to weed out undesirable applicants rapidly?
□ Have employment standards been established in written form?
□ Have interviewing procedures been standardized and have interviewers been carefully selected and trained?
□ Are tests used in the selection and placement of new employees?
□ Are the tests related to the jobs for which the prospective employee is applying, and do they accord with federal government requirements?

- Does the personnel department check local credit investigating organizations to obtain information that might be helpful in evaluating applicants?
- Does the personnel department check former-employment references?
- In checking references, has the personnel department developed a list of specific questions that should be asked to obtain information to help in evaluating the applicant's potential?
- Is a manual or booklet given to each person who is employed to inform him of the company's rules and regulations?
- Are new employees required to undergo a probationary period? Does the personnel department check responsible supervision to make sure the requirements of the job have been satisfactorily met?
- Do the personnel files contain a full history of each employee, including data on special talents, ambitions, and personal achievements?
- Does the company have a program for helping employees solve personal problems?
- Are employees kept informed of management's objectives, plans, problems, successes, and failures?
- Do supervisors periodically review individual progress with employees?
- Does the company encourage and help employees to further their education?
- Does the company maintain a training program?
- Are the more progressive and talented executive personnel selected and enrolled in advanced management courses?
- Does personnel carry on a university recruiting program?

The Needs of the Worker

Management can be reasonably sure that its workers' needs are not being satisfied if the level of worker morale is low. Morale is reflected in the degree to which people cooperate voluntarily in group efforts toward group goals.

Managers are, and should be, deeply concerned with employee morale, if for no other reason than that morale directly affects productivity, safety, security, absenteeism, and turnover. The internal auditor must therefore be equally concerned with the attitudes of workers. The internal auditor, who is usually most comfortable with objective standards, units of measurement, and quantitative evaluations, is hard put to it to appraise that subjective quality in objective terms. Yet the importance of morale will not let him sweep the subject under the rug of his regular audit program. There are relatively objective appraisals he can make, and there are some subjective appraisals he should try to make.

Answers to the following questions might help the internal auditor make objective appraisals:

- □ Do supervisors observe their workers' behavior and periodically report to higher management on employee morale?
- □ Do safety inspectors consider the question of morale in appraising causes for accidents and do they report on their findings?
- □ Is there a program of nondirective interviewing by employee counselors in which the counselor makes no judgments and offers no interpretive or associative comments, but rather encourages the worker to express himself fully and honestly?
- □ Are all terminating employees given exit interviews, and is employee morale discussed?
- □ Are the number and types of grievances analyzed?
- □ How do grievances compare in number and seriousness with those in comparable organizations?
- □ Are production quantity and quality unduly affected by absenteeism?
- □ What is the degree of labor turnover, and how does the turnover compare with that of other departments in the organization and with other organizations?
- □ Are attitude surveys calling for anonymous replies carried out, summarized, and acted on?

The internal auditor can also make subjective appraisals; and although they may not be couched in quantitative terms, they can be valuable. In his audit assignments, the internal auditor usually works with the employees, observes their demeanor, working habits, relations to their supervisors, and feelings about their department and the organization. Also, he is subject to the same physical environment, and he can often find causal relations between deficiency findings and morale.

At the end of his audit assignment the internal auditor can prepare a record of impressions on such matters as morale, working habits, organization and staffing, supervision, interface with other organizations, and working areas. He can then discuss his impressions —he should not refer to them as findings—with appropriate managers and executives. The subjects are best handled informally and not included in the written audit report.[58]

The Internal Auditor—Appraiser and Subject of Appraisals

Performance reviews affect the internal auditor from the standpoint of (1) his own and his subordinates' performances and (2) the organization's personnel procedures and practices.

Performance of Internal Auditors

Appraising performance of internal auditors is complicated by the fact that no two audit projects are the same. It is further complicated by the many contacts the internal auditor must make at the various levels within the organization. Thus, besides technical and professional ability, the way the auditor deals with others can be extremely important. An abrasive personality can undo in one meeting the participative relationship the auditing department has been trying to build for years. On the other hand, the internal auditor who glosses over serious deficiencies in an attempt to be liked by the auditee can present an even greater hazard to both his organization and his profession.

The evaluations of internal auditors must therefore be considered carefully. To be effective, they should be frank, fair, frequent, and friendly. But not all evaluators have the innate or even the developed ability to perform useful evaluations. One auditor-in-charge may have a built-in bias against an assistant auditor, whereas another auditor-in-charge may regard the assistant with complete objectivity. Also, every audit assignment may call for different talents from the same auditor. An assistant or an auditor-in-charge may perform superbly in an audit of the accounts payable department and fall flat on his face in an audit of production control.

Hence, a compromise to the evaluation of internal auditors is to appraise the auditor after each audit assignment. The director of internal auditing should develop an evaluation form that gives appropriate weight to the various demands of the job. Here is an example:

Planning and organizing	20%
Fieldwork (working papers, testing techniques, evaluation of findings, etc.)	50
Oral expression	10
Writing ability	15
Meeting budget and schedule	5
Total	100 %

The various elements within those characteristics may then be evaluated as excellent, very good, fair, and unsatisfactory and a numerical rating given each. The measurements can be followed by an evaluation of other characteristics such as initiative, energy, pleasantness, cooperativeness, work habits, and readiness for promotion. Since those qualities do not lend themselves readily to quantification, adjectival ratings can be used. The numerical and adjectival ratings should be supplemented by the narrative comments of the rater; the comments can be more descriptive of ability and potential than the structured ratings.

At the end of a period—semiannual or annual—the evaluations of the various raters can be combined and the results can be discussed with the individual. Various forms and approaches are used to evaluate internal auditors. Whichever one is used, it should be applied consistently and should be fair to both the individual and the organization.[59]

Auditing the Performance Review Function

The internal auditor must understand that performance evaluations serve two basic purposes:

1. To determine the best possible utilization of the human resource.
2. To help the individual improve his value to himself and his organization.

The internal auditor must also understand that people generally dislike playing the role of judge of their fellow workers. And when the judging involves reducing the evaluations to writing and discussing defects in performance or character face-to-face with the worker, the chances are that the responsibility will be avoided or put off. Also, if the materials of evaluation are arbitrary, bookish, and not relevant to the work, the chances for successful evaluations become even more remote.

Accordingly, the internal auditor will want to determine whether:

☐ The personnel department has prescribed reasonable policies, procedures, forms, and records for the evaluative process.
☐ Evaluations are performed and reported on at prescribed periods.
☐ Adequate records are maintained.
☐ The evaluations are used when the employee is considered for raises or promotions.

□ Management has done a creditable job of indoctrinating workers and evaluators in the purposes and uses of the evaluations.

Internal Audit Groups

The internal audit team assigned to an audit project is a group,
and the psychology of groups is applicable to it. Large teams may
have their formal and their informal leaders. The formal leader—
the auditor-in-charge—is responsible for the conduct of the work and
the final report. But the success of his project will depend on how
well he welds together a successful team and how he elicits the cooperation of the members. In seeking cooperation, he must identify the
informal leader and deal with him.

Some team captains operate as autocrats. They lay out the program, parcel out the assignments, review and correct working papers,
deal alone with operating managers, and take over completely the
writing of the audit report. But standoffishness can impoverish the
job. Each of the team members makes contacts and develops understandings that may be useful and helpful to the team leader and the
other team members. Periodic meetings whereby each member can
contribute ideas that will further the audit purposes can be useful.
And if the team leader promotes a feeling of cohesiveness, the individual contributors can present lines of audit thrust not dreamed of in
the original program.

Similarly, in large internal audit organizations deploying a number of teams, periodic staff meetings can be helpful. They promote
a feeling of belonging. They can provide a sounding board for
ideas. The internal auditor reviewing the shipping department
might have some pertinent points for the internal auditor reviewing
accounts receivable. The internal auditor reviewing accounts payable might point to problems the auditor reviewing purchasing
should be aware of.

Staff meetings should be so structured that people are given an
agenda of what will be covered and the time allotted for interchanges
among members. They should also have their unstructured moments so that people will feel free to get things off their chests or contribute information to the group.

The internal auditor is also concerned with the groups in the organization: the ad hoc, temporary, or permanent committees set up to
carry out specific functions. He should be interested in whether each
such committee is given a formal written charter for all to see. Also,
he should want to know whether any of the committees have overlapping functions or whether some activities or functions that top man-

agement thought were covered have somehow slipped between the assigned responsibilities of contiguous committees.

Internal Audit Review of Groups and Committees

Certain functions within an organization do not require the day-to-day attention of an operating department yet may represent a responsibility that requires periodic attention and must not be forgotten. Safety and security matters, separate from the ongoing policing function, are a case in point. Management sets up committees to meet monthly or quarterly to consider matters of fire or disaster prevention. Charters are established; chairmen are appointed; and representatives from operating departments are assigned to the committees.

Having done its job of organizing the committees, management will usually turn its attention to more pressing matters. Usually, no one executive has the responsibility for seeing that all committees function effectively, cover all activities that need coverage, and do not overlap. The job of making such a review and analysis should fall to the internal auditor. If the auditor sees that committees are carrying out their functions as prescribed and are adequately covering the activities needing committee coverage, he can provide assurance to executive management. If, on the other hand, some relevant activities are not covered, he should make appropriate recommendations to management.

A case in point involved the review of safety and security in a large corporation that had a central corporate office and a number of operating divisions. The internal auditor of one of the divisions reviewed the charters, meetings, agendas, and reports of all committees involved with or charged with responsibility for safety and security matters. His findings showed that there were eleven committees concerned with such matters:

1. Corporate Disaster Prevention and Safety Committee
2. Divisional Disaster Prevention and Safety Committee
3. Divisional Disaster Control Committee
4. Divisional Industrial Security Emergency Planning Committee
5. General Safety Committee
6. Managers' Safety Committee
7. Workmen's Safety Committee
8. Fire Hazard Committee

9. High Hazard Committee
10. Isotope Committee
11. Skills Training Committee

The internal auditor prepared a chart showing side by side the names of the committees, the frequency of their meetings, the chairmen and the members of the committees, the detailed functions and responsibilities of each committee, the authority under which each committee was established, and citations to the implementing instructions.

For the first time executive management was able to see what it had wrought over the years: the interrelations among the committees, the overlapping responsibilities, and the necessary activities that somehow had been forgotten in developing the committees. As a result of his work and his report, the internal auditor provided certain assurances to executive management on the adequacy of its safety and security systems. At the same time he made recommendations for improvements and consolidations that became apparent when the entire record was spread out for management to see. He demonstrated the importance of taking a good, hard look at groups and committees within the corporate structure to make sure the groups continue to do their jobs and are disbanded when they are no longer needed. He also demonstrated the effectiveness of using the management viewpoint in making audit appraisals.

Appraising Creative Activities

The Creativity of Others

The internal auditor's review of the organization's creative activities, such as sales promotion, advertising, and research and development, is often centered on the control aspects. The auditor may determine whether plans have been devised, organizational structures established, approval systems prescribed, budgets prepared, and costs evaluated. But management's interest in creativity exceeds measurable performance. As it looks to the future it is also interested in the abilities of its creative and professional people. Are those people competent? Are they innovative? How do they compare with their counterparts in competitive organizations? The immediate managers of those people may have a vested interest in protecting their professionals by extolling virtues and hiding defects. The managers may not always be objective, but the internal auditor is. Executive management has, of course, a right to expert, objective evaluations of any activities that affect the organization's current and future operations. Properly done, such evaluations can be useful.

The key criterion in assessing professional ability is how the professionals are regarded by their peers. In the case of scientists, for example, a test of standing in the professional community is the frequency of publication of papers. In one audit of an international company's research department, the internal auditors analyzed the department's publications over a period of years. They found that 20 percent of the scientists and engineers had not published in two years. That was considered by all to be a signficant percentage. The matter was turned over to the department head, who agreed to determine the reason why some of his people published 12 to 14 papers a year and others published none.[60]

In the same research department, the internal auditors found that section supervisors evaluated the performance of their scientific and engineering personnel but failed to communicate the results to the employees evaluated. The major benefits of an evaluation of a professional by his peer were therefore being lost. The difficulty stemmed from the fact that evaluators look upon the job of employee appraisals with repugnance and try to avoid the embarrassment of bringing defects to the attention of their people. But the job still has to be done, and management has to be told if it is not being done.

On a more traditional note, the audit of the research-and-development activity had a direct effect involving a good deal of money. In their tour of the laboratories, the internal auditors counted six electron microscopes. Those monsters cost about $100,000 each, and a couple were not being used. Several weeks later, during a budget audit, the auditors observed that another laboratory division had listed in its budget the procurement of an electron microscope. The auditors brought the two division heads together, had one of the six microscopes transferred, and saved $100,000.

Whenever the internal auditor feels out of his depth in evaluating specialized and professional activities, he should enlist the services of a respected peer of the professional worker. In the world of academe, it is standard practice for professionals of known stature to be assigned to evaluate their peers. The evaluation is accepted as a matter of course by those evaluated and creates the least amount of personal problems. It is the experience of internal auditors who have been part of such evaluations that the resulting reports should be made orally to both operating and executive management and not be incorporated in formal reports.

Internal Audit Creativity

The modern internal auditor also is deeply involved with creativity. His creativity need not be the inspirational flashes of genius associated with the nuclear physicist. Nor does it have to be; for creativity has been defined as "the ability to formulate new combinations from two or more concepts already in mind."[61] Seen in that way, creativity is as available to the internal auditor as it is to the sculptor or the poet. Creativity is there within all of us; psychologists are convinced that all people are to some degree potentially creative—all ages, all cultures, and all fields of human endeavor.[62]

Imagination and originality, by and large, are qualities that all of us were born with and which made our childhood days a kaleidoscope of incredibly interesting dreams, experiences, and ideas. As the years went by some of those qualities may have dried up as we developed hardening of the attitudes and fell into patterns and ruts. Perhaps we learned that in this demanding world of ours there was no real independence, no complete freedom from fear. And in the absence of freedom from fear, imagination and orginality find the climate too severe to grow to fruition, much less survive.

The sensible internal auditor understands that in his position—that of the careful, conservative counselor—he cannot tolerate some of the mistakes other experimenters can afford to make. Management is looking to him for what is tried and true, not what may be merely an ephemeral wish or hope. Nevertheless, within the confines of his profession, there is still room and need for innovation—sound innovation, practical innovation. Management does not generally get critical of new ideas as such. It is critical of new ideas that don't work, of half baked ideas that need more time in the oven.

With that in mind, the auditor may still recall the imagination and originality of his childhood. But now he can harness them by using the reins of practicality, reasonableness, and usefulness Hemholtz, the German physicist, gave three elements of the creative process: saturation, incubation, illumination.[63] *Saturation* is soaking up the facts, observing, gathering information. *Incubation* is carried on without conscious effort. It means carrying the facts, observations, and information in the deep dark recesses of the subconscious where they come into contact with other experiences and other knowledge to form new combinations. *Illumination* is that flash of understanding, after the incubation, when the new ideas come at the most unexpected times to give us a key or a solution to a problem.

To the three elements of saturation, incubation, and illumination the internal auditor will add verification: evaluation and the elaboration or development of ideas. The internal auditor should not, dare not, take action until verification has been accomplished. But when it is carefully developed, creativity can take place almost anywhere in the broad spectrum of activities the internal auditor engages in.

The internal auditor may be innovative in the long-range audit program. There he may build up fences to help protect his company against fraud and theft. As indicated in Chapter 1, he cannot be held accountable for all manner of embezzlement, fraud, theft, and other unconscionable acts that the fertile minds of villains conceive no matter what devices have been constructed to stop them. The fact that the internal auditor has entree to all activities of his organization does not mean that he thereby constitutes himself an insurer against all unpleasantness. The concept is ludicrous on its face. No sooner is a defense raised when the devious mind of some thief will find a way around it.

The internal auditor cannot be held responsible for extraordinary precautions. But he can be held to ordinary precautions; he can be held for making sure of the steps that a professional internal auditor can take. Hence, he can start creating a shield, both for himself and for his company, by identifying the areas and activities that historically have been subject to risk.

Each company will be different and will present different forms of risk; the internal auditor, through research, survey, and knowledge of his company, should identify and list the forms. They will include such disparate matters as blank check stock, receipt of currency in the mails, bank reconciliations, deliveries bypassing the receiving department, sole-source procurements, drugs in the medical department, rotation of employee assignments, assurance that all people in sensitive positions take vacations, conflict-of-interest programs, and many others. Once identified and listed, the activities should be referred to and covered in a programmed examination or dealt with as a separate examination.

The internal auditor can create new ways of performing his fieldwork, perhaps by questionnaires sent out in advance of his arrival on the scene. He can develop means of employing the computer to take some of the drudgery out of auditing; computer systems can be designed with special loops to spin off particular types of transactions for special study or random selections for examinations. And in his examination of processes and methods, he can be creative by doubting and questioning all he sees. The fact that something has been done for a long time in the same way is no guarantee of its propriety. Here is an example:

> Large rivets and fasteners have to be used around certain doors in an airplane under construction. Before a fastener is installed, a hole is drilled for its shank. The hole is then countersunk so that the top of the fastener's head will be flush with the surrounding metal. The internal auditor found that inspectors were rejecting some of the installations. The reason they gave was that the heads weren't flush with the surrounding metal. Since there seemed to be quite a few rejections involving a lot of rework expense, and since feelings were running pretty high between production and inspection people, the internal auditor looked into the matter.

> He found that there were two kinds of rivets, both of which were perfectly acceptable. One had a so-called knife-edge head; when it sat in the countersink, it fitted snugly. Both to touch and sight, the fastener was a perfect fit. The other fastener had a blunt or rounded edge to its head. When it was seated in the countersink, it left a moat—a slight, almost imperceptible space around the head. When the inspectors looked at and touched the head of the rivet and the surrounding metal, they got the impression that the head wasn't properly seated and rejected the assembly.

> The internal auditor, using some creativity, demonstrated by using a straight-edge strip of metal that the fasteners were indeed properly installed. As a result, rejections fell off and extensive, expensive rework was avoided.

C. S. Whiting observed that three positive factors will permit creativity to show itself: constructive discontent, observation, and facility of combination.[64]

Constructive discontent. To be constructively discontented is to be dissatisfied with existing methods and never to accept "This is the way we've always done it" as gospel. It is to question, to ask why, and to refuse to be put off. But it must be *constructive* discontent: an urge to make better and not merely overthrow.

Observation. Observation comprises the gathering of facts, the watching of processes, the discussions with production workers, inspectors, engineers, and managers so that the process is understood and all sides have been seen.

Facility of combination. The ability to combine and recombine information in a variety of ways amounts to the facility of combination. It seems plain that the greater one's fund of knowledge, the more likely one is to be creative. The more hooks one has to hang the problems on, the more factors he has to combine and recombine.

One of the most significant assets the modern internal auditor can offer to the problem-solving partnership with management is his ability to be creative in attacking the problems that beset every organization.

CONCLUSION

Both the manager and the internal auditor must deal with workers. To deal with workers effectively, the partners in problem solving must understand the workers' needs, wants, abilities, and potentials. The two partners must understand both the psychology of the individual and the psychology of the group. Disregarding the group will not make the group go away. It must be considered, and its goals must be meshed subtly with the goals of the organization. When the goals are diametrically opposed, the group unit must be disbanded lest it do harm to the organization.

Managers and internal auditors alike must appreciate the importance of growth, innovation, and creativity to the organization and how to foster it and evaluate it. What is extremely important is that the internal auditor should seek to tap the wellsprings of his own creativity to help further the needs of the problem-solving partnership.

References

1. Gen. 3:23 and 2 Thess. 3:10.
2. E. B. Flippo and G. M. Munsinger, *Management* (Boston: Allyn & Bacon, 1975), p. 131.
3. Frederick Herzberg, *Work and the Nature of Man* (Cleveland: World Publishing, 1966).
4. T. J. Atchison and E. A. Lefferts, "The Prediction of Turnover Using Herzberg's Job Satisfaction Technique," *Personnel Psychology*, Vol. 25, No. 1, p. 61.
5. M. G. Wolf, "Need Gratification Theory: A Theoretical Reformulation of Job Satisfaction/Dissatisfaction and Job Motivation," *Journal of Applied Psychology*, Vol. 54, No. 1, p. 93.
6. C. R. Walker and F. L. Richardson, *Human Relations in an Expanding Company* (New Haven, Conn.: Yale University Press, 1948).
7. P. F. Drucker, *Management: Tasks, Responsibilities, Practices* (New York: Harper & Row, 1973), pp. 260, 261.
8. Ibid., p. 274.
9. R. E. Walton, "How to Counter Alienation in the Plant," *Harvard Business Review*, November-December 1972, pp. 70–81.

10. R. N. Ford, "Job Enrichment Lessons from AT&T," *Harvard Business Review,* January-February 1973, pp. 96–106.
11. M. London and R. J. Klimoski, "A Study of Perceived Job Complexity," *Personnel Psychology,* Vol. 28, No. 1, pp. 45–55.
12. R. W. Beatty and C. E. Schneider, "A Case for Positive Reinforcement," *Business Horizons,* Vol. 18, No. 2, pp. 57–66.
13. Harold Koontz and Cyril O'Donnell, *Essentials of Management* (New York: McGraw-Hill, 1974), pp. 309, 310.
14. Flippo and Munsinger, op. cit., p. 103.
15. Drucker, op. cit., p. 170.
16. Ibid., p. 179.
17. Ibid., p. 183.
18. Ibid., p. 171.
19. Ibid., pp. 174–179.
20. Abraham H. Maslow, *Motivation and Personality* (New York: Harper & Row, 1954).
21. Richard Kosmo and Orlando Behling, "Single Continuum Job Satisfaction vs. Duality: An Empirical Test," *Personnel Psychology,* Vol. 22, No. 3, pp. 327–334.
22. Chris Argyris, *Personality and Organization* (New York: Harper & Row, 1957).
23. Victor Vroom, *Work and Motivation* (New York: Wiley, 1964), pp. 17–33, 121–147.
24. Robert Dubin, *Human Relations in Administration,* 2nd ed. (Englewood Cliffs, N.J.: Prentice-Hall, 1974), pp. 126–129.
25. R. Centers and D. E. Bugental, "Intrinsic and Extrinsic Job Motivations Among Different Segments of the Working Population," *Journal of Applied Psychology,* Vol. 50, pp. 193–197.
26. J. A. Lee, "Behavioral Theory vs. Reality," *Harvard Business Review,* Vol. 49, No. 2, p. 24.
27. V. B. Day, "Managing Human Resources in the Seventies," *Personnel Administration,* Vol. 33, No. 1, p. 23.
28. G. A. Miller and L. W. Wager, "Adult Socialization, Organizational Structure, and Role Orientations," *Administrative Science Quarterly,* Vol. 16, No. 2, p. 154.
29. C. I. Barnard, *The Function of an Executive* (Cambridge, Mass.: Harvard University Press, 1951).
30. Flippo and Munsinger, op. cit., p. 129.
31. "Conversations with B. F. Skinner," *Organizational Dynamics,* Vol. 1, No. 3, p. 31.
32. Douglas McGregor, *The Human Side of Enterprise* (New York: McGraw-Hill, 1960), pp. 33–34, 47–48.
33. Rensis Likert, *New Patterns of Management* (New York: McGraw-Hill, 1961) and *The Human Organization: Its Management and Value* (New York: McGraw-Hill, 1967).
34. Likert, *New Patterns of Management,* p. 123.

35. Argyris, op. cit., pp. 187–200, and Likert, *New Patterns of Management,* chaps. 2, 7.
36. H. J. Leavitt and T. L. Whisler, "Management in the 1980s," *Harvard Business Review,* Vol. 36, No. 6, pp. 44–45, and Dubin, op. cit., p. 79.
37. Drucker, op. cit., p. 181.
38. Lester Coch and J. R. P. French, Jr., "Overcoming Resistance to Change," *Human Relations,* Vol. 1, No. 4, pp. 512–532.
39. E. A. Fleishman, "Attitude versus Skill Factors in Work Group Productivity," *Personnel Psychology,* Vol. 18, No. 3, pp. 253–266.
40. Likert, *The Human Organization,* pp. 31–38.
41. A. L. Patz, "Performance Appraisal: Useful But Still Resisted," *Harvard Business Review,* May-June 1975, pp. 79, 80.
42. G. C. Homans, *The Human Group* (New York: Harcourt, Brace & World, 1950).
43. D. E. Zand, "Trust and Managerial Problem Solving," *Administrative Science Quarterly,* Vol. 17, No. 2, pp. 229–239.
44. Flippo and Munsinger, op. cit., p. 222.
45. Kurt Lewin, *A Dynamic Theory of Personality* (New York: McGraw-Hill, 1935) and *Field Theory in Social Science: Selected Theoretical Papers* (New York: Harper & Brothers, 1951).
46. R. F. Bales, "In Conference," *Harvard Business Review,* Vol. 32, No. 2, p. 47.
47. Flippo and Munsinger, op. cit., p. 225.
48. Ibid., pp. 418–483.
49. Abraham H. Maslow, *Toward a Psychology of Being* (New York: Van Nostrand, 1962), p. 141
50. Flippo and Munsinger, op. cit., p. 136.
51. Bernard Berelson and G. A. Steiner, *Human Behavior* (New York: Harcourt, Brace & World, 1964), p. 227.
52. W. E. Deming, "What Happened in Japan," *Industrial Quality Control,* August 1967, pp. 89–93; J. M. Juran, "The QC Circle Phenomenon," *Industrial Quality Control,* January 1967, pp. 329–336.
53. W. F. Schleicher, "Quality Control Circles Save Lockheed Nearly $3 Million in Two Years," *Quality Management,* May 1977, pp. 14–17.
54. D. A. Whitsett, "Where Are Your Unenriched Jobs?" *Harvard Business Review,* January-February 1975, pp. 74–80.
55. T. R. Igleski, "Legal Considerations When Employee Fraud Is Evident," *The Internal Auditor,* January-February, 1969, p. 43.
56. C. B. Cheatham, "Is the Polygraph a Valid Internal Control Device?" *The Internal Auditor,* January-February 1974, p. 42.
57. D. B. Niestrath, "Catch That Thief!" *The Internal Auditor,* January–February 1974, p. 68.
58. L. B. Sawyer, *The Practice of Modern Internal Auditing* (Orlando, Fla.: The Institute of Internal Auditors, 1974), pp. 118, 119.
59. Ibid., pp. 66–77.

60. J. T. Reeve, "Auditing a Research Division," *The Internal Auditor,* January-February 1975, pp. 23–28.

61. C. W. Taylor, *Creativity: Progress and Potential* (New York: McGraw-Hill, 1964), p. 5.

62. Ibid., p. 178.

63. C. S. Whiting, *Creative Thinking* (New York: Reinhold, 1958), p. 6.

64. Ibid., p. 20.

PART II

The Skills
of Management

The successful manager is skilled in making decisions, communicating, measuring, and employing scientific methods. The successful internal auditor must be equally skilled so as to augment or complement the skills required of the manager. Such skills are generally considered to be a part of the process of management: planning, organizing, directing, and controlling. But because of their extreme importance to the proper functioning of the process, those skills will be discussed separately.

5

Decision Making

Decision making and problem solving. The futurity of decisions. The effect of management decisions. Selections made rationally. Conditions of decision making. How managers often decide. Types of decisions. The process of decision making. Traps for the unwary. How problems reach managers. Identifying the true problem. Objectives and constraints. Consequences. Facts versus hypotheses. The search for alternatives. Disagreements, creativity, and opportunities. Criteria for evaluation. Limiting factors. Cost effectiveness analyses. Uncertainty and quantification. When to use the decision process. The difficulty of selection. Group decisions. Where decisions should be made. Decisiveness. Rules for choosing from among alternatives. Action, the end result. Need to know. Steps in implementation. The internal auditor as a contributor. Recognizing problems needing decisions. Need for full access. The facts the internal auditor obtains. Determining objectives and anticipating constraints. Management consulting firms. The internal auditor's offer of alternatives. Weighing courses of action. Quantification and the internal auditor. Restriction on choices. Monitoring effective action.

DECISION MAKING AND THE MANAGER

The Anatomy of Decision Making

The Futurity of Decisions

Decision making is problem solving. If there is no problem—and in this context we include difficulties and conflicts in the term "problem"—there is no need for a decision. Whether to launch a new product, how to procure needed parts that are in short supply, and how to get the warring directors of sales and manufacturing to see eye-to-eye, all call for decisions.

But whether the matters requiring decision are called problems, difficulties, or conflicts, the means of resolving them have one thing in common: They relate to the future. A decision cannot affect something that has already happened. All decisions are future-oriented, and that is what keeps the results of decisions from being sure things.

Everyone makes decisions. We make decisions when we select the clothes we'll wear, the product we'll buy, the appointment we'll make or reject, the menu we'll prepare, and the lawyer we'll retain. What sets the manager's decisions apart is that they are made in a fishbowl. True, the doctor and the lawyer and the scientist make important decisions, but for the most part their bad decisions do not receive the attention accorded the manager's. The doctor's decisions affect only his patient and the patient's family. Aside from the relatively few cases that serve as precedents, the lawyer's lost cases are important to his client alone. And the scientist, working with trial and error, maintains that he can receive important information both from his successes and his failures.

The Manager's Decisions

But the manager's decisions are of a different kind. His day-to-day decisions affect most of the people within his own unit. His more important decisions affect people and colleagues in interfacing units. And his most important decisions affect the entire enterprise and perhaps the community as well. His decisions are supposed to have a high degree of effectiveness; 65 isn't passing.

Decision making is perhaps the manager's key skill. His impact on his organization is measured by the results of his decisions. Indeed, as pointed out in Chapter 3, the decision theory approach to management holds that decision making is the sole function of management.

Decision making is rational selection. It is not a mechanical job.

It is a taking of risks, because to anticipate the future is always a chancey undertaking. It is a challenge to judgment because it is more than a mere intellectual exercise and because it calls for vision and energy and for the deployment of the organizations's resources to achieve effective action.

Rationality

Yet complete rationality in decision making is rarely achieved. Rationality can relate only to what has already happened; and since the manager must deal with the future, he will have to settle for limited rationality. It can, however, be a well-founded rationality if the conditions of decision making are understood. They can be summarized as follows:

- □ The decision maker should be trying to meet some goal that he could not meet without taking positive action.
- □ He should fully understand the limitations within which he decides on the action he will take.
- □ He must realize that any choice he makes must be consistent with the goals he has set for himself.
- □ He must know that rarely is there one best choice, one best selection that will be all things to all men and will satisfy everyone. Instead, the final selection will most likely be a compromise between no action at all and some elusive Holy Grail.

More than that, the manager must keep in mind that every decision he makes must take into account his responsibility to manage the enterprise, manage the worker and the work, consider the community and society. Yet when one asks an executive how he makes decisions, he gets about the same answer as to the question: "How do you ride a bicycle?" The actual answers are usually like these:[1]

"I don't think we businessmen know how to make decisions."
"I don't know how I do it, I just do it."
"There's no formula for effective decision making."
"Thinking only causes mistakes."

In recent years, however, particularly in the nonroutine decisions, intuition is relinquishing its place to reasoning. Certainly there must always be a place for individual judgments, but the managers are turning more and more to attempts to reduce the number of occasions on which intuition is the sole basis for the decision. Ralph C. Davis puts it well:[2]

> A man who has nothing but background is a theorist. A man who has nothing but practical experience is a business mechanic. A professionally trained executive is one in whom there is an effective integration of these two general types of experiences, combined with adequate intelligence.

Classifications

Decisions and approaches to decisions can be classified in a number of ways. Here are some of them:

1. There are planning decisions and controlling decisions. Planning decisions make the rules. Controlling decisions enforce the rules. Planning decisions specify organizational objectives, develop programs, and set policies and procedures. Controlling decisions call for the steps to be taken to bring performance into line with the standards specified in the plans.

2. Decisions can also be classified as:

Routine Repetitive decisions that follow well-defined patterns and established procedures.

Nonroutine Unique problems that require individual analysis and solution, including those that are concerned with people.

Ends Broad decisions that are concerned with goals and objectives and are often nonrational; that is, they are influenced by the politics of a situation, the setting of objectives for an organization, or the personal drives of the executive.

Means Specific decisions that relate to the ways by which goals and objectives are reached. They should be rational or they will not be effective or efficient.

Strategic These decisions involve the relations between the organization and its environment or concern such matters as product mix and diversification.

Administrative Under this head come organizational decisions that include establishing authority, determining the flow of work, and deciding where to locate facilities.

Operating Here may be grouped the decisions related to pricing and marketing and those concerned with production.

3. The bases for decisions may be classified as:

Nonquantitative. Those based on intuition, facts, experience, and considered opinions.

Quantitative. Those based on such mathematical techniques as operations research, linear programming, simulation, Monte Carlo, queuing, and gaming. They will be discussed in Chapter 8.

Experience and Decision Making

Managers who use and defend the intuitive approach to decision making point to the success of the decisions they have made and to the effectiveness and efficiency of their operations. That kind of intuition may be a valuable asset and certainly should not be abandoned entirely. But the intuitive manager must recognize that intuition is based on learning from experience. Such learning is usually random rather than structured and extensive. The intuitive manager is limited by the experiences he has had, not by all the possible experiences that may be germane to a particular decision. Then, too, whether he likes it or not, he must recognize that, although all managers have learning experiences, there is no certainty that they learned from those experiences. Besides, conditions change, and the problem under consideration probably is not exactly the same as the successfully solved problem dredged out of experience. Decision making is often identified with the final choice. Actually, it is a process. The process has been defined from the standpoint of the executive and from the standpoint of the decision.

Simon says that executives divide their time among three activities, all of which relate to decision making:[3]

1. Finding occasions for making a decision.
2. Finding possible courses of action.
3. Choosing courses of action.

Those activities are related to the stages in problem solving that Dewey described in 1910:[4]

1. What is the problem?
2. What are the alternatives?
3. Which choice is best?

But arriving at a decision takes more steps than those described by Simon and Dewey. Drucker comes closer to it with these:[5]

1. Defining the problem: determining whether there really is a problem. Identifying the real issues, estimating when a solu-

tion must be reached, and estimating what it will cost to solve the problem.

2. Defining expectations: clarifying what will be gained by solving the problem and setting the goals which must be considered in all the steps of finding the most satisfactory solution.

3. Developing alternative solutions: Which of the options available best meet the goals and are surest to avoid that which is undesirable and unexpected?

4. Knowing what to do with the decision after it is reached.

Drucker points out that if a manager pays attention to those four rules, he will keep from falling into such traps as:[5]

☐ Finding the right answer for the wrong problem.

☐ Making the decision at the wrong time. The premature decision may not take into account enough knowledge. Postponement, which is also a decision and sometimes a bad one, can be irrevocable and may defeat the goals that the manager is trying to achieve.

☐ Making decisions to act that result in no action. To leave such a decision unimplemented is an abortion.

For the purpose of this chapter, we have expanded the steps in the decision-making process to include the evaluation of the developed alternatives and the making of the final choice. Accordingly, the portion of this chapter devoted to the manager's decision making will be subdivided under the following topics:

Recognizing and defining the problem
Defining expectations
Developing alternative courses
Evaluating possible courses
Selecting the best choice
Taking action

Some readers may pounce on the absence of the classic statement associated with decision making: "First get all the facts." But modern writers find that injunction irrelevant. The future holds no facts; it holds only the proving or disproving of hypotheses. The rule must be changed to "First define your problem and your expectations." By so doing the manager can focus on the historical records that are essential instead of being deluged with data that may have little or no relation to the basic issue.

Recognizing and Defining the Problem

Problems are brought to the manager's attention in many ways. Some surface routinely as the manager reviews reports that compare actual occurrences with occurrences that have been scheduled and budgeted. The significant variances rise like flares to capture his attention. Others are brought before him by the operation of well-designed controls and checks, the most important of which is the functioning of an alert internal auditing staff. The broader the scope of the internal audit program the more certain the executive can be that problems throughout the organization—not only in the accounting areas—will be brought to his attention. The internal auditor's role in the decision-making process will be discussed at length later in this chapter.

Some problems arise from the setting of new objectives, and they are self-generating. New objectives, goals, and product lines foretell the problems that are bound to accompany them, and the executive has at least an inkling that in those activities decisions will have to be made.

Some problems burst unexpectedly in the manager's face: contract cancellations, catastrophic acts of God, death of key people, an unexpected flood of orders. But by far the largest volume of matters calling for decision come before the manager in the following three ways:[6]

1. *Decisions or directives passed down by higher authority.* Executive decisions and directives require implementation. That implementation calls for decisions at the lower level, and sometimes the higher decision was made without giving full consideration to the circumstances that prevail where the implementation must be carried out. The manager may be hung on the horns of a dilemma. Carry out the executive decision and create chaos, or refuse to carry it out and be found insubordinate. Those are the situations that try managers' souls and create great actors; for some managers have the consummate skill of making insubordination appear to be the highest form of loyalty. Usually the dilemma occurs because the manager responsible for the action was not included in the process that led to the higher decision. We shall speak about that problem later in this subsection.

2. *Submissions by subordinates for management decision.* It is a sad fact that most people would rather respond routinely to stimuli than take the responsibility of making decisions, so they pass the decisions to the boss. Also, conflicts or jurisdictional disputes in the lower ranks bring pleas for decisions, but the good subordinate understands his

responsibilities and his authority to make decisions. He settles on his own the matters within the compass of his assignment and seeks help only when matters are clearly outside that compass. Again, however, most people would rather leave the deciding to the boss. The wise manager must let it be known that he expects self-reliance and initiative from his subordinates, and so he forces his subordinates to make the appropriate decisions. Similarly, he does not create a climate in which he insists on making every decision, large or small, or in which the penalty for mistakes is so severe that decisions are avoided.

3. *Decisions imposed by the situation.* Many decisions are required neither by the imposition of superior decisions nor by submissions from subordinates; they are an inherent part of the responsibilities defined by the plan of organization. The first two kinds are not elective; the manager will have to respond one way or another. The situational decision is a matter of choice, however, and it is by far the most significant test of the manager's executive ability. Situational decisions are made on the manager's own initiative; and when initiative is lacking or when fear of failure is overweening, the tendency is to avoid the decision. The hesitant manager fears the consequences of a wrong decision more than he fears those of no decision. He is the manager who benefits most from an understanding of the anatomy of decision making and the principles that, if followed, are calculated to lead to acceptable solutions.

Problems, whatever their source, do not come with clear, incisive labels on them. Difficulties that identify themselves as one thing on the surface often mask the true identity of the underlying problem. The manager may then commit the cardinal sin of rendering the right judgment on the wrong case.

The first question that the manager should ask himself when faced with a problem or difficulty that presents itself or is presented to him is this: "Is a decision necessary?" If it is likely that the matter will clear itself or, although annoying, is of no importance and if corrected will not make much difference, the best course for the manager is to leave things alone. Strangely enough, not everyone abides by that seemingly self-evident truism. The project manager, with the help of a dedicated team, may accomplish miracles of production effort under adverse circumstances but then daub himself with pitch by dismissing an employee for some minor infraction just to prove that he runs a "tight ship." The heroic efforts are then shadowed by a decision that need not have been made because the problem did not warrant a decision. It really meant nothing in his grand scheme of things, and the result was out of proportion to the difficulty.

The rule the project manager should have followed is really a simple one:[7] *Act if on balance the benefits greatly outweigh the costs and the risks.* A corollary to that rule, of course, is: *Act or do not act, but do not hedge or compromise.* If a disease warrants a cure, prescribe the full dose. Half a dose is worse than none. Cutting off one finger when the whole hand is gangrened inflicts all the trauma and provides none of the benefits.[8]

The first phase of decision making, therefore, is diagnosis: to identify and clarify the problem. Too few managers fully practice or even understand that element of decision making, yet it is clearly the first sure step toward the solution of the right problem. Failing to give adequate attention to that step may lead the decision maker in the direction of a solution of the wrong problem. Peter Drucker tells a tale of the perils of improper problem identification:[9]

> A company was having great difficulty meeting its production schedules. Shipments were late despite a great deal of overtime. In desperation, management decided on plant expansion to ease production problems. Large sums were budgeted for the expansion and plans were being laid. Then somebody decided that perhaps the real problem had not been identified. When he started asking questions the key issue was unearthed.
>
> The fault lay not with production but with sales. Salesmen were promising rush deliveries to all customers, marginal customers as well as good customers. No priorities were being set. Orders were being rushed through no matter whose orders they were. As a result of the problem identification, the salesmen were given new instructions on rush orders and priorities. The orders of marginal customers took a back seat. And production was able to meet schedules.
>
> Management took a small risk, or course, that some marginal customers would be lost. But the greater risk of losing good customers because of missed schedules was avoided.

Some managers, accustomed to the intuitive snap judgments that they feel have worked for them, may reject the thought of spending large amounts of time in problem identification and definition. They are probably right if they are thinking of problems that are routine or will have no serious impact on their organizations' operations. But when decisions involve long stretches of time, considerable expenditures of funds, and the lives of people, the time so spent is economical in the long run. It is a sad waste of energy and funds to make decisions about the wrong problems. As many a manager is aware, there always seems to be time to correct the mistakes and so little time to forestall them.

Defining Expectations

After the problem has been identified and defined, one further step is needed before the search for alternatives: The objectives to be achieved by the decision—what the manager can expect to see accomplished by a decision on the issues and what hazards are faced by taking some new course of action prompted by the decision—must be identified.

Defining the problem is the first step, of course. But the most precise definition will not identify the objectives to be met by the decision, isolate the obstacles to the decision, or point out the constraints laid upon courses of action. And those objectives, obstacles, and constraints may have a profound effect on the relevance of the alternatives available to the decision maker.

The objectives must be in consonance with the overall organizational objectives. A decision that may appear brilliant, practical, and feasible may founder on the shoals of executive veto if it runs counter to executive policy. Similarly, an otherwise valid decision may prove to be a useless exercise if there are no resources for carrying it out. So the decision maker should take certain constraints into account before he embarks on his search for solutions:

Policy constraints. A manager's decision on a new product may be constrained by a company policy that all such decisions are to be made by the board of directors.

Financial constraints. The decision for plant expansion may be blocked by the utter unavailability of funds.

Technological constraints. The decision to provide added strength and resiliency to a product may be barred by the absence of any materials that offer such qualities and the lack of funds to develop them.

Contractual constraints. Decisions involving workers may run directly counter to union agreements.

Government constraints. Government is a factor that lurks in the background of many decision processes. A perfectly reasonable decision to merge two firms may run afoul of laws concerning restraint of trade. Similarly, the influence of the government must be considered in seeking decisions involving such matters as pricing, financing, and stock options.

Physical constraints. Decisions on plant expansion may be meaningless in the absence of any space in which to expand.

Personnel constraints. Decisions calling for special qualities in people cannot be carried out unless those qualities are available or procurable.

The consequences of decisions also must be taken into account before opening the field to certain alternatives. Every decision expectation must be concerned with "what if." Every decision involves some change. Every change has a ripple effect. And the ripples can turn to tidal waves for the unwary or those who failed to ask the right what-if question.

King and Cleland cite a case of "second-order consequences" that had some rough ripples as a result of what appeared to be a perfectly reasonable decision.[10]

> The Australian Yir Yorunt aborigines had from time immemorial used stone axes as their primary cutting tool. Missionaries, in the hope of improving the life of the Yir Yorunts, gave them steel axes. But the missionaries decided to give the steel axes to all the Yir Yorunts, men, women, and children. What the missionaries failed to take into account, however, was that stone axes played important roles in the lives of the aborigines, over and above their use in cutting wood. The men were the ones who had always owned the stone axes; and these were held to be symbols of masculinity and generated respect for the elders.

> Older men, having less respect for missionaries, were not likely to accept the steel axes, but as they saw them in the hands of others, it soon became obvious that the steel axes were far more efficient. So the elders, once respected, were forced to borrow steel axes from women and younger men. And thus the previous status relationships, so important to the stability of a culture, were thoroughly upset.

Certainly a manager cannot be expected to be a Delphic oracle able to anticipate every contingency or be aware of every constraint. That is why the intuitive decision maker who usually rides the crest of successful decisions can sometimes be capsized by the unexpected waves. But in most large organizations, planning staffs are available to explore the contingencies and the constraints. Their advice and assistance on major decisions should be sought before the decision is made, not after.

At the same time there can be a tendency for some planners to live in ivory towers, out of touch with reality. The wise manager, in seeking counsel from such staffs, should make the realities known to the planners and create a good marriage between planning and doing. "First get all the facts," a common exhortation to decision makers, puts the cart before the horse. If followed, it may produce factual information on a host of irrelevancies, including matters that should not concern the decision maker because they are excluded by constraints or adverse contingencies or because they run counter to the expectations of the decision maker.

But opinions and hypotheses that relate to decision expectations should be encouraged during this step of decision making. Facts relate to the past, hypotheses to the future. Hypotheses are born of experience with similar circumstances and are an integral part of decision making. The manager should entertain such hypotheses, but he should demand that they be well thought out. He should ask the proposers of the hypotheses what must be known to test hypothesis validity, how the validity can be tested, and how the hypothesis can be measured. Those are the "facts" that are relevant.

In the conflict of opposing opinions and hypotheses, the purpose and expectations of the decision emerge. The next step, the creative development of alternatives, can take place in greater safety.

Developing Alternative Courses

Whenever a decision is called for, there are at least two alternatives: overt action and no action at all—to change things or to leave them as they are. But it is a mistake for the manager to jump to the conclusion that he has only two choices.

It is rare for a number of alternatives to be lacking. In fact, it is a good idea for every manager to take the position that, if there seems to be only one way to go, it is the wrong way. Some decision makers have an unfortunate tendency to see only the extremes—the either-or situation. They are usually the people who pride themselves on their intuitive decision making and their snap judgments. They see no value in the difficult, often mind-bending search for potential alternatives.

Koontz and O'Donnell speak of the experience one of them had in such a situation:[11]

A firm was losing money because production was inadequate. Survival depended on increased output to reduce costs and serve an expanded market. But the losses had shrunk both capital and credit. The equipment needed for expanded production just could not be financed. The sole course of action appeared to be no action at all; and that meant bankruptcy. With that end facing them, the officers went to work and found two other alternatives:

1. A manufacturer had the needed equipment. It had been bank-financed, and the manufacturer had been unable to sell it. The bank agreed to let the manufacturer sell the equipment to the firm without

down payment, accepting two-name paper instead of the one-name notes already held.
2. A competitor of the firm had new equipment on order and offered to sell the old machines without requiring a down payment.

The workable alternatives don't come a-begging for attention. They must be hunted down; and that hunt has more than one purpose in decision making. The best thought-through decision may be rendered inoperative by changing, unforeseen circumstances. There should be an alternative waiting in the wings if the star is unable to perform. Drucker offers interesting support for this thesis:[12]

> Both the Schlieffen Plan of the German Army in 1914 and President Franklin D. Roosevelt's initial economic program in 1933 were disproved at the time they were supposed to be effective.
>
> The German General Staff had concentrated on one plan only; it had no alternative plan to fall back on. Hence, when the Schlieffen Plan failed, there were no other well-thought-through alternatives. And the ensuing series of gambles all failed.
>
> On the other hand, while Roosevelt's first plan was based on orthodox economics, he had people working on an alternative plan. The collapse of the banking system showed economic orthodoxy to be suicidal for the times. He then switched to a more radical policy, based on economic and social reform. He had a well-conceived, alternative policy to follow.

The soil from which innovative alternatives grow must be planted with the seeds of discontent and disagreement. A meeting of people anxious to avoid conflict and please the boss produces few alternatives, because by definition a number of alternatives implies different, and perhaps diametrically opposed, approaches to a problem. Tough, hard disagreement that raises the competitive instinct forces innovativeness. It is up to the manager to foster that fruitful disputation by permitting people to disagree with him and with each other in the search for alternatives. The consensus and compromise come later.

Also, in the search for alternatives, the manager must not brush aside the novel options and thereby stifle creativity within his organization. Creative thought needs freedom and "thinking time." That is another reason for avoiding the haste and stress of snap decisions, decisions made under pressure at the last moment. Creativity is enhanced when it is rewarded—if only by the appreciation of the manager for new ideas and if there is a reduction in levels of stress. That is the sort of climate the manager must generate to permit the growth of viable alternatives: the appreciative consideration of innovative proposals and the absence of severe penalties for novel ideas, which do not always work.

In the development of alernatives, the wise manager is also looking for opportunities. Hence, he should not stop with the seemingly obvious alternative; other alternatives may provide not only the solution to the problem but also an opportunity for novel courses of action. Drucker cites a case in point.[13]

> A small plumbing supply manufacturer had both excellent products and customers. Sales kept climbing, but profits remained the same. The manufacturer could not produce efficiently in his old location, and space constraints blocked expansion. The only alternative which came to mind was to build a new plant. But he had not considered the financial constraints and he had not searched for other alternatives. The new plant was built, the manufacturer became overextended, and he went out of business within the year. He could have considered other alternatives, some of which might have been excellent opportunities to move in new directions and improve his financial position. He could have:
>
> □ Subcontracted some of the work under appropriate quality control.
> □ Rented a new plant instead of building one.
> □ Given up the inadequate facility and had all his goods made by an outside supplier.
> □ Become a distributor for another supplier.
> □ Merged with another manufacturer.
>
> With the opportunities they offered, any of those alternatives could have been preferable to the position in which he finally found himself.

The successful search usually produces some alternatives that seem equally appropriate. If that were not so, there would be no problem of choice. The best alternatives would stand high above the rest and would automatically eliminate the others. But rarely is there one clear-cut solution that provides without doubt all the answers to a problem. The alternatives must be weighed and evaluated to determine which offers the most benefits with the fewest side effects.

Evaluating Possible Courses

With a number of alternative courses laid before him, the decision maker must measure each alternative by the standards of the decision objective within the constraints posed by existing circumstances. The easy way is to select the course that he proposed himself or personally likes. But the effective decision maker gives each alternative its day in court. He tries to understand why others proposed different courses. It could well be that they had a different understanding of the problem. And perhaps theirs was the better understanding.

All knowledge is less than perfect because of human or technical limitations. If all knowledge were complete, ultimate, and immutable, the totality could be spun into the computer and the readout then accepted as gospel. But knowledge is not perfect, and for that reason the decision maker has a function to perform in evaluating the alternatives before him. That evaluation may take subjective or objective forms.

The subjective form does not necessarily imply an intuitive ranking of alternatives. Certain criteria that are available to the decision maker may provide the subjective evaluation with some rationality:

The availability of resources in men, material, money, and machines.

The amount of risk faced in seeking the expected goal.

The costs to be borne in achieving the hoped-for results.

The time frame within which the decision and its implementation should take place.

As has been pointed out, decisions relate to the future and no "facts" can assure future conditions. But researchers are exploring techniques that may guide the decision maker in assessing what the uncertain future may hold relative to his decision.

□ G. L. S. Shackle believes the best alternative is the one that offers the least "potential surprise." The executive must make a subjective judgment that the alternative selected will result in no unpleasant surprises.[14]

□ L. F. Savage developed a similar concept in the "regret" criterion. To the extent he does not meet his maximum goals, the decision maker will experience regret. The difference between the maximum payoff and the payoffs resulting from various conditions measures the degree of regret.[15]

□ Abraham Wald suggests the "maximum criterion." Following the principle that "whatever can go wrong will," the decision maker assumes that the worst will happen to each alternative. He then chooses the best of the worst states.

□ Leonid Hurwicz's approach to uncertainty is to use weighted combinations of pessimism-optimism. The decision maker assigns a level of probability to his conception of the best and the worst of available courses of action.

Those approaches do not yet provide hard and fast rules for today's decision makers, but they do show the thinking being applied to the evaluation in the light of uncertainty. The techniques make use of probabilities that can be objectively measured, but the probabilities assigned usually come from the subjective feelings of the decision maker based on judgment and experience.

In weighing his alternatives, the decision maker must account for limiting factors. Those are the factors that block the accomplishment of a desired objective. Until they are identified and removed, the objective cannot be met. The factors can be tangible: time, fixed costs, operating costs. They can also be intangible: labor relations, technological changes (the unknown unknowns), political climate, the economy, strikes, and the nature of people.

Finding the limiting factor can sometimes be a difficult task. But, as Drucker points out, we can break through surface symptoms and come to grips with the real problem by isolating the critical factor, the strategic element. Drucker offers this illustration:[16]

> In one firm, eight men in rapid succession were given the job of executive vice president. All either left or were removed. In desperation, the president interviewed all eight in an attempt to determine why the job seemed to be too much for eight highly qualified people. He learned that the critical factor was himself. He had not been permitting those men to do their job. He had issued orders to vice presidents without informing the incumbent executive vice president. He had all vice presidents reporting to him. He just couldn't keep his hands off operations. Each executive vice president was forced to function in the dark, and he inevitably stumbled. The strategic element was responsibility without authority. The solution eliminated the limiting factor. This was done by elevating the president to chairman of the board and selecting a new president from among the eight former executive vice presidents.

Between the subjective evaluation and the objective, mathematical evaluation lie evaluations that can be weighed by cost-effectiveness analysis. The technique is used to determine the best choice when the objective sought does not have the clean specificity of such qualities as sales, costs, or profits. Among the objectives may be those of reducing pollution or training unemployables. But certain standards still may be used to measure effectiveness in such activities. For example, if the general objective of the decision were to improve employee morale, the alternatives to be evaluated would be those best calculated to reduce turnover, absenteeism, or the number of grievances. To the inputs might be added the judgment of qualified experts. The features of cost-effectiveness decisions are generally as follows:[17]

- □ Objectives are generally imprecise.
- □ Alternatives are concerned with systems, programs, or strategies.
- □ Although not always subject to quantification, the measure of effectiveness must be directly related to the objectives and must be set in as precise terms as feasible
- □ Costs are traditional measures, but nonmonetary terms also may be used.
- □ The decision criteria involve trade-offs or call for achieving desired objectives with available resources at the least possible cost.

Aristotle said: "Every situation has its own degree of certainty, and a well-trained man accepts that degree and does not look for a greater one." The higher the certainty the more simple the decision making. The lower the certainty the more difficult the decision making because of the impact of variables and nonpredictable factors.

When uncertainty reigns, the theory of probability can be employed to determine mathematically the degree of certainty that postulated events will take place. The physical sciences have long relied on mathematics. The methodology of quantification is now being adopted by decision makers to evaluate the probability of success of available alternatives.[18]

Research analysis is the scientific approach to decision making. It centers on the search for relations among the more critical variables of a problem and on the constraints and premises that bear on the goals to be sought. It is, in effect, the pencil-and-paper approach to decision making. Those matters will be touched on in Chapter 8.

Selecting the Best Choice

The right answer—the perfect answer—appears only in mathematics. Two and two makes four, and on that there is no room for debate. But in selecting from alternatives in a business decision, the decision maker must deal with uncertainties. An element of imagination and vision must be added to the process. The decision maker must meld what he knows to what he expects will happen. He must integrate past, present, and future. And his ability to do that well and consistently is a measure of his success.

Making the final decision is a lonely task. It is also a risky task, so some managers turn to group decisions. And there may be some merit to that route. It gives the group a feeling of belonging, and it improves commitment to carry out the decision because the group participated in the selection. The complexities caused by our galloping technology cry for input from different disciplines to find the right direction. A shared responsibility enhances chances of cooperation. All members of the group, when they see that their differing attitudes have been considered, feel that they have been dealt with fairly and not arbitrarily.

But the arguments against decision by consensus may be more powerful than those for it. Clearly, a certain amount of cooperation can be assured if the group is made part of the development of alternatives and if its members know that the alternatives they propose will be given careful consideration. The ultimate selection from among those alternatives does not lend itself to debate, however. A committee moves with the speed of its least-informed member. Some members speak louder than others. Some stand in awe of others and are fearful of making their choices known. Committees generally lead to vacillation and delay; and the consensus solution may be a mediocre average instead of a best and innovative choice.

In the final analysis, the authority for any particular decision lies with the responsible individual even if that individual is sitting with other council members. But that does not mean the selection of the best alternative should be made in mahogany row. The final decision should be made at the lowest feasible level and as close as possible to where the work is being done and the implementation will take place. Executives must learn when to let go. Many of them carry all the decision-making prerogatives with them as they move up the corporate ladder. That can create bottlenecks and overburden top executives with excessive detail.

Besides, if top management reserves to itself all decision making, it may very well make a brilliant judgment on an operating decision but not be aware later of the sudden hazard when things do not go according to plan and swift changes must by made. It is really all a matter of degree. Some decisions are routine. Others, by their nature, should be moved up to higher levels. Here are some guidelines:

Range. Is the commitment long- or short-range? How readily can the course be changed if unfavorable results become apparent?
Effect. Does the decision have impact on only the decision maker and his organization or on other organizations as well?

Values. Does the decision concern ethics, morality, or social and political beliefs? Does it affect human beings?

Rarity. Does the decision concern recurrent affairs, or is it rare and unique?

With our institutions and technology growing more complex, it becomes all the more important that the authority to make particular decisions be clearly spelled out and assigned to those who are capable of making wise choices. Decision making calls for a particular temperament. It has less to do with learning and intelligence than with decisiveness. For example, the brilliant scientist may be a poorer decision maker than the pragmatic executive. The scientific discipline creates indecisiveness because of the strictures it places on the scientist to question everything that is not supported by scientific knowledge.

The manager, however, must be decisive without the support of full knowledge. He never has "all the facts." Besides, he is dealing with futurity and uncertainty, and so he must be willing to rely on his subjective feelings of "conviction," "certainty," and "self-reliance" under the most uncertain conditions. Having made the decision, he must speak positively about it, no matter what his inner feelings are, so that others will feel confident that the best decision was made.

The selection process becomes still more difficult when it is concerned with aims and ends. The ends and aims are usually affected by nonrational factors as distinguished from profit-based goals, which are supported by the rationality of quantification. The nonrational decisions that involve morality or social considerations cannot be called right or wrong by scientific standards, but they have to be made. The executive is better equipped to make them than the moralist or the sociologist. Both the latter become entangled in the web of social responsibility, which is rarely clear-cut, and they lack decisiveness. The executive must take action that may call for aiming at one social goal at the expense of others. The Gordian knot must be cut; rarely is there time to untangle it.

The executive usually calls upon his intuition or his experience in making the final selection. Unfortunately, intuition implies an absence of analysis; intuition cannot be explained. If the basis of the ultimate selection is not clear, even to the decision maker himself, the chances for success become dimmer. Similarly, experience can be helpful or dangerous. Many people have experiences without gaining from them. Good decisions are tested against future events, whereas experience is rooted in the past. It may well be that experience is given greater reliance than it deserves in decision making.

But there are some rules the decision maker can follow when the time comes to make the final choice, rules that make use of but do not rely wholly upon intuition and experience:[19]

1. *The decision must contribute to achieving stated goals.* The alternative that best meets the established goal or objective is most likely to resist the eroding effect of time.

2. *Employ creativity.* The best solution may be a novel one, a grouping of familiar ideas in a new and novel way. The decision maker should not hesitate to leave his warm, accustomed bed and brave the chill morning of innovation.

3. *Every decision must be converted to action.* The choice selected must be capable of being implemented by existing or available money, men, and materials.

4. *Consider the ripple effect.* Every decision brings change, and the change often extends beyond the circle of the intended and expected decision field. So the decision maker must consider what can go wrong and how seriously it can go wrong, what safeguards should be employed and their cost, and how to monitor the results.

5. *Maintain stability.* Continually opening decisions for revision leads to frustration. Unless new facts or views become extremely compelling, the decision made should be let stand.

6. *Trial runs can determine feasibility.* Full resources need not always be committed at the outset. A trial run can point up unexpected defects, or a series of checkpoints can be established to guard against disastrous and irreversible effects.

7. *Decisions should not be made before their time.* The manager should not vacillate. He must be decisive, but the more time he has to make his final decision the better the decision is likely to be. The effort spent on the final selection, however, will be reduced if sufficient time and thought were allotted to developing the alternatives from which the selection must be made.

8. *A decision should not be defaulted.* The worst action is deciding not to decide. Needless delay may result in a waiver of the decision making, and that will create a vacuum that others may have to fill.

9. *The decision maker must recognize that everyone will not be pleased.* Someone usually disagrees with the decision. That is a condition that the decision maker must live with. After he has reached his decision, he must try to explain his thinking and win cooperation. He will have to show that, in the face of uncertainty, he may not be able to maximize but instead must, as Simon puts it,[20] "satisfice"—take a share of the market rather than all of it, make an adequate profit rather than a maximum, or obtain a fair price rather than the highest price.

Taking Action

The end result of any decision must be action. Defining problems, establishing expectations, developing alternative courses, evaluating possible courses, and selecting the best choice are sheer exercises in futility without action. Many a brilliant task force has pointed out the unmistakable way to go—but nobody went. Often it was because people were not presold or informed or made a part of the decision process.

Anybody who is needed to make a decision effective—or who could cripple it—should be part of the decision process. The alternative could be disastrous. The decision maker must understand that his decisions may not be acted upon unless the actors receive their scripts early on. Drucker gives an example of the results of violating the need-to-know precept:[21]

> A decision was made within a company producing industrial equipment to discontinue a model which had long been in production but whose sales were falling off. The customers who owned the model were dutifully notified. They recognized that the model would soon be unobtainable, and those who liked it hurriedly placed orders for the equipment against the day that it would be unavailable. Accordingly, there was a brief but sharp spurt in sales.

> In the meantime, the company's buyer who was assigned to procuring parts for the discontinued model was unaware of the decision not to produce it any more. His instructions had been—and to him still were—to buy parts in ratio to sales. The upturn in sales sent him scurrying to buy more parts. And the company wound up with enough parts in inventory for 8 years of production, none of which would take place.

Every decision must provide for implementation; and whenever action is desired, there must be feedback to make sure the action is appropriate and effective. The armed forces have long known that. When an order is given to a subordinate, the superior or his aide personally verifies that the order was carried out. He never relies on reports from the subordinate. The skepticism does not necessarily stem from distrust of the subordinate; it stems from distrust of communication.

Once the selection from among alternatives has been made, the decision maker must then consider:

The sequence of steps to be taken in implementing the decision.
The people who should be charged with carrying out each step.

The controls to be installed to see that the steps are taken.
The clear line of communication to those charged with implementation.
The tangible results expected.
The reports required to provide feedback on the action taken.

DECISION MAKING AND THE INTERNAL AUDITOR

The Internal Auditor's Responsibilities

The modern internal auditor can be an important contributor to the decision-making process. His position in the organization, his objectivity and independence, and his analytical ability combine to make him an indispensable part of the problem-solving team. He has much to offer in all but one of the steps in the process. That one step is the final selection from among the choices open to the decision maker. That is a line management function, not a staff function. For the internal auditor to make the selection would be to usurp line prerogatives. Also, it would tend to erode the auditor's own objectivity and independence. His Statement of Responsibilities makes that point clear when it says: "Objectivity is essential to the audit function. Therefore, internal auditors should not develop and install procedures, prepare records, or engage in any other activity which . . . could reasonably be construed to compromise the independence of the internal auditor."

Making the selection of a course of action for the manager could compromise the internal auditor's independence. The internal auditor owes it to the manager to suggest *a* course; he should never insist on *the* course. But in the remaining steps he can provide a signal service.

Recognizing and Defining the Problem

The busy executive is worried not only by the problems he is aware of but also by those that may be lurking in the dark corners and have not yet come to light. He rests a little easier, therefore, if he knows there is an independent force dedicated to shining a light into the corners and spotting the problems that need management attention. The charter that gives the internal auditor access to all records, areas, and personnel within the organization adds an extension to management's antenna. When that access is restricted, the antenna's reach is correspondingly reduced. Management gains, therefore, by eliminating restrictions on the internal auditor's activities.

The extent of the antenna's reach can be measured by the internal auditor's long-range audit program. Many internal auditing groups prepare long-range programs that cover spans of three to five years and list the specific audit projects to be undertaken. An indication of the depth of coverage for each audit project is seen in the number of audit man-days assigned to particular projects. The long-range audit program provides guidelines to the auditor and assurance to management about the activities to be examined. Management is thus made aware of the corners in the organization to which the audit lamp will be directed and can add corners of its own if it wishes.

Two examples out of many highlight the service the internal auditor can provide in identifying and defining problems. Both examples are from Mintern.

During an audit in one of his company's plants, the internal auditor saw that cartons of finished goods were being invoiced at amounts which assumed that all the cartons contained uniform quantities. He made tests of carton contents over a period of time. And he found that on the average the cartons contained about 10% more than the invoiced quantity. At the internal auditor's recommendation, management issued instructions to prepare invoices for actual quantities shipped. The identification of the problem resulted in annual savings of $113,000.[22]

An internal auditor for a manufacturing company was making an audit of perishable and durable tools. While checking tool inventories in the tool cribs, he observed that one expensive tool used to install fasteners was causing difficulties for production workers. There seemed to be a constant parade to the tool cribs for replacements of that tool. The production workers complained pungently to the tool crib attendant; but since repairs were not his responsibility, he turned a deaf ear, replacing the broken tools with new ones and ordering replacements and repairs as needed. The internal auditor began to dig deeper and finally identified the problem.

□ Repairs on this tool were costing $225,000 a year.
□ Excessive breakage was caused by misuse in some instances and poor tool design in others.

The internal auditor then brought the matter to the attention of the appropriate manager with the following results:

□ The production workers were instructed in the use of the tools.
□ Improvements were made in tool repairs.
□ Some tools were replaced with tools of heavier design.
□ Fundamental weaknesses inherent in the tool were investigated by the manufacturer.

As a result, repair costs were reduced by $150,000.[23]

As we have pointed out, management decisions relate to the future, and so for the manager to "get all the facts" is irrelevant. The internal auditor, however, in identifying and defining the problems needing management attention, must get all the facts needed to establish that there is a problem and that it warrants attention. He must know the population he is dealing with, in this case the number of tools, their value, and the cost of repairing them. He must isolate the causes leading to the problem, because he knows that no problem will ever be truly solved unless its causes have been identified. In this case, the causes were employee carelessness, poor tool design, and ineffective repair practices. He must know the effect of failure to solve the problem. In this case it would be employee frustration, lost production hours, and excessive expense.

The internal auditor, if he has truly arrived in his organization, is often called upon by executive management to perform management studies in addition to his programmed audits. The executive, on seeing the need for improvement in some areas, may ask the internal auditor to evaluate conditions, determine their seriousness, and recommend solutions. But the assignment of the study to the internal auditor may be an impulsive statement of what is desired from a frustrated manager who has not had or did not take the time to think the matter through. Throwing his hands up at some perceived difficulty, or upset by the inability of other staff people to solve it, he may simply say to the internal auditor, "Take a look at so and so and tell me what you think."

The wise internal auditor will not jump on his steed and go galloping off in different directions. He will first determine whether there is a problem and, if so, how he conceives it. Then, having identified and defined the problem, he will carefully present to executive management a thorough analysis of what he sees the problem to be, how he will carry out the study to provide the information he thinks management needs, and how much the study will cost. Very often management's conception of the problem becomes crystallized when the auditor defines it.

Defining Expectations

The experienced internal auditor sees, as the first rule of operational auditing, determining the objectives of an activity or an assignment before he lays out his audit plans. Without the lodestar of objective, goal, or aim, it is easy to get off course, and that is often why managers find the right solution to the wrong problem.

The internal auditor can help management chart a straight course and avoid the hidden reefs of constraints during the decision process. Constraints are not restricted to laws, executive policies, and technology. They may surface—often too late—when a decision in one department of an organization runs afoul of existing practice in another. And the internal auditor can be very helpful in identifying those constraints.

Nobody in an organization has the intimate, extensive knowledge of practices and procedures that is possessed by the experienced modern internal audit staff. Executive management has a general knowledge of operations throughout the organization. Operating management has an intimate knowledge of its own operations and perhaps of operations in contiguous departments, but not of operations in departments with which it has no contacts or only rare ones. And the deficiencies that internal auditors bring to the attention of surprised operating managers indicate that manager knowledge may be intimate but not necessarily complete.

Only the far-ranging internal auditor is aware of practices throughout the organization, and to exclude him from the decision-making process is to don blinders deliberately. For that reason, wise managers will ask their internal audit staff to read new policies and procedures and changes in operating instructions. The object is not to obtain internal audit approval for those matters; rather, it is to learn whether the internal auditor is aware of constraints that might impair the success of proposed actions. This is not to say that the internal auditor can be a guarantor of that success; it is merely to say that, if he has knowledge of some impediment to the sought-for accomplishment, he will make management privy to that knowledge.

Similarly, executive management should think long and hard before it bypasses the internal audit function in favor of a management consulting firm to help solve some management problem. It is not that consulting firms are without experienced, able personnel. They are capable of fine analyses and suggestions. What they lack, however, is the intimate knowledge of the organization. This author has observed expensive, extensive management studies by outside consultants that culminated in thick, hard-cover reports that contained dozens of recommendations. The trouble is that generally only a small percent of those recommendations were adopted. The recommendations may have been valid enough in principle. But often they were not relevant to the particular operation in the particular organization.

As a member of management study teams staffed by the organization's internal auditors, the author has found that a rejected internal auditor's recommendation is a rare exception. The ingredient for success is usually a knowledge of the constraints within the organization that would make otherwise rational recommendations inoperable.

Developing Alternate Courses

Some writers on internal auditing hold that the internal auditor should identify problems but not make recommendations to solve them. The reason cited is the auditor's potential loss of objectivity and independence. Such a position runs counter to both the internal auditor's Statement of Responsibilities and good sense. The Statement, under the heading Objective and Scope, lists "Recommending operating improvements" among the activities the internal auditor should carry out to attain his overall objectives. And denying management the benefit of his experience with workable solutions would seem to be an abdication of responsibility.

The internal auditor has no business telling management that his recommended course is the one course to follow. That involves him in the selection process, where he does not belong. What he should offer is one of the courses the manager should evaluate and consider before making his final selection. Here is one example of offering a course of action:[24]

Incoming raw materials are usually tested for conformance to specifications. The internal auditor during a routine test found that his company's inspectors often omitted these tests. He asked why and was told that the specification tolerances were so wide that materials invariably fell within an acceptable range. For example, the supplier might have been committed to a stated specification of .9. But the inspector's instructions permitted acceptance of a broad leeway—like a range of .7 to .11. Even at .7 the quality of the material would not adversely affect the quality of the company's processes. What had been overlooked, however, was the fact that the supplier would charge a higher price to meet a quality of .9 than a quality of .7. So the internal auditor suggested considering negotiation in appropriate cases with suppliers to ease the specifications and thereby reduce prices.

The internal auditor did not prescribe how much to ease the specifications, which materials to apply the revisions to, or what suppliers to negotiate with. Those were management decisions. Management moved ahead to renegotiate specifications with suppliers, and the eased requirements resulted in substantial savings in the cost of raw materials.

Evaluating Possible Courses

The internal auditor can and should provide managers with assistance in weighing alternative courses of action. He has many products in his inventory to use in assessing the courses available. His knowledge of company records and his ability to analyze values can be brought to bear, as witness this situation:[25]

A company had switched from coal to oil as fuel for steam boilers. Yet the coal inventory was carried on the books at purchased cost. Disposal had been recommended. But no evaluation had been made of the economics of that course. The market value was deemed nil; and still the inventory had been maintained.

The auditor encountering the situation made the appraisal for management. He learned that a market value did indeed exist, and at 75% of book value. Besides, he found that maintaining the inventory cost about 12% of book value for taxes, insurance, pile turnover, and the like. He also found that the company could recover 56% of the book value after paying delivery charges.

When the auditor presented his evaluation to management, he suggested two alternative courses:

1. Reduce inventory to the recoverable amount, thereby saving substantially in taxes.
2. Dispose of the coal if the cost of keeping it for backup purposes was considered too high.

Management decided to sell the coal. The cash recovery after taxes was about $25,000, and annual maintenance expense was eliminated.

It will be observed that the internal auditor did not make the decision. He helped management make it through his proffered courses of action and by his evaluation of available courses, including the course of doing nothing.

The internal auditor need not be a specialist in operations research or in other quantitative methods. But he should have a broad enough knowledge of all management techniques to know where to turn and whom to consult in order to aid managers. The author became involved in just such a stuation:

Executive management received a proposal from a young budget manager to use multiple regression analysis to estimate overhead rates. The budget manager had a master's degree in business administration and a thorough command of both quantitative analysis and computer programming. He had developed the formula and the computer program and had presented the proposal to the executive in a detailed report. The executive was stumped. He was not technically competent to evaluate the program himself, but he did not want to reject out of hand a plan which might cut hundreds of man-hours from the development of overhead rates. Yet he could not bring himself to make a decision solely on the recommendation of his young budget manager.

He turned to the internal auditor and asked for help. The internal auditor was not an expert on the subject either. But he knew where to look. In a book of mathematics for management, he found a multiple regression problem comparable with the one at issue. The problem provided detailed input data, formulas, a computer program, and the correct answers.

At the internal auditor's request, the budget manager introduced that problem's data into the computer, using his own program. The internal auditor observed every step of the input. After the lights had flashed and the tapes had whirled, the computer displayed the answer—and it was not correct. So the budget manager had his computer program reviewed and a programming error was found. With the error corrected, the auditor's data were again fed into the computer. This time the answer in the book and the one provided by the budget manager's program were identical. Buttressed with this support, the executive adopted the corrected program.

Selecting the Best Choice

As we have pointed out, selecting the final course of action is a lonely task. It is a management decision, and it can rarely be shared —certainly not with the internal auditor.

The internal auditor is the monitor of the organization's controls, and he must monitor and evaluate with objectivity and independence. He loses that objectivity when he espouses a single course of action, so he must be careful to avoid being associated as sponsor with any one course. Such an association could come back to haunt him if he should later review the results of the action and find them wanting. It is human for the internal auditor to want to be able to say, "That is what I told top management to do, and that's precisely what they did." But the path is strewn with traps. There is no need to walk it. That auditor's partnership agreement with management doesn't require it or even sanction it.

Taking Action

Once the decision is made and implemented, the internal auditor must deal with it as he does with any other important activity in the company. He must appraise the control system. He must evaluate the effectiveness of the action taken. He must see to it that managers are provided with the feedback that will assure them that what they ordered came to pass. The best-laid plans oft go astray. That is the reason for the modern internal auditor, and here is a case in point.

> In any large manufacturing process, product changes are a way of life, even though they are the bane of the production manager's existence. Every change has its inexorable ripple effect. And every care is, or should be, taken to make sure the ripples do not unduly rock the organization boat.
>
> As a part of the decision to make a product change, there must be an instruction that every engineering revision be communicated to the purchasing organization. Engineering changes often affect the parts or materials in the product. And as a result new parts and materials will have to be purchased in time to meet production schedules.
>
> As a part of a regular audit of the engineering organization, an internal auditor examined a sample of significant engineering changes and traced every ripple the changes caused. He found that the changes had been communicated to Purchasing so that new parts and materials could be procured to help implement the change. But to management's dismay he also found that the orders for the superseded parts and materials had not been canceled, so the company was receiving both the new needed items and the superseded needed items. Needless to say, corrective action was swift in coming.

The internal auditor can be management's safeguard in helping to monitor the results of decisions and make sure desired effects are achieved. And with the broad scope of his review program, he can provide managers with a feedback mechanism that is needed to round out the decision-making process.

CONCLUSION

The steps in decision making are similar to those in problem solving; they call for identifying and defining the problem, defining the expectations or objectives of the decision, developing alternatives and evaluating them, selecting the best possible choice, and then taking action. The key to decision making is the element of futurity; it is too late to make decisions about the past. So uncertainty and risk are always involved in decision making. Quantitative techniques are, however, available to measure the degree of risk.

The internal auditor can help the manager in the decision-making process because of the broad scope of his activities within the organization, his analytical ability, and his understanding of modern evaluative methods. One step of the process is outside the scope of his responsibility: selecting the final choice. That is a management prerogative, and any attempt to usurp would lead to loss of objectivity and independence of the internal auditor.

References

1. J. G. Longenecker, *Principles of Management and Organizational Behavior* (Columbus, Ohio: 1973), p. 134.
2. R. C. Davis, *The Fundamentals of Top Management* (New York: Harper & Brothers, 1951), p. 55.
3. H. A. Simon, *The New Science of Management Decision* (New York: Harper & Row, 1960), p. 1.
4. John Dewey, *How We Think* (New York: Heath, 1910), chap. 8.
5. P. F. Drucker, "How to Make a Business Decision," in W. T. Greenwood, ed., *Decision Theory and Information Systems* (Cincinnati: South-Western Publishing, 1959), pp. 53–62.
6. Henry Albers, *Principles of Management: A Modern Approach* (New York: Wiley, 1974), pp. 244, 245.
7. P. F. Drucker, *Management: Tasks, Responsibilities, Practices* (New York: Harper & Row, 1974), p. 476.
8. Ibid., pp. 466–470.
9. Drucker, "How to Make a Business Decision," pp. 54, 55.
10. W. R. King and D. I. Cleland, "A New Method of Strategic Systems Planning," *Business Horizons,* Vol. 18, No. 4, pp. 55–64.
11. Harold Koontz and Cyril O'Donnell, *Essentials of Management* (New York: McGraw-Hill, 1974), p. 90.
12. Drucker, *Management,* p. 473.
13. Drucker, "How to Make a Business Decision," pp. 59, 60.
14. G. L. S. Shackle, *Uncertainty in Economics* (Cambridge: Cambridge University Press, 1955), p. 34.
15. L. J. Savage, "The Theory of Statistical Decision," *Journal of the American Statistical Association,* Vol. 46, pp. 55–67.
16. Drucker, "How to Make a Business Decision," p. 55.
17. Koontz and O'Donnell, op. cit., pp. 92–94.
18. E. B. Flippo and G. M. Munsinger, *Management* (Boston: Allyn & Bacon, 1975), pp. 544–550.

19. G. R. Terry, *Principles of Management* (Homewood, Ill.: Irwin, 1972), pp. 133–136.
20. H. A. Simon, *Administrative Behavior* (New York: Macmillan, 1957).
21. Drucker, *Management,* p. 477.
22. H. J. Mintern, ed., *How to Save $14,500,000 Through Internal Auditing* (Orlando, Fla: The Institute of Internal Auditors, 1955), p. 247.
23. Ibid., p. 114.
24. Ibid., p. 136.
25. Ibid., p. 134.

6

Communications

The importance of communications. The manager, center of the communications network. Communications defined. A giver, a receiver, a message, and symbols. The recipient communicates. Perception, expectation, and action. Symbols of communication. Forms of communication. Feedback. Follow-up systems. Opportunities for communication. Transferring pictures. Bridging differences. Communicating with clarity, believability, and integrity. Communicating through asking. Communication and the internal auditor. The translator for management. Appraising upward communication. Reviewing management reports. Appraising policies and procedures in terms of validity and compliance. Appraising downward communication. Personnel policies. Internal audit reports. When to report. Elements of a deficiency finding. Elements of a formal report. One-page summary reports.

COMMUNICATION AND THE MANAGER

Importance of Communication

The textbooks generally classify communications as a function of directing, but its importance to the enterprise cries for separate treat-

161

ment. If some omnipotent power were bent on surely destroying an organization, it need but transform the organization into a tower of Babel, confounding "their language that they may not understand one another's speech." Then would the people be scattered and the organization abandoned.

That is more than a flight of fancy. Clarence B. Randall, former president of Inland Steel once said, "The businessman today must be able to write and speak the English language with clarity and felicity, or stand aside and let his chair be occupied by someone who can."[1]

That does not mean that all who communicate well are sure to be good managers. Successful communication is not the cause of good management; it is a result. A competent manager will almost invariably be a good communicator. Indeed, what may be considered a problem in muddled communication may be a matter of muddled management. Barnard said that the first function of the executive is to establish and maintain a system of communication. The executive must act as the center of a communication network and receive and disseminate information needed to keep the enterprise functioning effectively.[2] Without such a network the manager would be incapable of functioning, like a human being without his own network of veins and arteries carrying blood to and from the heart.

Communication is equally important to the manager's subordinates, who exchange ideas, concepts, needs, purposes, and problems through personal communication more effectively than through any other means. In the absence of open communication, common and personal goals become difficult to achieve—because they are not mutually understood. Too, planning often fails because those responsible for or carrying out plans do not have access to information about high-level objectives or policies. As a result the subsidiary plans are either not made or are inexactly implemented. The line of communication from top to bottom must remain unbroken if the members of the enterprise are to understand and work toward common objectives.

If communication is so significant to the proper functioning of an enterprise, why is it a topic which only recently has been feverishly explored? Perhaps because the ancients felt that, since everyone seemed to be engaging in communication, everyone was fully aware of communication's essentiality. But everyone is not aware of its significance, nor does everyone fully appreciate how its presence can lubricate the mechanism of the enterprise and its absence permit the rust of impotence to form.

A dramatic example of the benefits of good communication was reported by Texas Instruments in 1966:[3]

Texas Instruments found that new assemblers were having difficulty in learning their jobs. Three months was considered sufficient to develop an adequate level of competence. Yet the level was rarely being achieved within that span. The root cause was traced to anxiety about the unknown. And that cause brought about high rates of turnover, excessive training time, high levels of tardiness and absence, and unacceptable quality of work.

So Texas Instruments inaugurated an experiment. One group of new employees was given a full day of orientation instead of the usual two hours. The expanded orientation period was specifically directed to reduce anxiety. The new employees were told of the kind of hazing they could expect from the old hands. They were briefed on the idiosyncracies of their future supervisors, and they were urged to take the initiative in communicating with their supervisors. For example, they were told that one supervisor was friendly despite the aura of strictness that he wore; he was a shy man, but he really liked to talk to subordinates who made the first overtures toward him.

At the same time, control groups received the same kind of indoctrination as before, and the difference in orientation methods was not known either by the experimental group or by the control group.

The results were astonishing to management:

Training time was cut in half.
Training costs were cut by two-thirds.
Absenteeism and tardiness were cut in half.
Waste and rejects were cut by four-fifths.
Costs were cut by 15% to 30%.

The lesson learned in communicating with new assemblers was then carried up to new supervisors and managers. They too were anxious about how well they would do in in their new assignments, dealing with experienced subordinates. Texas Instruments devised a plan whereby seasoned operators helped train new supervisors. This had several salutary results. The supervisor learned to rely on subordinates for problem solving. The subordinates were given an interest in the success of the new supervisor. And the supervisors, anxiety reduced, felt sufficiently competent to communicate openly with their managers instead of keeping to themselves problems which they felt guilty about.

In this chapter, we shall seek to define communication, examine its symbols and forms, explore both the problems and opportunities it presents to managers, and discuss the internal auditor's place in the scheme of the communications network.

Communication Defined

Within the definition of "communication" lie both the essence of communication and the reason why communication is difficult to accomplish. It derives from the Latin *communicare*, "to make common, to share, to impart, to transmit."

To achieve communication, there must be a commonality, a complete sharing of ideas, facts, and courses of action. But static commonality will not be enough. For communication to take place there must be an interaction between or among people. It is the interaction that distinguishes communication from other transmissions, and it is interaction that stresses the desired effect of a message: action on the part of the receiver.

In every communication there is always a giver, a message, a receiver, and symbols. The giver wishes to convey what he has in his mind to the mind of the receiver by couching a message in appropriate symbols. The success of the effort to communicate depends on a minimum of distortion during the process of communication.

Until that is understood, there can be no communication. The early sages understood well the elements of communication. Their understanding was encapsulated in the riddle posed by the Zen Buddhists, the Sufis of Islam, and the Rabbis of the Talmud. They asked: "Is there a sound in the forest if a tree crashes down and no one is around to hear it?"

The right answer, of course, is no. The crashing of the tree creates sound waves. But nothing is heard until those waves impinge on the receiving eardrum and are converted into sound. The ancients understood the phenomenon that escapes many of us today: It is the recipient who achieves communication. If he cannot receive, there is no commonality, no sharing, no communication.

Communication differs from information. Information is logic. It is mechanical. It makes no demands. Communication does make demands. Its elements are perception, expectation, and action.[4] Unless the receiver perceives, there is no communication. Perception, roughly, is the awareness that a living, sentient thing has of its environment. That awareness is developed by all of us in different ways. It is molded by heredity, environment, family, friends, teachers, predilections, biases, and prejudices.

What cannot be perceived cannot be shared, and the effort to achieve communication fails. So the person who is sending the message must comprehend the receiver's ability to perceive the message before the message is understood. And when the perception is absent, the sender must first help the receiver perceive before he transmits the message.

People will tend to select from a message that which fits their needs. And they will tend to "recode" the message to fit into their perception. The result is often distortion and no communication at all. Try to communicate the color blue to a person blind from birth. It is impossible. The same impossibility is true of any message that does not fit into the receiver's perception. So the manager who issues an instruction or announces a policy that does not fit into his subordinate's perceptions is merely crashing a tree in an empty forest.

Another indispensable element of communication is expectation. People hear or read what they expect; if it is not what they expect, they do not hear or perceive it. The recipient looks to fulfill his expectation. The unexpected is rarely received at all. It is ignored, or it is misheard. That is why it is so important both for the manager in his instructions and the internal auditor in his reports to set the stage, explain what will be said, and then use terms and concepts that fall within the range of perception of the recipient.

Finally, communication is action, communication is purposeful. Ideas are transmitted to achieve a particular response. Therefore, the communication must be so couched as to facilitate the response. If the communication is to warn against some anticipated peril, the terms and structure must convey urgency, directness, and the inherent dangers. If, however, the purpose of the message is to achieve goodwill, it must be so planned and couched as to promote good feelings.

In communicating, whatever the medium, the question must be, "Is this communication within the recipient's range of perception, is it what he would expect to hear, and will it promote the action desired?"

Symbols

All language is made up of symbols. The spoken words are symbols; the written words are symbols; and so are smoke signals, Morse code, shorthand, bits on magnetic tape, proofreaders' marks, mathematical notation, and lines on a blueprint. So too are a manager's frown, raised eyebrows, or darkening scowl. Semantics, the science of language, is concerned with the study of symbols and their meaning.

Like maps, symbols are labels for the object or the concept; they are not the object or the concept itself. And therein lies the difficulty in communication. When two people observe the same pencil, then the same picture is likely to impinge on two brains. But if one person says "pencil" to another, the picture in the other's brain may be of a wooden pencil with or without eraser, a gold pencil, a silver pencil, a black pencil, or a small brush for fine art work.

As terms become less concrete, the chances that the same symbols will evoke different concepts in different people increase in geometric proportion. The meanings of words are influenced by association. And increasing the opportunity for personal association correspondingly increases the probability that different people will look at the same map and see different terrains.

So the manager is more likely to achieve communication if he uses symbols less capable of being misunderstood: pictures instead of words, concrete words instead of abstract words, examples to reinforce principles, and illustrations to illuminate procedures.

Forms of Communication

Choosing the right form or channel of communication may be as important to the effectiveness of the communication as the information presented. A manager has many channels to choose from. If he picks the right one, he may meet his objective. If he picks the wrong one, he may meet hostility.

For example, a controversial subject should not be sprung for the first time in a formal staff meeting. It would be more politic to obtain informal support from colleagues before the meeting opens. Similarly, hearing about an important change in a major program from the newspapers creates employee resentment. Being told of such changes informally before the public hears about them puts the employees in the know and enhances the feeling of belonging. On the other hand, an announcement of changes in a retirement plan demands a formal communique; the subject is too important to all employees and too readily misunderstood to be communicated without a formal, carefully thought-out presentation.

Every enterprise uses various forms of communication. Here are some of them:

1. *The chain of command.* Messages may be given orally or in writing, and formal messages travel down through the established organizational levels. Oral communication is quicker, but the messages can be thoroughly garbled by the time they reach the ultimate recipient. Some limited studies have been made of communication penetration. Starting with a board of director's meeting—ranked at 100 percent—the penetration of a statement passed by the board and com-

municated from the president to the vice president to the department director to the foreman to the worker had dwindled to 20 percent.

Written chain-of-command communications are as effective as the writer's ability to make himself understood. One executive would ask his two teen-age daughters to read every instruction he wrote before he published it. If they failed to understand what he was driving at, he would rewrite it until they did.

2. *The order.* Among the most important forms of communication to the employee is the order. That is the form managers use most often to get specific jobs done. It is essential to the execution of management tasks, but it is often badly communicated. It should tell what is to be done, who is to do it, and when, where, how, and why.

The successful manager considers all those elements in his orders so that there will be no misunderstanding about what is to be accomplished. He knows that the order should be subjected only to the interpretation he intends to give it.

The order "Test the incoming shipment of bolts 100 percent" may lack a host of elements that could easily lead to confusion. When is the shipment coming in? Who is the supplier? Why 100 percent for this shipment, when bolts are usually sampled in receiving inspection? What priority should be given to the tests? Where will the bolts arrive? How should they be tested—by standard or special tests?

3. *Posters and bulletin boards.* The bulletin boards and posters should not be used as primary devices, because many employees refuse to read them. In one instance internal auditors found that receiving inspectors were being informed of new test requirements by revised instructions posted on a bulletin board. When the auditor queried the inspectors about the new specifications, he found that a considerable percentage were unaware of them.

4. *Company periodicals.* A bright, attractive periodical can do much to convey information about the company. Employees soon learn, however, that generally only self-serving declarations, statements that are consistently beneficial to the company, are permitted in the paper. Specificity and accuracy are therefore desirable. And since people love to see their names and pictures in print, a periodical can play a significant part in the company's social life.

5. *Letters and inserts.* The personal letter addressed to the home gives the employee a feeling of importance. Pay inserts insure exposure at the very least, but the communications are usually read rapidly and with partial attention. They should be written clearly and simply.

6. *Employee handbooks and pamphlets.* During the orientation process and when special programs such as pension and insurance plans are introduced or changed, handbooks and pamphlets are often given to employees. Unfortunately, many remain unread even though the employees sign statements that they understand the contents. If the pamphlets are considered important enough, supervisors may have to hold meetings with their subordinates to discuss them and then test the subordinates' knowledge about the information.

7. *Annual reports.* Annual reports were originally prepared for the owners, but more and more they are being expanded to provide information to employees as well.

8. *Labor unions.* The union can be helpful in combining with management to offer information or persuasion on some significant issue. That can boomerang, however, if the employees got the notion that the management-union relationship is not in their best interests.

9. *The grapevine.* The grapevine is the underground railroad of communication in an organization. It exists wherever people work together; much of what an employee learns within an organization comes from the informal network of communication that springs up in all enterprises. An employee receives his information from the employee at the next desk, from his wife who may have picked it up from another employee's wife, from the coffee break chatter, from social activities, and from daily associations in the company. There is a bit of the town crier in all employees.

The grapevine produces rumor aplenty, but it also carries fact. A study was conducted to trace thirty rumors occurring in six different companies. Sixteen turned out to be just that—unfounded rumors. But nine turned out to be fact; and the remaining five were at least partly fact.[5]

Opinions about the grapevine vary. Some executives regard the grapevine as closely related to poison ivy. Others see it as playing a positive role that should be enlisted. They counsel that management cannot possibly plan every channel of communication in the network. So why not use the informal network? If the canny manager would make use of the grapevine, however, he should recognize the "informal communication" leaders and keep them well informed. Thus he can help the grapevine transmit more accurate information.

The greatest drawback of the grapevine is its capacity to disseminate inaccurate information. The best antidote for the poisoned grape is a dose of truth. When false rumors are rife, managers should hasten to counter fiction with fact. Some companies print both the rumor and the truth, but that may tend to underline the fiction and insure its remembrance. Some organizations use the company newspaper to scotch rumors in a column of letters to the editor. Employees are encouraged to make inquiry on any subject relating to the company that may interest or concern them. Authoritative answers then tend to dispel the unfounded rumors.

10. *The meeting.* Probably the most used channel of communication is the meeting. Indeed, it has been said that the manager who is not attending a meeting is either going to one or is leaving it. Untold man-hours are spent in meetings and untold man-hours are wasted there because the chairmen do not handle the meetings effectively. Yet there are some commonsense rules for chairmen that can improve communication and reduce the length of meetings.

- Use meetings when all else fails. Don't substitute them for deciding simple issues or using the telephone.
- Inform the conferees in advance what will be discussed, what is expected of them, and what material to bring.
- Set a specific starting date and time and estimate the duration of the meeting.
- Tell the conferees about the purpose of the meeting. Is it to inform, to consider a proposal, to arrive at a decision, or to offer advice?
- Develop a meeting agenda and consider the questions that the conferees might raise.
- Make sure each conferee is informed, and have your secretary call him in advance to remind him that his attendance is expected.
- Use visual material to convey complex data, but don't let the "dog and pony show" take the full time of the meeting.
- Don't allow monopolies of conversation, and require each member to express himself. If his comments are not needed, he probably should not have been asked to attend the meeting.
- Don't let the meeting get off track. Stick to the specific issues and get the wanderers back home.
- Sum up significant points. Ask if your summation accurately conveys the thoughts expressed. Make sure all understand what has been said.
- Do not permit telephone calls to be transferred to the meeting room, but allow the quiet delivery of notes in emergent circumstances.
- Present facts before offering or asking for solutions.
- Write up all proceedings of the meeting, including action items,

persons responsible for action, and dates of completion. Distribute copies to the conferees and to their superiors.

Studies have been conducted to determine which forms of communication are most effective. Interestingly enough, the speediest are found to be first the grapevine and second oral communication received from the supervisor and the manager. The least effective are memos, letters, and bulletin boards. It appears, therefore, that face-to-face communication is far superior to other forms if speed is desirable. In accuracy and permanence, however, the written word must take precedence.

Feedback

Good managers leave little to chance. They are fully aware of the ease with which communication breaks down, messages are misunderstood, and orders are ignored. Many a business communication is like a message scrawled on a piece of paper, corked in a bottle, and tossed into the sea. Feedback is the means by which managers learn whether their communications have been effective. Feedback returns to the sender the signal "Message received and understood" if the message has been clear and the recipient is on the proper wavelength.

In face-to-face conversation feedback may be a light of comprehension, a puzzled look, or a blank stare. The perceptive manager can tell whether he is getting through or whether he needs to say things another way, amplify his statements, illustrate them, or ask whether they are fully comprehended. The face-to-face discussion has a better chance of achieving understanding if the sender is watching for the signs of feedback.

Written messages require feedback built into them or into the communication system. There is no assurance that a query will be answered or that a request will be carried out as expected. It is rare indeed that the desired action will be prompt and satisfactory. The manager should as a matter of course have a follow-up system for all his written communications. When a written message asks for some action, a copy should be placed in a tickler file and marked with a follow-up date. On the appointed date the recipient should be called or written to again, with a request for information on the status of the inquiry or request. The individual who receives and acts on each message as requested is unique. The manager's feedback loop must take that into account.

Achieving Communication

The Difficulties

Successful communication, like a successful marriage, requires an earnest willingness to share. From the sender's standpoint there must be an aggressive willingness that plows through obstacles until the goal of understanding is achieved. Successful communication also requires a willingness to understand, fully understand, the process of communication. Without that understanding, there is merely a clashing of symbols that emit noise without achieving comprehension. Let us therefore summarize some of the concepts that may help the manager cope with his problems in communication.

The pivotal term in communication is "perception." When that term is fully comprehended, the difficulty of achieving successful communication is finally realized. Perception means seeing the same picture in the same way—sharply focused and undistorted. No two mental cameras are the same. No two learning experiences are the same. No two sets of biases, predilections, prejudices, families, and friends are the same. Yet each set affects perception, how the individual perceives both what he is told and how he is told it.

Seen in that light, true communication, the transfer of an identical picture from one mind to another, along with the words and accompanying music, is an utter impossibility. At best the picture will be an approximation, but how can even the approximation be gained? The answer lies in determining how the recipient perceives the message and adjusting the focus as necessary. So reasonable communication is achieved less by sending messages than by receiving them, less by speaking than by listening, providing for feedback, and by earnestly trying to find out just what picture was thrown on the recipient's mental screen by the message.

A friend of ours, president of a small business, was stimulated to try an experiment after we had expounded on the hazards of achieving communication. It was his practice to provide new hires with an orientation course about the company and its processes. After our conversations about communication, he had his new hires for technical and administrative positions carry a small notebook with them and record their impressions each day for a period of time. And each day he read the record they had made.

The results were eye-opening. The perceptions often varied widely from those he thought the new hires had. He was gaining an insight—and sometimes a humbling one—into his ability to communicate. But he was beginning to achieve reasonable communication, because he was making the effort, because he was earnestly trying to share, because he was not only sending messages but listening as well, and because he was not only giving instructions but obtaining feedback on how effectively he was instructing.

Misunderstandings are bound to occur in the communication process. They can be the result of many differences: in vocabularies, in the meanings associated with certain words, and in the status of the people sending and receiving the messages. All of them place impediments in the path of communication. Direct conversation is therefore the best way of removing the blocks; it not only permits speaking and listening, statements and questions, and recapitulations and restatements but also permits the use of nonverbal symbols that heighten understanding and signal comprehension. Often it is the light in the listener's eye, and not the spoken word, that reflects the extent of comprehension.

Written Communication

Yet the written word, with its permanence, preciseness, and the opportunity it provides for analysis, is essential to the communication process in large organizations. But the writer of messages must take the hazards into account. One of those hazards is failing to recognize that communication is also expectation. As we have pointed out, one hears what one wants to hear or expects to hear. So written communication must always set the stage, focus the expectation, and tell the reader what he should expect to see. And that is only part of the story.

Written communications must have clarity, believability, and integrity. The writing must be as clear and simple as it is possible to make it. Simple words. Concrete words. Words that bring pictures to the mind—the sharp, clear pictures that the sender wants to flash on the receiver's mental screen.

A message could merely say, "This project exceeded budget by $10 million." But how much more graphic is the picture if the message were to say: "The budget was exceeded by $10 million, which is equal to a man working 40 hours a week, 50 weeks a year, at $5 an hour for 1,000 years."

The message must have believability. It must carry the aura of accuracy and propriety. Getting the message is difficult enough; its transmission should not be garbled by doubts as to its authenticity. Verifiable specificity commands believability.

The message must support the integrity of the organization.

Among other things, that calls for the executives to buttress the positions of their subordinate managers. And unless emergent circumstances demand simultaneous messages to all in the organization—like a bomb threat in a building—the messages from on high should not bypass those in intermediate positions who have a need to know.

Perceptions

The great leap in understanding comes from the superior's comprehension of the subordinate's perceptions: his values, beliefs, hopes, and goals. That comprehension comes only when the superior tries to get into the skin, the heart, and the head of the subordinate. And he can do so only by receiving messages, not sending them.

Superiors should ask their subordinates to record carefully and thoughtfully how they see themselves in the organization's scheme of things, how they perceive the superior's position, how they can contribute to organizational goals and objectives, what standards they should seek to meet, how they can measure themselves to see if they have met those standards, how they should be expected to perform, and what they should be held accountable for.

Such communications seldom fail to surprise the superior, whose perception is rarely the same as his subordinate's. But they do show where bridges need building. They show where the downward messages got garbled in the transmission and how badly the subordinate misconceived the superior's job, its complexitites, and its constraints. The superior and the subordinate may not see eye to eye. But the veils may start to lift and there may be at least an approximation of communication.

Clearly, the subordinate's proposals may need to be overriden. At least, however, the subordinate knows he's had his day in court and the superior is aware that the decision he is making is overriding the subordinate's beliefs.

There is no reasonable communication when the message goes from boss to worker; communication is achieved only when it goes from one of us to another of us.

COMMUNICATION AND THE INTERNAL AUDITOR

How the Internal Auditor Can Help

Communication is the internal auditor's food and drink. Without it he cannot do his job properly, and he cannot adequately convey the results to those who need to know. He must be able to communicate both to obtain information and to pass the information on.

The checker of numbers, sitting alone and incommunicado in a corner, is an anachronism. He does not play the role management expects of the modern internal auditor. The role he does play gives little emphasis to listening, speaking, and writing—primary tools for the comprehensive internal auditing job. He must be a first-class communicator to learn from others what the conditions are and then to explain to others how the conditions deviate from standards, how they may be improved, and how they may be corrected.

Sometimes the conditions are complex, esoteric, and technical, and they may be enshrouded in arcane language known only to a select few. So the internal auditor must be a translator for management. As he rides the circuit in his organization, he sojourns for a while in strange lands with strange languages. He must learn those languages so as to be able to speak them fluently.

He must be conversant with the following:

Remainders and reversionary interests in the legal department.
Drawback, demurrage, and switching costs in the traffic department.
Packing sheets and receiving memos in the receiving department.
Work-in-process and process costs in the accounting department.
Contaminated metals in the scrap department.
First-article inspections in the quality control department.
Traveling requisitions and acknowledgments in the purchasing department.
Attachments and garnishees in the personnel department.
OSHA in the safety department.
Interperiod tax allocations in the tax department.
Euro-dollar issues in the treasury department.
Area quotes in the contracts department.
Budget realizations in the production department.
Design change control in the engineering department.
Tear sheets in the advertising department.
Program loops and accumulator registers in the data processing department.

All of these—plus an anthology of other terms—are compounded by a proliferation of form and procedure numbers, abbreviations, acronyms, and nicknames.

The internal auditor must therefore be able both to appraise management's systems of communication and to communicate his findings clearly and understandably to management. The remainder of this chapter will be devoted first to the internal auditor's appraisal of the information system within the enterprise and second to his reports, which inform managers of the conditions that are not brought to light by the information systems.

Appraising Operating Reports

Managers in large companies function and make decisions largely on the basis of information received from operating levels. The decisions are generally no better than the information on which they are based, and that information, flowing to the decision maker, may leave its recipient either parched or inundated.

Clear, current, accurate, meaningful reports are desperately needed, but the perfect report is a rarity. The executive, poring over the data he needs to help him plan, direct, and control the activities of his organization, is generally at the mercy of the report writers. And often the reports can be more like self-serving declarations than full statements of existing conditions.

The professional internal auditor, analytical, objective, and unbiased, is the chief defense of the report recipient. When the auditor has done his job, the executive can breathe more freely for knowing that the data on which he may be staking his managerial reputation are reliable. Every internal auditing organization should have a complete and constantly updated listing of "management" reports—the reports prepared in the operating departments and destined for the organization's top executives.

The list should be referenced to regular audits scheduled in the long-range audit program. To make sure that there are no slip-ups in the review process, each "permanent file," the repository of all information relevant to repetitive audits, should contain instructions to review appropriate management reports. To further insure against slips, each internal auditor embarking on an audit assignment should fill out a reminder list that provides for the steps to be taken in any audit, and in that reminder list should be an instruction to determine which management reports are relevant to that audit and to review them. But the loop is not closed until the audit supervisor makes it a practice to review the reminder lists for compliance.

The management reports, because of their significance in successful decision making, are among the known "risk areas" in an organization. An auditor cannot be held responsible for a risk area that a prudent practitioner has no reasonable way of identifying. But management reports come within the purview of the internal auditor's responsibility, and the auditor owes a duty to management to review them regularly.

An individual internal auditor, on beginning an audit of operations, should determine which reports are issued and received within the organizations whose activities he is reviewing. They may not be the kinds of reports submitted to the organization's top echelons, but they may be of significance to operating managers. And the internal auditor can provide the operating managers a service by reviewing the reports.

The extent of the internal auditor's review of reports will depend on the nature of the reports themselves, but generally the auditor will be concerned with elements of accuracy, timeliness, and meaningfulness. Let any one of those elements be missing and the report may be a waste of time, effort, and money because it will be valueless to the recipient.

An audit of a report that is expensive or significant enough to warrant a thorough review might go something like this:

1. Determine the purpose of the report and learn the names of the report's recipients and scheduled due dates, the source of the data on which the report is based, the process used in preparing and reviewing the report, and the cost, in man-hours, of preparation.
2. Test the report for accuracy by comparing it with source data and recomputing its calculations.
3. Test it for timeliness by comparing due dates with release dates for a reasonable period.
4. Test it for meaningfulness by:
   (a) Evaluating the format to determine whether it summarizes and provides the information needed to carry out the report's purpose.
   (b) Questioning recipients as to the usefulness and derivable benefits of the report.
   (c) Determining the regularity with which report preparers question report recipients as to a continuing need for the report. In one case the head of an accounting department queried executives about their need for a 37-copy report. All of them said they needed it. But the chief accountant had his doubts, and the next month he withheld all the copies. He never received a request for the report, so he stopped preparing it altogether.

Appraising Policies and Procedures

Superiors promulgate policies and procedures that subordinates may follow, circumvent, or pay lip service to. Whether those policies and procedures are successful therefore depends largely on how well they are understood and accepted by subordinates and how relevant they are to real-life situations. Hence, superiors should have a healthy interest in how well their policies and procedures are faring at the working level.

Without professional help, obtaining that information may be a catch-as-catch-can affair. Part of every internal audit program is devoted to appraising adherence to existing policies, procedures, and other instructions. And the internal auditor is usually concerned with more than mere compliance; he will evaluate the relevance and propriety of executive instructions under changing conditions.

The internal audit program can take many forms. The simplest is testing transactions by comparing them with the standards set up in operating instructions. For example, in an audit of purchase orders, the internal auditor might test compliance with rules such as these:

- All orders valued at over $1,000 require at least three written bids.
- Lists of potential bidders must be reviewed by the buyer's supervisor.
- Orders valued at less than $100 require no signatures other than the buyer's, but orders of greater amounts must be approved at designated levels, depending on the amounts involved.

Those are but a few rules among very many that apply to the purchasing function. The internal auditor's test of a sample of purchase orders is designed to appraise compliance with the rules. But the auditor would also ask questions such as these:

Is the $1,000 level for written bids reasonable? Should it not be $500 or $5,000? The volume of orders and the existence or absence of other checks might make the $1,000 rule no longer practicable.

Is the review of bidder lists for each purchase reasonable? Do the reviews of all lists result in inundating supervisors so that the lists get no more than perfunctory approval? Would it be better to have a general list of all approved bidders that the buyers must use and ask for supervisor approval only in exceptional cases?

A level of $100 for orders issued solely over buyers' signatures may seem reasonable on its face because of the small amounts involved. But it has been found that repetitive orders under $100 can represent large total amounts, and they can be the dark little corners in which favoritism may lurk. Hence the question whether the supervisors regularly select random samples of such orders for review and evaluation. The uninspected inevitably deteriorates.

Inspectors of products must work under a host of rules and regulations, standards, and specifications and they must have an intimate understanding of those rules, regulations, and so on to do their work accurately and with dispatch. One internal auditor selected a sample of important rules that such inspectors must follow and quizzed the inspectors on how well they understood their instructions. The results discomfited the inspection manager but brought about improved training programs.

Appraising Downward Communication

As we pointed out earlier, superiors often have difficulty in communicating successfully with subordinates. The communication gets distorted, filtered, and diffused by the time it reaches the ultimate recipient. The internal auditor can put his finger on the pulse of downward communication and inform managers how well the communications are reaching the people for whom they were intended.

Hired consultants are often employed to listen to employees, but the internal auditor is eminently suited to carry out the same function. Here is an example of the usefulness of the technique:[6]

> Because of economic conditions, management of a company had been forced to hire new employees at rates which were higher than those paid older employees. And on occasion, to avoid short-term layoffs, some employees were transferred to other jobs. Management had thought that it had ably communicated the reasons for its actions to its employees and had even expected applause for its efforts in preventing the short-term layoffs.
>
> But production dropped. And puzzled management could not tell why. A consultant was hired to find out. He questioned 600 employees over a 6-month period. The results of the questions showed that there were strong feelings on the part of many employees that work standards were too high, that older employees resented the higher wage scales of the new, and that the temporary transfers to avoid layoffs were resented, much less applauded.
>
> As a result, management undertook a broad communication and action program:

□ Methods men were set to roaming around the factory floor to be available to employees on questions about standards.

□ Vacations were lengthened for older employees to compensate for the higher wage scales necessary to recruit new employees in a tight labor market.

□ Service clubs were established for older employees. A new plant organ was developed to improve the social life in the plant and instill a pride in company products.

□ A rotation system was installed in conjunction with the temporary transfers, and management carefully explained the alternative, which would have meant layoffs.

Obviously the sensitive, tuned-in manager might have arrived at the same solution. But the sad fact is that he often just does not have the time, and perhaps the skills, to carry out such an appraisal program. Therefore he needs the skilled internal auditor, his problem-solving partner. And the professional internal auditor needs a thorough grounding in the behavioral sciences to conduct such an appraisal.

Personnel policies are often the bone in employees' throats. And generally it is not so much the policy itself as the way employees perceive it that causes resentment. Personnel policy audits have been undertaken to assess that perception. The policies are listed and employees are interviewed to obtain their views on the policies. The data gathered are arrayed and summarized, and the internal auditor may consult with behavioral scientists in the personnel department to interpret the information gathered and recommend action to solve any problems identified by the audit.[7]

Audit Reports

Of all the skills the professional internal auditor needs, communication must surely top the list. The most brilliantly developed findings, the most innovative, cost-saving recommendations may lie moldering in the internal auditor's working papers unless the auditor can communicate them successfully to the person able to act on them. Ability to communicate effectively takes training and effort; it requires ingenuity and innovativeness; and it calls for an understanding of what managers want and need and how managers think. It also calls for the realization that managers at different levels have different needs, different understandings of conditions, and differing spans of time they can spend on reading audit reports, to say nothing of different perceptions, expectations, and responsibilities for action.

All those things the professional internal auditor must take into account in communicating his findings and getting his recommendations accepted. And he must use the most appropriate forms of reporting to obtain attention and achieve correction. His reporting process should not be reserved exclusively for the formal, final report that concludes the audit assignment. Communication for the auditor should be an always thing.

At the very outset of his assignment the internal auditor should report orally to the operating manager on how he proposes to carry out his audit project: what he plans to cover and what he plans not to cover. Through that communication he can avoid such astonished questions from the manager at the end of the project as: "You mean to tell me you fellows never looked at our XYZ unit . . . training program . . . indirect expenses . . . procurement policies . . . reporting system . . . etc., etc.?"

The communication process is carried out when the internal auditor detects a condition that needs prompt correction; and reporting unsatisfactory conditions calls for special techniques and qualities. Certainly, the internal auditor should not become enmeshed in minutiae. Minor defects not warranting management attention should be discussed with operating personnel, corrected on the spot, and reported only in the internal audit working papers. They should not be used to take up the time of the busy manager.

But significant findings usually demand prompt action to correct the unsatisfactory conditions that were found, and the urgency of the situation can be conveyed to the manager if the auditor performs a professional job. The techniques of developing findings and the elements of a properly presented finding are as follows:

1. *Statement of condition.* This statement should describe the condition and its scope. It should, for example, indicate the population involved: the total value of purchase orders, the total number of people on the payroll, the total number of safety boxes, the total number and value of cars and trucks, the total number and severity of accidents, and the total volume of blueprints. The information puts the finding in perspective and indicates its importance in the company's scheme of things. The statement should show exactly what happened, objectively and fairly, with verifiable specificity.

2. *Standards.* The internal auditor should show not only what happened but what should have happened. He must show the standards or criteria for the particular operation and the path that should have been followed. He must always be ready to tell the operating manager: "'This is the way it should have happened according to the rules and regulations, and this is the way it did happen.'" An understanding and agreement between the internal auditor and the man-

ager on the standards the internal auditor used in measuring the effectiveness of an operation is pivotal to an agreement that things are not what they should be.

3. *Effect.* Every manager confronted with a reported condition calling for action has the right to ask: "So what?" And every auditor reporting an unsatisfactory condition should be prepared to answer that question in terms of dollars or man-days lost or potential hazards that should be avoided. The effect of the condition should be presented in such a way that the manager becomes convinced that he may not achieve some of his own objectives if the condition is not corrected.

4. *Cause.* Rare indeed is the manager who does not pose to the internal auditor a question like "How in the world did this happen?" The auditor should be prepared to show the cause or causes for the condition. Besides, the purpose of determining cause goes beyond satisfying someone's curiosity; for no problem is truly or permanently solved until the cause is isolated and identified—the cause that, if not corrected, will surely permit the condition to recur.

5. *Recommendation.* The problem presented to management calls for a decision. As we discussed in Chapter 5, each decision is a choice from among alternatives, and the internal auditor can help managers by offering feasible alternatives. Thus the internal auditor has a duty to offer a recommendation for management's consideration. The recommendation should be feasible, economical, and workable. Perhaps it will not be followed, but that does not matter. Management must make the operating decisions. The internal auditor is not responsible for having his recommendations put into effect; he is responsible for seeing that the conditions get corrected. If the manager takes a different path, he has that prerogative. The internal auditor's responsibility lies in keeping the finding open until the condition is corrected, no matter how the manager decides to correct it.

Interim reports of a condition—presented during the course of the examination—can be made orally or in writing. The complexity of the condition will generally dictate the medium. What is significant is for the matter to be reported promptly so the defect can be corrected without unnecessary delay.

The final, formal report should be testimony to the internal auditor's communication abilities. It must demonstrate his understanding of: "Who are my readers and what do they need or want to know?" If he has demonstrated his ability to communicate, the internal auditor will have a wide following of interested readers from managers at the operating levels to executives who guide the destiny of the entire organization.

The operating manager and his superior generally want to know what the auditor covered and what he did not cover, what he found to be satisfactory and what he found to be unsatisfactory, and what they can do to correct unsatisfactory conditions. And generally they want the information in sufficient detail that they have a comprehensive picture of what the internal auditor found. For that reason, the formal audit report generally contains the following elements:

1. *Introduction.* This section of the report should, obviously, come first. It sets the stage. It defines the area, activity, function, or organization that was reviewed. Familiar activities—receiving, purchasing, accounts receivable, for example—need little introduction, but volume statistics about the number of employees, transactions, and dollar amounts help put the operation in perspective. Less familiar activities—research and development and tool liaison, for example— may require some explanation to improve the reader's perception.

2. *Purpose.* This sets out specifically what areas or activities the internal auditor planned to cover. It develops the reader's expectations of what he can hope to see discussed in the remainder of the report. In effect, it is a map of where the reader will be led.

3. *Scope.* This section is particularly helpful in defining the limitations on the internal auditor's detailed examination: He covered purchases in the last three months only; he looked at invoices in excess of $500 only; he examined tool cribs in plants A and B, but not in plant C; he reviewed payrolls for hourly but not salaried employees; he reviewed the control systems but made no tests of transactions. The section should also show, of course, the reasons for any limitations on the audit coverage.

4. *Opinion.* Some audit organizations report exceptions only. Their reasoning is that top managers operate on the management-by-exception principle. We think that is wrong. It portrays the internal auditor as a predator instead of an objective evaluator. And it denies management the benefit of the internal auditor's overall appraisal of the activity audited.

The *external* auditor's formal report is not a mere catalog of defects. It expresses a responsible opinion on a company's financial position. Why then, should not the internal auditor express a responsible opinion on the operations he has reviewed?

If the opinion is satisfactory, executive management need not read further. If it is satisfactory, with certain exceptions, or unsatisfactory, the executive may wish to dig more deeply into the exceptions and assure himself that appropriate corrective action is being taken.

Expressing an overall opinion provides a service that may assure managers of satisfactory operations, alert them to problem areas that have been detected, or sound a call to action when emergent circumstances warrant high-level attention.

5. *Findings.* The findings support the opinion. They may be satisfactory and provide information on the steps the internal auditor took to assure himself that conditions were free of defects. On the other hand, they may be unsatisfactory and be accompanied by explanations of the conditions found, the standards or criteria from which the actions taken deviated, the causes, the effects, and the recommendations for improvements. Also, each statement of finding should include the reaction of the operating manager to the finding and the action the manager proposes to take.

The elements just described make up a comprehensive audit report. Such a report may be long and detailed to provide operating managers with the information they need. In a large company, in which hundreds of audit reports may be issued in a year, it would be a physical impossibility for executive managers to read each report in detail. Yet the audit reports describe the company's administrative health and are important sources of information for executives on company operations.

The internal auditor should therefore provide executive management with a summary statement that offers a quick overview of the auditor's opinions and findings. Many auditing organizations give that information in a one-page summary that becomes the first page of the internal audit report. The summary can be constructed to offer opinions about and brief explanations of the results of internal audits. One approach is to provide opinions on the three elements generally constituting the scope of the auditor's work: compliance, efficiency, and effectiveness. They may be defined as follows:

□ *Compliance.* How well the auditee complied with laws, regulations, policies, procedures, instructions, and other standards of performance and whether those standards of performance are still valid.
□ *Efficiency.* How promptly and economically the auditee carried out his assigned tasks.
□ *Effectiveness.* Whether desired results were being achieved, whether assigned missions were accomplished, and whether the work done was consonant with the entity's overall objectives and plans.

To provide opinions on those qualities, the internal auditor would have to be aware of the organization's objectives, determine whether appropriate plans, policies, procedures, and systems had been devised to meet those objectives, determine whether people met acceptable standards of cost, quality, and schedule, and whether people were complying with acceptable practices and procedures.

A one-page summary for an audit report covering marketing activities is shown in Figure 1. The summary provides opinions on the five marketing activities covered in the audit. Opinions are given, by adjective ratings, under the three elements of compliance, efficiency, and effectiveness. The rating of B, C, D, or F is followed by the number of the deficiency finding, identified under the heading Deficiency Finding, that caused the rating to be assigned. The meanings of the ratings appear in the legend at the bottom of the summary page.

A minor deficiency is one that requires correction and warrants reporting to management but cannot be said to prevent the activity from meeting a major objective. A major deficiency implies failure to meet one or more of an activity's major objectives. A complete breakdown of an activity's functions would merit a rating of F.

The deficiency findings cited briefly are referenced to the page numbers in the body of the report, where the conditions are discussed in more detail. Management is also interested in the status of the corrective action taken to cure the defects reported, and that information also is provided in the summary.

The comments, near the bottom of the summary, are extremely important. They place the audit findings in perspective. A catalog of errors, unrelieved by positive comment when warranted, can give a completely erroneous impression to executive management and can result in misguided punitive action.

In the illustration, the comments indicate that the chief difficulty —one often found in technical organizations—was administration. When the man in charge is concerned more with technical activities than with his people and his systems of control, the kinds of findings cited are almost inevitable.

Summary statements such as the one in Figure 1 can provide valuable insights for the executive without demanding too much time. With such an overview, executive managers may become as interested in reports on the organization's administrative health as they now are in the reports of its financial health.

CONCLUSION

The manager who cannot learn to communicate had better move over and make room for one who can. Each manager must be the center of a communication network passing messages upward and downward. Through communication he creates understanding and

Figure 1. Internal audit report on a marketing division.

Activity Reviewed	Compliance	Efficiency	Effectiveness
Marketing research	A	C (1)	C (2)
Advertising	B (3)	A	A
Sales promotion	A	D (4)(5)	A
Credit	A	A	A
Customer service	A	A	C (6)

Deficiency Findings

(1) Marketing research was performed exclusively through field polls and questionnaires at a cost of $57,000 when substantially the same information was available from the U.S. Census Bureau and trade reference guides (page 3).

(2) The data that cost marketing research $350,000 to gain through market-testing product Q were already available in trade publications (page 3).

(3) The advertising department, instead of the purchasing department, dealt directly with suppliers in a number of instances in violation of company policy 123 (page 4).

(4) Orders for sales promotion material were not issued on time, and as a result excessive overtime and transportation costs were incurred (page 6).

(5) Costs were not being monitored, and hence the sales promotion manager was not informed that the sales promotion program overran budgets by $63,000 (38 percent) (page 8).

(6) Instructions to customers on the use of company products were written in technical terms not readily understandable to the layman (page 9).

Corrective Action

Corrective action was completed on findings 1 and 2 through revised procedures. Findings 3 and 4 were corrected through improved instructions to employees and closer supervisory review. Corrective action was initiated but not yet completed on findings 5 and 6; written reply is requested.

Comments

Despite the six deficiencies we observed, we believe that people in the marketing division are highly motivated and technically proficient. The advertising and sales promotion products are of excellent quality and have received commendations of merit in trade publications. Prompt action was taken and is continuing to correct the conditions we found; and while we consider some of the conditions to be serious deviations from good practice or policy, we believe that they are not material when considered in terms of the marketing organization's overall mission. The marketing director has assured us that he plans to devote increased attention to administrative matters in the future.

Legend

A—No deficiencies   C—Relatively major deficiency
B—Relatively minor deficiency   D—More than one major deficiency
     F—Failure to accomplish major missions of the activity

promotes action. Precise downward communication—the flashing of the same picture on two or more minds—is a virtual impossibility because no two people have the same perception of things, the same backgrounds, the same qualities, and the same feelings. An approximation of communication can be achieved if managers can comprehend the channels of communication, the symbols of communication, and the barriers to communication and if they try aggressively to reach their employees.

Internal auditors can play a significant role in the communication system by evaluating and appraising the channels of communication, by determining whether management's communication of policies of procedures are being complied with, and by assessing whether instructions communicated are still valid. Internal auditors must be adept at communication to be able to report their findings clearly and compellingly to the various levels of management within the organization.

References

1. C. B. Randall, *The Randall Lectures* (White Plains, N.Y.: The Fund for Adult Education, 1937), p. 11.
2. C. I. Barnard, *The Functions of the Executive* (Cambridge, Mass.: Harvard University Press, 1938), p. 226.
3. E. R. Gomersall and M. Scott Myers, "Breakthrough in On-the-Job Training," *Harvard Business Review*, Vol. 44, No. 4, pp. 62–72.
4. P. F. Drucker, *Management: Tasks, Responsibilities, Practices* (New York: Harper & Row, 1974), p. 483.
5. Robert Hershey, "The Grapevine—Here to Stay but Not Beyond Control," *Personnel*, Vol. 43, No. 1, pp. 62–66.
6. A. A. Imberman, "To Avoid a Strike," *Personnel Journal*, Vol. 48, No. 11, pp. 890–894.
7. Michael White, "Participation by Preference," *Personnel Management*, Vol. 7, No. 5, p. 25.

7

Measurement
and Evaluation

Measurement must relate to performance. Evaluating people: the weakest link. Management inventories and data banks. The beneficial side effects of proper evaluations. Trait-based measurements, quantitative measurements, and the amalgam of the two. Plans and programs. Indexes and input-output ratios. Standards, the yardstick for measurement. Structured and nonstructured work. The purpose of appraisals: to improve. Financial measures: profit as a percent of sales, return on investment, residual income, earnings per share, cash flow per share. Standards and internal auditors. Objectives, goals, and long-range audit programs. Internal audit appraisals of the administrative health of the organization. Measuring operations by identifying objectives and the related controls. The internal audit standards of effectiveness, compliance, efficiency, and economy. Appraising management inventories. Assisting managers in financial measurements.

MEASUREMENT AND MANAGERS

Performance

The ultimate test of a manager's ability is performance. That and that alone is relevant to the organization's aims and needs. The manager may be endowed with sterling qualities that dazzle the eye: ambition, charisma, dedication, drive, forcefulness, and initiative. But all those qualities are merely surface glitter unless they are wrapped around a central core of demonstrated performance.

A manager is truly measured, then, by how well he performs. And his effectiveness as a manager emerges only as a direct result of the performance of the people who look to him to lead them. "Wherefore, by their fruits ye shall know them." The green-leafed tree with its abundant blossoms makes beautiful promises, but the edible fruit is the proof of performance.

Productive managers are the organization's most valuable resource. It must be weighed as carefully as such other resources as money, inventions, and marketable products, yet it is often measured less thoughtfully than the cost of stationery.

Management Inventories

Weighing and measuring remains the weakest link in the organizational chain. Although the valuation of product inventories has become almost an exact science, the evaluation of management inventories and potentials is still pretty much a groping in the dark. Many executives evaluate their management inventory as of the present or for the short range: Is this worker capable of managing? Should this manager of the general accounting department be promoted to controller? We've just lost one of our branch managers; who should replace him?

How much more comfortable and secure is the executive who has a properly evaluated management inventory that names candidates and lists their strengths and potentials. It is useful for each segment of the organization to have a chart of the key people in that segment. After each name might be two facts (age and number of years in the position) and an assessment. (Ready for promotion. Promotable within one to three years. Has the potential for promotion. Does satisfactory work but is not promotable.)

Some companies maintain data banks of skills that include education, current and previous experience, and performance ratings. Obviously, such an inventory needs periodic updating and objective valuations.

Thoughtful attention to the management inventory has some valuable side effects. It forces an organization's executives to think through its objectives and reevaluate them as circumstances present new opportunities or obstacles. It requires executive management to ask itself: "What are the specific responsibilities of our managers and workers and how important are they in meeting organizational goals?" "What tasks should be undertaken, and how shall people be held accountable for their completion?" "How can we help people help themselves and thereby build a better management inventory?"

The failure to answer the last question is the reason for many appraisal breakdowns, the reason why appraisals of and by managers remain a chronic weakness. Evaluations should not be the province of the superior alone. The subordinate manager and the worker should be provided with the information that will help them appraise themselves. A person usually takes affirmative action on what he himself perceives and not on what he tries to see through someone else's eyes.

Trait-based and Quantitative Measurements

Executives and managers have long recognized the need to appraise their people. Varied means of appraisal were developed, but they often did more harm than good. They were based on traits rather than performance. They asked superiors to evaluate such qualities as judgment, dependability, attention to detail, qualities of leadership, and getting along with people.

True, such qualities are highly desirable, but their appraisal is highly subjective. They are colored by the appraiser's biases and predilections. They require the appraiser to play God without anything resembling superhuman insights. Indeed, the appraisals may be untrue or, if they are true, they may be unconvincing to the person being appraised. They lack objectivity. They lack predictability. And when they directly affect the appraised person's economic interests—salary increases or management compensation plans—they can lead to dissatisfaction and bitterness.

Fair-minded executives, feeling that trait appraisals require them to toy with people's souls, tend to lean over backward by giving high trait ratings. In support of that thesis, a rating of Navy officers showed that some 98.5 percent were outstanding or excellent and only about 1 percent were average.[1] Trait-based measurements have therefore generally fallen into disrepute.

Many executives then replaced trait appraisals with evaluations "by the numbers." Certain mathematical goals are set for the manager and the worker, and accounting reports then determine whether the goals have been met. The method is obviously more objective. After all, a number is a number is a number, and it can readily be compared with another number. But there is more to people and jobs than numbers. And when managers have the numerical crutch to lean on, they may let the numbers do their deciding for them. Then only blacks and whites predominate. The person either reached the quantitative goal or didn't. Inequities, inconsistencies, and external forces are disregarded. The appraisal becomes a robot performance.

Enlightened management, however, has arrived at an amalgam in evaluating managers—and more particularly potential managers— that combines both objective appraisals of performance and judgments on the qualities of management. The managerial qualities cannot be overlooked. There is a temperament that resides in the true manager that is lacking in the technician. The superb technician can easily meet and exceed personal performance goals that are set for the average worker, but as a manager he must meet those goals through his people. The managerial temperament provides the aura of confidence that people feel and that makes them feel comfortable under their superiors. It is comparable to the judicial temperament that some able attorneys have and others have not: the ability to sift evidence quickly and surely, the ability to judge people, the ability to ask the right questions, the ability to make a quick decision—one that is usually correct—and then cleave to it.

Measurements for Managers

What, then, is a reasonable measurement for managers and for potential managers? Fundamentally, measurement is the acertainment of the quantity or capacity of some well-defined entity. The entity must be identified. Its characteristics must be established. The units of measurement must be determined. Finally, a count must be made of how many times the unit is contained in the entity.

It sounds simple, but when the entity is a manager, a human being, his inherent capacities cannot be measured by such yardsticks. Yet his *productivity* can be measured. Measuring characteristics in terms of production can be translated into determining how the individual manager did what was expected of him. And that expectation can be translated into objectives, goals, policies, programs, indexes, and standards.

"Objective" stems from the Latin and is literally a thing thrown before the mind—some purpose to be gained. It is often general in character, and it is usually expressed in broad and qualitative terms extending over long periods. As an example, suppose we plan to increase our penetration into the world market of Texas-size belt buckles.

"Goal" stems from the French *gaule*—a "stick" or "pole." It has a tangible, quantifiable connotation and governs a shorter, well-defined term: We plan to market 200,000 buckles in the coming fiscal year.

Plans and programs are the elements of work scheduled to achieve established goals: We will produce belt buckels in lots of 1,000, using existing equipment. We will inspect them on a nondestructive basis. We will mount an advertising program in both developed and developing countries in selected media.

Indexes and input-output ratios are measures that are useful to managers in weighing performance. An input may be the number of sales calls; the related output the number of sales; and the input-output index the sales per sale call. Similarly, an input may be the number of employees on the workforce; the output may be the number of employees leaving the organization; and the input-output index may be the employee turnover rate. In our present example, the ratio might be the number of belt buckles handled each hour by each worker producing the buckles.

Standards are the desired goals or measures—the ratios that the workers and the manager should equal or exceed. A worker should be able to produce 20 acceptable buckles an hour. The belt buckle production manager's workers should be able to produce 4,000 acceptable belt buckles a week.

Each organization and each unit within the organization must develop its own objectives, goals, plans, programs, indexes, and standards. And only to the extent that they are clearly understood, acceptable, and attainable will they be met by worker and manager alike.

Standards

The keystone in the structure of measurement is the standard—the statement of results expected of an operation, the yardstick by which performance will be measured. Few factors are as important in weighing performance. For how are the worker, the manager, and the executive to know whether they have done a good job if they do not know what a good job is?

If standards are appropriately set, appraisals of performance become easier to make and are more readily accepted by the evaluator and the one evaluated. The unfairnesses of trait-based measurements are avoided. The capricious, subjective, often biased likes and dislikes are replaced by thoughtful judgments guided by reasonable standards.

Some standards are relatively easy to construct. In repetitive activities, for example, time-and-motion studies supply measurable standards on clearly calibrated yardsticks. But if an item is custom-made or requires a high degree of judgment to produce, effectiveness of performance is more difficult to measure. Managers may shy away from developing standards that cannot be readily quantified. There is little choice, however. If performance is to be objectively measured, then acceptable, reasonable, and usable standards must be set.

Tasks should be divided between quantitative (structured) and qualitative (nonstructured) work. The quantitative work can be measured; the qualitative work must be judged. Yet all processes, whether they are simple or complex, mechanical or thoughtful, have certain elements in common:

- ▢ The incoming work is received into the processor.
- ▢ The processor acts upon the work.
- ▢ The processor operates under certain controls or constraints.
- ▢ The work leaves the processor as "output."
- ▢ The results of the output produce a feedback mechanism that influences the input: Satisfactory output will maintain or increase input; unsatisfactory output will have an adverse effect on input.

The nature of the work, quantitative-structured or qualitative-nonstructured, is generally evidenced by certain attributes in the processing cycle. The following tabulation provides clues to those elements:

Properties	Structured	Nonstructured
Input	Invariant; no disturbances to input	Variable; random disturbances
Processor	Machinelike	Man or man-machine system
Control	High reliability	Wide range of reliability
Output	Predictable; structure stable	Unpredictable; statistically unstable
Feedback	Self-organizing	Output not automatically reintroduced

After its nature is determined, the job must be divided into manageable segments. As each segment is examined, it should be questioned:

□ Why are we doing this job?
□ How necessary is it to meet the established objectives for the job?
□ What units capable of being measured or judged make up the segment?
□ What is the hallmark of a job well done for this segment?
□ How do the worker, supervisor, and manager know when the job is done well or poorly?

If at all possible, the individual whose work is to be measured should participate in the setting of both objectives and standards. His willingness to be measured by the standards has a better chance of improving if he takes part. That does not mean that his proposals or decisions will prevail. The manager must have the last word; for he has the final responsibility. But the worker or the subordinate manager can feel that his thoughts, needs, and capacities have not been overlooked in the process.

The very process of setting standards can be beneficial. The job is analyzed; it is put in perspective relative to the entity's needs. There is dialogue between manager and subordinate. The purpose, importance, priority, and relations of the job to other jobs are explored. Ways of doing the job better, quicker, and more economically are bound to come up. The individual takes a fresh interest in and has an improved attitude toward his job.

For some jobs the task of setting measurable standards can be frustrating; but if enough thought is given, some criteria can be developed. After all, each job has some purpose, or else it should be eliminated. And if that purpose can be defined and spelled out clearly, there will be some way to determine when that job is achieved efficiently and effectively. Often the boss himself may not be able to set relevant standards. But, if he enlists their aid, his subordinates, those who are on the firing line and intimately know the work being performed, may be able to propose some kind of standards. True, the boss may have to review, change, add to, or even veto the proposal. But from the dialogue may emerge ways by which all can see whether efforts have achieved expected goals.

It is so much easier to measure that which is quantifiable that standards for the nonquantifiable or partially nonquantifiable are often ignored. Attention is then focused on what can be readily measured by the numbers and turned away from that which can not be. Yardsticks to measure the performance of a seamstress, a buyer, a salesman or a draftsman are readily constructed. On the other hand, performance yardsticks for a secretary, a doctor, a scientist, or a vice president of industrial relations are not easily calibrated. Yet the need for the objective measurement of such positions is as important as, or maybe even more important than, the need for measuring those previously mentioned.

Each job has its hallmarks, its techniques that can be performed well or badly, its elements which, when put together, show a goal to be achieved. Not all the elements are tangible or mechanical. The manager's job, for example, includes more than technical skills. The chief engineer in an aircraft company must be expert in the technical fields of aerodynamics, stress, weight, and producibility. In addition, because he is responsible for the work of others, he must be proficient in the fields of planning, organizing, directing, and controlling.

Those elements are the heart and marrow of management. If the chief engineer is good at only the technical aspects of his job, then he may be nothing more than an elevated technician; he is certainly not a manager. And requiring managers to be measured by standards related to the principles of management has the happy faculty of making better managers of them.

Appraisals

Setting standards without appraising results is like buying the groceries but not making the dinner. Appraisals represent the final purpose of the measurement process. They should not wait for the end of the job, however, or for the end of the year. Managers should probably be appraised at least every quarter against verifiable goals and standards. That which is going off track can be corrected more easily and economically than that which has left the rails entirely.

Appraisals call not only for the ability to compare one number with another but also for the application of wisdom and understanding. Often the standards and criteria—set for events in the future—may not have been accurately established. Unforeseen events, the unknown-unknowns, can provide 20-20 hindsight, but they can also result in unfair evaluations. The appraisal process calls not only for a review of performance but also for a look at the yardstick used to measure performance. Were the goals really attainable? Did unanticipated factors completely frustrate the attainment of goals thought reasonable when set? On the other hand, did luck play a part, so that under the circumstances the poorest of managers could have reached the promised goals?

Here is an example of the dangers of evaluating by the numbers without taking other relevant factors into account:[2]

A number of production control supervisors had been removed from their jobs for failing to set production schedules which would bring about scheduled deliveries and make the best use of facilities. The performance evaluation system in use had led to the transfer or dismissal of the supervisors because deliveries were late and facilities were ineffectively used.

A frustrated management called in an independent agency to determine whether the computer could do a better job of scheduling. As in many computer feasibility studies, the analysis disclosed inherent defects that not even the computer could cure. It seemed that the manufacturing division comprised a number of sections, some of which did their own scheduling. From the managers of these sections the supervisor could get no adequate information. So when he prepared schedules for other divisions, he was working in the dark. He was being frustrated by an organizational deficiency. This was ultimately cured by a reorganization which put all production scheduling in his hands. Evaluations which took into account these frustrations could have pointed up the problem.

Appraisals, like other functions, do not sit in a vacuum. They too have purposes. And the chief purpose is to improve performance. The purpose is not to demean or embarrass people, to exhibit biting wit and sarcasm, or to punish—unless the punishment is calculated to stimulate improved performance. The purpose is not to dwell on weaknesses but to undershore strengths for the greater good of the individual and the organization. We all have our weaknesses. When we're in managerial jobs, we've probably passed that point of development at which easy changes in character or characteristics can be made. We'd just as soon not belabor the weaknesses we're heir to. But we're proud of our strengths, and we'll accept any recommendation to reinforce them, add to them, and give them more muscle. We'll work hard to increase our strengths. By and large, we'll reject and resent any discussions of our weaknesses.

Evaluation, therefore, should be regarded by both the evaluator and the one evaluated as a learning process for development. And the process works best when the evaluation focuses on the problem and not on the individual. Failing that, there is little learning and less improvement.

Financial Measurement

The financial branch of the organization is fortunate in dealing with a unit of measurement that is commonly accepted: the dollar, the pound, the franc, the yen, the mark, and the ruble, to name a few. Financial executives have a variety of financial yardsticks for measuring organizational performance. Ordinarily, measurement is applied to "divisions" within a company that represent responsibility centers having compatible products, services, and markets.

Measurements encompass both the manager and the operation for which he is responsible. The results of such measurements may be different. The measure of the operation is a mechanical one. The measure of the manager may have to take into account matters outside the manager's control, such as executive decisions, fire, flood, strikes, and shortages. Commonly used yardsticks and some problems in their application are, very briefly, as follows:

Profit as a percent of sales. Along with sales increases and decreases, profit as a percent of sales is probably the most commonly used index of financial health. It is readily available and easily comparable with forecasts and similar figures for prior periods. But it has little usefulness in comparing the results of one division with those of another or determining true profitability in each division. Yet it can be a useful early-warning system.

Return on investment. Although return on investment is considered a simple and valuable measure of operating efficiency, in practice the variants in use can make its application quite complex. Yet within the total organization, common methods should apply to all the divisions of the organization. Some companies tend to oversimplify ROI computations, particularly when investments, fixed-asset valuations, and controllable and noncontrollable expenses are concerned. That may make for easier understanding by the executive, but statistical accuracy may be reduced. Some middle ground needs to be established.

Residual income. As a profitability index, residual income answers the complaint that ROI induces divisional managers to emphasize the *ratio* of profits to investments and underplay the *total* of dollar profits. Hence the managers may abandon projects that promise increased earnings but will show small ratios. Residual income, however, is an index that shows the dollar contribution to the corporate weal. It is computed by allocating to each division the organization's current cost of capital and determining the consequent positive or negative amount of divisonal residual income. Emphasis on residual income ties in directly with the organization's objective to maximize earnings on stockholders' equity.

Earnings per share. The earnings per share index is concerned with the appeal that the company's stock carries with its investors and in the marketplace. Certainly, the executive gives high priority to improving return on investment and raising the profit level. But good market performance cannot be overlooked, and concern with earnings per share will direct the executive spotlight toward the larger problems. More current attention should be given to a division that accounts for two-thirds of a company's earnings, but has low profitability, than to a profitable division that accounts for but a small fraction of the company's profit per share.

Cash flow per share. In a manner similar to earnings per share, cash flow per share figures are computed by dividing divisional cash flow by the number of the company's outstanding common shares. The device can be useful in determining which division is contributing most to the company's well-being. A sustained high cash flow is a good index of satisfactory contribution. The cash flow per share yardstick is receiving increased attention because reported profit may have questionable validity as a result of the relative elasticity of "generally accepted accounting principles" and the application of "creative accounting." For example, depreciation allowances may often be considered inadequate because they are based on original asset costs and may not cover actual replacement costs. On the other hand, maintenance costs charged to current expense keep current facilities in repair and prolong their life. Hence, depreciation costs in terms of cash flow per share, as they affect reported profitability, have no relevance.[3]

All these yardsticks have their uses, but, like any other measurement devices, they need careful interpretation. When management performance is appraised, variances must be evaluated by whether they were controllable by the manager.

MEASUREMENT AND INTERNAL AUDITORS

Standards

Within the scope of measurement and appraisal, the internal auditor can contribute to organizational performance in two ways:

1. By measuring his own performance so that he may improve his efficiency and effectiveness.
2. By providing executives with new means of measuring the administrative health of the organization.

Internal auditing has its own criteria and standards of excellence. The truly professional internal auditing organization makes them known to its people and measures the performance of its personnel against them. The subjects covered are planning the audit project, organizing the work, directing and carrying out the audit steps, controlling the audit resources, and reporting the audit results. For each of those subjects there are criteria for judgment and standards for measurement. For example, some criteria calling for objective judgments from an audit supervisor are as follows:

□ Were audit programs geared to the key objectives of the operations audited?

□ Were working papers developed in a professional manner?

□ Were all audit findings fully developed in terms of determining operating standards, gathering facts, evaluating effects, assessing causes, and recommending improvements?

□ Were audit man-hours expended only on material matters?

□ Was the audit report properly supported by the evidence accumulated in the working papers?

□ Was corrective action taken or initiated during the audit?

□ Were cooperative relations maintained with the auditee?

Some of the standards that the supervisor can use to measure the work of the auditor quantitatively are these:

□ Was each programmed audit step carried out or otherwise accounted for?

□ Were working papers accurately and completely cross-referenced?

□ Was the approved audit report format employed?

□ Was the audit accomplished within the man-days budgeted?

□ Was the audit completed by the scheduled due dates?

Appraisals

The director of internal auditing can make use of all the objectives, goals, and standards to appraise his own organization and to permit executive management to appraise its performance. Such performance appraisals can be presented in oral and formal performance reports that say: "Here are the matters that, with your knowledge and concurrence, we set out to do; and here is what we accomplished."

The value of performance appraisals can be enhanced by imagination and innovation. Through performance reports, the director of internal auditing can not only appraise his own accomplishments but also use the opportunity to provide executive management with objective summaries of information not elsewhere available: information on the administrative health of the entire organization with which top management can apply new yardsticks of performance to appraise its operating managers.

Executive managers receive reports on the entity's financial health. The reports are developed by the controller's organization and are validated by the external accountant. Ordinarily there is no counterpart to those reports to cover evaluations of other operations in the organization.

But because internal auditors make wide-ranging appraisals of operations, they are in a position to offer objective, quantitative indexes of the entity's operating performance. Each of the internal audit reports normally expresses an opinion. That opinion may be favorable or unfavorable. (See Chapter 6, Communications.) The opinions are most likely supported by audit findings. But the opinions and the findings are indexes of the effectiveness of the operations reviewed, and they can be arrayed quantitatively according to area and subject matter. The array can be given additional meaning if comparisons among divisions of the entity and against operations performed in prior years are made. Trends portrayed by graphs can be particularly helpful.[4]

Appraisals of administrative health can be made especially useful to management by pointing to the causes of deficiencies described in the audit reports. A host of defects haphazardly listed can portray serious weaknesses within the organization, but they can also be confusing and valueless to executives concerned with the steps needed to correct the basic problems. If, however, the listing emphasizes the causes, the reasons, and the endemic difficulties, then they may aid executives in planning for improvement and in decision making.

For example, assume that internal audit reports described 550 different deficiencies during the past year. Let us also assume that the individual defects had been corrected during the audits or soon thereafter. But in the background may lurk a basic problem that is not being corrected because it is not being addressed, and executive management is not addresssing the problem because the problem has not been identified.

But suppose the internal auditing organization were to classify the 550 deficiencies according to cause and were to report them to top management, under the four functions of management, in the table on the following page. The signposts raised by the causes listed point unmistakably to operating managers who are not carrying out their management functions. Whether sales are good or profits are high

Cause	Number
Planning	
Need for control not recognized	55
Management decision not to take action	50
Failure to develop policies and procedures	40
Organizing	
Failure to assign appropriate authority	60
Failure to assign appropriate responsibility	50
Failure to assign appropriate priorities	30
Failure to assign sufficient personnel	5
Failure to provide adequate equipment	5
Directing	
Failure to provide coordination	60
Failure to provide adequate training	55
Poor morale	5
Controlling	
Insufficient management attention	60
Failure to see that standards are met	40
Failure to obtain feedback	20
Human error	10
Employee attitude	5
Total	550

or return on investment seems satisfactory, the fact remains that conditions could be still better if managers were doing their job of managing. The individual deficiencies must have had an adverse effect on costs and profitability, and the catalog of causes hints why.

Measuring Operations

If the internal auditor is to perform a management-oriented audit, he must think like a manager; he must structure his audit along management lines. Hence, he must be concerned with the same tools, the same principles, and the same methods that the competent manager uses when he looks at his own performance.

The internal auditor's first job, therefore, is to identify as specifically as he can the objectives of the organization he is reviewing: the organization's purpose, reason for being, and desired contribution to the well-being of the entire entity. And that is not as simple as it sounds. Many an internal auditor—and manager as well—confuses objectives with activities. The resulting audit is then designed to see whether the activities are being carried out in accordance with established procedures.

But that is not the be-all and end-all of internal auditing; it would not satisfy the able executive who installed internal auditing in the organization. What the executive expects to learn from the internal auditor is whether the operations under review *achieved their objectives* and, incidentally, whether those objectives were achieved efficiently and economically. Clearly, then, the first step is to learn what the objectives are. If the objective of an accounts payable operation is regarded simply as processing invoices for payment, the ensuing audit may probably be restricted to matching invoices with receiving memos and purchase orders and verifying signatures evidencing executive approvals for services.

But a different audit might result if the true objectives are identified and used in the audit appraisal. Those objectives may be regarded as follows: To process for payment what is due when due, distribute expenditures to appropriate accounts, and facilitate conservation of the organization's funds.

Seen in that light, the audit may take a different turn. The auditor may start asking himself questions that are management-oriented and keyed to the operation's central objectives. For example:

□ How do people who sign invoices for services assure themselves that the services have actually been received?

□ What studies have been made to determine the point at which lost discounts are counterbalanced by improved cash flow?

□ How are accounts payable clerks instructed on account distributions and changes in the charts of account, and how is the accuracy of account distributions monitored?

□ How promptly does accounts payable receive copies of purchase order change notices from the purchasing department?

□ Should feasibility studies be undertaken to computerize the accounts payable function?

□ What contacts have been made with companies using the computer for accounts payable processing?

The usual detailed verifications are still appropriate. Indeed, they are essential. But if the audit were to stop there, some important insights might be lost.

Even so simple a matter as petty cash is elevated to a management view if the true objectives are identified. The objective is more than making cash available for small purchases. It will include that, of course, but the complete statement might make the auditor's thoughts rise above paper verifications. For example, the objectives of petty cash may be to:

□ Provide cash for expenditures too small to warrant application of formal disbursement procedures. (The auditor should know when the cost of controls over formal disbursements warrants the use of petty cash funds instead.)

□ Restrict funds to an amount that will cover normal expenditures. (The auditor should determine what is normal and what is the least amount of petty cash needed to meet normal needs.)

□ Provide funds for a reasonable period. (The auditor should determine the optimum period between replenishments of the funds.)

The catalog of activities in the fields of human endeavor is almost endless. The practices and the circumstances may differ widely, but in each case the audit approach must be the same: The first and most important step is to determine, in concert with the manager, what the manager's objectives are or should be. Once the objectives have been identified, the internal auditor must determine the means devised or needed to achieve them and the controls needed to see that what has been planned will indeed come to pass.

For example, one of the objectives of the purchasing organization is to buy goods and services at the right price. And one of the means of achieving that objective is a system of competitive bids, when they are appropriate, from acceptable suppliers. The system of control needed to see that the objective is met may include a bidder's list of suppliers who have been approved for quality and financial stability. Another is the requirement that supervisors review requests for bids to see that all appropriate bidders have been asked to bid. Still another is the requirement that all requests to bid be mailed and all bids obtained be received by someone other than the buyer. Those precautions provide assurance that the buyer will not play favorites by discarding some requests to bid before mailing them and some submitted bids after receiving them.

The audit measurement process is completed when the auditor examines a representative sample of purchases to determine whether the system is working as intended and evaluates any deviations for materiality and cause. He then brings his findings to the attention of management and, as the case may be, either provides assurance that the system is a good one and is working effectively or recommends improvements to prevent the recurrence of any significant deviations from acceptable standards of control and performance.

The internal auditor generally uses four standards in measuring performance. A brief discussion of each follows, along with examples of actual audit findings that relate to the standards.[5]

Effectiveness. Is the operation that is being performed necessary to the objectives of the unit and the organization? Does it mesh with the overall organizational objectives? Is it the right operation to meet those objectives? And is it meeting them?

> An internal auditor investigated production control practices because of production line stoppages; in other words, production control was not meeting its objective of keeping the line moving on schedule. He found that the dispatching of material to the line was not being controlled. For example, materials were being sent to the wrong areas, and nobody was checking bins for adequate supplies until shortages occurred. New orders were being placed to cover line shortages. In his own investigations the auditor was able to locate and put into use parts whose replacement would have cost $22,000. As a result of the auditor's recommendations, the production control procedures were overhauled and improved.

Compliance. Are operations conducted in accordance with applicable policies, procedures, and instruction? And are such directives still valid to meet current organizational objectives?

> An internal auditor was verifying compliance with procedures set forth in a manual dealing with emergency situations. The manual called for specific assignments to individuals designated by name. The internal auditor found that three of the 25-man squad of security people were no longer employed. Of ten men questioned, only two had adequate knowledge of their responsibilities and only five had copies of the manual. Meetings were to be held every six months to review practices and procedures. Seven of those questioned said that they had never attended a meeting, and three said that there had been no meetings in three years. No one could remember a fire drill. The internal auditor was unable to report savings in terms of dollars, but his report of conditions sent a chill through top management and prompted speedy corrective action.

Efficiency. Are the resources of people, money, and materials being used and managed with the least possible waste and extravagance? Are operations being carried out in a manner best calculated to achieve desired results?

An internal auditor was evaluating the need for preemployment physical examinations. During a period of 18 months, 7,025 examinations were given at a cost of $65,670. Only 35 applicants had been rejected, and 18 of the 35 were rejected for pregnancy and varicose veins. The remaining 17 were rejected for heart trouble and high blood pressure. At the internal auditor's suggestion, the medical history questionnaire was expanded to obtain an indication of potentially serious problems, and examinations were required only in those cases. Savings were estimated at $30,000 a year.

Economy. Are operations being carried out in the least expensive way while still meeting acceptable standards and the objectives set?

An internal auditor asked a transportation manager the reason why all trucks were equipped with four-wheel drives; he saw no logical reason for such equipment for the entire fleet, since most of the work was being performed on paved roads or flat terrain. As a result of the questions, the transportation manager established a policy of equipping 50 percent of the fleet with two-wheel drive and 50 percent with four-wheel drive. Savings amounted to $270,000 a year.

Management Inventories

As we pointed out earlier, a periodic summary report to management on the administrative health of the organization can point to incipient or widespread ailments. Almost invariably, the major causes of defects are management-related. People who are elevated to management jobs don't always know how to manage. The promotion or transfer of a good manager may leave a gap that is filled by a poor one because backup talent had not been developed or even been considered.

In each audit he makes, the internal auditor deals with managers and supervisors, develops organization charts, evaluates productivity, becomes acquainted with management strengths and weaknesses, and assesses the capability of employees now and for the future. As a result of his in-depth analysis of operations, the internal auditor develops some shrewd impressions of the inventory of both managers and workers. Certainly, it is not within the auditor's responsibility to report formally on his evaluations of individuals. Such evaluations are the responsibility of the individual's supervisor.

Besides, if the internal auditor started reporting on individuals, he would create antagonisms and hostility that would make his internal audit task almost impossible to accomplish. But as a counselor to operating managers he could point informally to the desirability of developing, within a department, branch, or division, a management inventory. The inventory would specify a backup for each significant position—insurance that the loss of an individual would not result in the collapse of a function.

For example, in an audit of personnel services, an internal auditor found that the task of dealing with wage garnishments and credit letters was the responsibility of one employee, who acted without supervision because nobody knew anything about her job. The manager was unconcerned because the employee was doing a superb job. She was handling some 160 garnishments, 5 summonses and complaints, and over 500 credit letters a month. She dealt with company counsel, marshals, and sheriffs, and she knew them all by name. She had a complete and detailed working knowledge of what was involved in the often complex actions, including the relevant legal aspects. She had grown with the job and she handled it competently and knowledgeably. But everything she knew was stored in her head. Not another individual in the company, including the company's legal counsel, had any idea of the steps required to carry out the varied phases of her job. She had not recorded or imparted to anyone else what was needed to perform her tasks. When she was on vacation or was ill, the work simply piled up until she returned to her desk. Her death or separation from the company would have resulted in utter chaos.

The internal auditor, in appraising the activity, made a detailed flow chart of the steps required to carry out the employee's function. He then presented it to the department manager and suggested that it be used to develop a manual for the garnishment and credit letter function. He further suggested that the indispensable employee be assisted by another employee, if only on a temporary basis, to learn the system and forestall catastrophe in the event the key employee went elsewhere.

In another situation, an internal auditor, reviewing a facilities engineering function, observed that 85 percent of the people in the department were within five years of mandatory retirement For some reason, the chief facilities engineer, who was abundantly aware of the condition, had not communicated the potential problem to his own superior. The audit report corrected that defect and resulted in a more appropriate mix of ages in the department.

Besides the appraisals of people inventories conducted during regular audits, the director of internal auditing might offer to conduct a management study throughout the organization to see whether key positions are backed up with knowledgeable replacements and executive management is supplied with an up-to-date record of its management inventory.

Financial Measurement

The yardsticks of financial ratios discussed earlier in this chapter are useful tools, but like any other tools they must be sharp and they must be accurate. Most important, the results must be properly interpreted.

The data used by executive management in connection with financial measurement come from accounting and financial records translated into summary reports. The reports are put together by human beings or summarized from computer printouts. The probabilities of error, missing data, misinterpretation of instructions, and misconceptions of management needs represent an everpresent danger.

Hence one of the functions of the internal auditor is to keep a watchful eye on the manner of information gathering and reporting. The auditor will want to know if people developing information are aware of the purposes and uses of the reports they are putting together. He will want to examine the worksheets used and see how accurate they are. He will be concerned with cross-checks and fail-safe mechanisms to insure accuracy. He will make sure people are employing such simple but important techniques as initialing and dating the working papers they develop so that accountability is assured. The internal auditor's job, reduced to essentials, is measurement. Managers should find the internal auditor an expert ally in honing its own measurement techniques.

CONCLUSION

The ability to manage is important, but how well his people perform to meet goals is the true measure of the manager. Performance is the key. And to learn how an individual performs, be he manager or worker, it is necessary to determine what the person is supposed to do and how well he is supposed to do it. That calls for objectives and goals and for criteria and standards. Only then can an individual's performance be measured objectively both by himself and by others. The criteria are usually qualitative and must be judged. The standards are usually quantitative and can be measured. Established financial measurements are employed to measure profit performance of an organization. Each of the forms of measurement has its uses and its weaknesses.

Internal auditing is an operation that can measure and be measured in terms of goals and standards. The program of internal audits can also produce indications of the administrative health of the organization through summaries of audit opinions and audit findings. The internal auditor's standards of measurement must take into account the objectives and goals of the operation reviewed, and the audits should be designed to measure effectiveness, compliance, efficiency, and economy. The internal auditor can provide an important service for management in assessing management and people inventories and in assuring the accuracy of financial measurements.

References

1. Harold Koontz and Cyril O'Donnell, *Essentials of Management* (New York: McGraw-Hill, 1974), p. 267.
2. D. C. Basil, *Managerial Skills for Executive Action* (New York: AMA, 1970), p. 215.
3. R. N. Stillman, "Measuring Divisional Performance," in R. F. Vancil, ed., *Financial Executive's Handbook* (Homewood, Ill.: Dow Jones–Irwin, 1970), pp. 649–653.
4. L. B. Sawyer, *The Practice of Modern Internal Auditing* (Orlando, Fla.: The Institute of Internal Auditors, 1973), pp. 460–462.
5. Ibid., pp. 332–326.

8

Scientific Methods

High hopes and not so high results. A scientific method that survived centuries. Management must still manage. Operations research—the uses and methodology. Answering the "what if" questions. Questioning the questions. Forms of operations research: regression analysis, probability theory, queuing theory, Monte Carlo simulation, linear programming, inventory management, breakeven analysis, PERT, CPM, dynamic programming, game theory, exponential smoothing, line of balance, Markov process, and sensitivity analysis. Benefits to the internal auditor. Statistical sampling. The sampling plans: attributes, variables, dollar unit sampling, discovery, stop or go, judgment, and acceptance sampling. The selection techniques: random numbers, interval, stratified, and cluster sampling. Sampling rules and cautions: evaluations, defining the population, determining error rates. Selecting areas to audit through ratio, change, and trend analysis. Variations among elements and units. Illustrations of useful ratios. Assisting executives by assessing quantitative analysis applications. Protection from improper uses of qualitative techniques.

SCIENTIFIC METHODS AND MANAGERS

The Complaints

Many a disgruntled manager, after failing to reap expected benefits from quantitative analysis, has growled, "This new-fangled management science is a lot of malarkey." He may have been justified. The high hopes for applying systems methodology, long used in the physical sciences, to management decision making and planning have often gone aglimmering. The dreams that mathematical formulas and computers will replace managerial decisions may have vanished with the cold dawn of unredeemed promises.

But to say that "this new-fangled management science is a lot of malarkey" is to miss the point of some potentially valuable techniques. It is to be resentful of the ad that says "this car practically drives itself" because blind acceptance resulted in a mass of metal wrapped around a tree. A driver still needs to drive, and a manager still needs to manage.

To understand the purposes and limitations of "management science," we should first put the term in perspective. Management science, or as it is usually termed, operations research, seeks to solve business and economic problems mathematically. The approach is generally through models that represent the operation or system being examined. The model is usually reduced to mathematical formulas that seek to take into account all relevant variables. The number of variables in a business situation often makes the formula so complex that it can be solved only with the aid of computers. And the ordinary manager, faced with the awesome combination of arcane formulas and mysterious computers, either abdicates his managerial responsibilities to the scientists or avoids the scientists altogether. Hence the grumble: "These new-fangled. . . ."

Early Models

Actually, management science, formulas, and models are not newfangled. One scientific method reaches back into the fourteenth century, and managers have been using it ever since. Through the years it has remained a powerful and indispensable servant. The formula associated with the method is:

$$\text{Assets} - \text{liabilities} = \text{owner equity}$$

The model is double-entry bookkeeping. It represents the value of an enterprise. It is simple, symmetrical, logical, and beautiful. It is not the enterprise itself, the concrete and steel and blood and brains of the physical plant and its people. But it is an accurate representation of the financial structure made in quantitative terms that are readily understandable to those schooled in business.

If man has indeed demonstrated his ability to produce an enduring, useful mathematical model of a business, is there validity to the disappointed manager's grumble about scientific management? Yes and no.

The Difficulties

True, many problems come equipped with enough variables and interrelations to call for mathematics that exceed the grasp of most managers, even those who can be termed mathematically literate. In fact, John von Neumann, a mathematical genius, discovered that his awesome mathematical limits were soon reached during his development of the game theory.

But a manager does not have to be a bookkeeper or a mathematician any more than an author has to know how to construct a typewriter. Anyone can use a tool without knowing how to build it, but he should know what the tool can or cannot do. The double-entry system will not foretell the future. If properly used, it will accurately portray the past. It will tell of past profits, losses, receipts, and disbursements. And that information can provide the base from which the manager—not the double-entry system, mind you—will seek to anticipate what is yet to come.

That is not to denigrate bookkeeping. It merely describes bookkeeping for what it is: a tool of management, not management itself. So the data and the analyses supplied by the tool are but a beginning. The intelligent manager must go on from there.

Further, the manager cannot hope that the tools will provide, at the touch of a readily available button, the information he needs. Useful answers are generally prompted by useful questions. The manager and the manager alone must take the responsibiliy for determining what information he needs to run his organization and make reasonably successful decisions. Scientific management can provide answers to appropriate questions. But the manager will have to ask the questions.

Many a business trundles along without an adequate cash flow forecast—the peaks and valleys of money available to pay the bills. But the basis for such a forecast—receipts and disbursements—is available from the double-entry system. Again, the information received is a sound beginning, but the forecasting requires the input of variables that often only the manager can supply.

The double-entry system will furnish historical costs about a product on which to base estimates of the costs of a similar product. The historical costs may be valid and accurate—about the past. But the manager, the risk taker, must add in such variables as competition and inflation and his plans for the entity itself before the estimate achieves a reasonable level of reliability.

Similarly, the scientist, with his formulas and computers, can provide reasonable answers if the manager provides information on the estimated value of certain variables that are difficult to quantify and if he requests from the management scientist what he knows the scientist can supply. He must understand the scientific tool—what it can and what it cannot do.

The schisms between the manager and the scientist often widened merely because neither was fully aware of the other's responsibilities and limitations. The manager who asked for operations research formulas to govern an entire enterprise failed to take into account the enormous number of interdependent elements in a business—not only internal constraints, like varying degrees of skill and dedication of its people, but also external constraints like government and the economy. The management scientist, therefore, can provide useful information if both he and the manager understand the function of scientific management. It is a tool for analysis; it provides information, not categorical answers. But the analyses can be extremely useful.

Uses of Operations Research

Some companies have been successfully using operations research (OR) methods; among them are American Airlines, AT&T, Chase Manhattan, Du Pont, Eastman Kodak, General Electric, General Motors, Gulf Oil, Metropolitan Life Insurance, PPG, U.S. Steel, and Xerox. All have saved thousands of dollars through the scientific approach, and the approach has other benefits as well. The structured method gives managers insights that are not gained from intuitive, darts-at-a-dart-board decisions. The approach, which categorizes the OR methodology, is as follows:

1. State the problem. Articulate the objective of the search. Identify the variables, both those within management's control and those that are uncontrollable. Determine the constraints under which the operation functions, such as limits of productive capacity and lack of qualified personnel. Often the exercise of thinking through the problem in such a fashion can remove blinders from the manager's eyes or at least alert the manager to the difficulties he will face.

2. Build a model. The model, in mathematical terms, should represent the real system. There are basically three types of models that represent systems:

(a) The *iconic* is a scaled reproduction, like a model bridge or a model railway.
(b) The *analog* portrays one kind of property by another property that is graphic in character, like solid or broken lines on a map representing different kinds of roads.
(c) The *symbolic* is portrayed in mathematical terms. Symbolic models are most used in OR work and are constructed by mathematicians. But the input, the probabilities that some things will or will not happen in the real world, must be supplied by the experienced manager or by consultants such as economists, industrial engineers, and actuaries.

3. Test the model. Try various values, subject to control, to see what the results would be. Too often what shines on paper fades in real life. So the model should be applied to known, proven historical data to see if the results derived from it are the same as those determined from actual experience. Make any needed revisions as a result of the tests.

4. Put the model to work. Obtain alternative solutions to the problem for which the model was designed. The reliability of the solution will, of course, depend on how faithfully the model represents the real system. Select the best solution among the alternatives.

5. Put the solution into effect. Apply it to the system. Determine its effectiveness. See if it has indeed fulfilled its promise. And, most importantly, update it as needed; changed conditions must be incorporated in the model to represent the changed system.

Opportunities Available Through OR

The What-If Questions

If the manager and the scientist fully understand their own and each other's role, OR can be a powerful tool. Farseeing managers, looking over the horizon of a year or a decade, are constantly asking themselves the what-if question. What if we reduced prices? What if we increased prices? What if we changed credit terms? What if we located a warehouse in Ashtabula? What if we closed our warehouse in Cucamonga? What if we phased out product X? What if we changed our product mix? The assumptions could, of course, be put to work immediately by executive edict, or they could be tested. Testing assumptions can be an important service that the management scientist can render for managers. But the manager must ask the question and work with the scientist to make sure there is complete agreement on objectives.

The fact that the manager has asked it does not make a question the right one. The scientist, in concert with the manager, must make sure the right question has been asked before putting to work the extensive, expensive process of quantitative analysis. The manager may have asked, "What if we were to mechanize the costly manual inventory system in warehouse D?" Perhaps the question that needed asking is: "What if we eliminated warehouse D altogether?"

The manager is the ultimate decision maker. He should not, therefore, seek solutions from the OR scientist. He should ask for alternatives together with the risks attached to each. The scientist provides numerical responses. The manager must weigh each response in terms of its effect on the entire enterprise—its aims, its people, and its responsibilities. That is hardly a job for the scientist.

The manager should seek understanding rather than formulas and mathematical answers. When he understands the results of the scientist's work, he retains command. He retains responsibility, which he can never delegate or abdicate. The powerful tool of OR is in his hands, not in the hands of the scientist. OR is the instrument of management, not the exercise of the mathematician. And if the manager understands what it has to offer, when it can profitably be used, and what useful applications of it are available, then he can make it do his bidding, just as double-entry bookkeeping does.

In the subsections that follow, some of the more common forms of quantitative analysis are described. Space does not permit a thorough discussion of each, but there are books aplenty on the subject that explore it thoroughly.[1]

Regression Analysis

Regression analysis is the most widely used analytical technique for describing relations among variables. It measures the change in one variable when one or more related variables change. Simple regression is applied to the study of two variables; multiple regression relates to three or more variables.

Regression analysis is based on the principle that one variable, called the independent variable, will affect the behavior of a dependent variable. For example, there is a direct relation between packaging costs and the volume of packaged items. Increase the production of packaged items (the independent variable) and the packaging costs (the dependent variable) should increase because, clearly, there are more items to package. Hence, regression analysis would help the manager predict packaging costs at varying levels of production.

Whenever there is a consistent relation between two or more variables, regression analysis can be used.

Standard computer programs are available to compute both simple- and multiple-regression analyses. The technique has been used to:

- □ Study price behavior.
- □ Forecast general and administrative (G&A) rates.
- □ Analyze market demand for a product.

But the manager must be aware of the controls needed and the hazards attendant upon the use of regression analysis.

The reliability of the relation shown by regression analysis must be tested. The degree of correlation between the variables is measured by what is known as the coefficient of determination. A high coefficient shows good correlation; a low coefficient shows poor correlation. But there are hazards even in determining reliability. An apparent high correlation can be the result of too few observations made during the analysis, and there is always the possibility that two or more sets of observations may indicate a relation when in fact no such relation exists. As in all things, the manager must apply his judgment and experience to see whether the results presented by the scientists agree with his own expectations and make sense in the real world.

Relations that existed in the past may not persist in the future; external constraints may alter them. The manager working with the scientist must evaluate the validity of the relations and satisfy himself that what was true yesterday will be equally true tomorrow. Constraints like inflation, potential government controls, unavailability of materials, and discontinued demand must be considered.

Hence, when the manager is unable to make his own checks on the results of the regression analysis, he should call in an independent observer to do it for him. Later in this chapter, we shall recount an example of internal auditors being used for that purpose.

Probability Theory

In many cases the value of one or more variables is not known, yet decisions must be made despite uncertainty as to outcomes. By using probability theory, the manager can estimate the likelihood that the value of the variables will be at certain levels.

For example, based on experience, a manager can estimate that there is a 75 percent probability that demand for a product will exceed $25,000 in December and only a 25 percent chance that it will exceed that amount in January. Using such estimates does not remove the risk, but it points out the degree of risk the manager faces and offers him a guide that may help him minimize the hazards.

In making use of probability theory, the steps are usually these:

1. Identify the available choices open to the manager.
   Example
   Produce one of three products, since facilities are not available for all three. Product X will appeal primarily to the mass market, product Y to the middle-class market, and product Z to the upper-class market.

2. Determine the probable result of each choice.
   Example
   Net profits for each product are estimated as follows:

Choices	Mass	Middle	Upper
Product X	$100,000	$ 30,000	$ 10,000
Product Y	16,000	100,000	30,000
Product Z	10,000	50,000	150,000

3. Assign probabilities to the achievement of the net profits, based on judgment and experience; that is, assign the probability of achieving profits from each of the three markets.
   Example

Choices	Probability
Mass	.5
Middle	.3
Upper	.2

4. Calculate the expected value of the estimated results by multiplying each expected profit by the probability of achieving it. Then sum the results.
   Example

Choices	Mass	Middle	Upper	Expected Result
Product X	$50,000	$ 9,000	$ 2,000	$61,000
Product Y	8,000	30,000	6,000	44,000
Product Z	5,000	15,000	30,000	50,000

5. Select the choice with the highest estimated result.
   Example
   Product X appears to be the most likely choice, based on estimated profits and the likelihood of achieving those profits in the three markets.

In real life the problems and choices are much more complex; here the example has been made arithmetically simple for the purposes of illustration. In some applications of probability theory, a decision tree is used. The branches springing from the trunk—in the case just discussed there would be three branches—display alternative results and the probabilities of meeting them in graphic form that is more easily visualized.

Certainly, an exercise in probability theory would not be warranted when the amounts involved are small, but the theory is now being put to use in industry. For example, at General Electric all investment requests exceeding $500,000 must be accompanied by an assessment of the probabilities of success. Ford, Du Pont, and General Mills also use probability theory as an aid to decision making.[2]

Queuing Theory

The queuing theory, also called the waiting-line theory, helps managers decide how to staff service facilities. It has been used in providing optimum service at minimum cost whenever "customers" must wait in line for some form of service: at banks, tool cribs, loading docks, supermarket checkout stands, hospital clinics, insurance adjusting offices, repair departments, and the like. Too few attendants can result in customer dissatisfaction or customer idle time. Too many attendants can be unnecessarily costly and inefficient.

Actual experience is used in queuing theory computations: the rate at which customers arrive and the time required to serve each customer. The information needed can be gained by observation with the use of stopwatches, and the sample results can be projected to estimates that provide reasonably sound bases for determining staffing and facility needs.

Monte Carlo Simulation

In many cases, analytical solutions based on observed data—as in queuing theory—are impossible because the data are unavailable or too expensive to obtain. It is therefore necessary to simulate actual conditions.

For example, in a large city, data on the frequency and length of telephone calls may be extremely difficult to accumulate. Accordingly, a model is developed. The number and length of telephone calls are simulated by using random digits that correspond to the random placing of telephone calls. In earlier days, experimenters used modified roulette wheels to estimate the expected frequency of events, hence the term Monte Carlo. Recently random-number tables have been used.

Here is an example of the use of Monte Carlo simulation: In a supermarket the manager could determine from his records the expected sales volume of quarts of milk. But he could not know how the demand by customers fluctuates over a period of days, weeks, or months. By using the Monte Carlo method, random digits for moments in the period under study would simulate the random customer demand and help the manager decide on the amounts of milk he should have available at all times.

Linear Programming

Resources in any entity are rarely, if ever, unlimited. Managers must decide how to allocate limited resources of men, money, materials, and equipment to provide the best contribution to earnings. Managers must determine what their objective is—maximize profit or minimize cost, for example—and then solve the problem by mathematics. Linear programming helps solve the resource allocation problem, but the problem must have certain characteristics.

1. A stated objective.
   Example
   To reduce transportation costs between factories and warehouses when a company's factories must deliver to scattered warehouses.
2. Resources are limited and can be put to alternative uses.
   Example
   Several factories, each with a maximum output capacity, must deliver goods to a number of warehouses, each with minimum requirements.
3. The elements of the problem must be subject to quantitative measurement.
   Example
   The factory outputs are known. The warehouse needs are known. And the cost of transportation from each of the factories to each of the warehouses is known.
4. The relation must be linear; that is, all elements must be proportional.
   Example
   A 12 percent increase in the distance shipped must cause a 12 percent increase in transportation costs.

The H. J. Heinz Company was one of the first firms in the United States to use linear programming. It was distributing products from

6 plants located throughout the country to 70 warehouses that were widely scattered. One of the difficulties was that, in the eastern half of the county, demand exceeded production capacity and, in the western half, capacity exceeded demand. When it substituted linear programming for seat-of-the-pants allocations, H. J. Heinz saved thousands of dollars in freight bills.[3]

Inventory Management Techniques

Decisions on inventory are common to most entities in varying degrees. Retailers must maintain stocks of goods to meet customer needs. Manufacturers must maintain stocks of raw materials, parts, and finished products. Offices must maintain stocks of stationery. Hospitals must maintain stocks of medical supplies. Lack of needed inventory can result in loss of customers, line stoppage, or serious dislocations. Excess inventory results in unnecessary investments in goods and in excessive storage space, handling costs, insurance, spoilage, and shrinkage.

Somewhere a balance must be struck because, as every manager knows, as order quantity increases, order costs drop and inventory costs rise, and vice versa. The goal of inventory management, then, is to minimize the total of all associated costs: both the costs of carrying inventories and the costs of not carrying them. Hence the inventory manager has two decisions facing him: How much to order, and when to place orders. In deciding how much to order the manager must consider:

1. Needs for a period of time—month, quarter, year.
2. Setup costs—issuing purchase orders for procured materials or setting up equipment for production runs of manufactured products.
3. The costs associated with carrying the items for the need period.

In deciding when to order, the manager must consider:

1. Lead time—the period between placing the order and receiving the goods.
2. The demand for the goods during the lead time period.
3. How sure he is that the lead time and demand can be reliably forecast.

Formulas are available for determining economic quantities, lead time, carrying costs, and stock-out costs.[4]

Breakeven Analysis

To assess the effects of alternative courses of action, managers often use breakeven models. The models relate total cost to total revenue. The values are recorded on a chart, and the point at which benefits equal costs is the breakeven point. After that point, when fixed costs have been absorbed, profits begin to expand with increased output. Breakeven charts are useful in determining:

The possible effect of raising or lowering prices.
Effects of changed plant capacity.
Whether a new product should be added or an old one dropped.
Whether a firm should lease or purchase a fleet of cars for salesmen.

Any situation that permits a plotting of costs versus anticipated benefits can make use of breakeven charts, but the charts do have limitations. They may not be useful for long-term decisions, since costs that are stable in the short term may very likely vary over the long term; they may not provide reliable information when the environment is dynamic and fluid. A simplified breakeven chart is shown in Figure 2.

Network Analysis

Managers often find it necessary to control complex, interrelated systems that are nonrecurrent, as in large programs or projects. They need control measures to insure coordination, to see that essential steps are not forgotten, and to make certain that step A will be completed before step B begins. That need gave rise to the demand for some means of visualizing the system. A view of the network of steps and actions can disclose places where resources can be redeployed and both cost and time can be reduced.

Network models make use of a set of points connected by lines. The paths indicated by the lines represent the work to be performed to achieve system goals. The network can be useful in controlling projects involving many activities that must be coordinated or must be completed before other activities take place.

Two networks to assist management were devised at about the same time: 1957 and 1958. The Program Evaluation and Review Technique (PERT) was developed by a team of experts from Lockheed and Booz, Allen & Hamilton and was used on the Polaris project. Originally, PERT was chiefly concerned with time. It is de-

Figure 2. Breakeven chart.

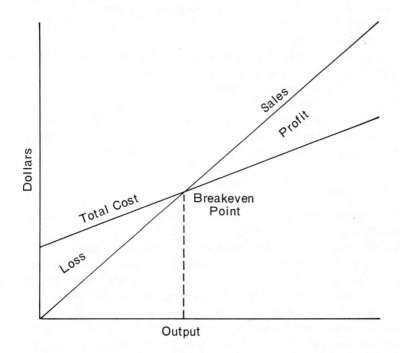

signed for projects in which time spans are uncertain. The network emphasizes events. Cost was not considered. But for the Polaris project PERT helped cut two years from the scheduled span, so cost reduction most likely did result.

The Critical Path Method (CPM) was developed by operations researchers from E. I. du Pont de Nemours & Company and the Univac division of the then Remington Rand organization. CPM's purpose was to help schedule and control activities concerned with constructing chemical plants. It is used when there is reasonable certainty as to time spans, and it emphasizes activities. Cost is a major concern in CPM networks. As the name implies, the path is critical because a delay in the completion of any activity in the path can mean a delay in meeting project objectives.

PERT and CPM models have common elements and are developed in much the same way.

1. Define the objective to be achieved.
2. Specify the time and/or cost factors that must be controlled.

3. Determine the order in which tasks are to be accomplished.
4. Estimate the time required to complete each activity.
5. Design the network.

Clearly, the network, as a management tool, is useful only in complex projects. Also, the manager must understand that the model's success is contingent upon the reliability of the information on which the network is based and an understanding of the methodology. Often, the discipline required to plan PERT and CPM networks can have significant benefits without going through the mathematics. Several books provide thorough guides to the application of network techniques.[5]

Other Techniques

Other quantitative techniques, less well known, have been used as management tools. Some of them are as follows:

Dynamic programming is termed a "maximization theory." It is used when a whole series of states of action take place and a decision on each state is dependent on the decision made on the preceding state. It permits a mathematical determination of the period-by-period consequences of decisions. It can be used to calculate the desirability of incurring temporary losses for the sake of long-term gains. For example, through dynamic programming a manager could calculate the benefits of expanding large sums on research and development and incurring losses during the immediate period in the hope of making much greater profits in later periods.

Game theory is used to establish a basis for decisions in a competitive environment. It takes into account the consequences of the action by one party upon the actions of an opponent who is choosing from among alternatives. Game theory goes beyond the classical theory of probability, which is limited to pure chance. In game theory, strategic aspects, that is, aspects controlled by the participants, are stressed. The theory is therefore well adapted to the study of competition in which there are present several common factors such as conflicting interests, incomplete information, the interplay of rational decisions, and chance.

Exponential smoothing is used to correlate later values with earlier ones in the same series. It is used to base predictions on past observations and give the greatest weight to the latest observations. It can be applied to determining the production of optimum lot sizes to meet forecasted sales.

Line of balance (LOB) was developed in industry and applied by the

Navy in World War II as a means of comparing achievement with scheduled performance. A chart indicates, on a calendar time basis, the number of units to be completed. Another chart shows progress and displays the planned and actual activity of a project at a given time. Finally, a production plan shows the activities to be performed in comparison with a time to completion.

Markov process, like regression analysis, is based on mathematical probability principles and combines objective fact and subjective judgment. The process has been used in market research, hospital planning, and realiability engineering.

Sensitivity analysis is used in connection with linear planning. In formulating and solving linear programming problems, one makes certain assumptions, at least initially. It is assumed that all values of the coefficients are derived from the analysis of data and that they represent average values or best-estimate values. Accordingly, the method is useful in analyzing the sensitivity of the solution to variation in the coefficients or estimates of the coefficients. Said differently, one seeks to determine the ranges of variations of the coefficients over which the solution will remain optimal. Sensitivity studies of this sort are known as parametric linear programming.

SCIENTIFIC METHODS AND THE INTERNAL AUDITOR

The Benefits

Quantitative analysis gives the internal auditor a chance to help himself and his organization's managers. He can help himself through the thoughtful use of statistical sampling and other quantitative techniques. He can help executives and managers by verifying the data used in scientific decision making, validating quantitative techniques, providing protection against the misuse of mathematical procedures to the detriment of his organization, and recommending appropriate techniques.

The modern internal auditor with a master's degree in business administration has a working knowledge of mathematical analysis. His work throughout the organization and his familiarity with the computer show him how to put that knowledge to practical use. And although he may be deficient in abstruse calculations, he knows where to turn for help and what questions to ask. He should not keep management in the dark about those qualifications. His combination of objectivity, independence, learning, and understanding can make him a powerful ally when the chips are down, and managers should learn to turn to him when the need arises.

Statistical Sampling

Audit Sampling

Auditors have for years sampled transactions instead of examining all of them. And from the sample results they have drawn conclusions about the population of interest to them: all the travel vouchers or shipping tickets or sales slips or receiving memos or purchase orders or canceled checks or requisitions for some specified period. The auditors knew that there was a risk in sampling, but they were willing to take the risk in deference to the shortness of life and the limit on funds an organization could afford for the examination of transactions. And so auditors would select some haphazard group or bundle of items and verify their validity.

The trouble was that the auditor could not measure the risk he took; he could not tell whether it was big or small. He could not defend his sample objectively; he could not demonstrate that it was a reasonable representation of the whole. True, he would try to reduce the risk by examining all expensive items and sampling the rest sparingly. But the large items are often given reviews by several levels of management, whereas the small ones, reviews of which are sparse, may be the very ones mishandled.

Mathematicians and statisticians, on becoming interested in auditing as a proper field for statistics, pointed out the errors of the auditor's ways. A haphazard groping for transactions was no guarantee of a representative sample. The auditor's simple "point projection" —if 10 percent of the sample is in error, then 10 percent of the population is in equal error—was just plain wrong. And, of extreme significance, the scientists demonstrated that the time-honored 10 percent sample could be woefully inadequate or ludicrously expensive. For example, under certain conditions of desired sample reliability, a population size of 50 will call for a sample size of 31 and a population of 100, only 50 items more, will call for a sample size of 46—50 percent more than the size of the sample for 50. *But* a population of 10,000, to have the same desired sample reliability, requires a sample of only 86 and a population of 500,000—50 times greater—calls for a sample of only 87.[6]

As auditors became more mathematically literate, as they learned to make use of the enormous capabilities of the computer, they turned more and more to the benefits offered by statistical sampling and learning various sampling plans and selection techniques. Some of the more useful plans are as follows:

Attributes Sampling

This plan provides information on "how many." It is concerned with yes or no, go or no-go results. It is used, for example, to estimate from a sample the number of purchase orders issued during a year without competitive bidding. It will not estimate the value of the orders issued without competitive bidding, merely the number of them. And it will not tell *why* competitive bids were not obtained. That must be tracked down by inquiry and verification.

Variables Sampling

The variables sampling plan provides information on "how much." It is most often used to produce an estimate in dollars. It can be used to estimate from a sample the dollar difference between book values and actual values of inventories. It is somewhat difficult to use, since sample sizes are dependent in part on the variability of the population. The more variable the population, the greater the difference in value between the lowest and the highest amounts of the items in the population, the larger the sample size to achieve the desired sample reliability. To measure that variability, auditors are required to compute the standard deviation of the sample and estimate the standard deviation of the population.

A relatively new form of dollar estimating goes under the various names of dollar unit sampling (DUS), cumulative money amount (CMA), and combined attributes variables (CAV). The dollar estimating plan, as the last description indicates, makes use of both attribute and variables sampling in estimating dollar values from a sample. Each dollar in a population is considered a sampling unit. A population of invoices totaling $1 million is considered to be made up of that number of units. If .1 percent of the population were to be examined, every thousandth dollar would be selected. Of course, if that dollar were "attached" to others in an invoice valued at $1,500, the entire invoice would be selected for examination. Proponents of the system argue that it provides greater sample reliability and insures the selection of all invoices over a given value. In the case just cited, since every thousandth dollar will be selected, every invoice valued at $1,000 or more would have to be examined.

Discovery Sampling

Sometimes called exploratory sampling, discovery sampling is used to identify, by a sample, at least one suspected item and to discontinue sampling when the item is located. Obviously, if there were only one suspected item in a population, the auditor would have to examine every single item to find it. But if he can stipulate some given number of suspected items—5, 10, 15, and so on—then he can select a sample that will give him some measurable assurance—90, 95, 98 percent, and so on, depending on the sample size—of finding at least one of the items in question.

Discovery sampling usually involves fairly large samples, and the hazard of overlooking an item demands high sample reliability. Its use is therefore restricted to areas of extreme risk to the organization: potential phantoms on the payroll, bank loans without collateral, duplicate payments, unauthorized shipment of goods, shipments not billed, and the like.

Stop-or-Go Sampling

Often an auditor may have used attributes sampling on populations that called for a large number of items to examine only to find, at the end of his toil, that the population could be considerd relatively error-free. As he looked back on his wasted energies, he wistfully wished he could have obtained some measurable assurance much earlier in the game. Stop-or-go sampling offers that objective measurement. He can start with a small sample of 40 or 50 items, no matter what the size of the population may be; and if he finds no errors or very few errors, he can discontinue sampling. He can state that he has objective assurance that there are no more than x percent of errors in the population at y percent of assurance.

If errors persist in surfacing, he can switch to attributes sampling, having lost no time by the stop-or-go exercise. An example would be to seek adequate assurance that misfiled accounts payable vouchers are fewer than some acceptable percent.

Judgment Sampling

Auditors often do not need objective, mathematical assurance of sample reliability. Indeed, a sample of a single item may satisfy an audit objective: If an auditor wishes to assure himself that a purported system is actually in effect, that all safeguards do in fact exist, he may conduct a "walk-through" of a selected item through the system to make sure that all the purported bases are there and that all were touched as the transaction flowed through the system.

On the other hand, one or two examples of misconduct may launch a "directed" sample search that pokes into suspected crannies and turns over specified rocks. No attempt will be made to attribute the sample results to the entire population. And therein lies the crux: Does the auditor need to attribute his sample results to the whole population? If he does not, judgment sampling, carried out in a reasonable fashion, may completely satisfy the audit objectives.

Acceptance Sampling

Acceptance sampling is widely used in industrial quality control work. It consists of selecting a sample from a given field. In practice, the selection is made from a lot of produced or purchased items in order to determine whether the lot contains more than a minimum number of unacceptable items. If the number of unacceptable items exceeds the minimum, the lot is rejected. If it does not, the lot is accepted. The method is largely numerical appraisal and does not provide for an estimate of the unacceptable items in the entire population. For that reason, acceptance sampling is not as useful to the internal auditor as the methods previously mentioned. Nevertheless, the internal auditor should be aware of acceptance sampling and the principles behind it so that he may evaluate the adequacy of the sampling systems used by quality control inspectors in their own tests.

Sample Selection

The six sampling plans we have just discussed tell the internal auditor how many items he needs for his sample, but he must use accepted sampling selection techniques to pick the sample items. Sample selection takes two forms: random and purposive.

Random sampling permits each item in a population to have an equal chance of being selected. It is completely unbiased; it is unaffected by personal preference. Purposive sampling, however, confirms a suspicion or probes a suspected area and is openly biased. Both techniques have their uses. For example, in an audit of accounts payable invoices, the auditor may take a random sample for the purpose of attributing sample results to population values. But then, because he may be suspicious of the work of one accounts payable clerk, he may take a purposeful or directed sample of that clerk's work.

Within the area of random samples, the auditor has several choices. Here are some of them:

Random-number tables are tables of randomized digits used to provide sample-item numbers. Random-number samples are rigorous and demonstrate complete lack of subjectivity when properly used. They can be used when numbers are assigned to the individual items. In some instances they are quite burdensome to use.

Interval sampling calls for the selection of every nth item after a random start. Interval sampling, or, as it is often called, systematic sampling, is usually easier to use than random-number tables. And if the auditor has satisfied himself that no items are missing from the population being tested, it can provide adequate assurance of random selection.

Stratified sampling helps divide the population into two or more strata or groups. Each group is then sampled or examined in its entirety. For example, accounts payable vouchers can be divided into two groups: high-value invoices and all others. The high-value invoices may then be examined completely, and the remainder may be randomly sampled. Stratification helps reduce the variability that so strongly affects the sample size needed to achieve the desired degree of sample reliability.

Cluster sampling is used when the location or filing of documents makes random-number or interval sampling burdensome or excessively expensive. It involves selecting clusters of documents and then sampling from the clusters—multistage sampling—or examining all the items in the clusters selected. All selections must be made at random. The clusters may be all the items processed during certain days, items filed in file drawers, or documents bound in bundles. The reliability of cluster sampling is generally lower than that of random-number and interval sampling, and the auditor may have to examine larger samples to make up for the lost reliability.

Sampling Cautions

To the auditor, statistical sampling is like quantitative analysis to the manager: a tool. It does not take the place of audit judgment. It simply provides the internal auditor with more reliable information. What he does with the information and how he uses it spells the difference between superior internal auditing and number juggling. In the following paragraphs we shall discuss some of the matters he must take into account in his sampling.

The internal auditor must know and fully comprehend the principles of statistical sampling. He must understand them well enough to be able to put them to proper use or to defend his decision not to use rigorous quantitative techniques. And, as we shall see later in this chapter, he must have enough command of the principles to point the finger at abortions of acceptable sampling techniques.

The evaluation of sample results calls for audit judgment, not sampling principles or computer technology. Carpenter's tools may be the same for two different people, but with them the tyro might build a lopsided table and a craftsman a masterpiece. Along with the numbers that he puts together statistically, the auditor must consider the system of internal control, the adequacy of management and supervision, and the quality of operating employees. He must analyze what happened, why it happened, and how the indicated conditions affect the organization. Finally, he must figure out what can be done to improve things if his sample indicates defects. He must be a management-oriented internal auditor first and a statistician second.

The internal auditor who is confident of his grasp of sampling principles will use random selection techniques when they are appropriate and employ directed, purposive sample selection when it best suits his audit purposes. He will know, however, that the results of a directed sample are not representative of the entire population. The directed sample gives a biased picture, the sort of thing that makes wise managers wary when eager assistants present "evidence" of a widespread malaise. Managers expect more objectivity from internal auditors than deliberately plucked examples.

It does not take a statistician to know that, when one is testing some population, he should have a pretty good understanding of what that population consists of. "Define your population" must be one of the cardinal rules of the auditor who embarks on a course of sampling. Will it be all the purchase orders for a year? Will it be just purchase orders valued over a given amount? Does the population exclude change orders? Does it exclude blanket orders stretching over several years? Does it exclude orders to foreign suppliers? Does it exclude subcontracts? Can the auditor be certain that no orders are missing from the population to be tested? In every sample selection, the auditor must identify to himself and to management precisely what he tested, because only to that population may he project his sample results.

An attributes sampling plan requires the auditor to make certain assumptions that are implicit in the formulas and the table used to determine the sizes of the sample to be used:

1. Confidence level: the degree of assurance desired that the projection of sample results will lie within a certain range. Confidence level is expressed as a percent—85, 95, 99 percent or some other degree of assurance.
2. Precision: the range within which the sample results will lie at the desired confidence level. It is expressed as plus or minus

some number or percent such as ±3 percent. Confidence level and precision are entwined. One cannot refer to one without mentioning the other.

3. Error rate: the estimated degree of error or other occurrence that exists in the population tested. The error rate is an estimate of variability in the population, and the greater the variability the larger the sample needed to provide representative results.

The auditor selects confidence level and precision to meet his requirements of sample reliability. The higher the confidence level and the narrower the range of precision the larger the sample size he will need. But that is a determination he must make to accomplish his audit objective.

Error rates, however, are conditions that the auditor believes exist in the population to be tested. If he underestimates the error rate, his sample will be too small and might not give a reliable representation of the population. If he overestimates the error rate, he may select too large a sample and thereby waste precious man-hours. Making the appropriate estimate calls for audit judgment in terms of the population under review. One gauge of the maximum error rates to be expected would be the point at which alarms would go off if the particular error rate were exceeded. For example, the error rate in a payroll could not possibly be very high without alerting the treasurer, the employees being paid, or the budget people.

Similarly, the auditor should not set needlessly high reliability goals. A reliability goal of 99 percent confidence level and ±1 percent precision calls for vastly greater sample size than for 90 percent confidence level and ±4 percent precision. For example, assuming a population of 10,000 and a 5 percent error rate, in the first instance the sample size would be 2,397; in the second it would be only 80. So the auditor will use his judgment. He will evaluate the system of internal control, the guidance and wisdom of the operating manager, the training and experience of the operating employees, and whatever fail-safe mechanisms management has constructed, and he will then stipulate reliability levels that are reasonable in the circumstances and not unnecessarily rigorous.

Whenever the internal auditor expects his sample results to be considered representative of the entire population, he must let each item in that population have an equal chance of being selected. Otherwise, the sample may not be considered randomly selected and the rules of statistical sampling will not apply. The fact that an individual item is difficult to locate or time-consuming to examine is no excuse for rejecting it and selecting another. The rules of statistical sampling are rigorous, and the auditor who does not play the game according to the rules may not proclaim that his results reasonably represent the population tested. Hence, neither personal bias nor population patterns must be permitted to violate the primary rule of statistical sampling: Every item must have an equal opportunity of being chosen for the sample.

Ratio, Change, and Trend Analysis

Applications

Where should the internal auditor put his powerful sampling tool to work? Where should he deploy his audit efforts? Like the manager, he must give priority to the areas of greatest hazard, but how is he to identify the areas? His long-range audit program will include the activities reasonably known to cause problems or those which, if uncontrolled, can result in serious losses. But what of the incipient sores that are not yet bleeding? How is he to identify them? How is he to offer his ministrations before the entity's blood flows in earnest?

Diagnostic techniques are available to perhaps identify ailments before they get too serious. They call for the analysis of certain indicators that point the internal auditor's nose in the right direction. They provide information of an overall nature on trends of important functions. The internal auditor might observe and analyze those matters during an audit of an operation. He is there, and he looks for all problems, actual and incipient. But his audits are intermittent. What about changes that occur between audits? What about matters not detected by the ordinary system of internal control? What about changes in programs, the aberrant conditions not included in normal tests, and the effect of external factors that are not internally controlled?

The analysis of financial data concerned with ratios, changes, and trends can be like a microscope in the hands of the competent internal auditor. It is designed to highlight what is abnormal, what is changing, and what appear to be unexpected variations. It is performed by critically examining the relations that exist between sets of financial and operating data either over periods of time or against some expected standards.

The internal auditor is alerted by unusual variations in ratios, unexpected changes, and abnormal trends. A ratio measures the relative magnitude of two related factors inside or outside an entity. The

changes that will interest the auditor are those that were not anticipated; the trends that concern him are those that do not follow an
expected pattern. Those indicators may help him recognize problems before they manifest themselves, are detected by management,
or are evident through inflicted damage. Recognizing and analyzing
a problem can go a long way toward solving it. There are three steps
in the analysis:

1. Selecting appropriate data.
2. Measuring changes and interrelations.
3. Evaluating the changes and interrelations and learning why
   they happened.

Every entity of any size has a host of such relations. Usually it is
not difficult to know what is considered normal or abnormal. That
information can be obtained internally from past experience with the
entity or externally by comparison with statistics available from various trade associations, the Small Business Administration, Dun and
Bradstreet, Robert Morris Associates, and others. Useful internal
data require just a little imagination to locate them. For example, the
use of packaging material should rise or fall in relation to the volume
of shipments. When unusual variations occur, there may be a need
to investigate.

External data are equally useful because they supply objective
standards not available internally. They are independent; and if they
are current, they may indicate experience during comparable
periods. Obviously, such information must be used with care. One
must account for different methods of computation, the nature of the
sources, varying policies, and the like. But when the differences are
accounted for, comparison of elements on a per unit basis can be useful. For example, the entity's cost to produce a unit may be $5 for
labor and $8 for material. Industry averages, however, may be $3 for
labor and $6 for material. Such variances warrant close investigation.

Variations are significant indicators. For example:

□ Relations between functions such as variances over time in the
relation of net profits to net sales or of cost of sales to inventories.
□ Lack of consistency between functions, such as increased scrap
sales but decreased production.
□ Differences in assumptions between management policy and actual practice, such as the amount of bonus payments for work at
foreign locations versus management's understanding of the

basis for such payments. For example, management may have been expecting reduced rates depending on the length of tour of duty whereas employees are paid continuing rates.

□ Variations from such standards as budgets and standard costs.

□ Changes over a series of periods in such ratios as net profits to net sales, miles traveled to fuel consumption, debt to interest expense, and sales to bad debt expense.

Comparisons can be made by relating elements to a totality or by company units.

Elements

The purpose here is to determine whether elements of some account or activity bear a reasonable relation to the totality. For example, each component of administrative expense must bear some reasonably consistent relation to the sum of all such expense. The auditor can measure current relations against past patterns and investigate significant differences.

Units

Unit costs can be useful in determining or establishing standards and analyzing variances. Some variances may be readily explained and may appear reasonable; others can point to problems. For example, changes in unit costs may be explained by material mix or by new methods of production. On the other hand, they may be caused by poorer material quality, increased rates of rejection, or inefficient production. Similarly, changes in labor unit cost may be caused by inefficiency, excessive machine downtime, or learning time.

Whatever variances he finds, the internal auditor must analyze them. Certainly, if management has already provided for a system of detecting and analyzing variances, the auditor need not reinvent the wheel. But he can determine whether the data used are valid and whether abnormal conditions were acted on. If management has not developed such a system, the auditor should recommend the practice as a regular, continuing tool. How much more valuable for managers to monitor their activities constantly than for the internal audi-' tor to do it intermittently. There is no substitute for self-control, and it is much more palatable than externally exercised control. The wise internal auditor will accompany his recommendation for a system of ratio, change, and trend analysis with a significant finding of such an analysis.

A great number of financial ratios are in common use; they include current ratios, current debt to net worth, working capital to sales, and cost of sales to inventory. Some that may be of particular use to internal auditors are the following:

The *sales to inventory ratio* could point up too little inventory to support a given level of sales or increased inventory accompanied by reduced sales.

The *average collection period* can be a good measure of the effectiveness of an entity's collection policy. The internal auditor can compare his findings with industry ratios to determine the reasonableness of collection policies and practices. A useful ratio can be computed by:

□ Dividing net credit sales by 365 to obtain average daily credit sales.

□ Dividing trade notes and accounts receivable, including those discounted, by the average daily credit sales.

□ Comparing the two results.

The *net income per unit of service ratio* offers a measure of profit per unit of available capacity: per room in hotels, per bed in hospitals, per ton-mile for trucks, per passenger mile for aircraft, per sales clerk in department stores, and per production worker in factories.

The *commissions to sales ratio* is a measure of an important cost of distribution. In the Equity Funding case, such a measure might have shown a sharp increase in "sales" without a corresponding increase in salesmen's commissions, since many of the "sales" were fictitious and did not involve the use of the sales force.

The *bad debts to sales ratio* is a measure of how good a job the credit department is doing—whether it is constant, improving, or deteriorating.

The *sales expenses to sales ratio* is a measure of the cost of the selling effort. It may point to an inefficient deployment of sales effort—continuing to cover areas or customers that produce too low a level of sales results.

We have provided only a brief overview of the value of ratio, change, and trend analysis to both internal auditors and managers. More detailed information can be found in available literature.[7]

Assisting the Executive

The Problem-solving Partner

The expansion in use of quantitative techniques has had its effect. Executives and managers with strong mathematical backgrounds take operations research problems in comparatively easy stride. They evaluate proposals based on quantitative techniques and can knowledgeably accept or reject them. Others are hoist on the horns of a dilemma: "I am faced by a technique that may well have great potential. It might save me money. But it's complicated and mathematical, and I don't understand it. Shall I reject it? I might lose out on something valuable. Should I accept it without understanding its inner workings? That goes against my grain, and I might live to regret it!"

The knowledgeable internal auditor can be a valued ally in such circumstances. He is objective; he has no axe to grind; he has proved his reliability. Many a manager in circumstances of doubt has turned to the internal auditor for assistance in having his doubts resolved. An actual example, cited in connection with decision making in Chapter 5, has equal applicability here and is repeated for the convenience of the reader:

A budget manager presented to the chief financial officer a way of improving forward pricing on products. The method involved the use of multiple-regression analysis and the computer. The chief officer was in a quandary. The budget manager was persuasive, but the officer was unable personally to validate the proposed system.

He therefore called on his internal auditors and asked for an opinion. The auditor assigned to the task doubted whether a detailed verification of the formulas and the EDP program would offer adequate assurance of the program's reliability or convince the executive. A search through the literature, however, provided him with two comparable problems that had already been solved through standard computer programs employing regression analysis.[8]

He provided the budget manager with the input data. The purpose was to see whether the manager's program would produce the precise answers found in the literature. The auditor observed the entry of the data into the computer and received a copy of the resulting readout. The answers so obtained disagreed with what was expected.

The manager reanalyzed his formula and EDP program and found an error that was responsible for the variances. With the error corrected, the multiple-regression program was successfully put to work.

The internal auditor can be a stout champion when his organization is under attack by other auditors. Two actual examples are illustrated. One involves statistical sampling, and the other involves ratio delay studies.

Statistical Sampling Study

Government auditors analyzed travel expenses of a company by means of statistical sampling. Travel vouchers were selected at random and examined. The differences between what had been recorded and what the government auditors considered allowable for the sample vouchers were then projected to the total population. The resulting extrapolation, reported as "overcharges," amounted to several hundred thousand dollars.

The government auditors issued a report to the company's financial officer setting forth the overcharges and asking for appropriate adjustments. The amounts involved were so large that the financial officer asked the company's internal auditors to review the statistical sampling methodology used.

The internal auditors met with the government auditors and were given an opportunity to review the working papers and the computer programs on which the requests for adjustment were based.

The internal auditor was able to point out some fatal defects in the sampling methods—violations of basic statistical sampling techniques. For example, the sample of travel vouchers were selected from those involving local travel only. Yet the extrapolation covered both local and foreign travel. The selection technique, therefore, did not permit each item an equal chance of selection. Other errors involved consistency of selection methods and were abundantly demonstrated. As a result, adjustments were made only for the expense vouchers actually examined and not for the amount originally claimed.

Ratio Delay Study

A team of government auditors performed a ratio delay study, also called work sampling, in five clerical departments of a company doing work for a government agency. Following a two-week study, the government auditors charged the company with significant "nonproductivity" in those departments. They projected the difference between observed activity and "acceptable" activity and computed estimated costs that could have been avoided for the year by less nonproductivity or idleness. The company's chief financial officer called upon the internal auditors for assistance in dealing with the government auditors' allegations.

Ratio delay studies employ a random sampling method of obtaining information about human and machine activities. They use random observations of individuals at work to determine the ratio of avoidable delays to total available working hours. The studies are based on the laws of probability and therefore rely on the principles of randomization and sampling reliability.

Reviews were made by two-man teams of observers entering the areas under examination at moments during the day that had been randomly selected. Also randomly selected were the names of the employees to be observed. Based solely on observation, the government auditors judged whether activity was (1) avoidably nonproductive (idleness), (2) unavoidably nonproductive, or (3) productive.

The observations for a two-week period were summarized and charted by the least-squares method. The charts displayed curves that rose sharply and then gradually leveled off. The charts portrayed early low points (little or no nonproductivity) that indicated the workers were fully aware of the presence of the observers, and then the line would rise to indicate greater degrees of nonproductivity as the workers became accustomed and indifferent to the observers.

The curve would then approach a straight line, termed the asymptote, which was supposed to project from the findings the "normal" level of inactivity in the department being observed. The information was analyzed by using General Electric's CURFIT time-sharing computer program. Data points represented the number of observed nonproductive activities divided by the number of observation periods in the sample for a day. CURFIT takes a set of data points and determines by the least-squares method how well they can be described with six types of algebraic equations (curves). Above each curve, the straight-line asymptote represents the value that the equation (curve) would reach if the number of observations were infinite.

The government auditors regarded the asymptote as representing the true level of nonproductivity. They had determined that 11 percent inactivity for the day was acceptable and that any amount over that point was not. After comparing the charts with the arbitrary 11 percent acceptable percent of nonproductivity, the difference, considered avoidable, was extrapolated to a full year. An example of one of the curves is as shown in Figure 3. The asymptote to the curve is 23 percent—12 percent above the standard of 11 percent. The extrapolation, running about a half a million dollars for the five departments, sent a chill through the company's executives, as could well be expected. And the failure to respond knowledgeably and convincingly to the charges could be a serious blow to the company's standing with government contract officers and adversely affect negotiations for future contracts.

The company's internal auditors reviewed the work performed by the government auditors and provided the information needed both to blunt the government's attack and to soften the government auditors' reports. Here are some of the arguments.

□ The two-week sample was not representative of the one-year population of activity. People tended to transfer frequently. Work tended to

Figure 3. Projected rate of nonproductivity (asymptote = 23%).

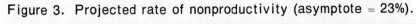
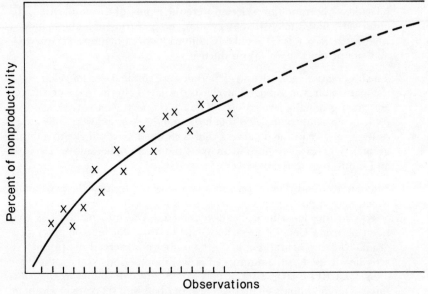

Observations

change. Seasonal cycles have a significant effect. Hence, every unit in
such a shifting population does not have an equal chance of being selected.

□ The government auditors subjectively selected one of the six CURFIT
curves that they considered most appropriate to their contentions, not
necessarily the one that was kindest to the company.

□ There is a considerable body of scientific opinion to the effect that
there is not necessarily a relation between the accuracy of a curve based
on past observations and the reliability of the curve for purposes of
forecasting.[9]

□ The standard of 11 percent selected by the government auditors was at
variance with criteria shown in respected publications on the subject.
For example, *The Management Services Handbook,* published by The
American Institute of CPAs Inc., indicates a level of 20 percent or less
is acceptable. That is in agreement with a similar percent shown in
Rober Lee Morrow's *Motion Economy and Work Measurement* (The Ronald Press, New York.)

□ Insufficient observations had been made to produce reliable curves.
Some of the rejected curves gyrated so wildly, because of too few observations, as to be meaningless. Those selected may have achieved their
form by happenstance.

□ The most serious indictment of the government report was the emphasis on numbers instead of activities. Ratio delay studies can be
helpful when they point to specific defects in operations or supervision

that management can deal with: people arriving late for work and leaving early, extended breaks, reading newspapers or magazines during working hours, lack of adequate facilities, and supervisors not knowing what their people are doing or where they are. The numbers alone— the percents and the unsupportable extrapolations—give irritation without offering causes of corrective action. A manager can do something about identified conduct, but projections of hundreds of thousands of dollars are usually meaningless in terms of correcting conditions. Statistics merely indicate the potential existence of a problem; they do not define it. In the situation just illustrated, the internal auditor's analysis of the work sampling study resulted in a revised government report that was much less damaging.

The internal auditor can be a useful partner to managers in assessing and interpreting statistics. The statistical tool is powerful, but it is still only a tool. The hand that wields it must be skillful, and the mind behind the hand must provide understanding.

CONCLUSION

Quantitative analysis—operations research—can be extremely useful when a manager is fully aware of its benefits and shortcomings. The knowledge and skill of the mathematician can help the manager reach his goals so long as the manager knows what his goals are and retains control over the scientific effort. Scientific method can test managers' assumptions, provide answers to what-if questions in mathematical terms, and present managers with alternatives. But the managers must ask the right questions and ultimately make the decisions.

Probability theory and statistical sampling can be powerful instruments in the hands of knowledgeable internal auditors. But they are a means to an end and not the end itself. The internal auditor must understand the techniques, but he is not obliged to use them exclusively. He can be a formidable ally to managers who are faced with mathematical problems beyond their ken, and he can provide a stout defense when the management sciences are improperly used against the manager.

References

1. C. W. Churchman, R. L. Ackoff, and E. L. Arnoff, *Introduction to Operations Research* (New York: Wiley, 1957).

D. W. Miller and M. K. Starr, *Executive Decisions and Operations Research* (Englewood Cliffs, N.J.: Prentice-Hall, 1965).

F. S. Hillier and G. S. Lieberman, *Operations Research,* 2nd ed. (San Francisco: Holden-Day, Inc., 1967).

H. M. Wagner, *Principles of Operations Research with Applications to Managerial Decisions* (Englewood Cliffs, N.J.: Prentice-Hall, 1969).

R. I. Levin and C. A. Kirkpatrick, *Quantitative Approaches to Management* (New York: McGraw-Hill, 1971).

J. S. Hammond III, "Do's and Don'ts of Computer Models for Planning," *Harvard Business Review,* Vol. 52, No. 1, pp. 110–123.

D. A. Heenan and R. B. Addleman, "Quantitative Techniques for Today's Decision Makers," *Harvard Business Review,* Vol. 54, No. 3, pp. 32–62.

2. R. V. Brown, "Do Managers Find Decision Theory Useful?" *Harvard Business Review,* Vol. 48, No. 3, pp. 81–83.

3. "The Answer: Linear Programming," *Business Week,* March 12, 1955, pp. 43–44.

4. "Internal Audit of Inventory Control and Management," *Research Committee Report No. 16* (New York: The Institute of Internal Auditors, 1970).

5. H. F. Evarts, *Introduction to PERT* (Boston: Allyn & Bacon, 1964).

   K. G. Lockyer, *An Introduction to Critical Path Analysis* (London: Pitman, 1967).

   J. J. Moder and C. R. Phillips, *Project Management with CPM and PERT,* 2nd ed. (New York: Van Nostrand Reinhold, 1970).

6. *Sampling Manual for Auditors,* Table A.3, published 1967 by The Institute of Internal Auditors, Inc., with the permission of the copyright owner, Lockheed Aircraft Corporation.

7. R. A. Foulke, *Practical Financial Statement Analysis* (New York: McGraw-Hill, 1968).

   L. A. Bernstein, "Ratio, Change and Trend Analysis as an Audit Tool," *The Journal of Accountancy,* September 1964, pp. 51–55.

   B. G. King, "Cost-Effectiveness Analysis: Implications for Accountants," *The Journal of Accountancy,* March 1970, pp. 43–49.

   J. M. Forsberg, "Forecasting and Trend Analysis," in R. F. Vancil, ed., *Financial Executive's Handbook* (Homewood, Ill.: Dow Jones–Irwin, 1970), pp. 402–416.

8. C. H. Springer, R. E. Herlihy, R. T. Mall, and R. I. Beggs, *Statistical Inference* (Homewood, Ill.: Irwin, 1966), pp. 44–57.

9. Henry Schultz, "The Standard Error of a Forecast from a Curve," *Journal of the American Statistical Association,* Vol. 25, No. 170, pp. 139–185.

PART III

The Process
of Management

Managers are responsible for planning the entity's destiny, organizing its resources to carry out those plans, directing its people and other resources toward the planned objectives, and controlling activities so that goals are met efficiently, economically, and effectively.

Internal auditors are responsible for seeing that managers are provided with current, accurate, and meaningful information that will assist them in carrying out their responsibilities.

9

Planning

Planning, the primary function. A modern development. What should the business be? Planning and improved performance. Planning versus forecasting. Strategic and tactical plans. The characteristics of planning. The patterns of strategic planning. The planning steps. Objectives: the primal directive. The three objectives of a business. Limiting factors. Premises: forecasting the future. The three types of premises. Data for forecasters. Principles. Policies. Procedures. Rules. Methods. Standards. Technofactors. Budgets. Participation in planning. The internal auditor's involvement in planning. Auditing the centralized planning function. Objectives and internal auditing. Defective planning mechanisms. Auditing planning in operating activities. Testing objectives. Standards for planning. Helping managers achieve change. Monitoring plans. Checking for compliance. Checking for the adequacy of procedures. Methods for improving methods. Auditing budgets. Budgets and people. A dearth of budget auditing.

PLANNING AND THE MANAGER

Nature of Planning

Definition and Purpose

Among the four functions of management, planning is primary. A manager cannot successfully organize or direct or control if he has

243

not carefully planned. As the old carpenter said: Measure twice and cut once.

Planning, like decision making, is the selection of a course of action from among various possible choices. The selection will be subject to certain premises that must be stated or predicted by the planner and to certain constraints that may be imposed by the environment. Hence, planning is future-oriented.

Logical as the need for it may be, planning is a comparatively modern development. Frederick Taylor laid great stress on it, but before World War II what planning was done was fragmented and poorly coordinated throughout the enterprise. Now many companies use comprehensive corporate planning and regularly create long-range as well as short-range plans.

A significant aspect of the revolution in management thinking is the increased interest in planning, the desire to bridge the gap between where we are and where we want to be. Many modern managers began deciding, well in advance of action, what to do, when to do it, how to do it, and who is to do it. They came to the realization that, with well-constructed plans, they could make things happen that might not otherwise happen or they could identify and forestall potential troubles. So the function partakes both of planning and controlling. When management sets forth desired ends, it uses the plans as a standard. When it uses the standards to ensure and measure accomplishment, it is controlling.

The future is ever uncertain, but managers must cope with uncertainties to achieve their ends. Plans therefore seek to minimize uncertainty and deal with the changes that the future is bound to bring. Planning focuses management's attention on objectives. Indeed, managers have no target to shoot at until they have decided on the objectives they must meet. But by coordinating the objectives and plans of components within the organization, managers can gain more economical operations through the elimination of redundancies and overlaps.

Planning takes time. It is a difficult mental exercise, and many managers find the intellectual process frustrating and constricting. It is no panacea, because it cannot predict the future with certainty, but it has many more pluses than minuses. It forces managers to think through what they must do to reach their goals: try to resolve uncertainties, determine relations between themselves and others in the oganization, allocate the ever-scarce resources available to them, set priorities, and, if nothing else, realize the need for lead time to gather together the means to get the job done.

At the higher levels of management, where overall strategy is framed, the planners must make the most important planning decision of all: What should our business be? Not what is it or what was it, but what must it be to survive? That kind of planning takes into account the one certainty: Things will be different. Thus the central purpose of planning is to see that the mistakes of the past will not continue into the future. The uncertainties cannot be precisely predicted, but some of them can be reduced to alternative courses of action.

Advantages

Planning has the chief advantage of giving purpose and orderliness to an organization's activities. In one company surveyed, a brilliant manager was serene in his confidence that he could resolve problems as they occurred. He was master of his fate, and he could bend circumstances to fit his will. So he planned little and instead spent his time supervising his ongoing projects. Those projects, by dint of prodigious personal efforts and exhortations, met their schedules, but his subordinate managers transferred to other areas at every opportunity.

A revealing study that validates the advantage of planning involved 36 firms representing 6 industrial groups. Of the 36 only 17 were found to have formal long-range plans. The results achieved by firms with formal plans were compared with the results of firms employing informal plans. In each case, the formal planners significantly outperformed the others in terms of earnings per share and earnings on total capital employed. And then, to confirm the findings, comparisons were made in the planning companies between performance before and after each company began its formal long-range planning. The favorable comparisons for the firms which used formal planning held true.[1]

Whenever the planner encourages advice from subordinates, he helps both them and himself. Cooperative planning motivates the subordinates to achieve by participating in and becoming committed to the plan. And it is a self-imposed and valuable check on the wise executive. Gardner has said:[2]

> Individuals who hold the reins of power in any enterprise cannot trust themselves to be adequately self-critical. For those in power the danger of self-deception is very great, the danger of failing to see the problems or refusing to see them is ever-present. And the only protection is to create an atmosphere in which anyone can speak up.

Among the less obvious advantages of planning is the process itself. It forces managers to look ahead and to seek out the need for change, to see more than one side by posing the what-if questions, to encourage achievement by setting goals, to encourage the broad view by seeking to fill the organization's needs, to balance the use of facilities by assigning priorities, and to help managers gain status by participating in an executive function.

Characteristics

Planning is not forecasting. Actually, it is simply because we are unable to forecast with sufficient reliability that planning is needed. Planning makes use of forecasts because the plans will be carried out in an uncertain future. But despite the uncertainty some position about the future must be taken. That position is the forecast; it is not a plan.

A forecast is objective and passive; it describes anticipated conditions over which the manager has no control. Planning is subjective and active; it declares an intention to take steps to do something that is under management control. Forecasts are often taken from open, available information; plans are usually proprietary to the organization that makes them. The forecast rejects uncertainty by taking a definite position; plans accept uncertainty by taking a middle course of action and hedging against adverse conditions. And, a major difference, forecasts are mechanically constructed from detail; plans are oriented toward a goal and the details are filled in afterward.

All planning can be characterized as strategic or tactical. The strategic plans are long-range. They are concerned with broad and fundamental issues; they peer beyond the horizon, and they pervade the entire organization. Tactical planning is short-range. It is primarily concerned with the most efficient use of available or allotted resources.

The longer the time element, the more strategic the plan. Usually, long-range plans are over 5 years; anything over 20 years is considered infinity. But that does not mean one cannot plan beyond that time. The tree that will not be cut for 90 years is part of a long-range planning program that starts today.

All plans, strategic and tactical, have common characteristics:

□ The plan is not a mere wish; it is a specific course of action tied to identifiable products, organizations, and individuals.
   Example
   Specific people in the marketing department will mount an advertising campaign for product Y.

□ A plan deals with action in the future on a decision made today. We will allocate $x of resources to the advertising program.

□ Plans must be carried out in conditions of relative certainty or uncertainty.

Example

Production planning of specific products can be done with relative certainty. But the plan to increase the distribution of product Y by penetrating a new market is fraught with uncertainty.

□ Planning is intellectual. It calls for imagination, thought, creativity, and foresight. Useful plans cannot be constructed solely from the debris of the past.

Example

Novel and innovative means will be needed to interest the public in product Y.

□ Planning involves all managers, and it never ends. It permeates all levels of the organization, and it must go on all the time. Plans are future-oriented, so they are essentially tentative, because the conditions planned for may not come to pass. Hence the plans must be constantly monitored and reappraised.

Example

Marketing, sales, engineering, production, finance, accounting, and personnel are involved in the plans for product Y. And the plans will be subject to change based on such factors as the public's acceptance or rejection of the marketing program and the availability of money, men, and materials.

Strategic planning practice generally follows three different patterns:[3]

"Satisficing." Stay with the status quo. Don't break with the past. It is more important to survive than to grow.

"Optimizing." Do as well as possible. Optimum plans are not always carried out, but one can try to get close. And the effort to achieve the best can yield valuable byproducts of information for future projects.

"Adaptivizing." Adapt operations to accommodate short- and long-range plans. For example, a company may have a cyclical demand that causes peaks and valleys of employment in the manufacture of its product. It might develop a long-range plan for another cyclical product whose valleys coincide with the first product's peaks.

Two other characteristics of strategic planning are flexibility and "suboptimization." Flexibility calls for plans that can change directions. The ability to switch must be built into the plan, and sometimes it can cost more in the short run to achieve savings in the long run. An example is spending more for movable partitions to cut the cost of relocating fixed partitions later.

Suboptimization requires trade-offs between competing groups. For example, sales and credit have different goals. Sales wants to sell all it can to whomever will buy. Credit will refuse to allow sales to marginal customers. Overall plans must coordinate the conflicting goals.

Steps in Planning

The steps in planning approximate those in decision making, since both processes involve a selection from among alternatives. And, as in decision making, extended analyses for minor plans are not cost-effective. But it is also not cost-effective to make sketchy analyses for plans involving heavy investments of men, money, and materials. Here are some of the steps toward successful planning:

Resources. Determine the resources available or attainable to carry out the plans: money, people, property, materials, equipment, and managers. When needed resources are neither on hand nor available, plans based on those resources are unachievable dreams.

Environment. Determine the environments—external and internal—in which the plans must be implemented. If they are hostile to the plans and there is no way of making them friendly, the plans have no chance of being carried out.

Opportunities. Evaluate resources and environment in relation to the opportunities available so as to produce the best fit of all three. At the same time, analyze problems that may affect plans to determine whether an apparently insurmountable difficulty can be an opportunity to produce an innovative, profitable result. For example, the need to reduce pollution can be transformed into an opportunity to reclaim chemicals whose value may exceed the cost of pollution reduction.

Objectives. Determine the aims, purposes, and goals of the enterprise when setting all objectives, both long- and short-range. Objectives are the foundation stones on which all plans rest. The short-range plans must contribute to the long-range plans. Thus, subordinates who develop subsidiary plans must have a sound understanding of enterprise objectives. And executive management is charged with the responsibility for meshing long- and short-range objectives. Inconsistent objectives can be disastrous. After World War II, Montgomery Ward's long-range objective was to enhance profitability. But Sewell Avery's short-range decision to curtail expansion frustrated profit enhancement and put Montgomery Ward far behind its more adventuresome rival, Sears, Roebuck. Objectives will be discussed more fully later in this chapter.

Premises. The premises are set at the highest level of management. They are the assumptions that form a framework around which estimated events that affect the plans are expected to take place. Everyone in the enterprise must use the same framework or the major and subsidiary plans may be uncoordinated. For example, if different units within an organization project widely varying inflation rates, the results may be a confused jumble of inconsistent plans. Premises also will be discussed later in this chapter.

Alternatives. Search for alternative plans. Every plan has alternatives. Often the problem lies less in listing the alternatives than in reducing the number so that only the mot promising alternatives will be analyzed. And the obvious plan is not necessarily the one to select. Often the least obvious plan is the best.

Evaluation. Weigh the various factors affecting each alternative. Each plan has its offsetting characteristics. An apparently profitable course may demand large cash outlays and promise slow payback. Another may be less profitable but also less risky.

Important to the evaluation is the period of fulfillment. The plan must take into account the day of accomplishment. If a program of three years calls for plant facilities, the cost should be written off within that time. The plan is for the future, but the decision must be made now. So if fluctuations are anticipated, some flexibility will have to be incorporated into the long-range plan. A plant to produce a single product may have to be made capable of producing other products as well if it is possible that the first product may not meet public acceptance.

Selection. After all reasonable evaluations have been made, the appropriate alternative must be selected. When the future holds threats, one or more of the discarded alternatives may have to be kept in inventory as a possible replacement.

Derivatives. Once the major plan has been developed, lay subsidiary plans. The plan to go ahead with a new product calls for subsidiary plans to hire, transfer, and train employees, design tooling, procure materials, and market the finished product. Each department's derivative plans must be put under the microscope to see whether they contribute to the established objectives and are compatible with other plans. If ten departments intend to spend $5 million and only $3 million is available, some adjustments will have to be made.

Control. Formulate the means of control, the reports, and the feedback needed to provide information on how well the plans are being carried out. Managers must be kept aware of progress, accomplishment, and roadblocks so as to receive current information on the progress of plans. Managers must be in a position to restructure plans that are not achieving the objectives.

Pretesting. Because past history is often wrong, inapplicable, or improperly interpreted, the plan should be tested before it is put into operation. Simulation techniques have been successful for the purpose. Given a known result, determine how well the plan would handle the past situation.

By and large, the easiest part of the planning process is the selection from available alternatives. What is truly difficult, what requires the genius of a master planner, is the honing of objectives, the shrewd selection of premises, and the communication of both premises and objectives to the people in the organization who must carry out the plans.

Objectives

Purpose

The health and survival of a company or an industry can hang upon the objectives the leaders formulate. Nothing is more important. In the 1960s Detroit saw the influx of small foreign cars, yet it failed to modify its objectives. An erosion of the American automobile market by a flood of small foreign cars was the result.

Objectives precede programs, policies, and all other management decisions. Thus they must be clear and they must make sense to the people in the enterprise. If they do not impel commitment, they may not be achieved. The student who is not truly committed to a college education may be sidetracked by a well-paying but dead-end job.

Objectives can motivate people. When they are moved by purposes that seize their imagination and understand their part in making the purposes come to pass, they become involved and committed. Their commitment to an objective can transcend their commitment to a job. A job is a means; the objectives set a goal. People often confuse the two; and when conditions change, they mindlessly keep following the book without knowing why it was written.

Similarly, many people follow the false grail of optimizing profits as the primary purpose of their business. There may be periods in an organization's existence when current profits must be subordinated to long-term aims. The major objectives of an organization are the fundamental standards by which the organization is judged. Optimizing profits is not a satisfactory constant. The true objective of the productive organization must take into account the employees and the social structure within which the organization functions. So the organization's three main objectives are:

1. To create something of economic value to a customer. No organization has a reason for being unless it can create customers and products of value for those customers.
2. To survive and to grow. Profits are needed to achieve the objectives; but the profits should be sufficient, not necessarily optimal.
3. To create values that are desired by the members of the organization. An organization is the sum total of its people, whose needs must be considered and satisfied if they are to make the organization grow.

Threading through the tapestry of key objectives is the central theme of what the business should be. Is SCM in the business of distributing typewriters or word makers? The typewriter need not be the only means of putting words before a reader's eyes or ideas into a hearer's mind. That fundamental determination points the way to desirable objectives and the goals that must be set to meet them.

- □ Is the business of the university to educate or to perform research?
- □ Is the business of a prison confinement or rehabilitation?
- □ Is the business of a church religion or social relationships?
- □ Is the business of a medical school training medical students or carrying on basic research?

Development

The development of objectives and subobjectives (goals) calls for the following steps:

- □ To develop strategy—the purpose of the organization.
- □ To determine broad objectives.
- □ To set goals that are designed to meet the objectives and are measurable.
- □ To make the objectives and goals operative by communicating them to the people who will achieve them.

Goal setting is made difficult by conflicting demands upon the organization: the demands of stockholders, society, customers, employees, government, and financial institutions.

□ The goal for higher wages for employees conflicts with the goal of higher return for stockholders.
□ The goal of higher production may conflict with society's needs for less pollution.
□ The commitment of more resources to research and development may paint a poorer picture to financial institutions.

An ever-present problem is to reconcile social demands and profit needs. The social needs cannot be ignored. If they are, the business may be visited with hostile action from activist groups and from the government itself. Management's social responsibilities are being felt more keenly with the passing years. But enlightened, innovative management can answer the needs of both society and its stockholders. Dow Chemical spent millions on antipollution, but it was able to consider pollution to be a wasted resource. In some of its plants it was able to recover enough chemicals to balance the cost of pollution abatement.

Ethical questions influence objectives; management cannot turn its back on the spiritual values of the culture. Many companies live in a fishbowl under the penetrating searchlight of the press. They cannot afford to let the water get murky. As a result, codes of ethics have been established by some groups to offer guides for business behavior.

What evolves is that no system is completely rational. None is completely controllable or predictable. Every organization in setting objectives and viewing interrelations must recognize that it floats in a sea of constraints and limiting factors.

Constraints.

The government imposes limitations on activities in restraint of trade through the Sherman Anti-Trust Act of 1890, which was followed by the Clayton Act of 1913, the creation of the Federal Trade Commission in 1914, and the Robinson-Patman Act of 1936. In the field of labor, constraints are imposed by the Wagner Act of 1935, the Fair Labor Standards Act of 1938, and the Taft-Hartley Act of 1947. In the field of commerce, constraints are imposed by the Securities and Exchange Commission, the Interstate Commerce Commission, and the Federal Communications Commission.

Limiting factors within the organization can frustrate the setting or accomplishment of objectives. They are in a constant state of flux and can change as objectives are set and the planning process moves on. In 1945, the General Electric Company mounted a large expansion program. Its primary objective related to such matters as organizational structure and production facilities. But other factors, not immediately apparent, made themselves felt. GE's Ralph Cordiner said: "Not customers, not products, not money, but managers may be the limit on GE's growth."[4]

The constraining interrelations and limiting factors, troublesome as they are, do not argue against planning and the setting of objectives. Rather, they show what the intelligent manager must consider as he lays his plans. And they will affect management's commitments to its objectives.

Management commitments to objectives vary. Some may be deep-seated and thoroughly supported; others may be lip service. Management's dedication to its objectives can usually be discerned by its allocation of resources. If it puts its money where its mouth is, the objective is real. But if, for example, it vociferously espouses an expanded safety program but reduces its staff of safety engineers, the program and its safety-directed objectives can be considered suspect.

Premises

Purpose

A plan is as good as its premises. A meticulously well-thought-out plan for a picnic that fails to take into account a forecast that rain is a 95 percent probability is a futile exercise. Premises are predictions. The longer the plan the less certain the predictions, but premises must still be established.

In one case a company president, imbued with the spirit of cooperation, decided that planning must begin at the bottom. Accordingly, he asked his subordinates for budgets, but he provided them with no premises. And when he received the departmental budgets, they were so inconsistent that it was impossible to put them together. Had he understood the importance of premises, he would not have asked for budgets without providing guidelines.[5]

Executive management must describe its premises explicitly; it must state what conditions or predicted uncertainties will affect the plans to be established.

Types

Premises fall into three basic types:

- Environmental. These deal with the economy, society, and the government.
- Competitive. These are concerned with such matters as the enterprise's future, the plans of its competitors, its anticipated share of the market, its projected return on investment, its new products and patterns of marketing, and its dedication to research and development.
- Internal. These identify the organization's strengths and weaknesses, its resources, the cost of its information, its productivity, its manpower and management, and its standing with its customers and in the community.

Environmental factors, particularly public policy, strongly affect planning and the premises for plans. Questions on which positions must be taken include these:

- Will the government be friendly or unfriendly to the field in which the enterprise functions?
- Are prices likely to be controlled?
- What government agencies affect the enterprise's operations and which of their rulings impinge on the plans?
- How much has the government budgeted for products sold by the enterprise?
- What changes in fiscal and monetary policies are likely?
- What new tax legislation is in the offing?
- What sort of investment tax credit will be available?

No business can live as in a walled city, protected from the outside. The competitive factors have a strong impact on the positions that planners must take. For example:

- Are competitors coming out with an improved or new product?
- On the other hand, does competitive weakness provide opportunities that should be seized?
- What is the projected market for raw materials and labor?
- What is the trend in labor rates?
- What is the expected population trend or the shift from urban to suburban living?

Among internal premises, perhaps the most important is the sales forecast. It becomes the official position of the organization. It is the basis for all the other forecasts in the business; on it are built production schedules, inventory and purchasing plans, personnel requirements, additional production facilities, and financial requirements. Once the sales forecasts are disseminated as premises by executive management, then forecasts and estimates can be prepared by the people responsible for production planning, engineering, industrial relations, accounting, finance, and marketing.

Sales forecasting methods generally divide as follows:

□ The jury of executive opinion—meetings and discussions at the top-management level; trading guesses about the future.
□ The sales force composite—obtaining input from members of the sales force.
□ Users' expectations—polling customers for their anticipated needs or unmet wants.
□ Statistical methods—using such techniques as trend cycle analysis (projections from historical sales data), correlation analysis (relations between sales and other economic and noneconomic phenomena), and mathematical models.

A considerable body of information, statistical and economic, is available to get the forecaster started. For example, *The Financial Executive's Handbook* lists many sources of statistics and information that can be useful in preparing forecasts and developing premises.[6]

The Subplans

Planning and plans are generally associated with broad objectives, programs, and projects. But under the wide umbrella of plans are the various subplans that translate, dissect, and communicate the organization's major plans for its managers and employees. They are the guidelines that lead operating people toward the aims and purposes of the enterprise. They subdivide from the general and conceptual to the specific and concrete.

Policies are regarded as being the apex of the pyramid of subordinate plans and guidelines within an organization, but policies are most likely to endure if they resemble fundamental principles. Hence the hierarchy of subplans starts with principles and goes on from there to policies, procedures, rules, methods, standards, technofactors, and programs. Illustrations of how some of these subplans carry out a major plan are as follows:

□ *Principle.* Ethical dealing with others is an obligation an organization owes to society.

□ *Policy.* Our employees are not to be financially interested in our company's suppliers.

□ *Program.* A conflict-of-interest program has been established to carry out this policy.

□ *Procedure.* A specified series of steps are to be followed to provide information about dealings with suppliers and potential conflicts of interest.

□ *Rule.* Any buyer who accepts a bribe or kickback from a supplier shall be summarily dismissed.

□ *Method.* The facts about any employee reporting a potential conflict shall be reviewed by the employee's superior, reported to the legal department for recommendation, and ruled on by the executive committee.

□ *Standard.* An employee shall not accept Christmas gifts from suppliers that exceed $5 in value.

Principles

Principles are general or fundamental truths. They are basic laws, doctrines, or assumptions on which other laws, doctrines, and assumptions are based or from which they are derived. They govern life and human behavior. And when policies, procedures, and rules are based on accepted principles, they have a greater chance of being accepted by operating people. A policy based on the principle of fair dealing will receive better general acceptance than one based on chicanery. In formulating policy, therefore, the policy maker should state the policy in such a way that it accords with principles acceptable in the community.

Of course, policies may have to be set in areas where the fundamental truth is unknown and where a principle has not been enunciated, approved, and accepted. In such situations the policy maker must rely on business judgment and intuition. Policies still must be formulated to provide direction and achieve uniformity even though an underlying principle is absent.

Policies

A policy is a basic statement tht serves to guide the action of people within an organization. It may or may not be in writing, but it establishes a position on a given set of circumstances. It avoids the need to make a new decision each time those circumstances arise. Yet it must allow latitude. An analogy is a freeway: a driver may not drive north on the southbound lanes, or vice versa. But within the northbound lanes he may take whichever one will best help him reach his destination. Similarly, a policy permits initiative and discretion—but within limits.

Policies set out the area in which decisions may be made, but they do not make those decisions. To that extent they are a grant of authority. Enduring policies are likely to be broad enough to give room for individual judgment and yet not be so obscure or vague as to require complicated interpretations. Their purpose is to help achieve objectives; to be acceptable, policies should take into account the suggestions of those affected by them. Policies are the springboard for other, subordinate plans: procedures, rules, methods, standards, programs, budgets, and, a new breed, technofactors.

Policies should call for the exercise of judgment. Consistency is important but so is flexibility. The two may seem irreconcilable, but careful administration will adhere to the broad guidelines while making appropriate decisions within the guidelines. A policy to promote from within should permit the hiring from outside under special circumstances, but to fill higher positions from the outside more than 50 percent of the time would be a violation of the policy.

Broad policies are geared to broad objectives, hence the final arbiter of such policies must be top management. Lower management may propose. Indeed, in matters requiring special expertise, it should propose. A personnel policy should originate with the personnel department, but the signature at the bottom of the policy should be that of the highest responsible manager.

Organizations use three types of policies. Here are some illustrations:

□ *Basic policies* affect the entire organization and are issued by top management.
  Example
  To sell a competitive product for every one sold by a competitor.
□ *General policies* affect a large part, but not all, of the organization. They may be issued by top or middle management.
  Example
  To procure goods from the company's customers, all other things being equal.
□ *Departmental policies* are relatively specific in nature and are usually issued by middle or lower management.
  Example
  Internal auditors making audits at suppliers' plants should call in every morning if that does not require a long-distance call.

Those who formulate policies should be aware of the standards for good policies. Some of them are as follows:[7]

□ Policies should be geared to and based on organizational objectives.
□ Policies should be based on known principles; to run counter to accepted principles—technological or behavioral—is to invite violation.
□ Subordinate policies should supplement superior policies and complement policies with which they must coordinate. Inconsistencies breed confusion.
□ Policies should take a definite position, be understandable, and preferably be in writing.
□ Policies should be stable and capable of standing the test of time. For the same reason, they should be flexible within reasonable ranges.
□ Policies should be sufficiently comprehensive to cover most situations within their scope. The purpose is to avoid repetitive managerial decisions.

Some policies, as anyone who has worked in a large organization knows, exist by managerial acceptance. The formal policy, being repeatedly violated without challenge, is replaced by informal policy. The written personnel policy may restrict the lunch break to 30 minutes; but if employees take 45 minutes and are not corrected or disciplined, the informal policy will prevail.

Similarly, comparable policies may be inconsistent within an organization. A person moving from production planning to industrial engineering, for example, will have to learn the varying policies that must be observed in his new environment. The new policies will govern rewards or punishment in the group, and they may be significantly different from what was experienced in the old group. For example, felicity of expression may not be important in production planning documents. In industrial engineering, where production regulations are spelled out, good writing may be strongly emphasized.

Policies may suffer from obsolescence as much as products do. Changes in objectives, strategies, competition, and labor contracts can directly affect existing policies. Any enslavement by the status quo can be destructive. Safeway, as an example, had built its reputation on quality and resisted food discounting. It feared that its reputation would suffer if it cut prices to meet competition. But as discounting spread, Safeway was forced to change its policy, and it moved aggressively into food discounting in 1970.[8] Policies are often revised as a result of analyses of quantitative data. Here is an example:[9]

> One company was subject to marked sales fluctuations. This resulted in layoffs of as much as one-third of its people during slack months. A militant union objected violently. The company resisted until pressures caused it to embark on a feasibility study. The quantitative analysis showed that relatively stable production would result if off-season sales were discounted—transferring the inventory cost to retailers—and that a 15 percent reduction in labor costs could be achieved through reduction in overtime during busy periods. The result demonstrated that it was not only financially feasible but advantageous to all to change the company policy to stable production.

Procedures

When policies establish general guidelines, procedures specify a chronological series of tasks or steps to achieve an objective. When policies are guides to thinking, procedures are guides to action. They give in detail the exact manner in which activities will be accomplished. Policies grant vacations; procedures show how to apply for them. Obviously, therefore, procedures should be in accord with related policies.

Although they should be specific, procedures should also possess stability. They should therefore be structured with thought to take all normal circumstances into account and require new decisions as little as possible. Each step should be complementary to the steps before and after it. Each step should fulfill a definite need to move employees toward desired objectives.

Procedures, by and large, apply to repetitive work. They have little value if each task differs considerably from other tasks. But in the typical large enterprise much work is repetitive and procedures, once established, can be followed day in day out. The manager is freed from making the same decisions over and over.

Procedures must be reevaluated periodically. To that end there is a tendency, when some new application requires coverage, to tack it on to the old procedure. A complete revision can often be the most economical approach when significant changes are needed.

Rules

A rule is the simplest type of plan; it allows for no discretion. Rules may or may not be related to a procedure. The prohibition against drinking alcoholic beverages on the job is an unrelated rule.

But a rule that says all incoming letters requiring response shall be answered or acknowledged within 10 days is related to the procedure covering receipt of and response to written communications.

Methods

Methods specify in detail how one step in a procedure should be performed. The series of steps in an employment routine is a procedure; how to check employment references is a method. The specified method, if properly devised, sets forth the best way to perform a task. It accomplishes uniformity of product and service and thereby improves efficiency. Methods reduced to writing can be helpful in training new employees.

The Gilbreths, Frank B. and Lillian M., stressed the importance of methods in management and developed what we now call motion study. Employees relate to methods more than to any other form of plan because they are the easiest to understand, are tangible, and are intimately associated with the employee's work.

When methods, such as job instructions, carefully define the task, set forth specifically the steps to take, and show the time required to complete them, the greatest output can be achieved.

Standards

A standard, although used in the function of controlling, is developed in the function of planning. It is a yardstick against which products or processes are measured to determine their acceptability. To that extent all plans can be considered standards, but in common usage a standard is applied to performance results. Maintaining a tolerance of plus or minus .0017 inches for a production part and using no more automotive fuel than a gallon per 18 miles are examples of standards.

There are two types of standards:

1. Those specifying the end result of an activity. A blueprint that sets forth precise tolerances is a standard. So is a budget.
2. Those specifying the nature of the elements of an activity. The requirement that a buyer secure at least three written bids from qualified suppliers and award the order to the lowest bidder is a standard; it is assumed that the buyer who meets that standard is performing an acceptable buying job in seeking to obtain the best price.

Standards provide effective means of control. When clearly devised and accepted by those measured, they offer an incentive to meet established goals. Also, when all elements of a process are held uniform by standards, output tends to increase. On the other hand, standards do freeze conditions, and to that extent they may impede progress toward ultimate goals. Moreover, they rarely adjust to the differences in individuals. Hence, standards should be developed to take those opposing results into account. Clearly that is not easy, but the standard setter should be aware of the potential conflict.

Technofactors

Technofactors are technical approaches to planning; they supply assistance to managers that more conventional plans cannot. They apply chiefly to time, cost, or material flow. Among them are PERT, PERT-COST (see Chapter 8), and RAMP (Review Analysis of Multiple Projects). When PERT and PERT-COST are used on a single project, RAMP is used to control more than one ongoing program. For example, a contractor constructing several buildings concurrently can watch all the work as a unit through RAMP.

Rhochrematics is a technofactor used in the management of material flow and is helpful in automation studies. It seeks to integrate the flow of material from original source through production and processing to the final consumer. Its proponents claim improved customer service, lower costs, and better use of working capital. It depends heavily on good accounting data, mathematical techniques, and the use of the computer.[10]

Programs

Because programs are designed to achieve some objective, they too are plans. A program is a combination of goals, policies, procedures, rules, and the allocation of resources to carry out some course of action. It may be major or minor; it may involve the development and sale of a new commercial aircraft; or it may be a project developed to certify all weld operators.

Large programs may involve many subordinate plans, each important to carrying out the entire program. A major program may be successful only to the extent that all derivative plans work well. A single element or procedure may cause a huge program to stumble or fail. In the first Ford-Carter presidential debate an insignificant audio component brought the entire program to an embarrassing halt for 20 minutes.

Budgets

A budget, in terms of planning, is a statement of expected results expressed in numerical terms. Indeed, the financial operating bud-

get is often called the profit plan. It can be expressed in any numeri-
cally measurable terms: dollars, man-hours, machine-hours, or units
of production.

A budget is also a control, but first it must be developed as a plan
or standard against which accomplishment can be measured. One
must plan before one can control. To that end budgets anticipate
operating results over given future periods and provide a basis for appraising performance as plans become translated into results.

Budgets of varying complexity are developed in almost every ongoing enterprise. The principal benefit lies in forcing the manager to
plan in precise terms the future of the organization he is responsible
for. The requirement for concrete numbers prevents vague general-
ities. The numbers have other benefits as well:

□ They emphasize the importance of careful planning; results inconsistent with the plans point up poorly constructed budgets.
□ They force executives to establish measurable objectives. A
  budget is meaningless unless the manager knows what he is
  budgeting for.
□ They increase participation in the planning process. Each
  lower-level budget is incorporated into the overall budget,
  which thereby embraces the plans of people at all levels of the
  enterprise.
□ They supply objective standards to measure the efficiency of
  manager and worker alike. The numbered goal makes comparisons easy.
□ They impel good planning. In effect, they are a facilitating
  technique and hence a result rather than the precursor of management planning.
□ They help sharpen the organizational structure. Effective budgets are not possible if the organizaton is not sound. Thus the
  budget process points to defects in the structure.

The larger the organization, the more diversified the budgets
needed to plan its course and control its activities. Over all, generally, is the planning or operating budget that establishes the relations between revenues and costs. It usually starts with a sales forecast; and after the forecast is officially approved, it becomes the sales
budget.

As the chief source of information, the sales budget provides the
data necessary to prepare the production budget. The latter sets
forth in quantified terms the number of finished products that will

meet the needs forecasted in the sales budget. The production budget is then used to prepare tooling, materials, purchase, and labor budgets.

The factory overhead budgets cover expenses not identifiable with finished products; they include rent, power, management salaries, and other indirect factory costs. Distribution budgets cover the cost of selling and delivering products. Administrative expense budgets cover general management functions at the headquarters office and the executive level. Cash budgets are designed to show the cash needed for operations and to prevent disastrous depletions; they are estimates of the cash receipts and disbursements during the budget period. Capital additions budgets detail expenditures for additional plant, machinery, and equipment, as well as improvements in existing facilities and replacements.

Some budgets are static; they remain the same during the entire budget period. But because budgets, like other plans, are future-oriented and because the future is uncertain, another form of budget is sometimes employed. When sales or production levels are unpredictable, a flexible or variable budget may be used. It provides for a range of volume levels and budgets that apply to the various levels within the range. Since budgets are also control devices, the variable budget permits more intelligent administration of activities based on varying levels actually encountered.

Budgets are absolutely essential to the functioning of the enterprise; their absence would probably mean chaos. Yet it is a rare organization in which budgets do not create a framework for conflict. Almost invariably the individual subject to a budget considers the budget unrealistic. The responses aroused are usually antagonistic and emotional. The staff people who develop the budgets are targets of dislike, and they become defensive themselves. Budget pressures evoke retaliation and devious means of producing inaccurate or self-serving results. The production supervisor with a tight weekly budget for manufactured items may hoard parts during a good week and release them during a bad one. The forces thus generated may in the long run diminish efficiency. That is not to say that budgets should be eliminated; for elimination would be completely destructive. It is to say that budgets involve more than numbers. They involve people as well, and the numbers can have repressive effects on the people.

The practices that management follows can go a long way toward minimizing if not eliminating budget problems. Management must recognize that some resistance to budgets is entirely normal and that some grousing does not necessarily mean an absence of cooperation.

Virulent opposition may be minimized by a democratic style of leadership. The participative approach can have a salutary effect in bringing the maker and the subject of budgets together. However, the participation should be real and not window dressing. He who is called upon to participate and is not then given a hearing is doubly resentful. He may believe that he has been manipulated, and in that climate no advantage accrues.

Argyris tells of a study in which a controller boasted of participation in budget preparation.[11] He would convene a meeting of supervisors at which the budget for each supervisor was presented and discussed. Then each supervisor signed his budget. If he later complained when his realized production fell short of budgeted performance, he was shown his signature as evidence that he had "participated" in budget preparation. Actually, the meetings did not evoke frank discussions; there was a mere nodding of heads. What went on inside the heads remained hidden. Argyris points out that participation in the real sense involves group discussion in which people are comfortable enough to be spontaneous and feel free to accept or reject something new. Obviously, budgets cannot be set by mobocracy, but wise leadership can let participants feel they have had their day in court and have received a sympathetic hearing.

Participation in budgets also means providing the supervisor or manager with the information he needs to control himself and learn why variances occur. Hence, an unfavorable variance need not be considered a dereliction of duty when circumstances forecasted did not come to pass and there is a valid reason for the variance.

Controversy will never be eliminated from the budget process, but it can be lessened by participative management.

PLANNING AND THE INTERNAL AUDITOR

Where the Internal Auditor Can Help

The internal auditor who spent all his time verifying completed transactions for accuracy and compliance with procedures was not noted for being forward-looking. The modern internal auditor, like the manager, looks over the horizon for what is beyond. His ability as an analyst and appraiser can be useful to management in the planning function.

It is not enough for the internal auditor to verify compliance with plans, policies, procedures, and budgets. Compliance may be meticulous; employees may be following the book to the letter; but the end results may not be meeting management's needs because the book needs a new edition to bring it up to date. So the internal auditor must not only verify compliance with the regulations; he must also determine that the regulations are in gear with the organization's objectives.

With that outlook, the internal auditor can assist management at all levels through planning-related audits. The assistance can be especially helpful in audits involving:

The centralized planning functions of the enterprise
The planning functions within operating organizations
Compliance with procedures
Methods improvement
Budgets

Centralized Planning Function

Organizations have varied means of carrying out the long-range planning functions. Every executive and manager must plan his own activities, of course, but some plans involve all or many of the groups within the organization. In such cases, central groups are usually assigned to develop drafts of policies, procedures, programs, charters, and the like. Often, by executive indifference, those groups are left to wield considerable power within the enterprise. Also, since they represent a staff function, there is a potential for animosity between them and the operating functions.

Internal auditors become involved with those staff functions either because they audit staff departments directly or because they appraise the policies and procedures during audits of operating functions and learn how well or how badly they are working. Here are some of the matters the internal auditor should be concerned with in audits of planning functions as he questions the workability of plans, policies, and procedures developed by the groups:

- Are the plans, including policies, procedures, and programs, compatible with the related objectives of the enterprise?
- Do the plans improve coordination of various objectives?
- Do plans anticipate problems?
- How reliable are the forecasting and data gathering?
- Is the subject matter of the plans important enough to warrant formal planning?
- Do the benefits exceed the cost of drawing up the plans?
- Will the plans capitalize on the abilities and ideas of individuals capable of carrying them out?

□ Do the plans help achieve uniformity of action among interfac-
ing units?
□ Do the plans allow for initiative?
□ Are the plans properly communicated?
□ Will the follow-up methods make it possible to measure the
success of the plans?

Obviously, in such analyses, the internal auditor must have a
sound understanding of company objectives. He will rarely have that
understanding if his organizational status is low. Primary organizational objectives are promulgated at the highest levels in the enterprise, and the director of internal auditing must be able to convince
executive management that he can perform a high-level function only
if he is a part of the councils of executive management. He must be
privy to the minutes of the board of directors, and he must periodically meet with the audit committee of the board and with top executives as he lays out his long-range audit program and inquires where
he can best be of service. A knowledge of top management's thinking
improves the service the internal auditor can offer. It sharpens his
ability to detect defects in the planning methods and the plans themselves. Here, for example, are some of the signs that may indicate
defective planning mechanism.[12]

□ Insufficient top-management support. Is management really
committed to and involved in planning?
□ Inadequate line involvement. Is operating management sharing with the planning staff the development of plans for the
operating units?
□ Lack of relevance. Are plans attacking real problems, or are
planners in ivory towers, out of touch with reality?
□ Lack of use. Are plans being developed and then forgotten?
An important service the internal auditor can supply is to inform the planner how his plans are working.
□ Lack of direction. Is top management communicating to line
managers what the plans are supposed to be accomplishing?
□ Lack of realism. Do plans take the politics of the organization
into account? Do they suffer from weak analysis, inadequate
forecasting, or insufficient information? The internal auditor
is an experienced fact gatherer. He can provide considerable
assistance to the planner in devising significant plans.
□ Inadequate thinking through. Are plans merely a simple
projection of past experience? Do they take into account internal and external trends?

□ Insufficient recognition of contingencies. Have the planners asked themselves the what-if questions? What can go wrong most likely will.

□ Inadequate feedback and control. Are the plans moving the organization toward identified objectives, or are they merely workable mechanisms?

□ Poor communication. Is there a clear three-way communication among top management, operating management, and the planning staff?

□ Lack of integration. Are plans made up of uncoordinated parts? When planning is oriented toward goals, the sum of the parts is greater than the arithmetic total.

□ Too much attention to detail. Nobody can predict the future precisely; predictions can be only general and within certain ranges. Is excessive detail obscuring the goals and handcuffing those who must carry out the plans?

□ Undue rigidity. Is the breadth of long-range planning being confused with the narrower precision of budgeting? Excessive concentration on precise results undermines creativity.

The internal auditor can be especially helpful in bridging the gap between the planner and the doer. Internal auditors reviewing central planning activities can interview operating personnel to determine whether the plans are clear, understandable, and compatible with existing conditions.

It should be pointed out that the internal auditor's responsibilities do not include developing plans, programs, procedures, and rules for operating people. To include them would be to usurp a management function. Further, with respect to the plan he has developed and espoused, the internal auditor could no longer rely on his objectivity in future audits of the planned activities. But his objectivity is not compromised when he suggests control mechanisms for plans or reports on how well plans are functioning.

Planning Functions of Operating Activities

In every audit of a company, division, section, or group, the internal auditor will be concerned with the planning performed by the unit's manager. He can provide an important service to the manager by taking a fresh look at the manager's planning function and pointing out areas for improvement. And if the internal auditor and the manager work together as partners in making the evaluation, friction will be eliminated and improvement almost assured. Here are some of the matters they can consider:[13]

□ Determine the objective of the organization under review. Not until the auditor and the operating manager have agreed on an understanding of the objectives can they proceed with the next step.

□ Identify the plans which have been devised to meet the objectives and relate specific policies and procedures to those plans. The analyses may reveal redundant, missing, or inconsistent instructions.

□ Determine whether the objectives conceived at higher levels have been properly communicated downward and whether operating employees have been informed of the objectives and the related plans.

□ Determine whether the organization of work, personnel, authority, and responsibility is adequate to facilitate meeting the objectives.

□ Determine whether the plans provide for a feedback of information that permits the manager to make periodic comparisons between plans and accomplishment.

A cooperative approach to the examination can be an education to both the manager and the internal auditor, and the education can continue with the appraisal of the objectives after the objectives have been identified. In the appraisal process, the internal auditor and the manager should probe into the adequacy of the objectives. It is a probe that the manager should have made himself, but it is a rare manager who can be clinically dispassionate about his own creations. The internal auditor's presence and questions can improve the manager's objectivity if the internal auditor is careful not to arouse defensiveness. Here are some of the questions that should be answered:

□ Are the objectives capable of being misunderstood or misconstrued?

□ Are any significant areas not covered by objectives?

□ Have the objectives failed to consider the company's responsibility to its shareholders, the government, the community, and its employees?

□ Have people been made aware of the objectives?

□ Is there any incompatibility between the objectives of the unit and those of the company? Between those of the unit and of complementary units?

□ Does management just pay lip service to the objectives by not allocating resources to the accomplishment of objectives?

◻ Should existing objectives be divided or subdivided to make them usable, more clearly understood, and more easily met?
◻ Do existing controls provide for seeing that objectives will be met?
◻ Are objectives revised so frequently as to cause confusion and frustration?

Plans follow objectives, and plans also can benefit from analysis. For all significant plans and programs, the auditor should find out whether the manager considered such questions as these:

◻ Why must it be done? There should be a logical answer that meets the needs of the entire organization.
◻ What action is necessary to get it done? The action being taken may not be the logical one.
◻ Where will it take place? Is the location where the action is taking place the best location?
◻ When will it take place? Every plan must have a schedule and a due date. Long-range programs should have milestones of accomplishment.
◻ Who will do it? Responsibility must be laid on an identified individual or group of individuals.
◻ How will it be done? Have the procedures been clearly spelled out?

Internal audit appraisals involve the comparison of activities and functions with acceptable standards. The planning function is no exception. With the agreement of the manager, the application of standards can help sharpen the audit approach:

1. *Setting objectives*
   (a) Management should have a clear conception of the basic, long-term needs of the organization and should have those objectives reduced to writing.
   (b) Annual objectives should be in writing, and the commitment made should be submitted to higher management. The objectives should contain provision for:
       (1) Improvements in the organization's operations
       (2) Improvement of the organization's image
       (3) Cost reduction
       (4) Personal development of the manager and his subordinates

(c) Plans should be compatible with and improve coordination of company objectives.

(d) The manager should be able to identify specific, continuing major objectives of the organization, that is, those that should be met if there is to be no adverse effect on quality, cost, or schedule in significant areas of operation.

(e) More stringent control should be provided over the accomplishment of objectives that are most likely not to be attained if neglected or poorly striven for and that are difficult and time-consuming to supervise, rather than over objectives of lesser importance.

2. *Assigning responsibility*

(a) There should be a proper delegation of responsibility that provides for accountability to higher authority for the activities assigned and at the same time capitalizes on the ideas and abilities of individuals.

(b) Plans should provide goals that are subject to measurement and should provide reports on periodic measurement to insure the proper discharge of the responsibility assigned.

3. *Maintaining continuity*

(a) Long-range plans should provide for continuity of effort on major programs; the short-range plans should be concentrated on achieving interim milestones or accomplishing less-extensive programs.

(b) Plans should be made for continuing companywide training programs.

(c) Plans should be made to establish a companywide personal development plan for each employee that encompasses not only company training programs but also outside study and development.

4. *Reappraising objectives*

(a) The organization's plans, objectives, policies, procedures, and subplans must be reappraised periodically to make sure they remain consistent with the overall plans and objectives of the company, that they achieve uniformity among related organizations, and that their benefits outweigh their costs.

Reappraisals are often traumatic. Perhaps the most difficult task of the manager is to change thinking—both his own and that of his people. To many, change is fraught with peril. Better the devil we know than the devil we don't. But change feeds the muscle of every enterprise, and the internal auditor's stock in trade is change—to make better, to forsake the old ways that are not working. And the internal auditor can help the manager achieve change if he points out that change is more acceptable to the manager's people when:[14]

- It is understood by those affected.
- It does not threaten an individual's security.
- Those affected help create the change.
- It results from the application of established principles instead of from some personal order.
- It follows a series of successful changes, not a series of failures.
- It is inaugurated after prior related changes have been assimilated, not imposed during the confusion of other major changes.
- It has been planned and proved, and is not experimental.
- It affects people new on the job, not those old on the job.
- It affects people who share in the benefits of the change.
- The organization has been conditioned to accept change.

Planning decisions commit for the future. Goals may be well established; but roadblocks tend to arise unexpectedly. Managers must continually check on events to see whether changes in premises require changes in plans. The wise manager is aware of his supervisory responsibilities, but he may not have the time to check on events. The neophyte manager may not even be aware of the need for constant follow-up. But the internal auditor, as the expert on control, must be abundantly aware of the need for monitoring plans. He can be of special assistance to managers in the audits of operating activities. Here is an example.[15]

According to procedures developed in the sales department of a store, sales personnel were supposed to add the cost of outgoing parcel post and express shipments to the sales checks at the time of sale. That was the plan, but it was not working. The sales people did not take the time to consult the necessary manuals and rate charts to determine transportation costs, and supervisors were not monitoring the sales people to see if they were doing that job. When the internal auditors compared postage charged to customers with the actual cost of postage expense incurred, they found that the store was losing about $75,000 a year.

New systems were then installed. Scales were provided with direct dollar value readings from simplified shipping cost charts based on average rates. Determining shipping costs then became an instantaneous process which the sales people found simple to use. Annual shipping cost losses were sharply curtailed.

The internal auditor, like the manager, must be a profit planner. He must have the ability and authority to probe the economics, the operating methods, and all the other plans involved in making and selling the entity's product or service that may affect profit. The auditor is in a particularly advantageous position to make those probes. He can concentrate upon any of the organization's products or services and can cross traditionally functional boundaries of the enterprise to determine relations and decide on the needs of participating organizations. He can act as a catalyst to improve the planning practices of contributing groups. For example:[16]

> During an audit of a company's plant which produces farm implements, the internal auditor questioned the use of ¾-inch bolts and nuts on certain implements. He learned that the less costly ⅝-inch bolts provided adequate strength. The internal auditor raised the question with all organizations involved in planning and production. An engineering study was undertaken as a result; and after a period of testing, the smaller bolts were prescribed. Savings ran $19,800 annually.

Compliance with Procedures

Since time immemorial, auditors have verified adherence to procedures. They compare operating actions with procedural requirements in all areas of the enterprise, point out deviations, and recommend corrective action.

The organization that develops the procedures, usually staff people, rarely has the authority to review operations, detect deviations, and require correction. That is the function of operating supervision, but operating supervisors are usually involved with the day-to-day problems of assembling parts, producing products, or providing services. The internal auditor can therefore help operating management by verifying compliance with procedures and reporting significant deviations together with recommendations for improvement. Here is an example.[17]

> An integrated steel company operated coal mines located some distance from the steelworks. Coal was being brought from the coal mines to blend with the company's coal. Procedures laid down the specifications for the purchased coal. The internal auditor compared the specifications of the purchased coal with those prescribed by the companies. There was a considerable variance. Evidently communications had broken down between the various organizations in the company. One did not know what the other was doing. The internal auditor recommended closer cooperation and adherence to procedures. As a result a more eco-

nomical blend of coal was used, saving about $200,000 a year. The internal auditor did not prescribe the blend or know how to go about creating it. That is a management function. But he focused mangement thinking upon the problem; and that was enough.

Modern internal auditors go beyond reviews of compliance with existing policies and procedures. They question the policies and procedures themselves. As an internal auditor reviews an operation, his first concern is the objective. What is the operation supposed to achieve? His review will encompass the implementing procedures and seek to determine whether they assist or hinder the people who are performing the function.

Sometimes existing procedures may not achieve the needed goals, yet people are still following them because that is always the way things have been done. Now and again some alert manager develops new procedures for his own group that can be more productive than those followed by the rest of the organization. The internal auditor, observing the breakthrough, can make it applicable to other groups as well, sometimes with substantial savings. For example.[18]

In a branch audit, an internal auditor observed that the branch manager, instead of mailing all debtors' checks to the main office's central bank account for deposit, made a separate deposit by telegraphic transfer for large checks. When the internal auditor returned to his headquarters office, he analyzed the number of days between receipt of checks and deposits and found transit time ran from 2 to 4 days. He compared the cost of telegraphic transfer with savings of overdraft interest at 12 percent annually. At his suggestion procedures were changed throughout the enterprise to use telegraphic transfers for all deposits over $10,000. Savings ran between $70,000 and $80,000 annually.

Internal auditors can develop routine tests of procedures in all their audit tasks. By incorporating those tests in their audit programs and by routinely comparing procedures with the tests, they can provide a significant service to managers. Here are some of the standards:

    □ In every step of a procedure, there should be provision for accountability. A specific individual should be responsible for a specific step. Such a clear-cut assignment helps reduce overlapping, redundancy, conflict, and loss of accountability. Procedures should designate not only what and how but who as well.
    □ Each step of the procedure should be supported by adequate

manpower and equipment so that work will progress smoothly. Lack of balance among various steps can create bottlenecks.

□ Each operating procedure should have a coordinate control procedure. Provision for doing a job should include provision for monitoring progress and accomplishment.

□ Forms that initiate procedures should, as much as possible, be designed for use by all elements of the organization involved in the procedure. That eliminates the need for initiating new paperwork.

Analyzing procedures through flow-charting a process can graphically disclose failures to meet those standards. And by explaining the standards to managers, the auditor can improve future procedure writing.

Methods Improvement

The Gilbreths, through time-and-motion study, were able to find better ways of performing work. Their efforts were generally related to factory work, but their methodology is applicable to all work within an enterprise. The internal auditor's analytical ability can be put to use in revising methods—the steps in a procedure—and searching for work simplification or improvement.

Work simplification, in essence, is the application of common sense. It seeks to find more economical uses of human efforts, materials, machines, time, and space. The steps the internal auditor can take in work simplification are essentially these:

1. Select for work simplification analysis the methods that appear to be bottlenecks or to be expensive or time-consuming.
2. By means of flow charts analyze each step of the process.
3. Ask why the task is performed, where, when, how, and by whom.
4. Seek improvement by:
    Eliminating
    Combining
    Rearranging
    Simplifying
    Mechanizing
    Reducing physical effort and fatigue
5. Put the simplified process into effect. All that went before is a futile exercise if the ideas are not carried out.

In the following example, an internal auditor achieved significant improvements and savings by having the work rearranged.[19]

An internal auditor observed that expensive assemblies were being scrapped in the last phases of production. As he dug deeper he found that in this critical phase of the process the company was using inexperienced people. At the internal auditor's recommendation, only experienced people were assigned to those stages of assembly where large man-hours had already been invested. Estimated savings totaled $80,000 in the first year and, because of increased production, $600,000 over the next five years.

Budgets

In general, the internal auditor becomes involved with four different aspects of the budgeting process:

1. The establishing of budgets and updating the budgets as premises change.
2. The recording of actual costs.
3. The reporting of performance.
4. Management's use of performance reports.

The auditor's reviews of those aspects are performed both in the budget department and in the operating departments that are subject to budgets. In both areas the auditor can be of service to management. Here are some of the matters with which he will be concerned in the budgeting department:

- The authority given to the department by top management to obtain information from operating organizations.
- The clarity and comprehensiveness of the instructions and premises issued within the department and to contributing operating organizations.
- The scheduling of steps in the budget development process.
- The coordination of the elements of the budget.
- The format dictated by the budget department to contributing organizations to obtain information that can be readily put together.
- The review process by which budgets are evaluated by top management.
- The types of reports used to evaluate budgetary performance.
- The manner of adjusting budgets when premises change.

In any review of an operating department, the internal auditor will be interested in the department's budget—the manner in which the budget was developed and how the budget is used as a management control device. His interest will center on these matters:

□ What support was developed for the budget proposals sent to the budget department?

□ How does the operating department adjust operations to accord with budget changes?

□ What variances are found between budgeted and actual costs? Are they properly explained and are appropriate steps taken to correct excessive variances?

□ Are all people who are affected by budgets aware of the budgets?

□ Does the department manager receive sufficient accounting information to tell him how he is tracking against his approved budget?

□ What reviews are made of significant variances and what is done with the results?

Perhaps one of the more significant services the modern internal auditor can provide in connection with budgets is the effect the budgets have on people. The internal auditor, who has had experience with budgets for his own audit projects, is aware of the constraining effects budgets have. A budget can be likened to a belt on a loose pair of trousers. It constricts the wearer, but its absence brings total disarray. If the belt were imposed on the wearer by someone else, and if it were to be too short, the result would be resentment. If the donor were a person in authority, the resentment might not be exhibited, but it would still exist and fester. The wearer might try to obtain an extension to the short belt; and if he could not, the resentment would increase.

Yet the belt is a necessity. The wearer must live with it. But the hostility toward those who imposed the galling restraint is ameliorated if the wearer had a voice in its design, if his views on the size and shape were given a hearing, and if his complaints on how it wears and irks are considered.

The internal auditor, in his reviews of budgets and the difficulties in meeting them, can lend a sympathetic ear. He can determine whether the forms of budgeting are applicable to the budgeted activity. He can determine whether the particular conditions are considered in the imposition of the budgets. He can find whether the budgeted manager is receiving the kind of accounting information that will help him control his own activities. Many a manager has had to develop his own jerry-built information system because needed data were not available in usable form.

The internal auditor cannot, of course, eliminate budgets for an operating manager, but he can determine whether they are reasonable and sensible and whether they relate to the objectives of the activity and the enterprise. It is possible that suspenders could replace the belt and still do the job.

At another level, the internal auditor can glean, from a review of budgets, information that can be useful to management. His broad-ranging activities can give him an overview that can be helpful in reducing costs. Here is an example.[20]

> An internal auditor reviewed the capital appropriation budget of a multiple-plant company. He observed that acquisition of similar kinds of property—forklifts and over-the-road trucks—had been planned for several locations. The internal auditor asked if the acquisitions were coordinated to take advantage of group purchases. He found that communication between the outlying plants and the central office had broken down. Central purchasing said that it tries to take advantage of group purchases when matters are referred to them. But it seemed that such coordination was the exception, not the rule. The internal auditor suggested that the budget department furnish the purchasing department with a copy of the capital appropriation budget for all plants. There the budget could be reviewed for group purchase opportunities. The result was an immediate grouping of equipment under one order and a system for continuing the practice in the future.

In a recent survey by The Institute of Internal Auditors it was found that only 15 percent of over 100 large companies questioned used their internal auditors to perform audits of budgeting activities.[21] It is unfortunate that executive management does not call upon internal auditors more often to review one of the most significant control measures in the enterprise. The budget process is no more difficult than any of the other complex activities the modern internal auditor appraises. The rewards accruing from an objective analysis and appraisal of the budgeting process can be significant.

CONCLUSION

Planning is the process of deciding where one wants to be and what one wants to do. Plans come in many shapes and sizes from designs for multibillion-dollar projects to simple job instructions. What characterizes any plan is a present decision to take future action. In that light, plans include programs, policies, procedures, rules, methods, standards, budgets, and technofactors. All plans must start with objectives. It is not reasonable to act without knowing the purpose of the action. And since plans are future-oriented, they must be premised on forecasts of what the future is likely to hold and on what constraints the future will impose. Plans work best when the people designated to carry them out participate in devising them. That is particularly true when the plans are constricting, such as budgets.

The internal auditor's appraisal techniques can be as useful in reviewing plans as in reviewing plan accomplishment. When he reviews compliance with plans—an established application of internal auditing—the auditor should also be concerned with the propriety, applicability, and usefulness of the plan themselves. To that end he can serve management through methods improvement as he reviews the manner in which employees follow procedures. Many internal auditors do not audit the budget process. Executive managers and operating managers can benefit from an independent review of the budgeting activity both in the budgeting organization and in the units in which the budgets are imposed.

References

1. S. S. Thune and R. J. House, "Where Long-Range Planning Pays Off," *Business Horizons,* Vol. 13, No. 4, p. 83.
2. J. S. Gardner, "How to Prevent Organization Dry Rot," *Harper's Magazine,* Vol. 231, No. 1385, p. 20.
3. R. L. Ackoff, "The Meaning of Strategic Planning," *McKinsey Quarterly,* Summer 1966.
4. E. C. Bursk and D. H. Fenn, Jr., eds., *Planning the Future Strategy of Your Business* (New York: McGraw-Hill, 1956), p. 46.
5. Harold Koontz and Cyril O'Donnell, *Essentials of Management* (New York: McGraw-Hill, 1974), p. 65.
6. Patrick Conley, "Environmental and Competitive Information," In R. F. Vancil, ed., *Financial Executive's Handbook,* (Homewood, Ill.: Dow Jones–Irwin, 1970), pp. 386–391.
7. R. C. Davis, *Industrial Organization and Management,* 3rd ed. (New York: Harper & Brothers, 1957), p. 41.
8. "Last Lap?" *Forbes,* Vol. 107, No. 7, p. 21.
9. Melvin Anshen, "Price Tags for Business Policies," *Harvard Business Review,* Vol. 38, No. 1, p. 75.

10. G. R. Terry, *Principles of Management* (Homewood, Ill.: Irwin, 1972), pp. 243–246.
11. Chris Argyris, "Human Problems with Budgets," *Harvard Business Review,* Vol. 31, No. 1, p. 108.
12. W. D. McEachran, "Corporate Long Range Planning," in R. F. Vancil, ed., *Financial Executive's Handbook,* (Homewood, Ill.: Dow Jones–Irwin, 1970), pp. 489, 490.
13. R. E. Seiler, "The Internal Auditor's Appraisal of Company Objectives and Plans," *The Internal Auditor,* Winter 1960, pp. 9–17.
14. R. M. Besse, "Company Planning Must Be Planned," *Dun's Review and Modern Industry,* Vol. 64, No. 6, pp. 62–63.
15. H. J. Mintern, ed., *How to Save $14,500,000 Through Internal Auditing,* (Orlando, Fla.: The Institute of Internal Auditors, 1975), pp. 16, 17.
16. Ibid., p. 147.
17. "The Round Table," *The Internal Auditor,* June 1976, p. 65.
18. "The Round Table," *The Internal Auditor,* April 1976, p. 76.
19. "The Round Table," *The Internal Auditor,* March-April 1971, p. 80.
20. "The Round Table," *The Internal Auditor,* May-June 1971, p. 73.
21. R. S. Savich, *Internal Audit of the Budget Process* (Orlando, Fla.: The Institute of Internal Auditors, 1976), p. 1.

10

Organizing

Organizing: bringing people and processes together. Results of poor organization. Objectives and organization. Each manager an owner. Forms of organization. Specifications for good organization. The penalties of excessive centralization. The need for control in decentralization. When to decentralize. Subdividing the organization. Forms of departmentation. Projectizing—benefits and dangers. The trilogy of responsibility, authority, and accountability. To delegate is not to abdicate. The penalties of failing to delegate properly. Prompting the manager to delegate. How to delegate. The proper span of control—an elusive number. Service departments and functional authority. Problems and solutions in line/staff relations. Informal organizations—they won't go away. Power, politics, status, and roles. The advantages and disadvantages of committees. Ways of making committees effective. Charts: organization, activity, and procedural. Changes and the necessary traumas.

The internal auditor's involvement in organizing. Supplying control in decentralized operations. Are activities and objectives compatible with organizational groupings? Determining the coequality of responsibility and authority. Evaluating delegations. Checking spans of management, but subtly. Internal auditing is staff. The sensitive appraisals of informal organization. Auditing in diverse cultures. Audits of committees. Organization charts: a tool for internal auditors. The internal auditor—herald of change. The audit of staffing. Attacking overstaffing, but gently. How to audit an entire organization.

ORGANIZING AND THE MANAGER

Nature of Organizing

Definition and Purpose

To achieve its objectives and goals, the enterprise must bring people and processes together in logical groupings so that plans can be carried out efficiently and effectively. To be successful, organizing should establish appropriate relations among people to do two things: work together efficiently and gain personal satisfaction from assigned tasks.

Organizing is not a precise science. It has few if any principles inscribed on tablets of stone. It is affected by too many variables in terms of people and conditions to permit the organizer to develop groupings that will always insure best results. In the final analysis it can be judged only by the test of "Does it work?"

Importance of Organization

Good organization is no guarantee of best results. Bad organization, however, will almost surely guarantee bad performance because it is the breeding ground for employee conflict and frustration. But the need for good organization is not always apparent, nor is good organization always high on the list of management priorities. The need can be obscured by good people working heroically to meet budget, schedule, and quality standards despite the inept way in which people and processes have been brought together. Whatever their efforts, however, an illogical organization creates waste and inefficiency because of friction among people and wheel spinning within the processes.

If good people perform well in a poor organizational environment, they might be able to perform magnificently in a good one. Good organization has a synergistic effect—the whole becomes greater than the sum of its parts. It improves both individual satisfaction and work productivity. The individual put in the wrong job cannot be easily moved to meet the goals expected of him.

Elements of Organization

Good organization should include these elements:

□ Objectives and goals must be established because good organization has but one function: to carry out management's plans. Good organizing, therefore, derives from good planning, in which objectives and goals are developed.

□ Components possessing the needed skills and abilities must be gathered, because the wrong people or resources will frustrate rather than facilitate the process.

□ The components should be bound up in a system of relations that makes clear the responsibilities for given tasks and smooths the way for cooperation and coordination.

□ The resulting framework must be compatible with the environment, that is, the existing technology, society, ethics, and politics.

□ The final structure, with its inherent responsibilities, authority, and accountability, must be communicated graphically and unambiguously to those affected by it.

Over and above those essential elements, however, the organization that works best is one that permits managers to feel they are running their own businesses, meeting their own goals, and gaining personal satisfaction from the work they do, no matter how taxing the work may be. So each organization should provide room for discretion and for some freedom and self-determination. It should take advantage of whatever creativity resides in the members of the organization. And it should take into account individual capacities, likes, and dislikes.

Designing the Organization

Designers of organization should not get intoxicated by the symmetry of their design. Organization is not an end in itself; it is a means to an end. It is the vehicle that helps bring people to performance and job satisfaction. And that vehicle must be shaped to the purposes of the enterprise. Some of the shapes are as follows:

Skill. The product moves to the skills available. In a factory, a piece of metal moves from the cutting department to the forming department to the heat-treating or anodizing departments and to the final assembly department. In a university, the students move from the history professor to the math professor to the language professor.

Stage. A housing development is constructed in stages: grading the land, laying out streets, building foundations, erecting frames, raising roofs, and completing the interior work. Ship building also is done in stages.

Team. Different skills work on an assigned task. Teams are used in research projects, in hospital operating rooms, and in projects in industry.

Functional. The functional type of organized work includes both stages and skills. It works well in the small companies for which Fayol designed the functional organization. It fits comfortably into mass production. Its benefits include clarity of assignments, because everybody knows exactly what he or she should be doing, and so it provides stability to the organizational structure. Its drawbacks include resistance to innovativeness, so it does not build people. Contrast that with the team approach in which tasks change frequently and which calls for adaptability and inventiveness. In the team approach there is high freedom but no clarity of function. It is best for imaginative and managerial work. It works inefficiently in operating work.

The form of organization must fit the objectives of the enterprise —what the business is and what it should be.[1] For example, America's Sears and England's Marks & Spencer are in the same business, but their concepts of what that business should be are quite different. Marks & Spencer sees itself as developing upper-class goods for the working-class family. Sears views its business as being the buyer for the American family. Hence, in Marks & Spencer the research and development activity occupies a paramount organizational role. That is not true at Sears, where purchasing is paramount. In those similar companies, the organizational structures fit dissimilar objects.

Arranging the activities within the enterprise is a matter of relations. The best arrangement is to have as few relations as possible—all kept to a minimum, but each one working. In the Catholic Church, for example, one of the oldest and most successful organizations, there are only three levels of authority: the Pope, the bishops, and the parish priests.[2]

Principles for organizing are not ironclad, but some specifications for good organization do exist. When they are violated, difficulties are invited. When they are followed, the resulting organization has at least an even chance of being productive. Drucker lists these specifications:[3]

Clarity. People should know where they belong and where to go for information or instruction. Clarity does not necessarily mean simplicity. But if nobody can get from here to there without a detailed map, there may be confusion and impediments instead of assistance toward performance.

Economy. The structure should permit self-control as much as possible. The least number of people should be needed to keep the machinery of the organization going. The less input required to grease the organization wheels, the greater is the effort available for producing the end product.

Direction of vision. Organization should direct people toward the right performance—the one that will meet organizational aims. It should concentrate on productivity rather than on effort. It should be a guide toward results rather than merely toward working.

Understanding. All members of the organization should understand not only their own tasks but also the tasks of their subordinates, superiors, and colleagues. Thus organizational structure should help rather than hamper communication and coordination.

Decision making. An organizational structure cannot make decisions for managers, but it can improve or impede the process. Organization should therefore force decision making to the lowest level, depending on the circumstances and the significance of the decisions.

Stability and adaptability. Each member of the organization needs a "home"; no one performs well on a street corner waiting for a bus. The feeling of stability is important to the individual. Yet people do move from one home to another, and so the organization should not be so rigid that the ability to adapt to change is inhibited.

Perpetuation and self-renewal. The sands of time ever trickle away, and the mortal resources of the organization go with them. But the organization itself must endure. Thus the form of organization and the number of levels should not prevent a young individual from reaching the top rungs while still young enough to be effective. That specification calls for provisions to develop and test each individual for the next rung of the ladder.

There is a fundamental logic to the steps in organizing. For example:

- Understand the objectives of the organization.
- Form derivative objectives, policies, and plans that flow naturally from the major objectives.
- Identify the activities needed to meet the objectives; they are the building blocks of the organization.
- Group the activities into practical, workable units. Base the groupings on similarity, importance, and the human and material resources available.
- Assign qualified people, or people who can be developed to perform successfully, to the groupings. Clearly set forth their responsibilities. Delegate to them the authority necessary to carry out their responsibilities.
- Bind the group together both horizontally and vertically through authority relations and systems of information.

There is much controversy about whether organizations should be built around functions or people. Perhaps the answer lies in the form of organization needed to carry out the activities designed to meet objectives. In a task-oriented organization, people are brought together to apply their skills to the tasks. The team approach is task- and people-oriented. Since the teams do not have to possess long-term stability, they should be built around the best people available for the particular job.

But in an organization that relies heavily on stability, the structure should be built around functions. The organization might work for a while if it were built around people, but in time it might be difficult to manage and the replacement of managers might also be difficult. People's interests and abilities are often subject to change; functions are less likely to vary.

Centralization and Decentralization

Origins

In small businesses authority is usually centralized. The owner-manager retains authority and makes most decisions. But as the business grows, the principle of span of management has its inexorable effect. The owner-manager no longer can effectively make all the decisions. If he tries, he may run the business into the ground, because no human being can effectively run a large organization alone.

Henry Ford tried it. He insisted on keeping his finger on every activity. He had to fit every piece of the puzzle together. He delegated authority haphazardly and often reversed subordinates on decisions without consulting them. But the business had grown too big for one-man domination, and its profits slid alarmingly. Not until Henry Ford II took over the company in 1944, brought in a management team, and delegated authority to those managers was the company saved from being a poor third in the automobile market.

Sears, on the other hand, followed the policy of decentralizing and allowing more decision making at lower levels. That forced managers to accept more responsibility, function autonomously—under central control—and perform more effectively.

Reasons for Decentralization

Decentralization, as we know it today, was born in 1920; Pierre S. du Pont sired it when he reorganized the family-owned du Pont Company. Alfred P. Sloan, at General Motors, refined the process by providing decentralized operations with centralized policy control. The standard model of decentralized organization emerged later from the reorganization of the General Electric Company in 1950 to 1952.[4]

The functional form of organization is best suited to decentralization, although it can also work effectively with teams. It can divide large complex organizations into a number of smaller businesses that are relatively compact and simple. It is therefore oriented toward results, and it works well with both operating and innovative activities.

But decentralization does not imply complete autonomy for the suborganizations. Strong control at the top is still needed to decide what activities to enter into or abandon, to allocate resources, and to decide what markets to pursue and what products to develop and produce. Top management cannot operate; but it must control. Philips of Holland instituted decentralization with hundreds of subsidiary companies in sixty countries. It had a leadership role in a number of products from light bulbs to household appliances. Sales went up but profits went down. There was no control from the top. What happened was fragmentation instead of decentralization. Inventories were excessive and uncontrolled. Capital investment was unplanned. Overstaffing was the rule. Only when Philips installed centralized control, common measurement, and coordinated planning did profits improve.[5]

Decentralization does not work for every company. Many factors determine its applicability in a particular organization. Some of them are discussed in the following paragraphs.

Costliness of decisions. If the results of decisions may be costly—in terms of such matters as money, morale, reputation, and competitive position—authority tends to centralize. Top management will be afraid to delegate authority for such decisions. Moreover, when business is bad and economic conditions are at low ebb, there is a strong tendency to centralize rather than to decentralize.

Diversity of product line. Centralization works more effectively when a large number of subunits produce or market similar products. But if products are diversified and each subunit deals with a unique product, there may not be sufficient expertise about each product to permit effective centralization. Knowledgeable decisions can best be made by those closest to the product. That is one reason why large conglomerates must be organized along decentralized lines.

Uniformity of policy. The philosophy of some companies calls for strict uniformity of credit, quality, service, delivery, and the like. Top management feels more comfortable with the same standards, accounting practices, financial records, and statistics for all. Decentralization would not find a welcome home with such managers.

Size. The larger the enterprise, the greater the number of decisions that have to be made, the more levels between top and bottom, and the longer the time span between requesting and obtaining the needed decision. That does not mean that small organizations should not decentralize when the step is appropriate. It means that larger organizations are often forced into decentralization to achieve greater efficiency.

Geographic dispersion. When facilities are geographically spread out, it may be difficult for top management to exercise control needed in centralized management. Decentralization beckons because of the distances from the top-level decision makers.

Nature of business. Manufacturing companies, with their constant need to adjust to change, present more fertile fields for decentralization than centralization. Companies dealing in finance, however, find it easier to hold on to centralized authority despite size or geographic dispersion.

Desire for independence. Individuals may become restive and frustrated when faced with delays in obtaining decisions from centralized authority. Besides, most people seek independence and freedom to make their own decisions. Centralized management, however, would be reluctant to permit local decision making if the people were not competent to exercise the authority.

Nature of growth. Companies that grow from within find it difficult to decentralize; top management has always made the decisions and is reluctant to delegate decision making to others. Such a management philosophy, of course, tends to reject decentralization. If, on the other hand, the enterprise grew as a result of merger or acquisitions, and left the top managements of the acquired companies in power, decentralization comes naturally.

Ability to control. To delegate is not to abdicate. Top management must still remain responsible for the overall performance of the enterprise. Appropriate management controls must exist to permit decision making at the lower levels but also to provide accountability of subordinate decision makers.

External influences. Increased government regulation may affect top management's decision to decentralize. Indeed, the need for uniform interpretations and application of government regulations may require a decentralized organization to recentralize, if only in certain parts of its operations.

Advantages of Centralization

Probably the most important advantage of centralization is that the chief executive officer has increased power and prestige. His becomes the last word on more decisions. And the psychology of top management can demand that. Such an executive may want to see strict uniformity of policies and practices continued. Specialists at headquarters are fully used and are close to the executive level. Besides, top-quality specialists can be hired because there is abundant work for them. Duplication is minimized, as is the danger of functions deviating from standards for long periods before the deviations are detected. To that end, elaborate control devices are not required because management is closer to the enterprise operations.

Advantages of Decentralization

Decentralization relieves the heavy load on top management. Delegation of some of the executive's load tends to develop generalists instead of specialists and eases the transition into general management positions. Greater responsibility at lower levels for the various "businesses" within the enterprise tends to develop closer personal relations in each business and to instill greater employee enthusiasm and loyalty. Each member of the "business" has a more intimate knowledge of the work. Trouble spots can be more readily located because responsible managers are closer to operations. In multiunit or multinational companies, the local managers have a closer contact with and understanding of local conditions. From the standpoint of top management, programs can be tested in one subunit without incurring risks in the remaining subunits. Indeed, risks of loss of resources can be spread out and thereby minimized.

More managerial talent can be developed because more managerial positions are available. Business can be run on a profit center principle because each unit is given freedom to improve the profits while being held accountable for results. Lower-level decisions may be more rational, since they take local problems into account. Products may be more readily diversified because a complete project can be developed to carry the product from conception to production and distribution.

The Choice Between Centralization and Decentralization

In the final analysis, the decision to decentralize or to recentralize and the extent of each depend on the individual circumstances. No two companies or chief executive officers are entirely alike.

Beginning in 1956, American Can Co. had made a number of acquisitions, including Dixie Cup and Marathon Paper. It therefore developed a loose federation of almost autonomous organizations. But profits were disappointing. And so, between 1964 and 1966, the central office decided to tighten controls and move to greater centralization. The central staff was increased. It took over work previously handled divisionally, particularly taxes, law, purchasing, marketing, accounting, and advertising. Competition between salesmen of different divisions was eliminated. Costs went down and profits went up. Per share earnings of $2.70 in 1964 increased to $4.18 in 1966.[6]

In centralization versus decentralization, the law of the situation must apply. That is illustrated by a story told by Edwin R. Embree:[7]

> In a little town in Louisiana a teacher had been hearing a class read a lesson about birds in a standard textbook. To drive home a point about the lesson, she asked one of the boys, "When do the robins come?"
>
> The boy promptly said, "In the fall."
>
> The teacher asked the boy to reread the text. Then the same question and the same answer. Infuriated, the teacher insisted on a rereading and then thundered the same question. In tears, the frightened boy finally gave the answer the teacher wanted: "The robins come in the spring."
>
> And so they do—in Boston where the book was written. But in Louisiana, where the robins come to avoid the winter, they arrive in the fall. And the boy's knowledge of local conditions was superior to that of the text writer.

When decentralization is applicable and is practiced properly, it works well. General Motors has developed what many regard as excellent controls to measure the results of its decentralized operations. One is the costing system, which eliminates as much as possible such extraneous factors as cyclical fluctuations. Another is the rate of return on capital invested in each division. A third is an analysis of the competitive standing of the product of each division in the market. Divisions that sell principally to other GM divisions are measured by their ability to sell at lower prices than other suppliers. The impact of forces beyond a manager's control are eliminated as much as possible. At GM decentralization prevents infringement by top management on division decisions, yet fairly holds division managers accountable.

Departmentation

Departmentation designates a distinct area, division, or branch of an enterprise that is responsible for performance, has authority to carry out needed activities, and is accountable for results. Some com panies have few levels in the hierarchy but many departments, all set horizontally and all reporting to a single superior. Such structures are said to be flat. Other companies have a large number of levels with relatively few departments reporting to a superior. Such structures are called tall. The flat structure calls for better people and greater responsibility because the broad span of control prevents close supervision. But the flat structure has its drawbacks, because the fewer the strata the less opportunity for people to advance.

Tall structures provide closer control and greater opportunities for advancement, close supervision inhibits the development of self-reliant, innovative managers. Also, it results in greater costs, because there are additional managers and their staffs in the hierarchy. Finally, it complicates communication because of the filtration process that distorts messages as they are communicated from one level to another.

Basis for Departmentation

Organizations may be departmented in various ways: by number of people, function, territory, product, customer, marketing channel, project, and process or equipment. A brief discussion of each follows:[8]

Number. The simplest form of departmentation is number. It is useful in the armed services, universities, collectors for community funds, and laborers. It has the benefits of rapid expansion or contraction. It is useful, however, only at lower levels of management.

Function. The most common form is function; the basic enterprise functions in manufacturing, for example, are production, marketing, and finance. Function has the advantages that it is simple and logical, follows the basic principle of grouping specialists in a specific occupation, makes training easier, and provides tight control at the top over the subsidiary function. Its disadvantages are that responsibility for results is usually centered at the top. It narrows the viewpoints of the specialists. It does not tend to develop general managers, because the functional employee does not always see the business as a whole. And it reduces coordination between functions because each function is an island unto itself.

Territory. Departmentation governed by geographical areas is used, obviously, in enterprises having wide physical dispersion. All functions in an area are grouped under a territorial manager. That works best when it encourages local participation in decision making. The advantages, basically, are economical and may include lower freight rates, rent, travel costs, and labor. The disadvantages include the need for more and better managers (always in short supply) and duplication of such services as purchasing and accounting.

Product. In large enterprises with many product lines, departmentation by product has gradually been evolving. It offers the advantages of growth and diversity of products and services, offers a good training ground for generalists, improves the coordination of functional activities, and provides for strict accountability for each product. As in territoral departmentation, however, it requires more and better managers and intensifies problems of top management control. It also results in duplication of some services that could be supplied more economically at a central location.

Customer. In customer departmentation the customer is central to the way activities are grouped. Loan officers in a bank, for example, may deal with a restricted type of customer. Some departments of a company are concerned only with military products, others with civilian products. When it is appropriate, this form provides for greater customer satisfaction because particular customers or types of customers are dealing with specialists trained in their needs and activities. Yet problems of coordination can arise between the customer-oriented department and other departments organized in a different way. Also, facilities and manpower can be underemployed, particularly in periods of recession.

Marketing channel. Some companies have expanded the product orientation to marketing channel departmentation. That can be brought about by the needs of varied markets. The Purex Corporation, for example, learned that neither product nor territorial departmentation would work for it. Purex found that buyers and ways of doing business were different in the supermarkets on the one hand and the the drug chains on the other.

Processes and equipment. In departmentation by processes and equipment, experts or machines in specific processes are grouped to perform special tasks. Electronic data processing departments that perform work for other organizations are prime examples. So are special heat-treating and anodizing groups in manufacturing companies.

Projects

The project concept is a violation of the principle of unity of command, yet it can and does work under certain circumstances and conditions. It is a form of staff with functional authority. It focuses on a large task; it is assembled for the task and is disbanded when the task is completed. It has been used largely in the aerospace industry, in which a contract is let for a specific piece of hardware or research.

The project manager is responsible for completing an end product by using people administratively responsible to other managers. He borrows talents from research, production, sales, finance, and other departments to carry out his task. He exercises more authority than is customarily assigned to a staff manager. And his people are, in effect, reporting to two masters. The administrative manager determines who will work on the project; the project manager tells those people what to do and is responsible for budget, quality, and schedule. The administrative manager is still responsible for ratings and raises for his people, but he receives input on performance from the project manager. The disadvantage, of course, is the violation of unity of command; the advantage lies in permitting maximum use of specialization, which is focused on a task of great significance to the enterprise.

Project structures can and do work. But there must be full and free communication and a thorough understanding of tasks, functions, and responsibilities. Like all principles, unity of command can be successfully bent to specific uses if everyone understands the needs of the enterprise and of the people involved in and affected by the project.

Responsibility, Authority, and Accountability

Duties and rights determine what tasks a manager is to do and what powers he has to accomplish them.

Responsibilities

The duties are commonly referred to as responsibilities—the obligation of a person to carry out assigned activities. Responsibility flows down from superior to subordinate, and, although it can be assigned, it can never be relinquished. The superior, all the way up to the chief executive, still is charged with the responsibility to see that what is assigned to others gets done. The president who assigns the marketing vice president responsibility for a sales campaign is still responsible to the board of directors and the stockholders for the success of the campaign. He cannot say, if the campaign fails, "I gave the marketing man the responsibility and so the failure is not my fault."

Responsibility is a series of obligations that constitute a chain from superior to subordinate to subordinate. Responsibilities are a chain of relations established between organizational levels, and those relations create risks. The retention of final responsibility in the superior carries with it the fear that the subordinate will not perform as well as the superior. So many superiors fear to delegate some of their responsibility to others. They make themselves indispensable; and they do not, therefore, build strong organizations or strong people.

Responsibility stems from function, and function stems from objectives. The clearer the understanding of all concerned as to what are the objectives, the functions, and the responsibilities, the more readily are people willing to accept and carry out responsibilities.

Unclear statements of responsibility result in job dissatisfaction. A study of 290 employees, including managers and technical people, measured role conflict and role ambiguity with varying levels of job satisfaction.[9] It was found that the classical theory of clear assignments and structure, standards and measurements, and emphasis on output reduced the conflicts and the ambiguities. People usually like to know what they're supposed to do and how much, but they function best when they have participated in delineating their tasks and responsibilities.

Assignments of responsibility can create problems when:

□ There are gaps—when people are not sure who is to carry out a given task.

□ There are overlaps—when two or more people are made equally responsible for given tasks.

□ The assigned responsibility does not contribute to an accepted, understood objective—if the job has no meaning to the one responsible for it. That often occurs when the objectives change and the responsibilities remain the same.

Authority

Authority is a right to perform; it is a right to command; it is a right to enforce compliance. It comes into being from ownership, legal fiat, or status in an organization. New concepts about authority stress the "subordinate-acceptance approach." The manager must be accepted by subordinates; he achieves better performance by winning support, not by ordering it. Yet the ultimate authority must be there. In time of emergency the manager must have the "position authority" to command and to be obeyed. When fire erupts, there is no time for superior-subordinate debates.

Authority derives from responsibility. It is futile to grant authority when there has been no prior obligation—responsibility—to perform. Yet authority has certain limits. It is restricted by the technical expertise of subordinates and by objectives, plans, organization structure, statutes, agreements, and social pressures.

Like responsibilities, authority must be made specific if it is to have legitimacy. For example, a buyer may have the authority to issue purchase orders on his own signature for purchases under $100, but not if they are $100 or over. If the levels of authority are not clearly spelled out, confusion can result.

Top-management philosophy will dictate the extent of authority delegated. The more that centralization is required the less the authority granted. The greater the degree of centralization the greater the need for granted authority at the lower levels. In such circumstances there is less of a requirement for decisions to receive approvals, before and after, and managers are willing to risk the judgment of their subordinates and allow a certain amount of mistakes.

Of course, the law of the situation will affect the amount of authority granted. How large and complex is the organization? How competent are its people? How well have tasks been standardized and made repetitive? How geographically dispersed are the organization's activities? And, most important, how effective is the system of communication? Is communication full and prompt, and is decision making aided by adequate, accurate data? In fact, the ubiquitous computer will probably put brakes on the trend toward decentralization and the increased delegation of authority.

Coequality

Authority and responsibility must be coequal. Logically, there can be no responsibility for a task if the authority to carry it out is lacking. So authority regulates the amount of responsibility that can be assigned. In fact, when authority is less than responsibility, the latter tends to fall to the level of the former.

Parity of responsibility and authority has long been held to be a truism, but, as McGregor says, it rarely obtains in practice.[10] No manager has complete control over his activities. He is constrained by such uncontrollable factors as illness of key employees, contract cancellations, government action, changes in customer preference, and unexpected vagaries in business cycles, yet he is expected to carry out his responsibilities. Still, the superior who deliberately assigns responsibility and does not grant the concomitant authority is handcuffing the subordinate.

Accountability

Accountability derives from responsibility. A manager cannot hold a subordinate accountable for tasks or people he has no responsibility for. On the other hand, whoever has been given responsibility and coequal authority can be asked to account for carrying out his responsibilities and for his stewardship of the resources entrusted to him.

Single accountability implies one boss–one employee. It means that each person should be answerable to only one immediate supervisor. It is a part of the concept of unity of command. As we have seen, however, unity of command may sometimes have to be violated to meet the laws of the situation, as in project organizations. As a continuing matter, it should be followed, since it is the only way the diverse and varied units of the enterprise can be logically organized.

Documentation

Subordinates will feel more comfortable when their responsibility, authority, and accountability are set forth clearly in organization charts, statements of responsibility, and job descriptions. These documents help establish and control relations among people and can also be useful in indoctrinating and educating new people.

Delegation

Nature

Delegation is the means by which responsibility is assigned, authority is granted, and accountability is exacted. It occurs, or should occur, when superiors or organizations have more work than they can handle.

Actually, without delegation, organization is impossible. There is a limit to close personal involvement in or supervision of tasks. When that limit is passed, the discretion and right to carry out tasks should be given to a subordinate by a superior. It is axiomatic, of course, that only that authority which the superior possesses legitimately can be delegated. Unfortunate indeed is the subordinate who is granted authority by a superior who never had it.

Failure to delegate can be disastrous. Safeway under Lingan A. Warren, the autocrat who made all the decisions, showed a poor profit picture. But when stockbroker Robert Anderson Magowan took over, decisions were pushed down to the district level, profits were lifted, and sales increased. Magowan knew little about the food business, but he fully understood organization and delegation.[11]

All involved in it must understand that the delegation process does not mean abdication. It implies granting authority; it does not imply divesting the superior of responsibility. Similarly, the sensible subordinate understands that no delegation is absolute. When the boss says, "Here's the job. Use your own judgment. Whatever you do is fine by me," he doesn't really mean it. The subordinate had better follow the boss's policies and remain aware of his philosophies, or the authority will soon be withdrawn.

And the boss who makes such a statement is not practicing the fine art of delegating. True, he may be showing receptiveness to new ideas from younger, innovative subordinates. He may be willing to let go some of his authority; he may be willing to trust his subordinates to make some mistakes; but he must not let go altogether. He may not abdicate his own responsibility. To that end, each delegation must be accompanied by some sort of control, some form of feedback, so the superior still has his arms around his organization, no matter how unobtrusively, and still has the means of knowing when to pull in the reins and take over.

The rule must be: Delegate, but obtain feedback; follow up on what must be carried out; and don't be afflicted by unwelcome surprises because the reins were dropped completely.

Why Managers Don't Delegate

There are many reasons why managers don't delegate. First, of course, is their failure to assume the role of managership when they are promoted. There is the fear that, if they are not into everything with both hands and feet, they won't be justifying the trust placed in them by their own superiors.

Then too, their philosophy may militate against delegation. They may trust nobody but themselves. They may fear being exposed, because delegation opens up activities and may reveal shortcomings. They may, on the one hand, not trust their subordinates or, on the other hand, fear that subordinates may take over the managerial job. They may desire to dominate in all things, and part of that may be the unwillingness to accept the calculated risks that accompany delegation.

Studies of managerial failure put poor delegation at the top of the list of factors, which include psychological attitudes, lack of understanding of the principles of delegation, and failure to put known principles into effect. But as in many other aspects of management, when the benefits and methods of delegation are understood, better management results.

Getting Managers to Delegate

The climate in the organization may have to be changed before managers become willing to delegate. When the fear syndrome permeates the organization, managers feel that they must be on top of every detail for which they are responsible. They feel that every question asked of them by a superior must be answered promptly and in specific detail. That reduces them to collectors and hoarders of information, both significant and trivial.

There should be no onus to saying, "I don't know the details, but I'll get them right away." So the first task for executive management that wishes to promote intelligent delegation is to make the delegator secure and to develop a climate that is free of fear of not having all the answers at the managerial fingertips. Managers should be taught by example that there is a need for delegation, that managers who can say "I'm the most expendable person in my organization" are highly prized.

Managers must be encouraged to believe in delegation, intelligent delegation, to understand that it does not exist in a vacuum, but must be granted to subordinates wisely and must include only those tasks the particular subordinate is competent to handle or can be taught to handle with reasonable success.

Also, managers must know that good delegation is made clearly. Guidelines are needed; parameters must be set; expectations should be spelled out. Some executives may boast that their delegations are deliberately vague to encourage innovativeness and provide flexibility. That may be true at the outset of a task involving many unknowns. But if the vagueness is permitted to continue, the dream of a happy innovative team gives way to the nightmare of a dissident group of frustrated people.

Principles of Delegation

A clear understanding of the principles of delegation improves the success of decentralized authority. Here are some principles:

□ Clear definition of the job. The task, function, or activity should be defined, and the lines of communication for needed information should be thoroughly understood.

□ Scalar principle and unity of command. Each delegate must know his delegator. The chain of command must be clearly delineated. It should be understood that the chain of command may be ignored at times—but only to obtain information, not decisions. Failure to observe unity of command may result in conflicting instructions.

□ Retention of responsibility. Once a delegate receives authority, he should be compelled to use it. Laziness that brings the delegate constantly to the delegator for decisions he should be making on his own should not be tolerated. To that extent responsibility is absolute. Once the subordinate accepts responsibility, he may not evade it. And in turn he must retain the responsibility for the work of his own subordinates. He must also be taught that, when he or his people encounter problems that are urgent and significant, they must promptly bring them to the attention of higher authority.

□ Equality of responsibility and authority. When authority is granted, it should be keyed to the responsibility assigned. It should never be less or more than is needed to carry out the results expected.

□ Splintered authority. Authority must be used intelligently. A manager should not have authority to make decisions involving the organization of a manager on his own level. Both managers should, when occasion warrants, be able to get together and work the problem out between them. Under the scalar principle, it is true, the decision should be referred to a common superior. But too many such referrals will swamp that superior. Although splintered authority cannot be avoided, too much may indicate the need for reorganization.

Spans of Management

The need for delegation harks back to the inability of human beings to be personally involved with too many diverse activities and too many subordinates. But how many is too much? Many controls have been made of spans of management or, as it is sometimes called, span of control. Some studies say the span should be 4 to 8 immediate subordinates at the upper levels. But in practice there are wide variances. The American Management Associations surveyed 100 large companies for information on the subject. It found from one to 24 executives reporting directly to a president. Only 26 presidents had 6 or fewer subordinates. The median number was 9.

But the numbers alone have little meaning. More important are such variables as subordinate training, good planning, number of changes, use of objective standards, and the excellence or poverty of communication. All those variables contribute to the appropriateness of tall or flat organizations. Tall organizations have narrow spans but many levels. Flat organizations have broad spans and fewer levels. The tall organizations have closer supervision but take a long time for decisions and communication to filter down. They make tight supervision easier, but they inhibit delegation. The flat organization sacrifices closer supervision for the development of more self-reliant subordinates.

Span of management increases geometrically with the addition of new people or units. More is involved than the added bodies; there are the added relations and intercommunications. If a manager has one subordinate, the number of relations is simply one: superior and subordinate. But add one more subordinate and what happens? The boss has two direct relations. Also, subordinate A relates to B and B to A: two more relations. Further, the boss now has relations with A and B as a group or B and A as a group. (Dealing with B while A is present is different from dealing with A while B is present.) Thus, the number of relations jumps from one to six with the addition of one more subordinate.

V. A. Graicunas, a French consultant in management, developed a mathetical formula to calculate the rise in number of relations:[12]

$$R = n(2^{n-1} + n - 1)$$

where R = relations
      n = number of subordinates

By using that formula, a superior with five subordinates can be involved in 100 relations:

$$R = 5(2^4 + 4) = 5(16 + 4) = 100$$

What becomes important to the executive, therefore, is not only the addition of people to his organization but the geometrically increased demand on his time because of the number of added relations. And when the work is varied, the people inexperienced, and the delegation minimal, the demands on limited time can rise alarmingly.

Line and Staff

Nature

All people in an organization are connected by a line of command from the very top to the very bottom. A small organization has a straight line of authority from president to lowest worker; hence the term "line authority." That type of structure has much to commend it. It is simple; it can change direction; and it can make speedy decisions.

But large organizations are rarely simple. Retaining the direct-line concept increases levels and foregoes the use of specialists who can provide expertise the line managers do not possess. Hence the use of staff. A staff is a stick carried in the hand as an aid to walking or climbing. It performs as the climber uses or needs it. It does not perform by itself. It can be used or not as the climber wishes.

The concept of staff in organizations is as old as government and armies, in which it has been used since ancient times. More recently it has been used in business. And the simple concept has now evolved into a relation that puzzles theorists and frustrates managers.

Definitions by the score have sprung up, but none has provided the ultimate, finite meaning. The reason lies in the many variations. For example, "line" has been defined as the function that contributes directly to the fulfillment of the economic objectives of the company. Hence many people think of line as primary and staff as secondary in importance. Do the accounting and tax departments contribute directly to the economic fulfillment of the company's objectives? Ask that question of the production manager, and his answer will be an emphatic *no*.

Departments have been identified as line and staff according to functions, but that identification is not wholly accurate. It depends more on objective. A professor in a university is line, but if he is hired by a manufacturing department to carry out his same function —to teach people—he becomes staff. Office work may be line in an insurance company; it is staff in a manufacturing company. And even there the difference is not that clear. Between the director of office services and the lowliest clerk in that department there is a line relation. Line exists whenever a superior exercises direct supervision over a subordinate for the fulfillment of an objective.

But the relationship becomes line-staff whenever one individual or group is responsible for meeting an objective and making the decision to that end and another is responsible for advising and assisting —usually on request. Hence a staff function may be characterized as one that is separated from the primary chain of command—the decision makers who deal directly with the organization's end products— to give specialized service and make the operation more economical and efficient. The specialists in large organizations are necessary. But as Farquhar put it: "They should be on tap, not on top."[13]

There are different kinds of staff. The primary difference is between personal and specialist staff.

Personal

The personal staff have backgrounds similar to the background of the superior. They are the "assistants to" who take some of the load off the superior without having functional authority. They help plan, develop departmental budgets, obtain information, and make outside contacts to gain information, but never direct or order.

Assistants, however, as distinguished from "assistants to," share the line manager's authority. In relation to the president, however, an executive vice president is an assistant manager, not an assistant to the manager. He has definite line authority, although it may be subject to certain restrictions.

The general staff was initiated in the military to help a top manager handle enormous operations. In the U.S. Army, it comprises G-1, Personnel; G-2, Intelligence; G-3, Operations; G-4, Supply; and G-5, Controller.

Specialist

The specialist staffs are broadly divided into advisory, service, control, and functional groups. Advisory staffs present opinions and recommendations on such matters as law, taxes, and insurance. Theirs should be completed staff work. The superior should not have to develop information; he should be able to merely agree or disagree with a proposal in terms of the entity's objectives.

☐ Service staff is designed to avoid duplication. Examples are central purchasing departments and data processing departments.

☐ Control staff restrains line authority and includes such functions as credit, security, auditing, and inspection.

☐ Functional staff supplies information on how and when to perform an activity. For example, the production control department represents functional staff in a manufacturing organization.

Because of their widespread use and because of some misconceptions about them, it may be useful to discuss further the service staff and the authority associated with functional staff.

Service Departments

Service departments differ from true staff functions. They produce a tangible end product. A typing pool turns out letters, and an EDP department turns out data and reports.

One purpose of the service department is to centralize activities to achieve economies; another may be to improve control. Examples of the latter are a central buying group and a central unit dealing with the administration of contracts.

Service departments may partake of both line and staff functions. When they act as line, they make all the decisions made by line people. But when they act as staff, their decisions are restricted to research and advice; they provide line executives with the benefit of their staff expertise.

Sometimes service personnel are loaned to a line department or other staff department to provide more immediate service. Examples are cost accountants assigned to a manufacturing branch or a traffic expert assigned to a purchasing organization. By their very nature, those assignments, logical on their face, may lead to conflicts. The cost man may be asked to side with manufacturing in construing accounting department rules. The chief of accounting, it is true, gives the cost man his raises and promotions, but the chief must rely on the manufacturing manager for input about the cost man's effectiveness.

Service departments exist because centralization is supposedly more economical than decentralization. But that can be just theory, and most service departments are created on that theory. Rare indeed is the service department that is set up after the costs have been studied. Besides, there are other attributes than cost to be considered: the possibility of inadequate service, delays, poor communication, favoritism, and downright failure to act in emergencies. A careful analysis of individual situations may show that a line manager, given service people whose cost is equal to their budget allocation in a service department, may get the job done better. He knows precisely what he wants and how he wants it done. As an example, operating reports may be produced better, faster, and cheaper by people under the direct supervision of line management.

Functional Authority

Somewhere between line authority and staff authority is a blend called functional authority. It exists because it has to; in its absence the chief executive is flooded. It is actually a delegation to a staff's organization of a slice of the chief executive's responsibility and authority.

Functional authority is the right to prescribe processes, methods, or policies to other line or service organizations. For example, the accounting branch has the authority to prescribe forms or the preparation of personnel time records. The chief of accounting's authority to that end extends throughout the enterprise. It supersedes the authority of any line manager to develop similar forms.

Functional authority is possessed by the personnel manager to prescribe grievance procedures, by the safety manager to shut down the plant if he perceives a hazard, and by the production scheduler in telling production when to process or construct its products. Obviously, functional authority should be resorted to as little as possible. Just as it is a slice of the chief executive, so it slices away the authority of the line manager. It encroaches on the unity of command. It is possible to find an operating manager having to bow to a half dozen functional bosses. And with arrogance so ready to surface in staff people, that can be frustrating and counterproductive.

Conflicts

Whenever one activity invades the domain of another, defenses rise and conflicts are spawned. It is a matter of authority. The staff officer has the authority of ideas. The line officer has the authority of command. Let the staff officer step over the line and try to command and the battle is joined. The line officer can benefit from the ideas of the specialist, but he should not be asked to delegate his job to the specialist. That distinction is central to good working relations between line and staff. The specialist in efficient operations brought in to unearth waste and inefficiency must understand that, no matter how brilliant his suggestions may be, they will have to be sold, not told. He cannot strip away the authority of line managers. He will function best when he helps them help themselves. And if he convinces the line people that the suggestion was *their* idea, then he will have fathomed the true meaning of what staff has to offer: a staff for leaning, not leading, for assisting, not insisting.

The staff people must be guardians of the relations. Staff is the more expendable. If a hard conflict arises, executive management will most likely side with line, not staff. So staff should seek never to undermine line authority; it should be scrupulous in how it offers advice. To say, "Do this" infringes on line authority. Even to say, "Here's how I'd do it" can cause line to abdicate its own responsibility. If things go wrong, line can use the excuse "This is how staff said it should be done; don't blame me." How much better if staff asks "How do you think it should be done?" and then, when told, asks "Why?" and explores the reasons.

Staff can offer advantages to line: The actions of the line manager may become more scientific; his span of control may be lengthened; communication and coordination with peripheral organizations can be improved. At the same time, staff can increase the number and the complexity of organizational relations. Its people often tend to usurp line authority, even without setting out to do so, and the usurpation invites conflict. To avoid the evils of a redundancy of supervision, to preserve unity of command, and to hold line managers responsible for results, staff must be denied command authority. Staff has something valuable for line, but that something must be bought by line, not rammed down line's throat.

Improving Staff-Line Relations

No sets of rules work for all people, but an understanding of what might work may dampen the antagonisms that threaten to ignite in any line-staff relationship.

Staff must understand, first of all, the basic authority relations in the organizing function. Those relations should be clarified through a clear identification of the particular staff's duties and responsibilities. Especially clear must be the limitations on staff authority. The staff people who are specialists must be just that: competent specialists in their field. They must be capable of earning the respect of the line people. They should, if at all possible, have some line experience so they will not be accused of being ivory tower theorists without the gut feeling of what it takes to make and implement line decisions. They should be kept aware of what goes on in the organization, lest the textbook proposals run aground on the rocky beach of existing limitations on what is practical.

They should be held accountable for their own performance. They too should be required to deal with budgets, schedule, and quality—standards that they impose on themselves or are imposed on them. They should not be given special treatment merely because they are staff. Their suggestion should be carefully thought out; they should not make suggestions they would not have made if they themselves were responsible for the line operation. Also, the suggestions should not be offhand comments that are left to the line to be put into usable shape.

The stress should be on interdependence and not on separation. Both staff and line should be evaluated on what they accomplish in concert rather than on how they perform individually. Good organizing fuses together all segments of the organization.

Line should be made fully aware of staff's contributions. It should be required to listen, not necessarily to accept. But line should understand that staff can make them look good. In General Motors, for example, the product division manager consults with the various staff divisions before he proposes major programs or policies. He is fully aware that he doesn't have to, but he is also aware that with staff on his side his proposals have a better chance of acceptance. From the standpoint of staff, if the advice is sound, valid, economical, and feasible, it will generally be accepted. Yet staff should be independent. It should feel sufficiently secure, because of expertise and status, to offer independent advice and not merely what line management wants to hear.

Informal Organizations

Nature

In every organization, like the double exposure on a negative, is the wraith of the informal organization. It is not readily defined, but it exists. It is pervasive; it is dynamic; and it must be considered. It cannot be incorporated into the formal organization nor can it be given formal status, because ordinarily it does not recognize the formal chain of command. But the manager who ignores the informal organization may be courting trouble.

Informal organizations are composed of relations among its members that ignore the organization chart. A supervisor who has the authority, under the cloak of the formal organization, to issue direct orders to a subordinate may have an informal working relation that puts the two on a par.

Benefits and Drawbacks

That may not be all bad. The informal organization may benefit the formal one. It can fill gaps in the formal organization, and it can improve coordination among people. It can make the enterprise a more appealing place to work in. An offer of a more lucrative job may be ignored because the individual does not want to leave his or her "family." It provides a grapevine for information that does not come through the regular chain of command. And it may very well make the manager more sensitive to his people and help him gain more cooperation and productivity.

On the other hand, the activities of the informal organization may run directly contrary to those of the formal one. The informal organization may impose limits on the decisions the manager feels are best for the organization as a whole, and because of its unstructured, fluid pattern it can create uncertainty. The wise manager will know who its leaders are and avoid antagonizing them.

Power, Politics, and Status

The informal organization is little affected by formal charts or statements of responsibility. Instead, it is guided and governed by such informal qualities as power, politics, and status.

Power is the ability to apply pressures that are effective. There are many sources of power in the informal organization, but the most important is expertise. He who knows how or why will be sought out and respected no matter where he sits in the formal hierarchy. Indeed, people will seek to transfer from supervisors whom they do not respect.

Politics exists in every organization. It is a way of getting things done outside the formal network; it is also a way of advancing oneself in the formal organization. A five-year study was made of 149 managers in a large manufacturing company. The sample comprised the following groups:[14]

Promoted	47%
Lateral transfers	14
Remained on same job	22
Demoted	17
Total	100%

The characteristics in the promoted group were the ability to maneuver and to get cooperation from the group's own level rather than from below and the ability to deal with confused and complex responsibilities. Those represent the sign of the good politician, the accommodator, and the compromiser. The study showed that people willing and able to engage in politics are more likely to be advanced in large organizations. Their characteristics are useful in achieving reconciliation and getting the job done. If improperly controlled, of course, doing his own maneuvering can result in chaos. On the other hand, he who sticks like a barnacle to the rule book will be personally safe, but he will become known as a brass-bound bureaucrat who is more concerned with being right within the letter of the law than in accomplishing objectives.

Status is rank. The informal organization has its pecking order that may be irrelevant and unrelated to the formal hierarchy. But management should disrupt that order as little as possible. Here is an example:[15]

Employees riding to jobs in trucks had developed a pecking order based on seniority. The senior man rode in the cab. The crew sat in the truck in positions also dictated by seniority. The youngest sat next to the tailgate, and it was his menial task to open and close it. Ankle injuries resulting from jumping over the tailgate impelled management to require the man in the cab to open and close the gate. This created chaos. The *high-level man* doing a *low-status task!* Teams who solved the problem best were those whose supervisors let the informal organization work out the best way to follow the rule without disrupting the informal organization. In some cases the senior man was convinced that by undertaking to open the tailgate he was caring for *his* people.

Roles

Closely related to status in the enterprise is role: How a person is expected to behave in the position he occupies in the enterprise. The formal job description sets forth the enterprise's expectations, but the informal organization has certain expectations of its own. If the two roles are incompatible, conflicts are almost certain to arise. The new supervisor who has to make demands upon former co-workers is in a role conflict. So is the foreman who has demands for productivity from his supervisor and conflicting demands for quality from inspectors.

Conflict also arises when there is disparity between the individual's personal needs and the needs of the organization, whether formal or informal: the ambitious worker whose co-workers warn him against outputs above their norms, the young, eager college graduate given uninspiring jobs, the internal auditor asked by managers to overlook what in his professional soul he knows to be wrong. All those situations create conflicts, and conflicts hamper performance. They are not matters that the manager or the internal auditor can quantify and draw inescapable conclusions from, but they do exist and they are significant. Thus they must be weighed in determining causes of and means of correcting unwanted conditions.

Committees

Forms of Committees

A committee is a group of people who work together on some facet of a management function. There are hosts of committees in all forms of endeavor. Some are formal; some are informal. Some are permanent, some are temporary. Some are at low levels of management, some are at high levels. Indeed, at the highest level sits the board of directors. It will be discussed in Chapter 12. But be they high or low, formal or informal, committees have two things in common: They can often accomplish more than individuals working separately, and they can be a waste of time, money, and managerial talent.

Advantages

Committees can combine varied knowledge and experience. In doing so they can transmit knowledge among members, knowledge that otherwise would not be gained. The knowledge crosses organizational lines and can result in better coordination and cooperation. Varied groups that might not be represented in other ways may be heard from in committee deliberations.

Committees put together people of diverse talents, and through diversity they tend to overcome individual bias and prejudice. By being engaged in the deliberations, committee members become committed to carrying out the group decisions; and misunderstandings of what was intended can be dissipated.

Committees can be a good training ground for the newer members who are taught to speak before a group, engage in give and take around the table, and carry out assignments more willingly because they will be expected to report back on their accomplishments to their peers.

Disadvantages

Committees spend an inordinate amount of time on trivia; it seems that the more trivial the item on the agenda the more time spent on it. The reason may be that trivial items are more readily grasped, and so people can argue with confidence about them. The obscure and complex items are difficult to understand, and committee members are reluctant to show their ignorance before their peers.

Committees, if poorly organized or run, can be not only a waste of money but also unproductive. At Goodyear, the president called a meeting at short notice only to find that all those asked to attend were already at other meetings. So he asked for an analysis and received this information: More than 20 percent of attendants to meetings arrived late; only 85 percent took an active part; and 25 percent had no business there in the first place. The chairman was unprepared in 15 percent of the meetings, and more than 10 percent of the total meeting time was a complete loss because of late arrivals, interruptions from outside, and conversations not relevant to the meeting. And those figures put the matter in its best light, because committee chairmen and members knew they were being observed.[16]

Committees carry with them the dangers of compromise. A consensus, rather than a bold, innovative solution, usually results. Members may abandon what is new and different rather than fight for their ideas because of the pressures of other work or because they don't want to alienate colleagues. Then, too, committees are often chaired by superiors of the members, and the members may be reluctant to speak their minds to and disagree with their bosses.

It is easier to place responsibility on an individual than on a committee, but that problem can be alleviated to some extent by these two methods:

□ Whoever is given committee advice must go on record as either accepting or rejecting it.
□ Assignments for action should go to individuals who are responsible for carrying them out by agreed-upon dates and for reporting results back to committee members.

Making Committees More Effective

Committees cannot usually perform innovatively and with the dispatch of the individual, but some fairly simple rules may make them more effective:

□ Make objectives and authority abundantly clear.
□ Select a chairman who is knowledgeable and who is blessed with traits that will provide reasonable assurance of a smooth operation: willingness to hear people out, but knowing when to step in and exercise authority to get things moving again. Define the duties of the chairman, vice chairman, and secretary.
□ Limit members to those directly involved, those with a real need to serve and contribute. The average size is eight. Much over that and the committee becomes unwieldy; much fewer and the views may be too limited.
□ Have a formal list of members to make sure all are notified and all receive committee reports.
□ Prepare agendas and supply them to members along with the scheduled meeting dates.
□ Record all committee proceedings, assignments, and results.
□ Prepare summary reports to an appropriate executive. Set forth the number of meetings held, the people in attendance, the man-hours spent, the progress made, and the goals met.

Organization Charts

Organization charts are intended to show organizational relations. Some presidents are proud to say they don't need them, but the reasons against them are usually not valid. Like flow charts, they can graphically show up inconsistencies, gaps, and overlaps that need attention. But they may reflect what should be instead of what is; they may display status, not describe authority relations. For example, the staff man reporting to the president may occupy a separate box on the chart that is higher than the one for a director who has much greater responsibility.

The activity chart is a more descriptive form of organization chart. Besides showing organizational relations, it shows the processes and responsibilities involved in achieving a particular objective. It displays:

□ The actions, both major and minor, that must be taken to achieve the objective.
□ The organizations involved in the actions and which organization is to take which action.
□ The individuals in the organization who are responsible for the particular actions.

The procedural flow chart depicts each step in a function. The organization chart is tied in by broken lines to the pictured function: what each individual is to do and when, the documents involved in the process and where they are to go, and how the entire process ties together from beginning to end. One of the benefits of the procedural flow chart is to show management that a change in procedure may require a change in organization to accomplish needed results.

Organizational Change

No organization can stand still. Technology, ecology, needs of society, constraints of the government, products, and mores change. The enterprises affected must either change or regress, so an important part of the managerial function of organizing is to keep analyzing the key activities. Activities once thought essential and significant may have lost those qualities but still occupy significant positions. Also, every time an activity changes, the organizational structure may also have to change.

The analyses sometimes come too late. The decrease in productivity is not analyzed for causes until disaster is imminent or erupts. And often the defect is the direct result of poor organization that makes production swim against a stubborn stream. General Motors and Westinghouse made marked strides after their reorganizations in the 1920s and the 1930s, respectively.[17] Hence one of the jobs for the internal auditor is to see where poor organization inhibits productivity before the problem becomes too serious. He is responsible for warning of organizational defects.

Change should not be made for the sake of change itself. Lawrence says that ideal changes are those that satisfy these three dimensions:[18]

- Achieving organizational purposes; the organization should be able to accomplish its objectives more effectively.
- Achieving self-maintenance and growth; the change should have a positive effect on the individual's opportunities for growth and development.
- Achieving social satisfaction. Breaking up the social groups may bring about dissatisfactions and reduced productivity; on the other hand, building into the changed organization social and psychological factors can insure improved productivity.

Empire builders will, of course, always manipulate the organization to their benefit. The chief executive who is alert to incipient empire building can tell the would-be workers not to bother to extend their domains because his plans for change and rotation will see to it that they won't have the same positions several years later. Organizations can pull themselves out of the debilitating muck of the past if certain considerations obtain:

- Accept criticism. Don't inhibit people from pointing out defects in the organization. Self-deception is a grave managerial illness.
- Recruit people with new ideas, and let them be heard.
- Question old methods. People become cocooned in their own red tape. Their vested interests and self-imposed procedures become more important to them than the needs and aims of the enterprise.
- Look toward what can be; not to what is or was. The practice of looking forward leads to new ideas and motivates people to climb out of their ruts.

Yet excessive change can be destructive. It keeps people off balance and frustrated. But when change is necessary, it can be a positive rather than a negative force if those involved and affected are given their chance for expression, if their views are carefully considered, and if they know their well-being is taken into account.

Staffing

The Need

Some writers on management theory show staffing as a separate managerial function. For our purposes we show it as a part of the organizing function—manning the organization with people who can operate the enterprise competently. It includes recruiting, selecting, and developing people at all levels for all kinds of positions.

Qualified managers are in woefully short supply, and many who were good managers have lagged behind changing conditions and advanced managerial technology. John Mee, Mead Johnson Professor of Management at Indiana University, wryly observed: "All managers are in a foot race between retirement and obsolescence; the best they can hope for is a photo finish."

It is puzzling that companies that plan sales and expansions so meticulously plan for recruitment and replacement of their most precious commodity haphazardly. Many executives and managers avoid thinking about the staffing aspect of their job because it must take into account the most variable and complex of resources: people. But plan they must lest they wake up one morning to find that their most needed people will soon reach retirement age. And lack of planning results in strategic and tactical errors that could be avoided. Maloney cites some of those errors.[19]

- Beginning the year with a major program that is suddenly terminated at the same time that professionals are laid off.
- Trying to hire really exceptional people at ridiculously low salaries.
- Hiring people with specific training who leave after a little while because there is no work for them in their field.

Some simple rules for management staff planning should be considered by all executives:

- Determine the number of managerial posts available. Establish the population of management positions.
- Obtain an estimate of turnover in managerial posts. The past five years is a reasonable period.
- Classify incumbents and potential managers according to:
  Those soon to retire.

Those who will have to be replaced because they are not performing adequately.

Those who are performing adequately but are not capable of
handling a higher job.

Those who are or soon will be ready for promotion.

□ Consider the plans of the enterprise and allow both for expected changes in organization and for affirmative action requirements.

□ Decide on the number of trainees that can be absorbed in the
workforce or are needed to replace incumbents. Some companies use a 1 to 1 ration; others go as high as 10 selections for
each possible opening. The expected attrition rate will be a factor.

□ Determine the sources for recruitment. Consider such matters
as climate, distance, and family.

The Skills

The category of skills needed to be a good manager is difficult to
develop. Any attempts made in that direction have been largely futile because the categories tend to delineate good people, not good
managers. But, certainly, one quality of the good executive must be
to create a harmonious whole out of dissimilar disciplines.[20]   One approach to categorizing managerial quality is to examine three basic
skills: technical, conceptual, and human.[21]

Technical. The manager need not have the technical skills possessed by his subordinates, but he should know enough about the disciplines he manages to evaluate goals and objectives, adopt standards,
and know whether the standards are being met. Furthermore, in
making decisions related to the technical disciplines, he should know
enough not to be led down the garden path by the technicians.

Conceptual. Enterprise problems call for intellectual capacity to a
high degree: the ability to ask the correct questions and evaluate the
answers, the capability of keeping a number of concepts in mind and
evaluating both them and the nature of the people advancing them,
the intelligence to think problems through and come to a logical decision based on the matters presented in the light of enterprise objectives, and the ability to see patterns and relations.

Human relations. The manager must accomplish goals and objectives, and he must meet standards through the work of others. He
must, therefore, be skilled in understanding and motivating people,
but that skill will not substitute for the other two skills. The man-

ager's technical and conceptual skills combine in the process of making decisions; then the human relations skills take over to see that the decisions are implemented.

Many people who are placed in management fail because they lack certain qualities. They fail if they haven't the deep-seated desire to manage—to reach objectives through others and not solely through their own efforts. They fail if they haven't the intelligence to deal with the problems, concepts, decisions, and conflicts that attend any management position. They fail if they are unable to communicate with their peers, their subordinates, and their superiors; for inability to communicate is an invitation to chaos and frustration. Finally, they fail if they do not have the integrity to reject the shoddy end product: to know what is good and insist on only that which is acceptable—both the standards and the products by which the standards are measured.

Generalists and Specialists

The field of management needs both generalists and specialists. Throughout the organization there is, by and large, a need for more specialists, but at some level generalists are needed to reconcile the differing and more parochial views of the specialists. The sales manager sees problems through the sales viewpoint. The purchasing manager sees them through his own viewpoint. Perhaps neither will see them through the viewpoint of the entire enterprise, and that is where the generalist must have his leavening and catalytic effect.

Sources

Promotion from within is obviously favored by employees, but it can be incestuous, and it can breed a narrowness of view. Besides, many technically expert employees do not have the managerial bent. Open competition of recruits from both inside and outside the company calls for fair and objective evaluations by executives, and rarely will favoritism and politics be absent from such evaluations. Recruiting from the outside gives an infusion of new blood and new ideas, which often are desperately needed if the enterprise suffers from stagnation, but it does create problems of resentment among employees.

Scientific selection through tests is more of a hope than a reality. It has been tried, but there still is no sensational breakthrough in predicting success for managerial personnel. The ability to pick the winners remains a chancey thing. For that reason, it should be a firm rule that the manager to whom the successful candidate will report should have the authority to make the final selection. If the executive is to be given the responsibility for what happens in his department, he should have the authority to determine the human resources he needs.

When accountability for results is not clear-cut, committees may be used to make selections. That may be applicable to universities and to some government positions. Some of the items covered in an interview with an applicant are:

Total number of dependents.
Education.
Plans for continuing education.
Whether now employed.
Length of last employment.
Personal goals.
Professional organization in which applicant was or is an active member.
Offices held in the professional organization.
Approximate net worth of the applicant.
Minimum monthly living expenses.

Management Training

Both the organization and the manager have responsibility for continuing training. The universities cannot turn out the compleat manager. They can provide an understanding of managerial functions and principles, but by and large these principles, without real-life illustrations, have little meaning to the student. The teacher who can coat the principles with the tangy taste of real experience is rare, because he must be both an academic and a businessman.

Seminars attended by working managers can be useful if the leaders have both knowledge and experience. Often, however, the seminar attendant may accept the principles of improved management but find them rejected by his superiors when he returns to the job. Education should therefore start at the top. Then too the experiences taught in seminars are general; they do not always come forward in a familiar frame of reference. They may just be a set of case studies and principles hanging on neat pegs, but they could be unrelated to the attendant's personal experiences or needs.

For that reason, a good working relation between the manager and the modern internal auditor can be rewarding. The internal auditor, coming upon a condition in the manager's shop, can analyze it and relate it to violations of management principles or good business practice. He can relate the principle to the condition and explain it in such a way that the manager sees the problem, the cause, and the solution in a sharply defined frame that portrays the real world in which the manager lives. That is the true meaning of the problem-solving partnership.

ORGANIZING AND THE INTERNAL AUDITOR

How the Internal Auditor Can Help

Internal auditing is a managerial control that functions by measuring and evaluating the effectiveness of other controls. Those are among the first words in the Statement of Responsibilities of Internal Auditors. The internal auditor is therefore involved in organization in almost every audit he performs. To that end he can take two approaches: examine causes of deficiencies and, if they relate to defects in organization, suggest that management improve related organizational controls. That is the normal approach. The other approach is to direct the audit specifically to organizing and organizational control, that is, to:

◻ The design for carrying out particular activities to achieve enterprise goals.
◻ The means devised for reappraising the design in the light of changing goals.
◻ The means for modifying the design as needed.

The first method, the indirect approach, is the normal procedure that internal auditors follow. The second—specifically directed to the managerial function of organizing—is more rare. When executive management becomes disenchanted with the existing plan of organization, it usually turns to outside consultants. The consultants often do a creditable job because of their broad experience in the field, but they lack what the internal auditor has developed over the years: a personal knowledge of the enterprise objectives, goals, systems, and people. If internal auditors, management-oriented internal auditors, were to direct their efforts specifically toward the function of organizing, their assistance to management could become much more valuable. To that end they need the status and authority to carry out such audits.

Drucker tells us that there are certain activities within the enterprise that never should be subordinated to anything. They are what he calls the "conscience activities."[22]   Among them are planning, setting standards, and auditing performance against the standards.   Internal auditors, then, must report to persons who are in charge of the conscience activities so that they may measure and evaluate all activities within the entity, including the organization and the function of organizing.

Relating detected deficiencies to organizational deficiencies is useful, but greater managerial awareness of organizational matters carries the internal auditor to new and higher levels of sophistication and usefulness in the organization.   We shall now explore the internal auditor's involvement with the aspects of organizing described earlier in this chapter.

Designing the Organization

It has been a precept in internal auditing that the internal auditor should never design the system that he is to audit.   The reason, obviously, is that he would be loath to criticize his own creation.   But that should not deter him from reviewing proposed plans of organization or reorganization to determine whether they include the necessary checks and balances that provide a means of assuring executive management that activities will be carried out as intended.   Indeed, the Statement of Responsibilities of the Internal Auditor addresses that very matter.   It points out that an auditor should not develop and install procedures, prepare records, or engage in any other activity that he would normally review and appraise and that could reasonably be construed to compromise his independence.   But the Statement goes on to say that "His objectivity need not be adversely affected, however, by his determination and recommendation of the standards of control to be applied in the development of the systems and procedures under his review."

Nowhere is that determination more significant than in the development of electronic data processing systems.   Waiting on the sidelines to make postaudits can prove disastrous.   The internal auditor has too much to offer to hold back, or to be held back, during the early days when the system is being designed.   The computer specialist is concerned with equipment, programs, and efficient computer performance, but within the frame of the large picture those concerns are parochial.   The internal auditor, on the other hand, can offer a broad background that has concern for entity objectives and aims. He can provide a stabilizing influence that embraces the needs of the entire entity, not just data processing.

Here is an example of the disastrous effect of noninvolvement by internal auditors in the design of an EDP system:[23]

In one large railroad company, the internal auditors decided that it would be a good idea to have the computer reject inaccurate data—after the EDP system involving freight car records had been in effect for some time. The internal auditors worked up an audit test deck. Essential data were deliberately omitted. Incorrect data were deliberately added. For example, the test deck showed cars interchanged with the L&N when the railroad had no interchange with the L&N. The test deck showed interchanges with nonexistent railroads, with nonexistent car numbers, and in one instance a car interchanged on May 53rd. Any self-respecting computer program with appropriate edit routines would have screamed TILT when the test deck was introduced. But this program happily processed and printed out all invalid (among valid) transactions, including 22 days extra per diem for the car interchanged on May 53rd.

Management should therefore consider the internal auditor when new organizations and systems are in the design stage. The purpose is not to involve the internal auditor in the design itself. Instead, it is to make use of the auditor's knowledge of internal control to find out if any essential means of control are missing. That is his brand of expertise. As he audits a segment of an organization and reviews a system, his approach must be to ask himself, "What is the objective of this operation?" "How does it mesh with entity objectives?" "What controls exist or *should* exist to see that the objectives will be met?"[24]

And in analyzing the design of a new organization or installation, the questions will be pretty much the same. They are not always the questions asked by the designers of organizations, so that is why the managers should turn to the internal auditors early on.

Centralization and Decentralization

As we pointed out earlier, decentralization may be essential because of the need to reduce spans of management, but it will not work without adequate control from the top. The internal auditor can be one of the means of control that keeps decentralization from becoming abdication.

The internal auditor's services can be invaluable during the early stages when it is known that decentralization is inevitable. In companies that grow by merger, an internal audit team should review the organization and systems of the company to be taken over. When that company's systems of management are incompatible with those of the acquiring company, the auditor should report the facts and his recommendations to executive management.

In decentralization, conflict and frustration erupt unless the authority of the respective organizations and people is spelled out clearly. One of the steps the internal auditor should take is to develop a chart of management-approval authorizations. If the assignments of authorization are not specifically spelled out, the internal auditor should recommend a system of appropriate authority levels and leave to management the decision of just what the levels should be. If they are spelled out, the internal auditor should determine if they are being followed.

In employment, for example, the personnel manager may process on his own authority the employment of all salaried people whose salaries are less then $1,000 a month. Hires between that amount and $1,500 must be approved by a vice president; between $1,500 and $2,500 a month by the president; over that by the board of directors. The dollar amounts will vary among companies, but the principle should be generally applicable.

The internal auditor should be fully aware that decentralization does not imply complete autonomy. He should know that attainment of common objectives, coordination of effort, and decisions on certain policy matters must be centrally controlled. It is his job, as he moves through decentralized operations, to see that the principle is not being violated. The other side of the coin is that he must make sure that centralized control is not being duplicated. Here is an example of an internal auditor's finding that saved at least $1 million a year by eliminating duplication in a centralized operation:[25]

> A business had some 250 retail outlets. Accounting was centralized. The outlets submitted weekly statements of sales and cash disbursements to the central office. They also sent invoices to headquarters for payment. Each outlet then received monthly statements of operations. The outlets were not, therefore, to maintain accounting records of their own.

> But they did. The internal auditor found that each outlet had a clerk who kept an unofficial bookkeeping system so that questions could be answered when the monthly statements were received. The internal auditor found that those answers could be obtained for the managers of the outlets merely by expanding the income and expense codes of the chart of accounts. The monthly statement therefore was able to answer the detailed questions which the records of the unofficial bookkeepers were designed to answer. Now, instead of 250 bookkeepers, centralized machine accounting (equal to the compensation of only two clerks) provided the needed answers. Reducing the staff by 250 clerks saved about $1 million a year.

In another company, a central purchasing unit was organized to process, companywide, certain materials that were used commonly by the many subdivisions of the company. Suppliers contracted to supply the materials at reduced prices because of the volume of business. But in a companywide audit of purchasing procedures, the internal auditors found violations of the centralized purchasing system because buyers in the subdivisions had favorite suppliers whom they did not want to relinquish even though the prices were higher than those offered under the central contracts.

The internal audit, properly used, can provide one of the means of control that management must retain when it decentralizes its activities.

Departmentation

Departmentation, the grouping of activities to carry out objectives, is not often the concern of the internal auditor, but it should be. Too often the internal auditor accepts the department he is auditing just as it is and does not consider whether the activities are suitably arranged and whether the organization is most efficient in its present form.

The first task of the internal auditor should be to determine what activities are needed to carry out the department's objectives, whether they have been considered in designing the organization, and whether they are balanced in terms of departmental goals. One internal auditor found an element lacking in an organization, one that led to inefficient use of resources and excessive costs:[26]

In one company the development of new products was the responsibility of the vice president, engineering. Three engineers reported to him:

□ A research and development engineer developed the new product.
□ A manufacturing engineer designed the production methods and determined what production equipment was needed.
□ An industrial engineer determined the most effective work methods, decided on the number of workers needed, and set production standards.

Once developed, the product was transferred to the production area for manufacture. The products were then produced and delivered. But the company was plagued by customer dissatisfaction and high scrap rates.

It took a thorough, detailed analysis to determine the missing element in the organization. When a product was developed a prototype was built to make sure it would work. But the prototype, like most prototypes, was relatively crude. Rarely is a prototype designed for mass production. And products being developed had to be mass-produced. In this company, however, the item being mass-produced was the prototype model.

So parts did not always fit. Subassemblies did not always mate. Costs were sky-high and so was the scrap rate. And since production units varied in quality, customer dissatisfaction was equally high.

Mass production requires that the concepts of the research and development engineer be designed in greater detail and accuracy for production: Eliminate parts that might break. Stipulate parts and materials. Reduce the number of parts to simplify production. Restyle the product to appeal to the eye. And make sure dimensions are precise and mating points are exact.

So that was what was lacking: a design department, or at least a design engineer. The analysis, in terms of what activities a department must include to meet an objective, disclosed improper departmentation.

The internal auditor must be concerned with the management controls that are violated through improper departmentation. Two illustrations, which are far from rarities, follow:[27]

In one instance, a quality control manager reported to a production manager. But the objectives of the production manager are to turn out a volume of products on schedule and at lowest possible cost. The objective of the quality control manager is to make sure the products meet quality standards. Company objectives and customer satisfaction depend on all three of these attributes. But when costs rise and schedules are not being met, what would it avail the quality control manager to complain to his superior that quality standards are not being met and that work should be rejected or reworked?

In another case, a credit and collection manager reported to the sales manager. Their objectives conflicted. The credit manager was responsible for protecting his company from poor credit risks. The sales manager was responsible for high sales volume. Who wins out in borderline cases?

In both cases, the internal auditor should recommend that activities with potentially conflicting but with equally important objectives be given parity in the organization. Each should be in a department that has authority equal to that of the other. Otherwise, departmentation is not balanced, and that means that company objectives may not be met.

Departmentation should provide for cross-checks and should, by separation of duties, reduce the possibility of manipulation and embezzlement.[28]

In some companies, activities relating to record keeping, financial analysis, and custody of cash and securities are not properly grouped and separated. When the internal auditor sees the following organizational errors, he should recommend immediate separation of duties and activities:

◻ The person responsible for accounts receivable records is also receiving cash. He could manipulate the records so that they would never reveal that he converted the cash to his own use.

◻ The person in charge of cash records is reconciling the bank accounts. Cash might be diverted and the bank records, under his control, would not send up flares to highlight the impropriety.

◻ Under a project organization designed to supervise the construction of facilities, the construction accountant reports directly to the engineering manager responsible for the construction. The special interests of the construction engineer may vary from those of the accountant. The accuracy and propriety of construction payments are likely to suffer.

One internal auditor observed that customer complaints were received by various departments in the company. The complaints were dealt with haphazardly and unsatisfactorily. He recommended that a special unit be assigned the task of handling customer complaints in a timely manner and in accordance with clearly established company policies.

Responsibility and Authority

Early in an audit of an organization, the internal auditor should review the statement of responsibilities for the organizational unit. His concern here is twofold: to determine whether responsibilities assigned are consonant with the unit's mission and to determine whether the statement bears evidence of review and approval and is up to date.

Executive management has a right to expect that the statement of responsibilities it prepared or approved describes accurately what the unit has undertaken or has been assigned to do. If a contract administration unit is responsible for seeing that certain government regulations are incorporated into subcontracts with suppliers, executive management should not have to check to see that the responsibility is being carried out. But the internal auditor should determine whether that and all other assigned responsibilities are dealt with and are not left hanging in limbo. If an assigned responsibility is not being carried out by the audited unit, the internal auditor must determine whether there is a need for it to be carried out at all. And if there is truly a need and the audited unit is not the place for the activity, he should determine what other unit in the organization is or should be carrying it out.

The internal auditor should also look for divided responsibilities, which rarely work. When, for example, a number of different people in different units are approving expense accounts, confusion will most certainly result. Different policies and standards may be applied. One approver may demand receipts for everything; another might be quite relaxed about the requirement. Employees submitting travel vouchers and being subjected to differing policies might understandably be irked.

In some instances, the statement of responsibilities may be window dressing. The audited unit may have prepared and received approval for a statement that does not portray actual responsibilities. The statement may be a facade meant to impress superiors rather than express actual conditions. Since executive management rarely has the time to learn of those instances first hand, it assumes that the statement speaks the truth and that the unit is burdened with responsibilities that in fact do not exist.

Sometimes responsibilities are undertaken to the detriment of the company. In one case of record a product manager extended his responsibilities to include purchasing, receiving, and inventory storage. His attention was diverted from his basic mission. Just as bad, the company was being deprived of the checks and balances supplied by independent agencies responsible for those activities. The internal auditor analyzed the excessive centralization of responsibility and recommended realignment of the activities to restore the checks and balances.[29]

The internal auditor should be concerned with the coequality of authority and responsibility. In one situation the internal auditor observed that the purchasing department was held responsible to commit company funds for the procurement of all supplies and services. In an audit of the marketing branch, he observed that marketing personnel were making agreements with suppliers to obtain as sales aids valuable products used in merchandising and in advertising the company's goods. The marketing people would then ask purchasing to write confirming purchase orders to cover the transactions. Purchasing was frustrated. Under strict rules designed to maintain armslength, unbiased dealings with suppliers, it had the responsibility to make all commitments. Marketing had taken upon itself some of the purchasing authority without responsibility to abide by those rules. The internal audit report resulted in the return of authority to the purchasing department, where it belonged.

Delegation

Since delegation demands control, because responsibility cannot be relinquished, the internal auditor can become the delegator's best friend. Nowhere else in the organization can the delegator obtain objective, professional opinions on how the assigned tasks are being carried out. These are the questions to which the internal auditor wants specific answers about delegated authority:

- Does the delegate understand his responsibility?
- Is the authority commensurate with the responsibility?
- Is performance up to the delegator's standards?
- Have comparable responsibilities been assigned elsewhere; that is, is there an overlap in responsibilities?

Brink tells of a situation in which the auditor was helpful in working out a particularly sensitive problem for the chief executive officer of a company. Because of his close relationship with the chief executive, the internal auditor was asked to inquire into an impasse between two senior vice presidents. The internal auditor, under the authority given to him by the chief executive, explored the problem in conversations with the vice presidents and their aides. The inquiry disclosed a lack of understanding of the precise delegation of responsibility to the vice presidents, and that resulted in an operational problem caused by the overlapping of responsibilities.[30]

Spans of Management

The internal auditor, as the expert in internal control, should be well aware that knowledgeable supervision of subordinates is probably the best form of control yet devised. That form of control implies availability to solve problems. When the span of management is so broad that supervision is not performing its function, the internal auditor should make his observations known. But that is a matter that is difficult to quantify. It is not a fact that can be objectively supported and reported. Yet the internal auditor, as a professional observer of operations, obtains impressions during his audit of an activity that are as valuable as the data contained in his spread sheets crammed with tests of transactions.

Some auditing organizations approach formally the collection and communication of impressions on such nonquantifiable matters as supervision and morale. Those impressions are recorded in working papers and are then informally discussed with appropriate management people. Often the impressions serve to fortify vague feelings held by managers who are not closely tuned to ongoing operations, or at least not as closely tuned as is the auditor, who may have spent weeks in close contact with operations and the people carrying them out. The discussions can be as useful to managers as quantified deficiencies supported by reams of data.

Obviously, the discussions call for tact and discrimination. Let the auditor cry wolf once too often and he loses his credibility. But approached from the vantage point of management-level observations, the auditor's communication of his impressions can provide valuable input to executive management.

Zimmerman tells of an organizationl control problem that was threatening to founder a company until the problem was solved.[31]

> The president of a company manufacturing highly engineered, highly competitive consumer appliances was not an engineer himself. Nine people reported directly to him—not too wide a span, ordinarily. But in this company the span was too wide because the organizations represented by six of these people were highly technical: product development, manufacturing engineering, industrial engineering, quality control, production control, and production. The other three were personnel, finance, and marketing.
>
> The highly competitive nature of his products required the president to spend considerable portions of his time on marketing. Yet the other activities kept calling for decisions; and since the president was not schooled in those disciplines, the decisions were slow in coming and not always the best. New products took too long to develop, and manufacturing suffered from a high scrap rate. A competent, management-oriented internal auditor would have readily spotted the problem and suggested a solution: Place the six technical activities under a vice president of operations, reporting to the president. This was the solution. The span of management was reduced to four, the technically trained vice president of operations tackled and solved the problem of scrap rates and manufacturing costs and the president took his first vacation in years.

Line and Staff

The internal auditor must always keep in mind this salient fact: He is staff and not line. He must sell, not tell. Let him seek to usurp a line manager's responsibilities and his usefulness and that of the line managers are seriously eroded.

Yet the internal auditor, as one of the most significant monitors of a company's control system, has the responsibility for measuring and evaluating the enterprise's control system. When controls are weak, he must not relinquish his vigil until they have been strengthened. That would seem to be a contradiction, and many an internal auditor has overstepped his bounds and incurred the enmity of line management by not knowing how to deal with the contradiction. On the one hand, the internal auditor is told he must have sufficient status in the organization to have his recommendations considered; on the other hand, he is warned not to step over into line functions by issuing orders.

The solution lies not in what but in how. The internal auditor is responsible for reporting on what is wrong, on what conditions indicate weaknesses in control. The line manager is responsible for determining how the controls are to be strengthened. Obviously, the well-trained, experienced internal auditor will have ideas about how the condition may be corrected, and he would be failing to function as a problem-solving partner if he withheld that information. But never should he be heard to say: "Correct the condition this way." Rather he should say, "Here is the condition, here is the effect, and here are causes. The condition must be corrected. One of the corrective steps you may want to consider is this. But whatever steps you take, the condition must be corrected and we shall evaluate the adequacy and effectiveness of *your* corrective action." There is no stepping from staff to line in such an approach. There is only counseling and maintaining the staff function of guardian over the entity's controls.

Drucker emphasizes that aspect of staff work when he says that staff people—and this is particularly applicable to internal auditors—require the right temperament for the job and that people with that temperament are rare. They must want others to take the credit. They must help line people do the job of getting a defect corrected provided only that it is not immoral or insane. That requires a person who lets others take the bows for doing the job themselves rather than doing it for them and then pointing to himself with pride.[32]

Internal auditors often audit services used by the company: janitorial, legal, tax, maintenance, data processing, and advertising, among others. Some of those services may be rendered by company people; some may be obtained by purchase. The auditor can help executive management decide whether particular services should be purchased or performed in-house. Some of the matters he should be concerned with are:

□ Relative costs. These include (1) waiting time for outside services, (2) the frequency with which the services are needed, and (3) the overhead expenses that would be incurred if the service were performed in-house.

□ Divided attention. When services are purchased, it should be remembered that the supplier has other clients and that the auditor's company may be receiving a low priority.

□ What to ask for. Sometimes managers dealing with outside services are not quite sure what they need. They may not know what to expect of outside legal counsel, for example. In-house counsel may be able to provide assistance in determining what is needed in a given circumstance.

□ Management of services. The managers of the supplier's organization usually have the skill, experience, and background often lacking in managers hired for in-house services. That may be one of the greatest bars to performing some services in-house.

Each instance requires careful analysis that makes use of the internal auditor's ability to accumulate and array comparable costs and the line manager's determination of need for the services. Together, the internal auditor and the manager can compare both the measurable and the unmeasurable costs and benefits of the two alternatives.

The Informal Organization

The sensitive internal auditor working within an organization can soon discern the pattern of the informal organization that overlies the formal one. And that is not only a matter of individuals but also a way of thinking that does not display itself in the formal organization charts. An entity or an organization within an entity moves forward if it has vitality, if it is able to generate and regenerate thoughts, ideas, and innovations. The absence of vitality makes itself evident in a number of ways:[33]

□ People cling to old ways even though the environment is changing.

□ New goals have not been defined; the old goals are no longer challenging.

□ Thinking relates to action on the day-to-day jobs; it is not reflected in looking foward.

□ The company becomes institutionalized; it is different from the people who staff it.

□ The organization has the reputation for stability and security, not for being venturesome.

□ People rely on precedent instead of generating new ideas.

□ Supervisors are intolerant of criticism; they discourage independent thought.

In addition to dealing with the informal organization, internal auditors who travel, particularly those who make audits in foreign countries, face dealing with the cultures of those countries.

Culture is cultivated behavior acquired through social learning,[34] and it differs between New York and Texas as it differs between the United States and Japan. In the United States the internal auditor generally meets a philosophy that emphasizes the individual. In other countries, class distinctions may be more pronounced and there is a lack of the democratic atmosphere that characterizes the American economy. The auditor must take those differences into account and deal with them much as he deals with the chart of accounts or the organization chart.

In the United States promptness is a virtue, but in some countries it is customary to keep people waiting an hour or two before seeing them. Hours of work differ. In Greece, the workday is scheduled from 8:00 A.M. to 2:00 P.M. six days a week. In Latin America the midday siesta is a standard practice. Part of the internal auditor's planning for an audit in a foreign country must include an understanding of that country's culture: what is accepted, what is taboo. He will have to learn how to work around the impediments raised by that culture to his normal working methods. Knowing, for example, that he will be kept waiting for his appointments, he should stuff his briefcase with material that he can work on while cooling his heels.

In view of differing informal organizations, differing cultures, and the role that status plays in an enterprise, the internal auditor must be careful how he makes his recommendations. He must always be concerned with the needs of people. And those needs may not always square with the kind of mathematical logic that is the internal auditor's stock in trade. For example, a brilliant marketing executive whose efforts maintain the company's high share of the market may see himself as ruler of all he surveys. He may be most comfortable and do his best work with a coterie of yes-men around him—yes-men who contribute little in terms of their own productivity, but much in terms of the executive's productivity. The internal auditor who, with seeming logic, suggests the transfer of some of those people elsewhere—and has the suggestion adopted by the president—may find that the end result is the loss of an indispensable marketing director.

Committees

Committees are an important part of the functioning of a large organization, but their operations should not be beyond the sphere of the audit review. In fact, an internal auditor may sometimes be made a member of a committee to observe the committee's deliberations and point out committee decisions that may propose actions that run counter to the existing control system or do not provide for appropriate checks and balances. As he reviews the functioning of committees, here are some of the questions the internal auditor will want answered:

- □ Is the objective of the committee, its reason for being, made definite? Are there written specifications to guide committee members and keep the members from getting involved in matters outside their charter?
- □ Do members of the committee understand their roles? Are they a decision-making body? Or are they merely there to advise and counsel the chairman?
- □ Are the duties of each member made clear? Serving on a committee is a job like any other job. And people work best when they know what they are supposed to do.
- □ Is the committee too small to produce varied viewpoints or so big as to be unwieldy?
- □ Do members have equal status so none is dominated by another?
- □ Is an agenda prepared for each meeting?
- □ Are minutes prepared, and do they indicate that the purposes of the agenda have been carried out?
- □ Are assignments for action specific? Do they name individuals who are to perform the assignments. Are scheduled due dates set forth?
- □ Is there a means of following up on the assigned tasks?
- □ Does the committee report periodically to executive management on its activities and accomplishments? Are the reports supported by the committee minutes and other records?
- □ Do the committee's activities conflict with or overlap the activities of other committees?
- □ Is the committee still needed? Has it completed its mission without being disbanded?

If he uses the right approach, the internal auditor can address those questions to the chairman of the committee. That is the direct and most useful approach. If it turns out that many of the answers are in the negative, the very process of answering the questions may be an education to the chairman.

An internal auditor can sometimes undertake a companywide appraisal of committees that deal with comparable subjects. He can prepare a large chart that permits the delineation of the key attributes of the various committees, as for example:

Name of committee
Meeting dates or frequency
Chairman
Members
Detailed functions and responsibilities
Authority
Implementing instructions

Such an analysis will highlight overlaps, gaps, and inconsistencies, and it can form the basis for questioning the continued need for one or more of the committees.

Organization Charts

The absence of organization charts, statements· of responsibility, and job descriptions is usually an indicator of inefficiency. Communication is difficult enough in relatively simple matters. When one considers the multiple relations in a fairly large organization, pictorial representation becomes all the more important. If organization charts are well prepared, everyone is looking at the same picture. True, two people may read different things into the same picture, but at least they are starting at the same point.

When organization charts are lacking, the internal auditor should prepare them and then ask appropriate managers whether they truly portray the organization as it is. The charts will often be the first picture taken of the organizational structure, and they could be a surprise to the executive. The author was given a consulting assignment for a small industrial company. Our first request was for an organization chart. When the president asked "What is an organization chart?" we knew without even entering the company doors that we'd find problems. And indeed we did.

The president and one of his immediate subordinates prepared their first organization chart, and they did not need the consultant to make them realize that the organization was lopsided, that too many people reported directly to the president, and that the reason the president had to work 70 hours a week lay in malorganization. He had no relief until he restructured the organization so that he had a reasonable span of control and was able to delegate some of his duties to others.

Brink tells of an internal auditing organization assigned by its company to review the organization and operation of the local YMCA. A review of the organization disclosed the need for changes at all levels from the board of directors down. The recommendations for improvement included a complete set of organization charts and supporting job descriptions. The audit resulted in a major improvement in the effectiveness of what had been a badly managed operation.[35]

Change

As the robins herald spring, so the internal auditor heralds change. His questions, his insistent "Why this way?" generally precede recommendations for improvements, and those recommendations bespeak change. Yet organizational change is normally resisted by incumbents. For that reason, the internal auditor recommending change should gain the confidence of the auditee and make sure the recommendation is accepted before it ever appears in the audit report.

The internal auditor should also be concerned with the ripple effect of a single organizational change. No department in a company is a detached member; it is a part of a complete body. A shift in one part is usually felt in other parts, particularly the peripheral or interfacing ones.

Then too, internal control includes the form of organization—the checks and balances provided by preventing an operation from being under the complete domination of one individual or one group. Hence whenever management proposes an organizational change, the proposal should be submitted to the internal auditing organization for views on whether the change will erode or weaken internal control.

The internal auditor is in a particularly good position to consider the effects of change. Over and above his professional expertise in evaluating the adequacy and effectiveness of control lies his knowledge of the interrelations of units and groups throughout the entire entity.

Staffing

Every entity and every unit within an entity takes on the color of the manager's thinking and philosophy. To identify that color should be the first task of an audit of operations. What is the manager like? What is his background? How does he manage?

The manager who has been trained in or has a natural bent for management and its rules and principles runs a far different operation than does the technician elevated to management position. The former's organization will most likely be designed to meet entity and unit objectives. Each subordinate will know his place and his job, and, equally important, he will know the jobs of those around him and the job of his superior.

The process of auditing such an organization is far easier than auditing an organization run by a technician unaccustomed to manage. There the internal auditor may have to show the usefulness of organization charts and job descriptions and how they are developed. Furthermore, in such an environment, the auditor must be prepared, subtly, to teach and to counsel the manager on the principles of good administration.

The internal auditor can perform a useful service in certain aspects of staffing. A good management team must start with good hiring practices. The scoundrel on board was probably a scoundrel when he worked elsewhere, and one of the important means of restricting fraudulent acts is to restrict the hiring of those with a fraudulent bent. Yet often the personnel organization will hire people without even the flimsiest of background checks. When people are dismissed for improper behavior, the hiring process does not always provide for a means of preventing their rehire. Those are the sorts of controls the internal auditor is obligated to check in evaluating the adequacy and effectiveness of the entity's organizational controls.

Also in his audit, the internal auditor should seek to determine whether each managerial position is defined specifically; without standards it is difficult to know what to hold the manager responsible for. In fact, recommending the establishment of job descriptions for managers forces the managers to think through what should be done and who is to do it. To set up the standards by which they can measure themselves can be an excellent device in training managers to function as true administrators.

Other matters the internal auditor should consider when he appraises staffing are these:

□ What was the basis on which the complement of people within the unit was established? Is it a sound one?

□ Does the unit employ the right kind of talent? Is a clerk doing a job best handled by a technician? Or does an engineer do low-level administrative work?

□ Do people have jobs that challenge their capacities and make them stretch? Can they see daylight ahead for themselves? If there is a high turnover rate, the challenge may not be there.

The internal auditor will, of course, be concerned with overstaffing. Executive management expects it of him, but it is hard to document and difficult to convince local managment about. The proper audit approach, however, may pay big dividends for the organization. Here is an example:[36]

> An internal auditor, reviewing operations in an industry's distribution center, was certain the center was overstaffed. But he knew he would have difficulty convincing management of his beliefs. He suggested, and the manager reluctantly agreed, that they cooperate in flow-charting the various processes in the center. The flow charts were developed in connection with extensive interviews of the personnel. When they were completed, the manager could see for himself that:
>
> □ Procedures for processing orders could be simplified.
> □ A manually prepared stock card system duplicated an existing computer system and could therefore be eliminated.
> □ A number of reports could be eliminated.
> □ A reshuffling of duties could cut down on errors and improve efficiency.
>
> Faced with the uncompromising picture of what was and what could be, management agreed to changes which would eliminate duplication and unnecessary work and thereby cut the staff about 35 percent. Office costs were thus reduced by over $50,000 a year.

The Organizational Audit

The internal auditor schooled in principles of organization can approach the organizational audit with greater efficiency and less wasted effort. He knows what to look for and can detect the telltale signs of organizational decay. Here are some of those signs:

□ Failing to have a system of periodic self-assessment—not taking into account how future plans will affect the organizational structure.
□ Lack of clear objectives.
□ Failing to clarify relations among people and groups.
□ Excessive spans of management. Failing to delegate authority and thus having everyone reporting directly to the boss.
□ A multiplication of management levels so that communication and decisions take forever to filter down and each decision involves tortuous paper-pushing.
□ Recurrence of problems that find their roots in malorganization.

- Errors in the process of delegating:
  Delegating duties to people who are not knowledgeable.
  Failing to balance delegation; that is, pushing authority down too far or not far enough.
- Inadequate communication—up and down or from interfacing organizations.
- Poor intradepartmental communication.
- Confused lines of authority; one subordinate reporting to two or more bosses.
- Authority without responsibility, and vice versa.
- Bottlenecks that prevent people from meeting schedules.
- Decisions that are in disagreement with company policies.
- Not using assigned functional authority.
- Staff–line conflicts.
- Executives who have reached their level of incompetence.
- Clashes between departments and people.
- An excessive number of committees. An inordinate amount of the executive's time spent on committees. Poor committee work. Too many people on committees.
- Lack of a uniform policy on key issues.
- Putting the attention of key people on non-key issues and failing to set appropriate priorities.
- Overorganization—making organizational changes at the drop of a hat. Changes in organization are like surgery; they should not be lightly undertaken.
- Lack of checks and balances. Breakdowns in financial control.
- Failure to accomplish objectives.
- Lack of knowledge or skill at the management level.
- Too many coordinators and assistants. Their use may be the result of poor organization.
- Excessive tension or dissatisfaction on the part of managers.
- A great many specialists and no generalists or administrators.
- Lack of information about what is going on in the company; people find out what's happening in their own organization by reading the newspapers.

Internal auditors usually perform some form of audit of the elements of organizing each time they audit a department or operation. Rarely are they asked to perform an audit of organizational control for an entire entity. Yet such an audit or management study should be within the competence of the management-oriented internal auditor. The auditor should understand what questions to ask and what steps to take. Here are some of the questions that are pertinent to an audit of the organizing function:

- □ What are the provisions for preparing organization charts and statements of responsibility? How and how often are they updated? What provision is made to tie plans for the future into the organization chart?
- □ How is the development of the organization chart keyed to the objectives of the enterprise?
- □ What consideration is given to enterprise and unit objectives in developing statements of responsibility? To what extent do the objectives and statements agree? What gaps exist?
- □ What are the qualifications of managers to carry out their responsibilities?
- □ To what extent does the grouping of activities facilitate the meeting of objectives?
- □ What are the key activities of the organization? To which people has each of the activities been assigned?
- □ What is the authority of each manager? Was the authority placed close to the point at which action must be taken?
- □ How are managers made to understand their own work and that of others with whom they must interface?
- □ How is authority delegated? Are the delegates qualified to undertake their assignments?
- □ When delegations are made, what form of control is developed to provide feedback to the delegator from the delegate?
- □ How well are departments or units integrated? Which ones seem to operate without checks and balances?
- □ What consideration, if any, has been given to developing project organizations for major missions that are limited in their life span?
- □ What are the spans of control? Are any too broad or too narrow?
- □ What backup charts have been developed? How do they anticipate the need for replacements for the next 5 or 10 years?
- □ What system does the company use to replace managers and develop new ones?
- □ What means are used to measure the progress and potential of managers?

There are undoubtedly many ways to make an audit of an entity's organization, but here are some of the steps to consider:

1. Accumulate all written materials relating to the organization structure:
    Organization charts.
    Statements of objectives and responsibilities.
    Job descriptions.
    Performance appraisals.
    Qualifications for various jobs.
2. Review the materials to see if:
    They relate to entity objectives.
    They disclose gaps or overlaps.
3. Determine what is needed to do each job.
4. List the incumbent managers' qualifications in terms of education and experience.
5. Identify the requirements that were met and those that were not met; identify qualifications not needed in the present job and relate them to the requirements of other jobs; and indicate needed qualities that are not being met by the incumbent managers.
6. Suggest organization charts and job descriptions that might better fit the requirements and the existing personnel.
7. Suggest well-thought-out, detailed, changed procedures to replace those now in existence.

The scope and depth of such a study, the study's potential for major change, and the effect that drastic recommendations will have on operating personnel, together with the rule that internal auditors should not prepare procedures they themselves may later audit, call for two prerequisites for such a study:

1. Specific authority from a highly placed executive or from the audit committee of the board of directors to make such a study.
2. The inclusion on the audit team of a member of line management to insure balance and objectivity in the survey and the results and to write the changed procedures.

CONCLUSION

Organizing follows planning, and the form of organization must be keyed to the entity's plans and aims. Good organization is no guarantee of success, but poor organization will most certainly make goals much harder to achieve. There is a limit to what one human being can deal with personally; hence the need for decentralization.

That calls for the delegation of some of the superior's authority; but the authority must be coequal with responsibility, and responsibility may never be relinquished. The reins may be long, but they must always be gripped firmly.

Large organizations cannot escape the use of staff people to help managers, but staff must know its place and have its authority clearly defined. Staff should be on tap and not on top. Each formal organization has an informal one, and managers must learn to deal with it; it won't go away. Committees are necessary, but they should not be a necessary evil if their charters are clear and if they are properly organized.

Organizational change is inevitable, but the trauma can be relieved if the changes are properly approached. There are too few good managers around. Those that were not born with the knack need training, and the internal auditor can help. He should participate in the various phases of organizing, not to devise organizations, but to make sure they have appropriate checks and balances. Internal auditors are not often asked to perform comprehensive audits of the organizing function, but with proper techniques they should be able to inform executive management whether the organizational structure suits the purposes of the organization.

References

1. P. F. Drucker, *Management: Tasks, Responsibilities, Practices* (New York: Harper & Row, 1974), pp. 523, 524, 530.
2. Ibid., p. 547.
3. Ibid., p. 553.
4. Ibid., pp. 572, 573.
6. "The New Package at American Can," *Business Week,* No. 1933, September 17, 1966, pp. 94–100.
7. E. R. Embree, "Can College Graduates Read?" *The Saturday Review of Literature,* Vol. 18, No. 12, p. 4.
8. Harold Koontz and Cyril O'Donnell, *Essentials of Management* (New York: McGraw-Hill, 1974), pp. 149–168.
9. J. B. Rizzo, R. J. House, and S. I. Lirtzman, "Role Conflict and Ambiguity in Complex Organizations," *Administrative Science Quarterly,* Vol. 15, No. 2, p. 161.
10. Douglas McGregor, *The Human Side of Enterprise* (New York: McGraw-Hill, 1960), p. 158.
11. "The New Bosses: A Stockbroker Takes Charge of Food Chain, Lifts Profits and Sales," *The Wall Street Journal,* January 2, 1962, pp. 1 and 6.

12. V. A. Graicunas, "Relationships in Organization," *Papers on the Science of Administration* (New York: Institute of Public Administration, Columbia University, 1937), pp. 183–187.
13. H. Farquhar, "The Anomaly of Functional Authority at the Top," *Advanced Management,* Vol. 7, No. 2, p. 51.
14. F. H. Goldner, "Success vs. Failure: Prior Managerial Perspectives," *Industrial Relations,* Vol. 9, No. 4, p. 455.
15. N. R. F. Maier, A. R. Solem, and A. A. Maier, *Supervisory and Executive Development* (New York: Wiley, 1957), pp. 66–67.
16. "Too Many Other Rump Sessions," *Business Week,* October 15, 1960, pp. 187–190.
17. Ernest Dale, *The Great Organizers* (New York: McGraw-Hill, 1960), p. 83.
18. P. R. Lawrence, *The Changing of Organizational Behavior Patterns* (Boston: Division of Research, Harvard Business School, 1958), chap. 10.
19. P. W. Maloney, *Management's Talent Search: Recruiting Professional Personnel* (New York: AMA, 1961), p. 9.
20. C. H. Greenewalt, *The Uncommon Man* (New York: McGraw-Hill, 1959), p. 64.
21. R. L. Katz, "Skills of an Effective Administrator," *Harvard Business Review,* Vol. 33, No. 1, pp. 33–42.
22. Drucker, op. cit., p. 535.
23. L. B. Sawyer, *The Practice of Modern Internal Auditing* (New York: The Institute of Internal Auditors, Inc., 1973), pp. 221, 222.
24. Pauley, C. A., "Audit Responsibilities in the Design of Computerized Systems," *The Internal Auditor,* July-August 1969, pp. 22–32.
25. H. J. Mintern, ed., *How to Save $14,500,000 Through Internal Auditing,* (Orlando, Fla.: The Institute of Internal Auditors, 1975), p. 167.
26. R. R. Zimmerman, "Auditing the Organization Structure," *The Internal Auditor,* Fall 1965, pp. 66, 67.
27. Ibid., pp. 67, 68.
28. V. Z. Brink, "The Internal Auditor's Review of Organizational Controls," *Research Committee Report 18* (Orlando, Fla.: The Institute of Internal Auditors, 1972), pp. 38, 39, 45.
29. Ibid., p. 45.
30. Ibid., pp. 47, 48.
31. Zimmerman, op. cit., p. 63.
32. Drucker, op. cit., p. 536.
33. P. J. Taylor, "Appraising a Corporate Organization," *The Internal Auditor,* Winter 1962, p. 39.
34. F. M. Keesing, *Cultural Anthropology: The Science of Custom* (New York: Holt, Rinehart & Winston, 1958), p. 18.
35. Brink, op. cit., p. 47.
36. Mintern, op. cit., p. 162.

11

Directing

Directing: moving people toward goals through leadership, motivation, and communication. The complexity of the worker. A confluence of goals. Management's responsibility for motivation. The various motivators. The benefits and forms of participation. Constructive and destructive criticism. Creativity as a result of motivation. Compensation: the classic but not the best motivator. The expansion of fringe benefits. Production sharing and the Scanlon Plan. Leadership: stimulating people to work with zeal and confidence. The characteristics of leadership—not measurable but recognizable. Leadership styles: autocratic, participative, and laissez-faire. Leadership techniques: empathy, objectivity, self-knowledge, and legitimacy. Levels of leadership, from executive to supervisor. Giving orders. Directing change.

The internal auditor's involvement in directing. Auditing personnel administration. Evaluating the determination of manpower needs. Evaluating the orientation and training of personnel. Absentee and turnover rates as a gauge of effective direction. Reviewing personnel records, unemployment benefits, welfare, and other services. Internal audits of compensation. Internal controls over the entire compensation process. The internal auditor's involvement with leadership. Concern for employee utilization. Determining whether managers are carrying out their assigned functions. Human resource stewardship. The internal auditor and change.

DIRECTING AND THE MANAGER

Nature of Directing

Definition and Purpose

Directing, sometimes referred to as actuating, is the function of moving resources toward a goal. It is largely interpersonal, and so it deals mainly with stimulating people to do what is necessary to meet enterprise objectives. At its best, it will succeed in making people want to meet those objectives because achievement will satisfy individual needs and help people meet their own goals. At its worst, it creates resentment, foot-dragging, and sabotage.

Directing is a complex combination of actions and concepts that include leadership, motivation, behavioral patterns, and communication. Because of their special importance to the organization, we have devoted separate chapters to behavioral patterns (Chapter 4) and communications (Chapter 6). In this chapter we shall be concerned chiefly with motivation and leadership. Some of the concepts in Chapters 4 and 6 will be reemphasized as needed for a rounded discussion.

Importance

Rare indeed is the person who worships at the shrine of work for work itself. Usually people work to exchange effort for some gain that makes the effort worthwhile to them. They will contribute only enough of themselves to continue the exchange. Yet buried beneath that minimal effort is a tremendous wellspring of potential that is rarely tapped. Indeed, few people use more than a small part of their capability, so a goal of successful management is to show people how their own needs can be integrated with those of the enterprise and make them want to reach down to those hidden resources.

In an age of extreme competition, when comparable companies have access to comparable technology and markets, the difference in growth and profit can often stem from the difference with which the members of competing companies contribute to organizational goals. Therefore, management must, in its directing process, create an environment in which people are willing to do twice as much as they think they can.

Some people are self-starters and need no urging; they know what is needed and will drive themselves toward it. Others are willing but need to be told where, how, and how much. The great majority, however, need to be stimulated to contribute willingly and enthusiastically. The manager who can inspire that enthusiasm, day after day and month after month, is worth more than rubies. He is the leader whom people will follow. He is the motivator who wakens drives and creativity. And he is usually blessed with superiors who have developed a climate that encourages human growth.

Elements of Directing

Man's inherent complexity bedevils the function of directing. One hires more than the typist's fingers and the machinist's hands; one hires the whole typist and the entire machinist. And with the people come their backgrounds, likes, antipathies, prejudices, abilities, disabilities, and vagaries.

Man cannot be pinned down, dissected, and analyzed like a butterfly. Many behaviorists have tried, but no template for human beings has yet been cut. Nevertheless, the analyses have thrown some light on this complexity whose name is worker:[1]

- □ He is not only complex, he is variable. He varies from situation to situation and from stimulation to stimulation.
- □ He comes to the job with certain fixed views; yet he is capable of learning new motives through his experiences in the organization and through the effect his superiors and fellow workers have upon him.
- □ His motives may change from organization to organization and from department to department within the same organization.
- □ He may respond, and respond productively, to many different kinds of managerial strategies from the autocratic to the democratic.

It is true that the whole man is hired and brings along with him his diverse needs. Yet the only human needs the manager will be interested in are those that can be satisfied within the confines of the organization. No manager has the time, energy, resources, or ability to satisfy all of a worker's human needs. The purpose of the organization is not to be a worker's psychiatrist. Rather, it should be to offer the right environment for the fulfillment of relevant needs: those that will be satisfied at the same time that organizational needs are met.

The directing process, then, is effective to the extent that subordinates contribute to organizational goals, to the extent they perceive a flowing together of their personal goals and those of the organization, to the extent they feel responsibility for contributing to the organizational goals, and to the extent they feel that their own efforts will achieve those goals. So the superior must know the goals and understand the people.

The aim of successful directing, then, is not to open doors, but to show where the key can be found . . . not so much to teach as to awaken desires to learn . . . not to pave the path, but to portray the rewards at the end of it . . . not to set the standards, but to show how the standards can be set . . . not to be the monitor, but to help each subordinate develop his own inner monitor . . . not to give the answers, but to ask questions so that the subordinates are led toward finding answers . . . not to fulfill expectations but to paint a compelling picture of the satisfactions that come from self-fulfillment.

Motivating

Management's Responsibility

Every manager must motivate. Every manager must induce people to act in a certain way, and the desideratum of motivation is to inspire people to perform superlatively. That cannot be done either by simply getting out of the employee's way or by wielding a whip. The answer lies in reaching the motives within that will cause the individual to want to act in a desired manner. Hence managers are responsible for understanding employee attitudes—attitudes that have been acquired in myriad ways from a variety of sources. Chiefly, they result from past experience, from the groups with which the employee works, and from sources of authority.

Employee attitudes must first be understood and then be shaped if personal and organizational goals are to be met. For years managers operated on the principle that the only motivation worth considering was the financial reward. But if that is the only reward, people will in time give of themselves only enough to get by. That is particularly true when jobs are uninspiring and unchallenging. There must be a personal incentive as well if the superior is to bring out the zeal and enthusiasm that are waiting to be mined.

The Motivators

Douglas McGregor said that man is a wanting animal.[2] Man's wants are endless; let one be satisfied and another springs up. And what motivates man to work are the things that he feels will satisfy his wants.

Different people, clearly, have different wants. And any one individual will have wants that vary with the times, with the situation, and with the satisfactions achieved. The hierarchies of wants proposed by Maslow are as valid as the satisfiers and dissatisfiers proposed by Herzberg.[3]

Maslow's hierarchy demands satisfaction of physical needs before the social needs and relations with others emerge. And the psychic needs, the needs for recognition and for self-fulfillment, will ordinarily not make themselves felt until the more basic needs are satisfied.

Herzberg's studies disclosed that certain benefits offered by the employer do not satisfy needs; all they do by their presence is avoid dissatisfaction. Hence, company policy, administration, salary, and fringe benefits—the so-called hygiene factors—do not of themselves satisfy other than the very basic needs. On the other hand, their absence will dissatisfy, and dissatisfaction results in absenteeism, labor turnover, and low morale. The factors that do satisfy are achievement, recognition, the work itself, responsibility, and advancement.

Both Maslow's and Herzberg's finding must be considered in relation to the situation and the type of individual involved. Among knowledge workers, achievement on the job is the key motivator. When such employees do not feel achievement, and when the hygiene factors are sufficiently attractive to keep them from leaving the organization, people will just go through the motions. They will not extend themselves.[4]

Maslow's theory of the progressive satisfaction of human needs may not necessarily be applicable to managers; for such people may not need external stimuli to do a superb job. Contact with managers has demonstrated that, in many cases, all that managers need is the opportunity to perform and thereby satisfy both their own needs and those of the organization.

In a study of 82 scientists, the factors that satisfied the study's subjects had nothing to do with hygiene. What attracted and held them were interest in the work, the importance of the work, and projects that challenged them.[5]

The studies have resulted in no specific remedy for all the ills attributable to lack of motivation. But they have pointed up the variability of employees, the heights to which motivated employees can rise, and the difficulty of the manager's job.

Indeed, the manager who believes that job satisfaction will lead unquestionably to high job performance may be disappointed; studies have shown low correlation between the two.[6] Job satisfaction does not necessarily lead to high performance, but perhaps the correct conclusion is the reverse: High performance will lead to job satisfaction, and high performance will result from an appropriate system of rewards—not the hygiene rewards, but rewards that are directly linked to performance.

Obviously, all managers will try to move their subordinates toward some goals. The autocrat will do it with fear, punishment, and threats of dismissal. That may work for a while, or it may work when jobs are scarce and the workers are striving to fill their basic physical needs. But the autocratic style may not work when the autocrat turns his back or the job market benefits the worker.

The participative manager will try to offer rewards that fill the needs of the employee. And under proper conditions, production will be high if the worker has a true expectancy that he will receive those rewards. His expectancy is based on three factors:

1. He has the physical and mental equipment to accomplish the task set before him.
2. He feels sure that if he does the job in accordance with or better than the standards set, there will be a reward.
3. He is satisfied that the reward is equitable.

We have talked here of the tangible rewards, but many workers need more than that. Many jobs leave them with an unfilled need for "psychic income." That need can be satisfied if the worker feels that he has some effect on his own destiny: He would like some control over his own job so that he can shape it to suit his capabilities and aspirations, so that he can achieve recognition, so that the job is a challenge to be met rather than a bore to be tolerated, and so that he can feel that he can pull himself up to still better and higher positions.

Various types of motivators have been tried with varying success. Here are some:

Authority. The autocrat says: "Work or find other work." Authoritarian managers can obtain minimum performance with the whip, but the whip must be wielded constantly. It rarely motivates superb performance; and when it is set down, people slack off. In fact, strong unions and labor scarcity have largely caused managers to abandon it. They have begun to recognize that if the lashes are too severe, people will fight back. And in the long run flogging is destructive.

Competition. Under the merit principle, people are stimulated to excel their peers to gain higher merit ratings and earn promotion. But that form of motivation is notoriously difficult to administer, and objective measurements are almost impossible. The need for the individual to show himself superior to his associates can bring on resentment and adversely affect teamwork. In unionized plants merit has been superseded by seniority as a basis for advancement.

Zero defects. A zero defects program, if carefully established, publicized, and administered, can move people to work together to meet and exceed qualitative goals. By doing things right the first time, the escalating costs of rework and correction can be brought down. A number of success stories have testified to the practical worth of a good zero defects program.[7] In one sheet-metal shop it usually took 82 man-hours to correct errors committed during 13,800 production man-hours—a ratio of 168 to 1. After the ZD program was installed, it took only 16 man-hours to correct errors made in the same number of production hours—a ratio of 862 to 1.

Paternalism. Paternalism is the approach of the benevolent despot. "If I'm good to my people and provide them with the benefits I think they should have, they'll be grateful and work hard." But gratitude is a rare commodity. The benefits bestowed become benefits expected. They lose their gratitude-inducing appeal. They become just another hygiene factor whose presence does not satisfy and whose absence dissatisfies. Moreover, paternalism has one serious drawback in these more enlightened days: It assumes that the boss is superior to his workers and knows what is best for them. That may create more resentment than gratitude.

Implicit bargaining. Bargaining that is implicit differs from union-type bargaining. A tacit understanding develops between superior and subordinate: Live and let live. "You do your job, and I'll wink at the rules. You give me reasonable performance, and I'll see that you're protected." That may provide for country club living, but it does not stimulate superior performance.

Participation

Most people will extend themselves if they feel they are a part of the work they do, just as parents will usually dote on their own unlovely child and be indifferent to their neighbor's paragon. If the worker participates in developing and organizing the work, establishing standards, and setting goals, the job itself increases in stature and so do the worker and the manager. There is a challenge in clearing the high jump you have set. There is another kind of challenge in figuring out how to sneak under the bar set by others.

Participation adds dignity to the job. It marks the worker as a part of the decision-making apparatus, and it can reduce employee resistance. But management's offer of participation must be sincere. The worker does not need a doctorate in industrial psychology to detect insincerity. There are several approaches to participation:

□ *Suggestion system.* A suggestion system can be useful, but it generally affects only a minority of the employees.
□ *Multiple management.* In the multiple management arrangement, people participate in problem solving that goes beyond their normal assignments. For example, production committees made up of workers and managers might study ways and means of improving production efficiency and reducing production costs.
□ *Consultative management.* In a consultative management arrangement, managers bring their people into the management process. Instead of making authoritarian, unilateral decisions, they ask their people to participate in the day-to-day administration of the job. But the final choice must still be that of the superior. People like to be heard, but they also respect a decisive superior.

Participation is not a panacea. It may work with some people and not with others. The subordinate must be capable of becoming involved in the participative process, but some workers may fear and be suspicious of it. The atmosphere of the organization must provide a climate that is kind to the participative approach, hence the wise manager moves slowly and carefully in involving his people.

Also, participation may hold dangers. Unions may be jealous of their workers' loyalties and regard participation as a management ploy to win people over to the company's side. And, of course, emergent circumstances call for unilateral decisions. The worker expects strong leadership when danger threatens.

Criticism

Effective criticism can motivate people to improve; destructive criticism almost invariably accomplishes the reverse in the long run. For that reason criticism should be positive, and it will be more palatable if the evaluation process permits the subordinate to participate.

Rarely is criticism effective when it is approached in the white heat of passion. So the superior should avoid criticizing until he has asked himself what he hopes to accomplish. Having satisfied himself that the goal is improvement rather than the temporary satisfaction of telling someone off, he should then identify the problem. Approaching the problem impersonally can avoid defensiveness and resentment. The proper approach is not "Here's what you did," but "Here's what happened."

So that the subordinate will not be kept worrying about the unknown, the introduction should be followed immediately with the negative things that must be said. The negative things should be objective and specific. Examples of unsatisfactory behavior are important. Questions of fact should be thoroughly resolved, and then the subordinate should be asked how he can improve unsatisfactory behavior. Seeking participation can relieve tensions. The superior should help by suggesting ways of working out the problems.

The session should be ended with a high note: Point out the subordinate's good points and potentials. But the session should not be ended until both supervisor and worker feel that the problem has been fully and fairly explored.

Creativity

Creativity is closely tied to motivation. Creativity needs the right environment. It cannot be forced, but it can grow if the climate is right. When people are told that creativity is welcome, they will regard their jobs and their environment differently. They will find that new life is brought into their work. They will start to observe the matters that may have formerly escaped their attention. They may start thinking; they may relate ideas and experiences they thought were long forgotten. They will start generating different and alternative courses of action. They will no longer be hemmed in by the forbidding walls of precedent. They will start drawing upon forces they did not know they had—emotional and preconscious forces. They will learn to be flexible.

From the standpoint of the manager, creativity as such is not enough. The manager is concerned with innovation. Creativity generates the ideas; innovation puts them to use. In results management, most managers and workers will be on the constant lookout for ways of achieving goals while making the job more rewarding.

Most importantly, the manager should recognize creativity for what it is: Not necessarily the blinding flash of an Einstein's $e = mc^2$, but the developing of new ways of doing the same old things. More often, merely recognizing a problem and seeing the need for a better way is a creative act. Management is a creative and innovative pursuit. If managers provide the right environment, they can move their people to participate in a rewarding creativity.

Compensation

Motivator or Dissatisfier?

Compensation is the classic motivator, but managers find it difficult to make compensation more than a hygiene factor—one of Herzberg's dissatisfiers. As monetary needs are satisfied, they have less and less power to stimulate performance and more and more power to dissatisfy. If an executive in an organization is receiving a few hundred dollars less than a comparable executive, he loses sight of the fact that, after taxes, the difference in buying power is infinitesimal. He can be eaten by jealousy over the difference and become less effective as an executive.

Economic benefits motivate when they satisfy pressing needs. As has been said: Man does not live by bread alone—unless there is no bread. When economic goals are not the most pressing ones, they will motivate only under the following circumstances:

- □ High compensation should be a goal that is important both to the individual and to the organization.
- □ The individual must feel confident that, if he exercises energy and skill toward meeting organizational goals, he will gain greater compensation.
- □ The individual must be convinced that he has the personal equipment to improve, that improvement is attainable.

Compensation comes in three different forms: (1) base pay or salary for the job, (2) variable pay that is geared to the individual's productivity, and (3) supplementary pay that is not geared to either the individual or the job (fringe benefits). Thus, total compensation includes both base pay and extra payments. The base pay is what is publicly known. It is the value of the position; and it is the basis for the amounts of such other benefits as life insurance, travel reimbursements, and bonuses.

The means of compensation should have relevance. They should be meaningful in terms of the situation. A salesman's contribution is readily measured objectively; his compensation can be geared readily to performance that can be recognized by commissions. Conversely, the performance of a research scientist or a contract administrator cannot be measured readily, and hence it must be paid for through a straight salary.

Compensation plans may be what are termed shallow or steep. In an organization that is inherently conservative, one in which all managers follow the book and in which innovation and risk taking are not held in high esteem, compensation is shallow because variations in managerial ability are slight. But when the organization wants and rewards aggressive leadership and vision, a great differential among managers may be both appropriate and necessary.

Incentive Compensation

Incentive plans include bonuses, commissions, profit sharing, and incentive pay. The organization has no obligation to pay bonuses. The bonus is based primarily on company profits and is granted on the basis of salary and performance. The individual should have a clear understanding of the basis for bonuses, and the basis should be consistently applied. One drawback associated with bonuses is the passage of time between performance and payment. Positive, instant reinforcement is usually lacking; the reward does not mesh with the deed.

The subject of profit sharing is broad and ramified. Profit sharing can be a powerful motivator to some, but people who feel they cannot directly influence profits through their own efforts may not find it an incentive. Also, morale may drop when profits turn to losses or when profit-sharing funds decline in value. Commissions, on the other hand, are directly and visibly related to performance, and so they can be strong motivators.

Incentive pay is usually based on time studies if it is to be objective. If the studies could be completely accurate and scientific, incentive pay would be relatively simple to administer, but they are complicated by trying to get the measure of the normal output of an average person expending average effort under average conditions. That is a chimera, and the workers are usually abundantly aware that it is. Since the employee's compensation will be governed by the studies, it is no wonder that war is declared as soon as the time-study engineers enter the door.

Deferred Compensation

Deferred compensation includes contractual payments, stock options, and pensions. Contractual payments are agreements between employer and employee to defer payments of agreed-upon amounts until after retirement or after the term of employment. That form of deferred compensation can be mutually beneficial. The employer knows the amount he is committed for. The employee can receive compensation at a time when his income tax bracket may be substantially lower. Both employer and employee should be aware, however, of the government regulations covering deferred compensation.

Stock options are rights to buy a corporation's common stock at a specified price within a stipulated period in the future. They can be highly motivating to some managers who can see their efforts resulting in higher profits to the company and increased prices for their stock.

Pension plans have proliferated in recent years. The trend appears to be toward the noncontributory plans—those in which the employee makes no contributions to the pension funds. Pension plans have both benefits and drawbacks. On the one hand, they provide a degree of economic security for employees. Younger employees can see daylight ahead for themselves as older employees retire at stipulated ages, and the deferred compensation is greater because of the employer's purchasing power, greater than the kind of insurance the employee could procure individually. On the other hand, employees are deterred from leaving the company because the longer their incumbency the better the benefits. Also, inflation can seriously erode real purchasing power.

Fringe Benefits

The list of fringe benefits keeps expanding. A partial catalog includes medical and dental care, counseling and legal aid, group insurance, paid vacation and sick leave, time at seminars and conferences, educational assistance, scholarships, and paid association memberships. Those benefits are undoubtedly socially desirable, but their ability to motivate is questionable. They are not affected by job performance. Most companies provide the same or similar benefits, so the benefits provide little competitive edge in vying for an employee's services.

Production Sharing

Because individual incentives have rarely worked well, there has been a trend toward plans that appeal to the group instead of to the individual. Probably the best known production-sharing plan is a system that Joseph N. Scanlon, a union official, developed in 1938.[8]

Scanlon's plan was more than a way to administer an incentive program; his purpose was to provide a new, cooperative way of business life. For instance, machinists were to communicate directly with staff engineers. The approach was one of problem solving instead of rancor and animosity. To be avoided were the pressures of incentive wages, crash production programs, and autocratic leadership. The aim was to convey to all workers of the company the idea that their opponents were not the company's management but rather the competing firms that were getting a larger share of the market or making a similar product better and at lower cost.

The Scanlon plan required a series of departmental committees made up of the foreman and a union representative. The committee purpose was to obtain and process suggestions for improvement. In addition, normal labor cost per unit of output, based on past experience, was determined.

If greater cooperation and efficiency reduced costs below the norm, the amounts saved would be divided among the workers. Sometimes the savings would be divided equally between the firm and the employee group. The employees' share would be allocated to the employees on the basis of base pay. Most important, reward was directly and instantly tied to productivity, since bonuses were distributed each month.

Drucker has said that workers' participation plans, such as Scanlon's, work only when the enterprise is doing well; that it works only in profitable businesses.[9] Yet one of the first successful introductions of the plan was in a company that had its back to the wall: LaPointe Machine Tool Company in Hudson, Massachusetts. The workweek had been cut to four days, and the company was on the brink of bankruptcy. Part of the success of the plan there was attributable to a change in attitudes. Cooperation among all groups replaced backbiting and defensive self-protection.

At the Parker Pen Company, a unionized firm of 1,000 employees, incentive bonuses were paid in 142 of 168 months and ranged from 5.5 percent to 20 percent of payroll.[10] In a survey of 2,636 employees in 21 plants that adopted the Scanlon Plan, the employee role most emphasized was that of providing information through suggestions.[11] Under the plan, workers appear more interested in their company's health and seem to accept change more readily. Clearly, if an employee makes a suggestion for improvement, he will embrace the change that brings it about. The greatest defect in the plan is reported to be the lack of effect it has on the individual's own job. That effect, evidently, can be had chiefly through job enrichment or job enlargement.

The plan will not work for everyone. It is of lower value to middle and top management. There improvement in leadership styles brings about greater participation. But among supervisors, who often lack participative skills, the establishment of formal committees that must be consulted provides reasonable assurance of employee participation. Since formal participation is tied directly to the reward of money, the incentive to participate is strong.[12]

Probably the greatest contribution that Scanlon made was to show that management cannot consistently motivate people through gimmicks. Managers will motivate only when they create a climate that stimulates real cooperation throughout the entire organization.

One of the byproducts of a cooperative plan is improvement in morale. Morale was discussed in Chapter 4, Patterns of Behavior, and will not be explored here. Suffice it to say that morale is not necessarily a satisfier. It may not increase production, but high morale has other benefits. Personnel turnover and absenteeism are lowered. Grievances and work stoppage are reduced in number. Recruitment is made easier. And the task of the manager becomes less burdensome.

Leadership

Nature and Purpose

Management is responsible for giving direction to that which it manages. Resources available to the manager must be directed toward the greatest results, and the people must be led toward the greatest productivity and achievement. That is the function of leadership: to stimulate people to work with zeal and confidence. Zeal—intensity, ardor, and earnestness—is instilled by the inspiring leader. Confidence—technical ability—is evoked by the teacher who leads by setting good examples. The end result is getting ordinary people to do extraordinary things.

Leadership has three components: (1) he who leads, (2) those who follow, and (3) the situation that prevails. Always capable of making itself felt is a fourth component: irritation. People may not enjoy being told what to do, but many of them are not self-motivated and self-organized. They must be led and directed if enterprise goals are to be met. The leader may be liked or disliked, but he must be respected. In times of stress and emergency people look to their leaders. To the ordinary individual, emergencies are to be feared; to the leader they are opportunities to display abilities.

We know more about leadership now than we ever did before, but there is still no comprehensive theory and understanding of the function. The leader is a part of the group because he must pull his followers to heights they may not have believed attainable. Yet he is apart from the group because he holds their careers and their futures in his hands.

The wise leader uses whatever motivational system will get the job done. The fortunate leader is one who is blessed with a charismatic personality that inspires zeal in others. Above all, leadership is a process that is more emotional than intellectual or rational. Since people differ in what moves them, the leader must know his people and understand how to kindle their desires to achieve and how to keep the fires burning.

Thus the complex interaction of leader, led, and the situation will affect results. The same leadership behavior will not be effective in all situations. The leader who can assess the situation and adjust his style to meet it will have the better chance of meeting enterprise objectives.

It is a mistake, however, to assume that the happy employee is a productive one. A series of studies in a life insurance company, a railroad, and a group of factories manufacturing agricultural equipment encompassed the records of thousands of employees. The researchers found no correlation between job satisfaction and productivity.[13] The effective leader is not one who creates an aura of happiness; he is one who can instill confidence in his own ability, who understands those he leads, and who employs the motivational forces dictated by the law of the situation.

Characteristics

Executive ability cannot be cataloged or measued, but it can almost invariably be recognized wherever it exists.[14] Many theorists have sought to identify the qualities that make for a successful leader. Harrell sees the four major qualities as strong will, extroversion, power need, and achievement need.[15] Keith Davis sees them as intelligence, social maturity and breadth, inner motivation, and a human-relations-oriented attitude.[16]

Although all leaders have their own personalities, traits, and ideas about how to lead, the way in which they behave will be affected by the group they lead. The quality of performance of the led will affect the behavior of the leader. A study was conducted of random assignments of leaders to high-performance groups and to low-performance groups. The study showed that leaders of high-performance groups typically displayed more supportiveness of subordinates and that there was increased group cohesiveness and productivity. Leaders of equal ability were assigned to low-performance groups. They tended to manage autocratically, and the group produced unsatisfactorily as to quality and quantity of output. Leaders assigned to neutral control groups behaved in a manner somewhat between the two extremes.[17]

Many people who select and develop managers look for certain traits. That approach is open to criticism, since accomplishment, no matter how achieved, is more to be desired than particular traits. Nevertheless, the trait theory is as valid as any other theory extant. Here are some of the traits considered desirable in a leader:

Intelligence up to a point. High intelligence is essential to deal with problems and make decisions. Beyond a certain point, however, the possessor may be impatient with people with lower intelligence or may prefer to devote himself to abstract ideas and research.

Emotional maturity that includes objectivity, dependability, and persistence. The leader is energetic and willing to work long and hard. He has drive and is willing to give of himself. He is willing to support and sustain others.

Initiative—being a self-starter and being able to see what escapes others. This trait is predominant in executives; it is less often found at lower levels.

Communicative skills, including persuasiveness. The leader is able to speak and write forcefully. He is able to listen carefully and ask the right questions. He is able to convince people that they themselves want to accomplish what he wants accomplished.

Confidence. The leader exudes self-assurance. He is sure that hurdles present opportunities to jump, not an excuse to balk.

Perceptiveness in appraising others. The leader functions through others, so he must be able to understand his followers. Perceptiveness includes empathy: being able to put oneself in another's shoes and to see the situation as the other sees it. A leader knows people and is aware of their strengths and their weaknesses.

Creativity and originality. The leader must have the vision to find new ways and blaze new trails. Innovation is the sword that cuts the cobwebbed Gordian knot of custom and conformism.

Most managers master managerial skills more easily than leadership skills. Managerial skills are developed by following some basic principles of good administration. Leadership skills demand an understanding of human behavior and motivation, and that understanding is not vouchsafed to many. Few master leadership skills without trial and error and a good deal of heartache.

Leadership Style

Leadership style is a pattern of behavior that is designed to lead others, that is, to mesh the interests of the individual and the organization so as to pursue some set goal. Lewin classifies the styles as autocratic, participative, and laissez-faire.[18] The autocratic leader can be coercive or benevolent. The former attribute is associated with fear, threats, and command; the latter with tact, praise, and bribery through fringe benefits. When the autocratic leader becomes aware of the importance of individual commitment to a cause or program, he practices string-pulling and manipulation to convince subordinates that they are participating in decision making.

The participative leader has a higher regard for the capabilities of his subordinates than the autocrat has. He asks for inputs from subordinates without relinquishing his seat at the head of the table. His subordinates honestly feel that they can influence the outcome of decisions. It is doubtful, however, that anyone contends that the participative style will work in all situations.

The laissez-faire leader is hardly a leader at all. He passes the responsibility for decision making on to the group. He looks for the consensus and often finds chaos.

As employees become more educated, as labor unions become more powerful, and as the federal government makes itself more palpably felt, leadership styles will trend toward the participative. At present, the typical American style of business leadership is one of benevolent autocracy.

For a while the behavioral scientists were vehemently antiauthoritarian. Their goal was to see participative leadership take over in all situations. But they have begun to recognize that the manager, who is charged with achieving enterprise objectives, must use the style that is most effective for him in the situation in which he finds himself.

Participative management does offer professional people and higher-management personnel some advantages. It is less advantageous at the lower levels, where careful communication from a competent decision maker who is reasonably consistent and has a good feeling for people will achieve higher productivity. Even at higher levels, a leadership style that skillfully blends the authoritative and the participative will promote an atmosphere of stability and an impetus toward achievement.

It is probably the rare supervisor who will have complete control over the leadership style he wants to adopt. Usually his style is a reflection of the treatment he receives from his own superior. Fleishman evaluated leadership courses attended by foremen at International Harvester. During the training session, the foremen appeared to recognize the benefits and embrace the concepts of employee-centered leadership. But after they returned to their jobs, they reverted to former autocratic styles because they were unable to counteract the influences from higher up.[19]

Indeed, it seems that executives do not have the highest faith in the leadership abilities of their subordinate managers despite the fact that they feel their subordinates should be informed of what goes on in the company and should participate in decision making.[20] "Democratic management" seems to be a matter of degree. It is just less autocratic than other styles.

Leadership Techniques

The study of leadership is meaningless without the study of followership. Most people want to be led. Most people want to feel they are being guided and moved by a father figure—a person they can trust and be proud of. They want to be led by leaders who exhibit confidence, effectiveness, and a sense of purpose.

Leaders should act like leaders—not like followers or one of the boys. Envy may make followers grumble about the aloofness of some leaders, but they would rather have aloofness than vacillation and excessive desire to be liked. Followers, deep down, want their leaders to be more knowledgeable than they are, to be more conservative, and to stand slightly aloof. The leader should be aware of that need in the followers. And even though that aspect may not be natural for them, they should seek to cultivate it—but with believability. The leader must always be aware of the effect he has on his followers—the way the followers will interpret the unconsciously raised eyebrow, the secret smile, the careless word, the unmeant tone.

There is no magic potion that can create a leader; but if there were, confidence would be one of the chief ingredients. Confidence comes with experience and dedicated application, and it begets confidence. The leader who instills confidence in his followers by effective training, teaching, delegating, and criticizing is creating morale. When morale is high, the leader can move mountains and do no wrong.

The need to develop leadership skills at all levels of management is urgent. Managers who were not born with the skills must cultivate them through:

□ *Empathy*—putting oneself in another's place and actually tasting the other's emotions; truly understanding how others feel and what turns them on or turns them off. Empathy is hard to develop because managers are people too and have their own needs and desires. But if they want to be leaders, they must learn and want to fulfil the needs of their followers.

□ *Objectivity*—not taking action before analyzing the situation, not being moved to take irreversible steps before receiving input from those involved, not functioning by personal whim.

□ *Self-knowledge*—learning how certain words and actions may affect others adversely and seeking to avoid those words and actions.

□ *Legitimacy*—knowing what you're doing and doing it well. Success inspires people; it becomes their own success as they bask in the reflected glory. The unsuccessful leader is soon left for the successful one.

Empathy, sympathy, and understanding will usually bring results, but the law of the situation will often have to prevail. Examples may have to be made, and sanctions may have to be exacted. Insubordination, by and large, cannot be tolerated. When people are permitted to break a rule with impunity, all the rules will soon be ignored. Sometimes sanctions may have to be imposed to reinforce the superior's authority, and sometimes an individual may deliberately have to be punished as an example to others. Often a little talk may do the job, but there are times when more serious steps must be taken. One drastic example is attributed to Frederick the Great, the successful Prussian military leader:[21]

> He had issued a lights-out order and was making his rounds to see whether it was being obeyed. He saw a light coming from the tent of a captain. He entered the tent and saw the captain in the act of sealing a letter. The officer, terrified, dropped to his knees and begged forgiveness. Frederick asked him to resume his seat and add some words to the end of the letter. The officer obeyed and wrote as Frederick dictated: "Tomorrow I die on the scaffold." The next day he was executed. The example was harsh. But Frederick was concerned with the welfare of thousands of his soldiers whose security might have been compromised by an attack brought about by a careless light. The authority of the lights-out order as well as other orders was graphically if brutally reinforced.

When extreme measures are contemplated, the superior had better take into account how well liked the object of those measures is. And when he decides to move rigorously, he should be able to justify his actions.

Another successful technique of leadership is to keep in touch with reality, to go behind the top-level reports and documents and listen to the common man. Here is an example:[22]

> Charles Kettering was primarily responsible for the diesel engine. Much trial and error led to the development of a large diesel-powered vessel. As Kettering wandered down to the ways to look at it before it was launched, he observed a watchman staring intently at the stern. "What are you looking at?" Kettering asked. "The propeller," answered the workman. "What about the propeller?" asked Kettering. "Its size is off by at least an inch," said the man. "How do you know?" Kettering asked. "I know," said the workman. Kettering called on his architects to compare the actual size of the propeller with the approved drawings. The propeller was indeed the wrong size and had to be rebuilt.

Leadership and Organizational Levels

The leaders in an organization can be divided roughly into three groups of managers: top (executive) managers, middle managers, and supervisors. All managers are responsible for planning, organizing, directing, and controlling. Similarly, all managers must have technical, conceptual, and human skills, but at each of the three organizational levels the responsibilities and the skills are needed and used in different degrees.

Top management. The responsibilities exercised by top management relate chiefly to planning and organizing. Top managers make the basic plans and develop the broad organizational pattern. They formulate the decisions that have long-range effect. They defend the integrity of the enterprise. They reconcile the conflicts that constantly erupt within the organization. And they deal with the top-level people in other organizations.

The conceptual skills are of special importance at the top levels: they constitute the ability to visualize what the future may hold and the ability to relate different ideas and see their relevance to a given situation. Top managers must be able to understand abstract ideas, be able to develop and visualize models and relations, and be blessed with the clarity of vision that guides them in anticipating the consequences of planned action. The human skills are not as essential to them on a day-to-day basis, but they create the climate within the company that blows the chill winds of fear, the warm sirocco of languor, or the brisk breeze of zeal and accomplishment. And they move the middle managers to see that plans are carried out.

Middle management. "Middle management" is a general term applicable to all the levels of organization between the executives and the supervisors. In a flat organization there are few such levels; in a tall organization there are many. Middle managers have been referred to as the "fenders" because they are pelted by mud and muck from both sides. Their responsibility is to translate. They translate the abstract objectives and policies laid down by top management into the concrete goals and procedures to be met and followed by supervisors. They must also translate the concrete results their subordinate supervisors achieve into the general information that top management needs to make the executive decisions and hold the tiller of the enterprise.

Parsons suggests three levels of management function:[23]

1. An inner technological core in which supervisors can be protected from uncertainty and achieve rationality.
2. A middle management that acts as the intermediary and speaks certainty to supervisors and uncertainty to executives.
3. An executive level that relates to the uncertainty of the environment.

Actually, middle managers deal less with subordinate managers and more with their peers. Sayles found that a great deal of the middle manager's time was spent in dealing with nonsubordinates—coordinating, keeping the work flow moving, advising, and staying abreast of what is occurring in the enterprise.[24]

An American Management Associations survey of 536 middle managers in nontechnical fields found a surprising schism in the philosophies of middle managers and executives. Many middle managers were prolabor and were in favor of stronger prolabor laws. Indeed, 35 percent said they would consider joining unions. Their complaints concerned (1) the better economic gains made by blue collar workers than by managers, (2) the fact that they were not involved in important decision making, and (3) the lack of authority to carry out the responsibilities assigned to them.[25]

Supervisors. The supervisor is the only manager in the organization who has managers above him and nonmanagers below him. He stands between the Scylla of middle managers who want higher efficiency, effectiveness, quantity, and quality and the Charybdis of the workers who want protection from on high while receiving more for less. And to complicate further an already difficult job, he is often required to deal with the union steward—a force that strengthens with time.

Keith Davis's studies have produced five different viewpoints of the supervisor's function. Davis sees the supervisor as:[26]

The key man
The man in the middle
The marginal man
Another worker
A human relations specialist

The supervisor can be viewed as the key man because, to the worker, he is the personal representative of management. He is the one the workers deal with every day. He is the face of management. On the other side, what management knows about its people is what is gained from the supervisors. That key position is as significant as the linchpin that keeps the plow hooked to the tractor.

For the same reason the supervisor can be regarded as the man in the middle. His position of strength makes him a key man; his vulnerability makes him the man between opposing forces. He is caught between the expectations of the workers and the demands of middle management. Competing groups tug and pull at him, and he cannot fully satisfy either of the two groups if he is to do an effective job.

He can find himself in the position of a marginal man standing forlornly on the side if neither his workers nor his manager accept him fully or confide in him completely. Sometimes managers deal with their staff specialists instead of their supervisors and the workers develop their informal organizations and stand behind the shields of their unions. Add to that the often infrequent dealings with fellow supervisors and we find an individual who sits on a lonely hummock.

For a while many supervisors saw themselves as other workers, and in the 1940s many supervisors tried to join labor unions or create foremen's unions. But that was short-lived because the Taft-Hartley Act of 1947 reaffirmed their status as members of management by forbidding them to join employee labor unions. Their legal status was changed, but their elevation from the ranks of workers often occurs without a cutting of the umbilical cord. As a result, many a supervisor sees himself as just another worker with little more money but a lot more headaches.

Finally, the supervisor can be viewed as a human relations specialist. With staff people taking over the problems of scheduling and quality, he can regard the most significant part of his job as dealing in human relations.

The human relations aspect has been underscored in studies conducted by Likert and his colleagues in the Institute for Social Research at the University of Michigan.[27] The studies of supervisory practices covered public utilities, an insurance company, an automobile manufacturing company, a heavy-machinery factory, a railroad, an electrical appliance factory, and several government agencies. Two major criteria were used to evaluate supervisory effectiveness: (1) the productivity per man-hour or some similar measure of success in meeting production goals, and (2) the satisfactions derived by employees. Likert found little relation between productivity and how employees regarded the company. Absenteeism and turnover may have been affected, but not productivity. In fact, management had commonly assumed that a favorable attitude toward the company would improve productivity, but the findings of the study did not support the assumption.

On the other hand, Likert did find a definite relation between the kind of supervision received on the one hand and both productivity and individual satisfaction on the other. The high-production groups generally had supervisors who were employee-centered. The supervisors who responded that they gave greatest emphasis to production were from sections with low productivity.

Low-production sections had supervisors who kept a close watch over their workers and supervised in terms of procedures instead of goals. High-production centers were in the charge of supervisors who supervised more generally and emphasized objectives instead of rules. To establish the cause-and-effect relation, supervisors were switched among sections. Their approaches did not change, but productivity did. The former low-productivity section improved under employee-centered supervision; the former high-productivity section slipped somewhat under production-centered supervision.

Likert found that the employee-centered approach—general, goal-oriented supervision—did not imply a lack of concern with productivity. It meant merely that employee-centered supervisors knew they must achieve their productivity through people. They felt that applied pressure loses its force in time, whereas the goals stand as a grail, something to constantly reach for. He also found that high productivity did not mean low morale. Indeed, morale was highest in the section with employee-centered supervisors. So it would seem that today's supervisor should regard the elimination of some of his former jobs through increased technology and the computer as a signal to concentrate on the one factor with which neither technology nor the computer can deal: people.

Leadership and Orders

The order is the means by which people know what has to be done, and the leader should understand the techniques of giving orders so that his own orders will have a better chance of being followed. Managers should not make decisions calling for orders that will not be obeyed. If an order is refused or a decision challenged, the impasse may result in discharging an employee the executive very much wants to retain. The possible reaction of the employee should be taken into account, and a confrontation should be avoided by involving the employee in the decision making.

Orders should issue from the demands of the situation. They will be accepted with better grace if the source is attributed to the system. Indeed, if properly issued, the order can create a bond between supervisor and worker. The way the order is issued will have an important effect on how willingly it is carried out. It should be clear, so that it is understood. It should be concise, so that it is not beclouded by excessive detail and the employee can exercise some ingenuity. It should be consistent with the situation, with other orders, and with the worker's understanding of policies and procedures. And the tone in which it is issued should not be officious; it should not convey the impression of a superior pushing an inferior around. It should imply a request for assistance. To that end, if at all possible, the reason for the order should be explained.

On the other hand, the superior should not be in such fear of giving orders that he becomes excessively lenient. Leniency can be lunacy if it has no purpose. Indeed, the severe disciplinarian will be regarded as less severe than the lenient supervisor who suddenly becomes less lenient.

There is no perfect solution to problems of leading and exercising authority. The leader is contending with extremely complex relations between the worker and his superior, the worker and his colleagues, the worker and his union, and the worker and his upbringing. So the leader has less need of a set of rules than a method of analyzing the situation in which he must act and obeying the law of the situation.

Leadership and Change

Successful directing implies change. To lead a person in one direction often means that the person is being led away from another direction—the one he had in mind. That involves dealing with an intricate set of psychological mechanisms.

Change can be imposed. The authority of the leader can be brought to bear and force can be applied: "Do it my way or else." But that is rarely the best method, since the cost in human relations can be high. So an understanding of attitudes, of how a person tends to feel, see, or interpret a particular situation, is important. It is not change itself that is resisted; it is the methods used to require change.[28]

Simple changes can be accomplished by straightforward discussions with individuals. The effort should be to point out the value of the changes to the individuals and subtly induce an adjustment of attitudes toward acceptance of the changes. Sweeping changes may need more planning and the laying of groundwork. The leader may have to take the heads of informal groups into his confidence in order to pave the way. But even then the leader must move cautiously. He must be able to assess the temper of the group itself. He must feel confident that, after he has conditioned the heads of the groups to change, the group does not reject the leader. Groups have resorted to the character assassination of heads who have not properly understood their needs and desires.

Change often requires an admission of having done something wrong; otherwise, why the need for change? But if blame is not charged or implied, if both the leaders and the subordinates attack the situation and not the people, the possibility of successful change improves.

DIRECTING AND THE INTERNAL AUDITOR

The Internal Auditor's Involvement

When the internal auditor deals with planning and organizing, his appraisals can be completely objective. He can generally quantify his findings and support his conclusions with documented facts. Directing, however, is especially people-oriented; and except for certain hygiene factors, it often defies quantification. People do not fit into neat slots; they are not subject to simple addition and subtraction. Still, managers and leaders do need help and counsel in directing. And that function provides the management-oriented auditor with an unusual opportunity to move beyond the traditional role of evaluation by the numbers. He will have to tread more delicately than he does in his traditional paths; but as managers, owners, and the members of boards of directors turn more and more to his unbiased counsel, he will be impelled to take a hard look at the directing process.

We have explored the internal auditor's role in behavioral pat-

terns and communications in Chapters 4 and 6.   In this chapter we
will deal with his role in three other phases of directing.

The Personnel Department.   The personnel department is normally
responsible for determining the human needs of the enterprise—how
people can be motivated and how their needs can be satisfied.   Ordinarily, the department restricts its activities to the hygiene factors, to
the factors whose absence breeds discontent.   We shall concentrate
on the auditor's review of those activities, but we shall also touch on
appraisals of the satisfiers—the true motivators.

Compensation.   Payments to employees take a large slice of the entity's dollar and deserve thorough audit attention.

Leadership.   In terms of employee utilization, leadership is a fertile
field for the internal auditor, but of increasing interest are the leadership qualities of the managers whose performance is being evaluated.

Personnel Department

Function

The personnel department is a staff function.   It assists line managers in selecting, administering, developing, and rewarding people.
At its best it brings to bear a technical expertise in human relations
that is indispensable to the successful direction of human beings.   At
its worst it is a paper mill of policies and procedures, a deviser of gimmicks and pseudo motivators, and a mechanical administrator of
fringe benefits.   To carry out its true objectives, therefore, the personnel department needs to be staffed with people of judgment, wisdom, stature, and understanding.   And people with those qualities
are rare indeed.

The personnel department deals with people at all levels: the
hourly worker, usually unionized and generally in production areas;
the salaried clerks, not unionized and found all through the enterprise; and the management personnel, who include all salaried people other than clerks: technicians, professionals, and managers from
supervisors to executives.

Audit Approach

The internal auditor can best help management if he approaches
the audit of personnel activities—as he approaches any other operations—by first determining the operating objectives.   Everything the
department's manager does or seeks to accomplish should be keyed to
those objectives.

Obviously, the temperament, needs, desires, and aims of the chief executive officer will affect the aims of the personnel manager. And the internal auditor, in appraising departmental objectives, must do so in the context of the objectives set by the chief executive before he can be of any help to management. But by and large, the objectives of the personnel function are:

□ To identify manpower needs and availability and to train and develop manpower.

□ To administer the various personnel programs and benefits.

The internal auditor should see how well those objectives are being met. When they are not being met, he should find out why and counsel managers on corrective action. Those matters will be explored in the following subsections.

Manpower Needs

The jobs to be filled need precise description; otherwise, how could the organization recruit and develop people needed to fill the jobs? The internal auditor should therefore satisfy himself that Personnel has inventoried the needs of the entity and developed job descriptions that set forth the specifications for existing jobs and for jobs needed to carry out plans still on the drawing board. To look at the present alone is to permit the future to hold unpleasant surprises.

In making his evaluations, the internal auditor should review the entire system for an approach to analyzing jobs. He will want to know how the entire population of jobs—present and future—was determined. He will want to determine whether uniform criteria are used and, when necessary, whether reasonable weighting factors are employed to give appropriate significance to more demanding jobs. And he will expect management to provide for periodic reevaluations to deal with changing conditions. Also, the evaluators should be kept informed of complaints and grievances so that inequities may be corrected.

The internal auditor should be satisfied that personnel does not inhabit an ivory tower. All department heads should be consulted on their needs and on the manpower peaks and valleys. The internal auditor must therefore determine how well current and future needs are or will be matched with the proper personnel.

All significant jobs should have backup people ready to step into the shoes of incumbents if need be, and each executive should know that an inventory of backup people is available. Personnel, as counselor on people matters, should see to it that an inventory is maintained. The experienced internal auditor knows how many managers avoid such housekeeping functions, so he will expect a centralized agency, like Personnel, to assure reasonable, uniform backup inventories throughout the enterprise.

Manpower Development

People recruited usually need orientation to fit them comfortably into their new jobs and training to improve their capabilities. Orientation is generally the function of the operating manager, but the process can vary from department to department. On the one hand, orientation can provide an inviting welcome mat; on the other, it can frustrate the newly hired employee. The personnel department that takes its responsibilities seriously will provide guidelines to operating managers on employee orientation. The specifics will be job-oriented, but the general guidelines should reflect an understanding of human behavior and the needs of people. And people need to know how they can meet the particular needs of their employers.

The personnel department also has the responsibility for establishing programs, within available resources, to educate and train people to improve their capabilities. The internal auditor can evaluate those programs of orientation and training by measuring them against acceptable standards:

1. Orientation should include material that will inform the employee of his rights and obligations. Internal auditors can review the materials given to all new hires to determine whether they are complete and understandable.

2. Steps in orientation should give the employee an understanding of what the company expects of him and his job. Internal auditors can appraise the guidelines provided to operating managers and, on a test basis, determine whether the managers have developed and are using programs to provide orientation. The auditor can examine exit interview records to determine whether inadequate orientation may have influenced employees to leave the organization.

3. Employees should be made receptive to additional training. Auditors can review the programs designed to inform employees of available training. Those programs should make the training attractive and capable of improving the employee's ability to better his position in the organization.

4. Training materials should be professional and should be tested for usefulness and relevance. The internal auditor can evaluate the process of selecting and developing the materials and review em-

ployees' evaluations of the training courses. Internal auditors can also interview operating managers to determine how useful they consider the training their employees receive.

5. Hazardous and very technical jobs should require special training and certification. Such jobs may include materials handling, explosives handling, welding, and working with chemicals or with electrical and electronic equipment. The internal auditor will want to know that records are maintained of all personnel engaged in such activities and that methods are in effect to insure certification and recertification.

How effectively employment and development activities are being carried out is difficult to appraise objectively; but when they are deficient, they are likely to be reflected in high absentee rates that, in turn, result in high turnover rates. Such rates can be determined by the following formulas:[29]

Absentee rate:

$$\frac{\text{Total man-days lost}}{\text{Total man-days worked}} \times 100 = \text{absentee rate}$$

Turnover rate:

$$\frac{\text{Number of separations per month}}{\text{Average number on the payroll during the month}} \times 100$$
$$= \text{turnover rate}$$

A comparison of those rates with the rates in comparable industries or in other divisions of the company can furnish an index of employment and training effectiveness, provided due consideration is given to other variables.[30]

One audit of a regional branch office included an analysis of sales personnel turnover. The analysis covered new hires and terminations during a 13-week period. The internal auditors observed that the largest percent of terminations occurred after about 26 weeks of employment. Hence, the cost of training salesmen was not balanced by increased sales, since a large percent of the salesmen left almost as soon as they had been trained.

Management had not been aware of the excessively high cost of training in relation to the benefits received. The audit report was a warning to management to review its employment, motivational, and compensation practices to reverse a costly trend.

Personnel Administration

Many internal auditors regard the payrolls as the closest they should get to the personnel function, but the internal auditor is not fulfilling his own responsibility if he does not review the operations of personnel administration. Those operations may not directly affect the earnings statement. Indirectly, however, the impact is enormous, because it is concerned with people. And people, through their performance, affect earnings directly.

Because of the sensitivity and confidentiality of personnel administration activities, the internal auditor would be well advised to avoid any adversary relation with personnel managers. Instead, he should seek to pursue a participative audit: Agree upon the objectives of each function, determine the controls needed to see that the objectives are met, and identify the standards of good performance.

Each audit will call for individual programs that focus on the objectives, controls, and standards of the particular function. No canned checklist will help the internal auditor dissect the unique organism he is examining, but here are some of the areas that will pay dividends for an in-depth study:

Personnel records. Are the personnel records comprehensive; are they kept confidential and readily retrievable; and are they useful as histories of all employees? In one examination, the internal auditor found that personnel files charged out for updating were not controlled. As a result, there was no follow-up system to make sure that the histories of employees were being safeguarded.

Unemployment benefits. Are records on terminated employees accurate and complete, and are protests lodged against improper claims by employees who left involuntarily without good cause or were discharged for misconduct? Is the company paying no more unemployment tax than the law requires? The following example illustrates the benefits of alertness to legal provisions:[31]

> In one state, the employer's unemployment tax is based in part on these factors:
>
> 1. The percentage of decline between each year's gross wages paid over a 3-year period.
> 2. The percentage of decline between total quarterly wages paid during the 3-year period.
>
> When the ratio of decline is raised so are the rates. Two matters can adversely affect the ratio: A bonus paid in one quarter of a year. A seventh biweekly payroll, compared with six payrolls in the next quarter (usually occurring twice a year).

The state law allowed the bonus and the biweekly payroll to be allocated over the year in which paid, thus eliminating the unnatural increase and decrease during the year. But the internal auditor found that his company was not taking advantage of these allocations. He recommended a recomputation of rates for the last two years, and as a result his company received a substantial refund.

Welfare and other services. Included in welfare and other services are conflict-of-interest programs, credit unions, management clubs, social activities, employee purchases, suggestion systems, athletic programs, bonds, legal aid programs, and wage garnishment and credit letters. Those activities, like all other activities in the company, should be conducted in a businesslike fashion. Yet often, since they are people-related, those in charge of them may be pursuing objectives and following practices that are not in agreement with company policies. Audits should be made, therefore, to insure good administrative practices and adherence to the policies set forth by executive management. Here are some examples. The first is from Mintern.[32]

A company was receiving large discounts from local merchants. As a benefit to employees, the purchasing department accommodated them on purchases for such items as appliances. It issued purchase orders to the suppliers, paid the suppliers, and billed the employees. But payments from employees were often slow, tying up company funds and calling for the assignment of one clerk to handle the record keeping. The purchasing department was reluctant to press for payment from fellow employees.

The internal auditor made a simple suggestion to correct the condition: For $1.62 the purchasing department bought a rubber stamp which said "This purchase must be paid for in cash at time of purchase." The employees then took the purchase orders to the merchants—who refused to give discounts without them—received the goods, and paid the lower prices. The results were gratifying:

1. Employees were still being accommodated.
2. No company funds were tied up in employee purchases.
3. Collection problems disappeared.
4. The need for the clerk was eliminated.
5. Local merchants were saved the expense of billing the company.

In an audit of a conflict-of-interest program administered by the personnel department, the internal auditor found:

1. The personnel department was not following up to see that all people required to sign declarations that they were not involved in conflict-of-

interest situations had done so. Obviously, those from whom such declarations are not received may be the most suspect.

2. A number of employees who were newly hired, transferred between company divisions, or promoted to covered positions, had not signed the declarations, and there was no system to make sure such people did.

A company had organized a "recreation club" to promote employee welfare. An audit disclosed the following conditions requiring correction:

1. There were no alternates for executive committee members.
2. The blanket fidelity bond did not accurately indicate the people covered.
3. A resolution had been adopted to allow a welfare investigator to commit sums up to $100 per case in event of emergency, but the resolution had never been implemented. That caused undue hardship for employees in temporary need.
4. The recreation club's accounts, handled by one individual, had never been reviewed by the club's executive committee.

Compensation

Compensation administration puts a company in the middle of two opposing forces. On the one side is the need to offer compensation that will attract and hold competent people; on the other side is the need to remain competitive in the marketplace.

With those objectives in mind, the internal auditor perceives the need for certain control measures designed to see that the objectives will be met. Here are some examples:

□ Means of classifying jobs in accordance with relevant and sensible criteria.
□ Job compensation that is keyed to the particular classifications and at the same time is competitive with compensation for like jobs in other enterprises and departments within the auditor's enterprise.
□ Employee evaluations made periodically to fit performance to compensation in the range within the employee's classification.
□ Periodic reevaluation of all classifications and compensation to see whether adjustment to existing conditions is needed.

The internal auditor can determine the bases on which levels of compensation have been set. He can review the surveys made to determine whether they were thorough and whether conclusions drawn were based on sufficient and representative data. He can determine whether levels of compensation are reviewed and tested periodically. By analyzing records of grievances, he can find out whether employees feel that job analyses and compensation are fair. If the employees feel that they are unfair, he can find out why.

Leadership

Involvement

In terms of leadership, top managers can look to the internal auditor to assist them in providing information and counsel in answering, among others, these questions:

- Are the leaders at the middle-management level properly using the human resources subject to their stewardship?
- Are managers effectively carrying out their management functions?

The answer to the first question calls for relatively well-known auditing techniques. The answer to the second, however, goes beyond what is normally regarded as an internal audit responsibility and calls for tact, the development of standards, and a thoroughly professional approach.

Employee Utilization

The human resource is undoubtedly the entity's most important asset. The way it is used can mean the difference between the entity's success and failure. Yet internal auditing literature abounds with tales of employees wasting their time and managers being blissfully unaware of the waste. The internal auditor owes it to his organization to put the searchlight on such practices and to see that they are stopped. One approach auditors can take is as follows:[33]

- Analyze job classifications.
- For each job review data that show the levels of actual performance.
- Talk to both employees and their supervisors and observe on-the-job performance. Compare performance with what the job classification calls for.
- Evaluate performance to determine if the job is (1) carrying out company and departmental objectives and (2) duplicating some other job.

Here are three examples of audit findings resulting from translating those general audit objectives to specific audit steps:

> A message center was operating 24 hours a day to coordinate maintenance work on heavy machinery. The department manager wanted round-the-clock monitoring as a precautionary measure. The internal auditor found very low activity during swing, graveyard, and weekend shifts. He therefore recommended alternate means of reporting maintenance requests, and three positions were dropped from the monitoring service.

> Highly paid craftsmen were doing routine clerical work. The auditor compared job descriptions with work performance and substantiated his initial impressions. It seems that some organizational realignments had been made without considering the side effects. At the internal auditor's recommendation, the administrative work was transferred to existing clerical personnel and three craft positions were eliminated.

> After a company reorganization, the internal auditor flow-charted certain processes and found that the realignment of duties created overlapping and duplication. Besides, certain supervisory positions had less supervisory responsibility after the reorganization. The internal auditor presented his findings to management and thereby brought about the elimination of two administrative positions.

Those results were gained by (1) measuring work loads, (2) determining what people were supposed to be doing, according to their work classifications, (3) observing performance, (4) interviewing people, (5) studying organization charts, and (6) flow-charting processes.

In another situation a test of a payroll brought to light idle time that had never been identified as such and hence did not reach management's attention:[34]

> A statistical sample was taken from the 104,000 annual payroll payments. The test results showed that 10% of the employees paid in the sample had excessive idle time. These employees were charging their idle time to various indirect cost accounts.

> The problem lay in the fact that management was not identifying idle time. For example, research had decreased. To keep the researchers on the payroll, their idle time was charged for extensive periods to indirect expense categories, inflating those accounts instead of disclosing the charges for what they were: idle time.

> The internal auditors recommended reports to management which showed just how much idle time was being charged. Management could then make more knowledgeable decisions on workload scheduling, hiring and termination policies, and pricing under varying conditions.

Internal auditors, as experts in internal control, should be concerned with overcontrol as well as with inadequate control and thereby help management make the directing process more efficient. Here is an example:[35]

> An internal auditor observed that a toolroom was attended full time by an employee whose wages plus benefits totaled $9,000 a year. The tools being safeguarded were worth about $1,800 and, besides, shop personnel usually entered the toolroom and helped themselves. At the internal auditor's recommendation the job of toolroom attendant was eliminated. Security guards at the gates represented sufficient deterrence to prevent employees from leaving the plant with those tools.

Evaluating Leadership

Asking an internal auditor to evaluate leadership is like asking him to swim in shark-infested waters, yet deep-sea divers brave such waters when they believe the treasures awaiting them make the risk worthwhile. Researchers into the field of human-resource accounting (HRA) believe the internal auditor has a function in that process just as he has a function in accounting for other assets.[36] The researchers give some examples of the application of internal auditing techniques to protecting the resource that comprises the leaders within the organization.

□ Report the failure to follow a promotion-from-within policy—a failure that could affect morale of employees and leaders alike.
□ Prevent the luring away of leaders or potential leaders by appraising pension plans, fringe-benefit packages, or compensation plans and comparing them with industry standards.

Leaders in an organization may be torn between the organizational goals of steady income and appreciation of market price of stock, on the one hand, and the improvement of their personal lifetime income, on the other. When the goals diverge, the divergence may be manifested by dysfunctional behavior on the part of the manager. Since a significant element of the directing process is people, should not then the internal auditor be concerned with the behavior of people during his audit of that process? Mautz and Sharaf seem to think so when they say: "Unknown to the reviewer (audit function), the pressures which motivate the people in the 'system' may change sufficiently that they cease to act in an expected fashion, whereupon the internal control procedure loses its effectiveness."[37]

But the auditor's job, in the final analysis, is to measure; and to measure, one must have standards or at least questions to ask, questions that will elicit information about leadership style, the atmosphere in which the entity's systems function, and the use and maintenance of human resources. Rensis Likert gives us some clues:[38]

- To what extent does the leader exhibit confidence in his subordinates? Does he seek their ideas? Does he use the ideas?
- Do subordinates seem to be free to talk about their jobs to their superiors?
- To what extent does the leader make use of punishment, rewards, and employee participation?
- To what extent do subordinates feel committed to achieving organizational goals?
- In what way, if any, are subordinates made to feel a part of the drive toward meeting goals?
- How do subordinates report upward their accomplishments and problems?
- How is information on goal accomplishment communicated downward?
- How well do the leaders understand the problems, difficulties, and frustration felt by their subordinates?
- To what extent are subordinates involved in the decision-making process?
- From what sources are the bases and premises for decisions obtained—solely from the top or from subordinates as well?
- To what extent does the decision-making process motivate or disaffect subordinates?
- In what manner are goals established—by fiat or by group action?
- Is there evidence that the manner of goal establishment results in resistance to the goals by subordinates?
- Are review and control functions concentrated at the top, or are they fairly widely shared throughout the organization?
- Does the informal organization resist the formal one, or do both organizations seem to have the same goals?
- Are control systems used for policing or for self-improvement and decision making at the levels responsible for operations?

It may be some time before internal auditors routinely solicit answers to such questions and include the results in their formal audit reports. But the information about subordinate managers is of vital importance to the chief executive officer or to executive or group vice presidents. If properly and confidentially carried out, the making of such inquiries and the confidential communication of the results can add another dimension to the internal auditor's usefulness.

On the surface there may seem to be an inconsistency in advocating, on the one hand, confidential information about operating managers and, on the other, a cooperative attitude in which manager and internal auditor work together in a problem-solving partnership. But that is a fine line internal auditors have often had to walk. It harks back to the internal auditor's dual responsibilities: (1) To keep top management informed. Useful, objective, unbiased reports about middle managers constitute extremely important information to executive management. (2) To leave every place a little better than the internal auditor found it. That calls for cooperation with operating managers. The line is fine, but the approach must suit the audit objective. That approach is far different in the detection of fraud than it is in recommending operating improvements. When the business community is made aware of the auditor's responsibilities, the apparent inconsistencies become understandable facets of a complex job.

Change

Perhaps more than any other function in the organization, internal auditing is concerned with change. In almost every audit assignment, the internal auditor is interested in seeing existing operations carried out more effectively, more economically, more efficiently, more safely, and with more concern for the environment. And that calls for change. People fear change imposed by their own superiors; they fear it all the more if it is imposed by outsiders. The changes instituted as a result of an internal audit are feared all the more because they imply criticism that is brought to the attention of top management.

Hence the internal auditor of the classic stereotype, the cold, secretive, finger pointer, is rarely welcomed and his recommendations for change are seldom embraced. But the stereotype can be changed, and in many auditing organizations it has been changed. The reason for the change can be traced to the participative audit. In such an audit, the internal auditor changes his approach from that of the policeman to that of the consultant—the problem-solving partner. The internal auditor, from the outset, takes operating management into his confidence through open discussions about his preliminary survey, his audit programs, and his audit findings.

The findings are not used as a reason to say, "Look what you did," but rather as an opportunity to explore a condition and determine, as partners, how to improve it. The audit report does not say to top management, "Look what I found and what I recommend," but rather, "A condition was observed and operating management promptly corrected it or took steps to correct it."

Until participative auditing becomes the preferred audit method, the fear of change and the resentment toward the recommender of change will remain. But when operating managers and workers are brought within the circle that carries out the change, the moving force for change—the internal auditor—will be more welcomed than feared, because "his" changes will become "our" changes.

CONCLUSION

Management performs through people. And to the extent that people follow management's directions so will management achieve its objectives. But people will be moved to perform with zeal and confidence only if their own objectives are congruent with management's and if they have been trained to perform competently. So the purpose of the function of directing is to arrange a marriage between the needs of the people and those of the organization. Many things move people, but in different ways. The motivator that probably has the strongest force and the longest duration is the charisma of a true leader coupled with the individual's strong positive feelings for his job. Other things, like compensation, fringe benefits, and a good environment, may keep him on the job, but the great leader and the commitment to the job make him want to perform superbly.

The internal auditor can assist management by closely examining the "hygiene factors" or the compensation and fringe benefits. On the one hand, they should be competitive with those of other organizations. On the other, they should be reasonable, and they should not make an unnecessary drain on the organization's resources through waste, inefficiency, and ineffectiveness. In time, internal auditors will be asked to make reviews that many are now hesitant to carry out: reviews of the leadership capabilities of the managers whose work they now appraise. It is a thorn-imbedded road to travel, but the benefits to top management of an objective appraisal of those qualities may make the trek important and rewarding.

References

1. E. H. Schein, *Organizational Psychology* (Englewood Cliffs, N.J.: Prentice-Hall, 1965), p. 600.

2. Douglas McGregor, *The Human Side of Enterprise* (New York: McGraw-Hill, 1960), pp. 36–39.

3. A. H. Maslow, *Motivation and Personality* (New York: Harper & Row, 1954), pp. 43–46, and Frederick Herzberg, Bernard Mausner, and Barbara B. Snyderman, *The Motivation to Work* (New York: Wiley, 1959). pp. 59–63, 70–74, and 113–119.

4. P. F. Drucker, *Management: Tasks, Responsibilities, Practices* (New York: Harper & Row, 1973), p. 232.

5. Frank Friedlander and Eugene Walton, "Positive and Negative Motivations Toward Work," *Administrative Science Quarterly*, Vol. 9, No. 2, pp. 194–207.

6. L. W. Porter and E. E. Lawler, "What Job Attitudes Tell About Motivation," *Harvard Business Review*, Vol. 46, No. 1, pp. 118–126.

7. G. R. Terry, *Principles of Management* (Homewood, Ill.: 1972), p. 451.

8. F. G. Lesieur, ed., *The Scanlon Plan* (New York: Wiley, 1958).

9. Drucker, op. cit., pp. 190, 191.

10. F. G. Lesieur and E. S. Puckett, "The Scanlon Plan Has Proved Itself," *Harvard Business Review*, Vol. 47, No. 5, pp. 113, 114.

11. R. K. Goodman, J. H. Wakely, and R. H. Ruh, "What Employees Think of the Scanlon Plan," *Personnel*, Vol. 49, No. 5, p. 28.

12. R. E. Walton, "Contrasting Designs for Participative Systems," *Personnel Administration*, Vol. 30, No. 6, p. 38.

13. R. L. Kahn, "Productivity and Job Satisfaction," *Personnel Psychology*, Vol. 13, No. 3, pp. 275–287.

14. C. H. Greenewalt, *The Uncommon Man* (New York: McGraw-Hill, 1959), p. 65.

15. T. W. Harrell, *Managers' Performance and Personality* (Cincinnati: South-Western Publishing, 1961), p. 171.

16. Keith Davis, *Human Relations at Work*, 2nd ed. (New York: McGraw-Hill, 1967), p. 107.

17. G. F. Farris and F. G. Lim, Jr., "Effects of Performance on Leadership, Cohesiveness, Influence, Satisfaction, and Subsequent Performance," *Journal of Applied Psychology*, Vol. 53, No. 6, p. 496.

18. Kurt Lewin, Ronald Lippitt, and R. K. White, "Patterns of Aggressive Behavior in Experimentally Created Social Climates," *Journal of Social Psychology*, Vol. 10, No. 2, and Ronald Lippitt, "An Experimental Study of Authoritarian and Democratic Group Atmospheres," *University of Iowa Studies in Child Welfare*, Vol. 16, No. 3.

19. E. A. Fleishman, "Leadership Climate, Human Relations Training, and Supervisory Behavior," *Personnel Psychology*, Vol. 6, No. 2, pp. 205–222.

20. "How Bosses Really Feel," *Business Week*, March 2, 1963, p. 58.

21. Sir Ian Hamilton, *The Soul and Body of an Army* (London: Arnold, 1921), p. 100.

22. Douglas McGregor, *Leadership and Motivation* (Cambridge, Mass.: The M.I.T. Press, 1966), pp. 118, 119.

23. Talcott Parsons, *Structure and Process in Modern Societies* (New York: The Free Press, 1960), chaps, 1 and 2.

24. L. R. Sayles, *Managerial Behavior* (New York: McGraw-Hill, 1964), chaps. 5 and 6.
25. "Union Cards for Managers?" *Monthly Labor Review*, Vol. 94, No. 9, pp. 71, 72.
26. Keith Davis, *Human Relations at Work*, 2nd ed. (New York: McGraw-Hill, 1976), pp. 123–126.
27. Rensis Likert, *Motivation: The Core of Management*, AMA Personnel Series, No. 155, 1953.
28. Alvin Zander, "Resistance to Change: Its Analysis and Prevention," *Advanced Management*, Vol. 15, No. 1, pp. 9–11.
29. Norman Morris, "Auditing the Personnel Function," *The Internal Auditor*, March-April 1975, p. 28.
30. *The Internal Auditor*, Summer 1963, p. 77.
31. *The Internal Auditor*, August 1976, p. 69.
32. H. J. Mintern, ed., *How to Save $14,500,000 Through Internal Auditing* (Orlando, Fla: The Institute of Internal Auditors, 1975), pp. 180, 181.
33. M. L. Neal, "The Use of Personnel and Operational Auditing," *The Internal Auditor*, August 1976, pp. 26–28.
34. V. Z. Brink, J. A. Cashin, and Herbert Witt, *Modern Internal Auditing* (New York: Ronald Press, 1973), p. 670.
35. *The Internal Auditor*, January-February 1973, p. 71.
36. J. A. Castellano, R. A. Juenke, and H. A. Roehm, "The Role of Internal Auditing in Human Resource Accounting," *The Internal Auditor*, February 1977, pp. 51–56.
37. R. K. Mautz and H. A. Sharaf, *The Philosophy of Auditing* (Sarasota, Fla.: American Accounting Association, 1961), p. 145.
38. Rensis Likert, *The Human Organization: Its Management and Value* (New York: McGraw-Hill, 1967), pp. 13–24.

12

Controlling

Controlling defined. The link to planning and to objectives. The various forms of control. The elements of control: standards, comparisons, correction. Controls for nonmeasurable activities. Adequate control systems. Feedback. Standards and what they are used to measure. Controlling quantity, quality, schedule, and cost. Controlling the primary areas. Accounting control. Limitations to the numbers. Cost accounting. Budgets—plan and control. Forecasts for budgets. People and control. Control and conflict. Minimizing the adverse effect of control. Management by objectives. Self-control. The reasons MBO programs go wrong. The board of directors. The decline of boards as a controlling force. The mounting pressure on boards. Holding boards liable. Responsibilities of boards. Stock exchange requirements. The study of audit committees. The Foreign Corrupt Practices Act.

Internal auditors and controls. Understanding the objectives. Audits of operating controls. Internal accounting controls—The Arthur Andersen guide. People, control, and internal auditors. Controls and objectives. MBO and the internal auditor. Audit plans for MBO programs. The board of directors and internal auditors. The board's need to know. Relations with internal auditors. Standards for internal auditors. Internal auditing and due professional care. Management fraud: its nature, why it occurs, its symptoms, and what steps to take. Aroused interest in the internal audit function.

CONTROLLING AND THE MANAGER

Nature of Controlling

Definition and Purposes

Control is a guiding force; controls are the means of exerting that force. Control is exerted to correct deviations from the paths that lead to organizational objectives and goals and to remove from those paths whatever prevents efficient, economical, and effective performance. So the functions of planning and controlling are linked. Planning provides goals and standards. Controls measure performance to determine whether the goals have been reached and the standards have been met. The process of controlling is designed to correct any deviations and eliminate the roadblocks.

Everyone, from the chairman of the board to the lowest supervisor, uses control to make sure that what is being done is what was intended, but the means used at the various levels of the organization vary. The control exercised at the executive levels differs from that exercised at the operating levels. The two kinds are similar in that they seek to insure the meeting of objectives. What differentiates the two is the nature of the objectives. The varied forms of control can therefore be defined as follows:[1]

□ *Executive control* is directed toward the achievement of an organization's broad objectives. It encompasses the employment of appropriate means by the policy-making officers of the organization to direct, restrain, govern, and check on the activities of the organization for the purpose of achieving these objectives. The means used include, but are not limited to, methods of assuring the achievement or compliance with long-range objectives and goals, budgets and forecasts, policy statements, organization charts, and statements of function and responsibility. The means also include an internal audit function.

□ *Internal control* is directed toward the achievement of an organization's detailed objectives. It encompasses the employment of appropriate means at all levels of management to direct, restrain, govern, and check on those activities for which managers are responsible. Internal control comprises financial (or accounting) control and administrative (or operating) control.

□ *Financial control* includes, but is not limited to, the use of budgets, systems of authorization and approval, systems of accounts and analyses, and separation of duties, particularly the separation of the duties for accounting and record keeping from duties concerned with operations and physical control over assets.

□ *Administrative control* includes but is not limited to the use of production schedules, performance records, departmental budgets and forecasts, job assignment records, performance standards, logs, registers, forms, and check lists.

It seems obvious that, just as objectives may often overlap and coalesce, so will the different forms of control. It may often be difficult to tell when executive control becomes internal control and when financial control becomes administrative control. What is important is that control cannot exist in a vacuum. Its critical function is to see that some objective or goal will be met. Planning and controlling are therefore being treated, more and more, as integrated systems. One cannot work without the other.

Elements of Control

The essential elements of control are three:

1. Establishing standards that, when met, will provide assurance that relevant goals or objectives have been reached.
2. Comparing actual results with the standards.
3. Taking corrective action to return activities to the tracks leading to the desired goals or objectives.

Those elements have a quantitative thrust, yet controls are needed for both measurable and nonmeasurable events. The means used to retain good people are not measurable, yet they are significant because poor people do not an innovative, forward-looking organization make. Control is easy once one has the measure and the standard. Setting those standards is the most difficult task of management. Indeed, the more managers quantify that which is readily measurable, the less attention is directed toward the nonmeasurable, qualitative aspect of their resources—particularly people. And so the manager who truly understands what his organization is to achieve must appraise the qualitative, not readily measurable, performance of his people. He may have to develop reasonable criteria along the way, and he will have to acquaint his people with those criteria. But what may seem completely unmeasurable at first blush may yield to quantification if the problem is thought through. For example:[2]

The Royal Canadian Mounted Police (RCMP) administers the Solicitor General's law enforcement program. It enforces federal statutes and executive orders, performs services in crime detection laboratories, police information centers, and identification centers.

Since 1966/67, the RCMP has used performance indicators or standards against which to measure and evaluate police work. It weights outputs by staff hours taken to process the different types of cases. It then combines these weighted outputs to give a total output of the police operations. It shows efficiency of operations in terms of staff-hours per case. By providing standards and measurements in what might be considered nonmeasurable activities, it evaluates performance. But, more important, these methods have led to significant and worthwhile improvements. For example:

□ Shift scheduling helped the RCMP meet peak crime periods and reduce overtime costs.
□ Automation of the fingerprint system resulted in significant reductions of man-hours. The measurements showed the need for automation.
□ A time-reporting system showed excessive police time used to transport prisoners by car. By using aircraft, police time was released for other duties.
□ Civilian personnel replaced police officers who were doing administrative work, thus permitting police officers to do the work they were trained for.

For a further discussion of nonmeasurable work, see Chapter 7, Measurement and Evaluation.

Attributes of Adequate Control Systems

Each system of control, each means of control, should be designed specifically for the objective it is intended to reach. To that end desirable controls should meet the following specifications:[3]

Controls should be in tune with the needs and the nature of the activity controlled. Controls suitable for a chief engineer will differ from those for a draftsman. The closer the plan is meshed with the goal to be gained, the more effective it will be.

Controls should be timely. They should be synchronized with the events being measured. They should report events promptly when promptness is needed. But when events must mature, real-time response may confuse more then enlighten. The results of the market testing of a new product may demand daily reports, but the progress of a research and development project may be controlled through monthly or even quarterly reports. The desideratum in a control system is to detect deviations when they impend rather than report them after they occur. The third element of control is to correct deviations, so the timely report will alert management before the event strays too far from the track. Controls should therefore be forward-looking; a cash budget can control cash needs more effectively than a bank statement reconciliation.

Controls should be economical. They should never exceed the cost of that which is being controlled. Hence the manager should not seek to control the entire progress of every activity. Rather, he should focus and receive reports on the key points of key activities; the more the concentration on exceptions the more efficient the control. Control reports should provide the minimum information needed to alert a manager to action. The kind of information will vary, depending on the need. A warehouse manager needs daily information on inventory levels; a controller would be satisfied with that information every quarter.

Controls should be operational. They should lead to corrective action; they should eschew that which is merely interesting and focus on that which needs a decision by the user. They must always be directed to that person who can take the needed action, not solely to his superior. A vast chasm stretches between control and the domination of others. Reports should be sent to the persons who need them to direct their efforts to the results they are in a position to control. So the controls should reflect the organization's pattern; they must focus on the place in the organization where action can most promptly and effectively be taken. Moreover, the person doing the controlling must be authorized to do it. As in the management function of organizing, the line-staff distinction must be maintained. Staff people should measure and compare; line people should take the corrective action.

Controls should be simple. They must be understandable to those whose work is being controlled. Complicated controls confuse. They rarely work and they seldom survive. The manual that is simply stated and clearly illustrated will be used; the abstruse set of instructions will most likely be ignored. People who are a part of the control system should be told the objectives of their function so that they will recognize the significance.

Controls should be appropriate to what is controlled. Information should be precise when precision is relevant and attainable; it should be approximate when that will suit the user's needs. There is a danger in false precision. It can mislead rather than inform. An approximation is not made more accurate by being carried out to four decimal places. It is significant for an executive to know that some event can be described only as an order of magnitude or within a range rather than be cozened into clutching to his bosom some meaningless number and then demanding that events correspond to it.

Controls should be objective. Whenever possible, they should focus on events and not on people. The applicable standards may be quantitative, such as scheduled dates of delivery, or they may be qualitative, such as a training program to improve the quality of personnel. But in each case, the standard should be determinable and capable of being measured against.

Standards should be flexible. Flexibility should be built into the design of controls so that the controls will remain effective even though unforeseen events come to pass or premises change. The flexible or variable budget is an example of a control that will be congruent with the events it is designed to measure. The philosophy of the organization should lean toward flexibility in controlling, have less emphasis on rigid compliance than on stimulating imagination, and promote understanding of what not to control and an appreciation that making mistakes is a part of the learning process.

Controls should be acceptable. They should be agreed to by those whose work is being controlled so that people do not feel cribbed and confined. Those people should be asked to propose the means of control with which they would be most comfortable and which will accomplish the objectives of control.

Feedback

Feedback is implicit in the element of control that compares events with standards; it is performance information that is channeled back to management. That is the information that helps measure the adequacy and effectiveness of performance and triggers any needed action. A manager should have timely feedback, accurate feedback, useful feedback—the kind of information that will identify the problem and show him where it is so that he can correct it.

In informal organizations, managers can accomplish feedback through personal observation. In formal ones they must rely on structured reports, including financial statements, statistical analyses, and other formal documents. But even in large, formal organizations managers should not lose touch with people. They cannot get the visceral feeling of what is happening by reading reports behind desks in mahogany row. The experienced manager can obtain a wealth of information by occasionally walking through the operating areas, observing what is taking place, and engaging in casual conversations with people.

Standards

Standards represent the translation of enterprise goals into specific, measurable outcomes; they become the benchmark for acceptable performance. Standards are applied in the measurement of various types of performance. Here are some:

Output. Output standards specify quantitative performances such as machine-hours or man-hours per unit of output, units per day or week, or tons of steel produced per month.

Accuracy. Standards on accuracy specify quality of performance, such as agreement with specifications, fastness of color, or number of rejections.

Expense. The expense standards specify such things as material costs per unit, overhead per direct labor hour, or direct and indirect costs per unit of production.

Timeliness. Standards related to timeliness may cover production schedules, project completion, or meeting customers' need dates.

Capital. Standards concerning capital relate to the application of monetary units to physical items. They deal with capital invested, however, instead of operating costs. They relate more to the balance sheet than to the profit-and-loss statement. The standards include return on investment and such ratios as current assets to current liabilities, cash and receivables to payables, and turnover of inventory and notes or bonds to stock.

Revenue. The revenue standards arise from the monetary values assigned to sales. They may include revenue per airplane passenger mile, dollars per ton of sheet steel sold, or average sale per customer.

Determining appropriate standards is essential to measuring performance, but standards will not be effective unless they are placed at strategic control points. The earlier the point, the greater the assurance that deviations will be anticipated or detected and hence will be corrected.

Factors to Be Controlled

The four factors most likely to be controlled are quantity, quality, schedule, and cost. Each of the factors needs some form of surveillance to see that the standards for that factor are being met. For example:

Production. Is the factory meeting production quotas as desired specifications in time to meet sales commitments within established budgets?

Sales. Are sales quotas being met; is there a proper balance among the company's products; are salesmen making their calls on schedule; and are advertising and promotion costs reasonable?

Personnel. Is the workforce at reasonable levels; are the needed skills available and properly used; are work schedules met; and are wages competitive in the industry?

Certainly, management can set up strict and comprehensive controls and managers can sit on a network of feedback mechanisms over every function in the enterprise. But that tends to dilute the energies of the executives, who spend so much time in controlling that they have no time for the other three functions of management: planning, organizing, and directing.

Executives must therefore focus on the major problem areas in the enterprise. Control systems should be set up in certain primary areas, as in:[4]

1. Determining and improving the market standing of the organization.
2. Seeing that profitability meets forecasted needs.
3. Making sure materials are properly acquired and used.
4. Seeing that employees and managers meet established standards of performance, that their skills are being developed, and that their morale is satisfactory.
5. Providing assurance of adequate financial resources.
6. Maintaining needed productivity to remain competitive.
7. Assuring the acquisition and maintenance of physical resources.
8. Meeting the organization's responsibilities to society.

Accounting

Accounting is a well-known management control; indeed, organizations could not function without it. It is, in effect, a specialized language system that communicates information in numerical terms to executives and others. What must be remembered is that the language becomes merely noise unless it can serve to solve the organization's problems.

The significance of the numbers presented to managers can be determined only by understanding what lies behind the numbers. A manager may be told that net profits have declined over a period of time, but the information means little as a basis for decision making. The causes also must be understood. The reasons may be poor planning, need for tighter controls, or factors external to the organization that are attributable to neither planning nor control.

The manager must also be aware of the limitations on conventional financial statements. The changing value of the dollar blurs the apparent crisp accuracy of statements. When price levels escalate, the worth of assets is no longer realistic. To charge depreciation based on cost in such instances may drastically affect the ability to replace assets. The accountants must, of course, rely on and deal with historical costs primarily, but the manager must leaven the numbers with his judgment of what goes on in the world.

Inventory valuation presents difficulties. The first-in first-out method (FIFO) treats inventory as though the first item purchased will be the first item sold or consumed. But when that inventory was purchased at drastically different prices, the profits realized will not accord with reality. The manager will have to apply judgment to the inventory valuations.

Accounting information is purely numerical, but people are involved in all transactions. For example, an executive may compare two division managers on the basis of profit performance alone. The executive decision on rewards may be poorly founded if it is made without consideration of the fact that the lower profits in one of the divisions resulted from the death of a key executive, the unexpected introduction of innovative competitive products, or other factors completely beyond the control of that division manager.

Accounting information supplies information for control; it is not a control in itself. It may point to weaknesses, and only the manager can correct the weaknesses. But accounting is a powerful tool, and managers must understand the concepts and techniques associated with it. For example:

Responsibility accounting seeks to so structure budgets and costs that they match the specific responsibilities of a segment or cost center of an organization. A manager or supervisor needs a report on costs only if he can exert some control over the costs. That form of accounting provides better motivation to the operating manager, and it gives higher management a better basis for evaluating results.

Cost accounting systems focus on the detailed costs of particular products. Cost accounting answers such a question as "How much did it cost to produce the products we sold last week, last month, or last year?" That simple question can require a complicated accounting system to answer it, yet cost accounting is a major element in the control of a business. It provides information to develop budgets, price products, and control costs.

Standard costs describe what a particular product should cost to be produced. By measuring actual costs against standards, the levels of productivity and efficiency can be determined. Standard costs provide targets to shoot at. And when variances occur, they can call attention to possible deficiencies.

Direct costing, sometimes described as variable costing, is a cost accounting system that provides for assigning to a product being manufactured only the costs that vary with the volume of production—usually direct materials and direct labor. Fixed factory and other fixed costs are treated as period costs. Since variable costs are controllable primarily by the people responsible for manufacturing the product, the use of direct costing (apart from its value as an aid in making production planning and pricing decisions) can serve as a useful means of controlling the volume and efficiency of production work.

Budgeting

Budgeting involves both planning and controlling. As a decision of what will be expended, a budget is a plan: it is future-oriented. As a means of determining whether standards set are standards met, the budget is a means of control. Budgets have the significant benefit of forcing managers to plan and to control, to focus on measuring and appraising performance. But therein lies a weakness. Budgeting concentrates only on what can be quantified; it does not concentrate on quality.

The problem with budgets, and there are many problems, is not whether the controls they supply are necessary, but whether they are so used as to be effective. To develop budgets and to compare what is with what should be is salutary. But not to analyze significant variances and determine why they happened is to miss the whole point of budgeting.

Rigid budgets also miss the point. What starts out as a means of controlling operations winds up as a means of frustrating people. Budgets must be seen for what they can do and what they cannot do. When they are properly used, their benefits are undeniable. They offer to everyone in the company the views of top management. They tend to direct the efforts of the organization to the most profitable channels. They emphasize the useful, time-saving principle of management by exception. They charge individuals with specific responsibilities. They promote considered actions and reduce the number of snap judgments on cost effectiveness. They help identify weaknesses in managerial ability. They minimize unnecessary and top-of-the-head spending.

When they are improperly employed, budgets are treated as omniscient pronouncements instead of mere tools that require judgment to achieve results. They do not insure results; they merely provide the means to point out deviations. They are only as good as the standards implicit in them, and good standards are not easy to develop. They are not graven on stone like God's commandments; they are based largely on forecasts and hence are marred by uncertainty. They provide numbers, not interpretations. They need to be communicated to all concerned, sometimes a difficult need to meet. Their use requires skill and experience, and those are often rare commodities. They may hide inefficiencies when they are based solely on precedent, since overestimating becomes a practice when budget paring is expected. They seem so precise and unassailable that they tend to replace common sense. They can be a straitjacket, as when a sales department desperately needs engineering information to consummate a large sale but the engineering department protests that it does not have the budget to supply it.

If budgets are to work, operating managers must participate in setting them and then accept them without mental reservations. Managers should have the latitude to shift funds under their control so long as total budget is met and significant matters are not hidden. Standards are needed to translate budgeted amounts into rational needs for the manpower to show the resources needed to accomplish the budgeted work. And managers should not be subjected to across-the-board cuts, which are often evidence of inept planning and control.[5]

Budgets are no better than the data, premises, and plans behind them. They have been cursed and criticized since they were first conceived, but their importance should not be underestimated. They are the only way by which an organization's goals and plans are translated into recognizable, unvarying units. And they can be extremely useful guides for corrective action.

People

Managers have to face this hard fact: Machines don't mind controls, but people resent them. Control procedures are instinctively disliked because they disrupt the image people have of themselves, and most controls highlight what is done poorly, not well. People will seek to see the dark side of controls. They don't like the unpleasant criticisms controls may imply. They may refuse to see how their goals and the goals of the organization coincide. They may object to imposed standards of performance as being too high. Controls may be felt to be irrelevant; the salesman, for example, is intent on developing long-term goodwill while, at the same time, he is faced with current sales quotas. An outside group administering the controls becomes "the enemy."

Controls inevitably produce pressures, and pressures create conflict. When two groups are dependent on each other but perceive no compatibility in their goals, the resulting pressures bring animosity and ingenious ways of relieving the pressures while not actually meeting the goals.

Different managers use different ways to resolve conflicts brought about by reactions to controls. Some withdraw from the conflict; they retreat and engender contempt from the workers they seek to placate. Some try to play down the differences in order to smooth things over; they display insincerity in the process. Some try to bargain and compromise; they reach nobody's goals. Some impose their own values autocratically; they build up explosive pressure points. And some resort to an open, frank confrontation and exchange of information and views.

Studies have shown that the open exchange of information—confrontation—usually is most effective.[6]

By and large the adverse effects of control can be minimized if managers practice:

□ Participative management—encouraging employees to help develop controls.
□ Setting standards that are reasonable and objective, that set a range of adequate performance, and that are acceptable to the people controlled.
□ Developing general rather than detailed controls, so that employees can exercise judgment within broad parameters.
□ Using controls as a means to achieve goals rather than imposing strict rules that bring automatic punishment for infraction instead of for failing to meet the goals.
□ Keeping the goals simple, understandable, logical, legitimate, and keyed directly to what they are designed to achieve.

Management by Objectives

One form of control that has been practiced in recent years has been termed "management by objectives." The term was coined by Peter Drucker;[7] the concept is excellent and has had much success. It has also had disastrous results, and the reasons for the disasters may be attributable to the failure to remember Drucker's full title to his approach to management control: "Management by Objectives and Self-Control." Indeed, Drucker says that true management by objectives substitutes management by self-control for management by domination.[8]

Management by objectives (MBO) seeks to integrate company and individual goals: the company to achieve profit and growth, the individual to develop himself by contributing to company goals. But an MBO system requires prodigious effort to be successful. And there are enormous hurdles in its way:

- □ Many managers are functional experts. Their work is specialized and they enjoy their specialty. They would rather be concerned with their parochial goals than with the needs of the enterprise.
- □ Each level of management perceives the needs of the organization in different terms depending on the height of the level in the hierarchy. People at different levels may think they are talking about the same things when they speak of organizational objectives, but they are really speaking different languages. That is because, from different levels, one sees the same panorama in different detail. Methods of compensation among positions vary. The salaries of some people in the organization are fixed; the compensation of others is or may be tied to bonuses, commissions, or other factors that are based on performance.

Yet despite the hazards and roadblocks, MBO can make a big difference in the way people perceive their jobs and their commitment to their enterprise. That sharpened perception can lead to total commitment and improved performance. An effective MBO program, therefore, requires the following elements:

- □ Executive management must be sincerely committed to the program, must take an active lead in displaying that commitment, and must provide a climate in which the program can grow. Senior management must demonstrate its commitment by taking the time to establish systems for MBO, developing overall realistic objectives for the program, communicating the objectives to subordinates effectively, and permitting participation by subordinates in goal setting.
- □ The objectives of all units within the organization must be synchronized with the aims of the organization.
- □ Goals must be quantitatively expressed. They should be measurable; they should be attainable; but they should make people stretch to reach them.

□ The people being measured should be provided with information on their performance so that they can exercise self-control.
□ The orientation throughout the organization should be participative to gain commitment from subordinates. To that end:

Goals should be set mutually by superior and subordinate.
The way the subordinate perceives his own goals should be actively considered and merged with enterprise goals.
Goals should not be so inflexible that they cannot be adjusted for unforeseen changes.

□ The reviews of performance results should be used as a learning, and not a disciplinary, experience.

A good MBO program is pyramidal. Each level of the pyramid must be involved in the contribution the individual makes to the unit of which he is a part. The objectives of a district sales manager's job should contribute to the performance of the sales department. The objectives of the production manager's job are to improve the performance of the manufacturing branch. The objectives of an autonomous division are to improve the profitability and growth of the parent company.

Why then, do MBO programs so often go wrong? The answers are legion:

□ Executive management decrees an MBO program and does not participate.
□ The MBO program is not explained to its participants.
□ Unit objectives are not thought through because goal-setting guidelines have not been provided to unit managers.
□ Company objectives are not understood, are fuzzy, unrealistic, or inconsistent.
□ Busyness is confused with performance. Instead of setting goals, management merely sets out work to be done.
□ Goals are not measurable. Performance is therefore confused with traits or an appearance of hard work.
□ Goals are short-term, sometimes at the expense of the long range.
□ Goals are, on the one hand, continually being changed or, on the other, are so inflexible as to arouse frustration when basic premises or policies are changed.
□ Unit managers are not provided with accurate, current information to help them manage themselves.

With all their problems and hazards, MBO programs have worked. In 1961 the Purex Corporation installed an MBO program in fifteen manufacturing plants. The individual managers set their goals; control reports were provided for self-control; and the performance of the managers was periodically reviewed. The program resulted in substantial achievement, including individual plant productivity.[9]

The Board of Directors

Decline as a Controlling Force

Peter Drucker has said that the decline of the board of directors as a controlling force in business is a universal phenomenon of this century. He says that boards have in common one thing: They do not function.[10] He points to the fact that the boards of Rolls-Royce Ltd. in England, Penn Central in the United States, and Montecatini in Italy were apparently the last to know of the disasters that were about to strike their companies.

The BarChris decision, however, brought boards to a rude awakening. Many corporate directors were stunned by the judge's sharp attack on the lack of involvement in corporate reporting and the failure to ask questions about management's practices.[11]

Audit Committees

The courts' concern with board involvement is becoming sharper and more specific. In April 1977, a United States district court judge handed down a final judgment and order in the case of the Securities and Exchange Commission (SEC) against Killearn Properties, Inc., a Florida corporation. The order required the company's board of directors to maintain an audit committee composed of at least three members of the board who should be outside directors—not part of Killearn's management. The court also set forth specific responsibilities for the audit committee of the board:

1. Review the engagement, scope of work, and audit procedures of external auditors.
2. Review, with appropriate people, the general policies and procedures the company uses with respect to internal auditing, accounting, and financial controls. Audit committee members should be generally familiar with the company's accounting and reporting principles and practices.

3. Review with the independent accountants, upon completion of their audit:
   (a) Their proposed audit opinion.
   (b) Their perception of the company's financial and accounting personnel.
   (c) The cooperation they received in their audit.
   (d) How company resources can be used to minimize the time spent by outside auditors.
   (e) Significant transactions not normally a part of the company's business.
   (f) Any changes in accounting principles.
   (g) Any recommendations for improving internal financial controls, choice of accounting principles, or management reporting systems.
4. Inquire of both company personnel and outside auditors about any deviations from established codes of conduct of the company, and periodically review those policies.
5. Meet with the company's financial staff at least twice a year to review the scope of internal accounting and auditing procedures in effect and the extent to which recommendations made by the internal staff or by the independent accountants have been implemented.
6. Recommend to the board the retention or discharge of independent accountants for the ensuing year.
7. Have the power to direct and supervise an investigation into any matter brought to its attention within the scope of its duties.[12]

Some companies do not wait for the courts. For example, a special task force at Lockheed, after completing a comprehensive review of the company's activities, recommended on page 77 of the "Exhibits to the Report of the Special Review Committee of the Board of Directors, Lockheed Aircraft Corporation," that:

1. The audit committee of the board be expanded from three to four and possibly five members, all of whom are "outside" directors.
2. The audit committee review the internal audit function, its status, its quality of work, and its relationships with and responsibilities to management, the audit committee, and the board as a whole.
3. The committee define the role of the corporation's independ-

ent auditors, including their relationship with and responsibilities to management, the audit committee, and the board as a whole.

4. The committee be informed of all questionable transactions.
5. The outside auditor's personnel be rotated in their assignments.
6. The independence of the internal auditors from the activities they audit be insured.
7. A broad policy statement be issued respecting standards of integrity and ethics to be followed by employees of the corporation, and compliance with these standards be confirmed by either the internal audit department or the corporation's independent auditors.

Demands for audit committees are rising. In January 1977, the New York Stock Exchange adopted an "Audit Committee Policy Statement." It requires each domestic company with common stock listed on the Exchange, as a condition of listing and continued listing of its securities, to establish no later than June 30, 1978, and maintain thereafter an audit committee made up solely of directors independent of management.

In a research study by Mautz and Neumann, sponsored by Ernst & Ernst and supported by The Institute of Internal Auditors, Inc., the researchers surveyed proxy statements issued in 1975 by companies that were listed in Fortune 500 and Fortune 50s and registered on the New York or American Stock Exchanges. Of 604 proxy statements examined, 523 stated that audit committees existed, 53 stated they did not, and 18 made no mention of audit committees.[13]

And at least some of the audit committees have taken their jobs seriously. For example, *The Wall Street Journal,* on November 11, 1976, reported that Avis, Inc.'s audit committee conducted a study that showed that the company had made "improper, facilitating, or otherwise questionable payments to consultants, local government officials and others" of about $425,000 since January 1, 1972.

Responsibilities of Audit Committees

Different audit committees will undertake different roles and assume different responsibilities. One director sees that role as assuring stockholders and other directors that:[14]

□ Those responsible for auditing the affairs of the company have carried out their responsibilities.

☐ Both external and internal audit programs are appropriate.
☐ The reports of the external and internal auditors have been acted upon.
☐ The communications between the external and internal auditors are direct, uninhibited, and not subject to restraints by management.
☐ The auditors are receiving the full cooperation of top management.

The Mautz and Neumann report lists some of the practices that would contribute to the success of corporate audit committees. Here is the list of some of the practices, listed in the general order of importance according to the respondents to Mautz and Neumann's questionnaires.[15]

☐ The audit committee should have ready access to independent auditors.
☐ Independent auditors should brief the committee regularly.
☐ The committee should be provided promptly with relevant information.
☐ The independent auditors should notify the committee promptly about any problems encountered.
☐ Management should notify the committee promptly about problems.
☐ The internal auditors should have access to the committee.
☐ The committee should operate with an agenda and written statement of issues before its meetings.
☐ Audit committee members should visit company plants and offices.
☐ Internal auditors should promptly notify the committee of problems.
☐ Internal auditors should regularly brief the committee.
☐ The committee should have a written statement of its responsibilities.
☐ Management should regularly brief the committee.

The practices listed were the result of answers to questions asked of chief executive officers, nonofficer directors, internal auditors, and independent CPA's. The nonofficer directors and the internal auditors agreed that ready access of the latter to the former was a most important practice. The chief executive officers placed it lower in the scale of importance.

The Foreign Corrupt Practices Act

Despite the fact that some views are reported as less important, continued pressures on companies and boards of directors may make all these practices important and regular. For example, the Foreign Corrupt Practices Act of 1977 (Public Law 95-213, December 19, 1977, 91 Stat. 1494) amended the Securities Exchange Act of 1934 to add certain requirements that call for issuers (companies covered by the act) to maintain accurate records and to file certain reports.

The act calls for issuers to "make and keep books, records, and accounts which, in reasonable detail, accurately and fairly reflect the transactions and dispositions of the assets of the issuer." The law also requires issuers to "devise and maintain a system of internal accounting controls sufficient to provide reasonable assurances" about the execution and recording of transactions and the comparison of recorded assets with existing assets. The law forbids payments or gifts to foreign officials to influence their decisions. Any officer or director who willfully violates this law may be fined up to $10,000 and/or be imprisoned for up to five years.

Thus the problems of the directors mount, and the directors can get little comfort from expectations of insurance protection. *The Wall Street Journal,* on July 12, 1976, pointed out that, as suits against companies and their directors rise, the greater is the scramble for more liability insurance for corporate directors and officers, often referred to as D&O insurance. A survey disclosed that D&O coverage was obtained in 1975 by 82 percent of the companies listed on the New York Stock Exchange, up from 76 percent in 1974 and 70 percent in 1973. Average coverage rose to $8 million in 1975 from $7 million in 1974 and $6.4 million in 1973. The study's most significant finding was that the average payments to successful claimants under D&O policies rose to $865,000 in 1975 from $770,000 in 1974.

Protection

Directors and officers, says the *Journal,* have been held liable by courts for such vaguely defined acts as improvident investment of corporate funds, improper expenditure of corporate funds in a proxy fight, failure to obtain competitive bids for major purchases, and even failure to exercise "reasonable care" in the selection of a depositary bank that failed. New occupational health and safety laws as well as pollution and pension measures have also broadened personal liability.

Directors can obtain some measure of protection from audits made by external auditors, but many of the matters that place liabilities upon directors are generally outside the scope of the audits. Competitive bidding, safety and health measures, and pollution are cases in point.

A competent internal audit staff that is authorized to review all operations within an organization can provide an added measure of comfort to directors. They can do so by bringing to the directors' attention matters that present a hazard to the corporation. Reviewing company controls and practices concerned with competitive bidding, safety and health, and pollution is a part of many internal audit plans. As a result, it would seem fair to say that internal auditing, as it continues to expand its scope from financial auditing into audits of operations and is recognized as a strong deterrent force within a corporation, will have a beneficial effect in helping to obtain D&O coverage and perhaps even reducing policy premiums.

Sprinkler systems contribute to lower fire insurance premiums. Audit committees of boards are in desperate need of their own "sprinkler systems" to quench smoldering problems before the problems erupt into devastating flames. In the following section of this chapter, that aspect of the internal auditor's role will be explored further.

CONTROLLING AND THE INTERNAL AUDITOR

Nature of Controlling

Definition

The word "control" finds its roots in the process of auditing. It comes from the Latin *contrarotulus*. *Contra* means "against," and *rotulus* means a "roll." *Contrarotulus* was used in Roman times to describe the work done in the army to check accounts. One officer kept the roll of accounts. Another kept a duplicate roll so that one roll could be checked against the other. The current meaning is something that affords a standard of comparison or means of verification and also a restraining domination.

The skills of internal auditors grow as they depart from the ancient concept of *contrarotulus* to the modern one of standards of comparison. The ancient concept implies verification by comparing one document against another. The current definition invokes standards. And the concept of standards implies a means of determining whether a goal or an objective has been achieved—far different from checking one number against another.

Controls and Objectives

The most important message this advanced concept has to offer is that control does not stand alone. Control must be considered in relation to the objectives management is trying to reach, and the internal auditor must therefore know the objectives before he can properly evaluate the means of control.

Internal auditing is generally regarded as a "managerial control which functions by measuring and evaluating the effectiveness of other controls."[16] The internal auditor must know which means of control should apply to a given activity, and he should be able to key the means of control required to what he perceives to be the principal objectives of the activity under his review.

A system of control designed to achieve one objective may fail to achieve another, even though the activities involved are similar. For example, if the principal objective is speed of output, then the system of control needed will differ from that which would be required if the principal objective were accuracy. Daily performance reports must be issued promptly and estimates may suffice; the clock is in control. Financial statements must be precise; thorough verification is the control.

For the internal auditor to determine exactly what the objectives of an activity are may not be as simple as appears on the surface. On the one hand, management may not have issued a formal statement of functions and responsibilities for the organization or operation under review. Thus, the internal auditor may have no clue to the objectives that are sought to be achieved. On the other hand, detailed statements of functions and responsibilities in existence may be so comprehensive that they may well obscure rather than disclose the key objectives. If internal auditors let themselves be unduly influenced by such detailed statements, the auditors, instead of determining whether objectives are being reached, may merely be trying to see whether every single step prescribed has been taken. That misses the point of the management-oriented audit. Also, the audit may be needlessly expensive, since all objectives, not only the significant ones, might be analyzed in the same detail.

During the preliminary survey segment of the audit, therefore, the internal auditor should elicit from discussions with appropriate management personnel the major objectives and goals of the activity to be reviewed. Deciding what is major and what is minor is a matter of judgment based on the information gleaned by the internal auditor during the survey phase of the audit and a comparison of those objectives with what he knows of the broad objectives of the entire enterprise.

Audits of Operating Controls

If an internal auditor can determine significant areas of operations within the organization, identify their objectives, differentiate between major and minor objectives, determine whether the related systems of control are designed to see that the objectives will be met, and plan the audit accordingly, then he can feel that he is meeting his own objectives of giving management the greatest return for each audit dollar spent.

Two examples will illustrate the management- and objective-oriented audit of operations. One example is concerned with an operational audit of controls in an accounting function.[17] The second relates to an operation not normally evaluated by auditors.

> *Objectives.* The principal objectives of the accounts payable function may be regarded as authorizing payment for materials and services (1) actually ordered and received, (2) at prices properly agreed upon, (3) on the dates specified.
>
> *Controls.* The system of control should include form of organization, procedures, instructions, methods, and devices. They would operate in the following way:
>
> 1. To make sure that payments are made only for materials and services actually ordered and received, control through the following form of organization should be established: The accounts payable function should be separate from (a) stores, which issues requisitions for supplies, (b) purchasing, which places the orders, (c) receiving, which counts and verifies receipts, and (d) cash disbursement, which pays the bills.
>
> Control in the form of written procedures provides that accounts payable clerks are to receive and compare:
> (a) An approved copy of the purchase order for purchasing.
> (b) An original invoice on an imprinted billhead from the supplier.
> (c) An approved receiving report from receiving.
> (d) Executive certification of certain invoices to show receipt of services not covered by receiving reports or purchase orders.
> 2. To make sure that payments do not exceed prices previously agreed upon, control in the form of instructions should provide that the accounts payable clerks will compare invoiced prices with the prices

shown on purchase orders and on approved change orders. Control in the form of methods and forms should be provided to obtain an authoritative decision when there is a disagreement among the prices, quantities, terms, or items shown on the related purchase order. In such circumstances, the accounts payable clerks will make use of an invoice discrepancy report to request instructions from the responsible purchasing agents as to whether payment may be made.

3. To see that invoices are mathematically and clerically correct, the clerks will check them for accuracy and will total and recompute them as necessary.

4. To see that payments are being made at the right time, suitable control devices could be installed. Each accounts payable clerk might be provided with a set of folders, numbered from 1 to 31, corresponding to the days of the month. Invoices could be filed on receipt in the folder whose number represents the discount due date. Invoices would be paid by that date and, to conserve funds, no earlier than that date.

(Computers now often take the place of much of this manual work, but the concepts are largely the same.)

Tests. Having examined and appraised the system of control in the light of management's objectives, the internal auditor will then perform such tests as he considers necessary to determine whether (1) the system is working effectively and is achieving the principal objectives of the accounts payable function, (2) the means of control are unnecessarily elaborate, or (3) additional means of control are needed. The tests may include:

1. A sampling of paid invoices to see whether all necessary documentation has been received and considered prior to invoice payment, whether payments have been made at the appropriate dates, and whether invoices for services have been properly approved.

2. A review of appropriate approvals of invoice discrepancy reports and the basis on which those approvals were given.

3. A test of clerical and mathematical accuracy.

4. A sampling of folders to see whether the invoices have been properly filed, as well as an analysis of lost discounts.

Having tested the basic controls, the internal auditor might make certain additional tests to see whether the company's objectives are being met. For example, he could:

1. Check to see whether purchasing is sending change orders to accounts payable promptly. Delays might result in improper payments and supplier dissatisfaction.

2. Determine whether executives approving invoices for services have satisfied themselves that services have indeed been received in the quantities billed. Some executives have the tendency to sign perfunc-

torily what is placed before them, particularly if the charge is not
against their budget.
3. Analyze purchase orders to see whether they contain clear and explicit
   instructions regarding terms of payment. Accounts payable clerks
   often have to struggle with obscure provisions on the orders.

The second illustration deals with an actual audit of controls over
the activities of a materials and processes engineering department.
The department, in an aerospace engineering division, is made up of
engineering specialists, usually with advanced degrees in their special-
ties, whose primary job is to appraise materials—as well as the processes the materials undergo—used in aircraft and missiles: aluminum, stainless steel, titanium, beryllium, molybdenum, exotic plastics,
and the like. What follows summarizes some of the material taken
from the internal auditor's working papers and report.[18]

> The internal auditor found, during his preliminary survey, that the engi-
> neers in the department were assigned certain materials to analyze,
> usually upon requests from other departments in the company. They
> studied the materials by reviewing the available literature and putting the
> materials and processes through laboratory tests. They combed the mar-
> ket for sources of the materials by talking to suppliers, studying bro-
> chures, and exploring any other avenues that were open to them.
>
> And then they did several things. The one we are interested in here re-
> lated to their responsibility for issuing formal reports on their analyses,
> showing the characteristics of the particular materials and how they
> should be inspected when they come into the company's inspection de-
> partment.
>
> As the auditor saw them, the primary objectives of management in carry-
> ing out this responsibility were:
>
> 1. To obtain the best use of the efforts of the engineers. The engineers
>   were high-priced specialists, and the inappropriate use of their talents
>   could cost the company dearly.
> 2. To issue reports that were accurate and understandable. The reports
>   included information on how to test the materials when they were re-
>   ceived in the plant. The inspectors, who were not engineers, had to be
>   able to understand the inspection criteria.
>
> The forms of control that would be calculated to achieve those objectives,
> according to the auditor's research, might be as follows:
>
> *The Use of the Engineers*
> 1. An organizational structure in which the engineers were directly re-
>   sponsible to a supervisor or manager who was also an accomplished
>   materials and processes engineer.

2. A requirement that each request coming into the department for appraisal or test of materials or processes would be reviewed by the manager so that he could decide (*a*) whether the job should be done at all, (*b*) how much time it would take to complete, (*c*) what priority to give it, and (*d*) when it should be completed. Most of the jobs called for prompt action, usually within 60 days.
3. A simple job card showing the title of the job, the engineer to whom it was assigned, and the estimated man-days needed for completion.

Report System

1. A file of research materials behind each report so that someone—some other qualified engineer—could independently check on the accuracy of the report or that somebody else could continue with the preparation of the report if the engineer originally assigned to the job left the company or had to abandon the project in midstream.
2. The requirement that each draft of a report be reviewed by a supervisor, or some other reviewer, for accuracy, clarity, support, reasonableness, compliance with procedures, inclusion of all relevant elements, and the like.
3. A standard format for the report, preferably with established headings or sections, so that the writer will not omit anything essential and users of the report can immediately find the section that they need.
4. A list of approved recipients of the report and a periodic—at least annual—inquiry of those persons to make sure they still need the report.

Unfortunately, the controls in effect did not measure up to those standards. And the tests the auditor made proved the defects in the system.

The auditor took the job cards to an adding machine and totaled the number of man-days assigned to jobs on hand. The total disclosed that if not another job was received in the department, the work already scheduled would take a full year to complete. And new work was coming into the department each day.

Then the auditor discussed the reports with receiving inspectors, the people who had the greatest need for them. The auditor found that the inspectors were wasting a great deal of time trying to find the instructions they needed. The reports were voluminous and contained many sections; the inspection information was but one small part. Sometimes the instructions appeared in front of the report, sometimes in the back, and sometimes in between. Sometimes the instructions were headed Detailed Requirements, sometimes Sampling and Testing, sometimes Physical Properties, sometimes Test Procedures, and sometimes something else. When the manager of materials and processes was informed of the findings, he took the following corrective action on the two problems:

1. *Assignments.* The manager (*a*) developed backlog reports to show him the status of the workload, (*b*) made a survey of all the jobs in the backlog to decide which ones would be eliminated, (*c*) developed a new set

of criteria for the kinds of jobs that would be accepted for investigation, and (d) established a system of priorities for the work in process.
2. *Reports.* The manager agreed that the format of the reports needed some work. Accordingly, he established a standard layout for all the engineers' reports. The inspection section was clearly labeled and placed in the report so that it could readily be found.

As the engineering example indicates, the management-oriented internal auditor need not be a specialist in the activities he audits. But if he understands the relation between objectives and controls and is thoroughly indoctrinated in good business practice and in principles of management, he can make a meaningful, effective audit in any area of the enterprise.

Internal Accounting Controls

External auditors also are turning to the objectives-oriented approach to studying and evaluating internal accounting controls. Internal auditors who wish to coordinate their work with the work of the external auditors should be aware of that approach. In January 1978 Arthur Andersen & Co. published "A Guide for Studying and Evaluating Internal Accounting Controls." (Subject File AA 2880, Item 1.) The Guide states that the approach identifies the specific objectives that should be achieved by the internal accounting controls exercised in a broad area of a business.

The Guide points out that internal auditors can help organizations achieve the objectives of internal control. The internal auditors can facilitate the work of the external auditors by studying an organization's control systems for, in conjunction with, or independently of, the entity's external auditors. The Guide refers to the following four cycles or activities of a business:

Treasury. To receive capital funds from investors and creditors and to invest them as needed.
Expenditures. To acquire resources in exchange for the obligations to pay and to pay obligations to suppliers and employees.
Conversion. To hold, use, or transform assets.
Revenue. To distribute resources in exchange for current payments or promises of future payments.

A fifth cycle is concerned with financial reporting. Hence, almost every function involved in processing transactions or preparing financial statements can be keyed to one of the five cycles. The major exception is financial planning and control, which encompasses all of the five cycles.

Each cycle is made up of functions. A function is defined as a major processing task or part of a system that processes common transactions. Also, each cycle has specific control objectives. Those objectives relate to:

> *Authorization.* Compliance with established policies and standards.
> *Transaction processing.* Recognizing, processing, and reporting transactions and adjustments.
> *Classification.* Source, timeliness, and propriety of journal entries.
> *Substantiation and evaluation.* Periodic verification and evaluation of reported balances and the integrity of processing systems.
> *Physical safeguards.* Access to assets, records, critical forms, and processing areas.

To illustrate cycle objectives, the Guide gives 117 objectives listed under the five cycles and grouped according to the five elements just listed.

For example, under the expenditure cycle for a purchasing operation, within the Authorization objectives, the following objective, among many others, is listed:

> □ Vendors should be authorized in accordance with management's criteria.

Later in the Guide is a discussion of each of the cycle objectives showing the standards to be met to achieve a particular objective, the risk if the objective is not met, and techniques used to achieve the objectives. Some brief extracts of the matters relating to vendor authorization are as follows:

Selection Criteria
> □ Current and potential ability and willingness to provide quality, quantity, timely delivery, and service.
> □ Price competitiveness, considering unit prices, volume discounts, transportation and credit terms.
> □ Policies regarding related-party transactions, conflicts of interest, sensitive payments, and the like.

Examples of Risks If Objectives Are Not Achieved
> □ Payments made to suppliers not authorized to receive them.
> □ Late receipts, substandard materials, excessive prices.

□ Purchases made from related parties without senior management's knowledge.

Examples of Techniques to Achieve Objectives
□ Clear statements of criteria or acceptability of suppliers, and quality checks of suppliers by quality control inspectors.
□ Requirements for competitive bids, subject to stipulated exceptions.
□ Conflict-of-interest program calling for buying personnel to certify that they have not received gifts and that they are not affiliated with suppliers.

The Guide provides some excellent means of evaluating internal control systems. It is not a mere checklist, but instead provides the reasons for the controls and the risks to be anticipated if adequate and effective means of control are not installed. Further, it points out the difference between the external auditor's and the internal auditor's use of the Guide material. External auditors may limit their reviews of internal controls to those on which they expect to rely. In some cases it may be more efficient to verify account balances directly than to rely on internal accounting controls. Also, the account balances may not be material to the overall financial statement.

Internal auditors, on the other hand, may evaluate controls to determine compliance with company policies and procedures or to identify control techniques that are ineffective or redundant.

The cycle approach to evaluating internal accounting controls is being adopted by other accounting organizations as well. As this chapter was written, a Special Advisory Committee on Internal Accounting Control, formed by the American Institute of Certified Public Accountants, issued a tentative report, dated September 15, 1978, on internal accounting controls and used a cycle approach to illustrate an evaluation of internal accounting control.

Budgeting

The internal auditor's concern with budgets was discussed in Chapter 9, Planning. It will not be pursued here except to point out that the internal auditor's interest in budgeting as a control device is to make sure that budgets are properly used to that end. For example, if a manager compares actual costs with budgeted costs and leaves it at that, he is missing the entire point of budgeting as a means of control.

The internal auditor, therefore, should be concerned not only with comparisons but also with whether significant deviations are being evaluated, the causes for the deviations are being determined, and the information is being put to use to prevent repetition or to provide new premises for future budgeting. When those steps are not being taken by the manager, the internal auditor should make the evaluations himself and explore the reasons. Aberrations disclosed by deviations can often lead to the discovery of serious operational defects—matters warranting the attention of senior management.

The internal auditor should also be concerned with his own budgets—the amount of time expended on audit assignments as compared with the time budgeted. The evaluation should take place after each assignment is concluded to determine whether:

- □ The original budget was appropriate.
- □ The variances can be explained by changes in the premises on which the budget was set.
- □ The auditor in charge had lost control of the project and of his assistants.
- □ Time was wasted on unprofitable sorties into irrelevant areas.
- □ Budgets for future audits of the same projects should be adjusted.

People

Relation to Internal Control

People are a significant part of any control system. A system will run smoothly or will stutter and stop depending on the people controlling or being controlled by that system. The knowledgeable internal auditor will base his audit program and the extent of his tests on his perception of the people involved in the system. Consider two departments performing comparable work. Each functions under similar systems of control, but the quality of personnel and supervision differs.

In department A, the manager is reaching retirement and finds that his most compelling focus of interest. His supervisors are busy putting out the fires that result from poor planning. They have little time to supervise or train their people. Personnel turnover is high, as is the rejection rate for the product that forms the department's output, and morale is low.

Department B is staffed by an alert, experienced manager who practices planning, organizing, directing, and controlling. New hires are put through a comprehensive training program. Supervisors review the ongoing process and periodically test transactions to determine whether they meet standards. Control reports from supervisors to the manager provide an excellent overview of backlogs, rejections, self-evaluations, and improvements. There is little employee turnover, and morale is high.

There can be little doubt as to which department is more likely to have the better overall system of control and in which department the internal auditor would feel comfortable about minimizing tests of transactions. Obviously, the internal auditor's study of an activity's system of control must take people into account.

Relations to Objectives

The system of internal control will function effectively or poorly in direct relation to how well people understand the objectives of the system under which they are functioning. An example follows:

In a manufacturing company, the scrap sales yard was several miles from the production plant. During production, large quantities of metals were cut, turned, or drilled and thereby generated substantial quantities of scrap. Some of the metals, such as stainless steel, copper, titanium, and beryllium, commanded relatively high prices in the scrap market. Periodically, the carts containing the generated scrap were hauled from the production plant to the scrap yard. Each cart was tagged; and as it left the production yard, the guard at the plant gate was to record the exact time of departure on the tag. A guard at the scrap yard was then to record on the tag the exact time the cart arrived there.

An audit disclosed that the guard at the production plant was not recording the times the carts left the plant. When the internal auditor asked why, the guard grumbled that his chief was always coming up with rules that made no sense and that he didn't believe in wasting his valuable time on nonsensical rules.

The internal auditor then explained to him the objective of the control: The value of the scrap metal was high. There had been instances when the drivers, moving the scrap from one location to another, had left the assigned route to give the valuable scrap metals to unscrupulous scrap dealers in exchange for a few dollars. Recorded times were therefore essential control points. The exact time the trip between the two locations should take was known. If the difference between the times recorded by the two guards was exceeded by a predetermined percent, then the driver would be asked some hard questions and the scrap carts would be thoroughly checked. Once the guard understood the objective of the control system, he enthusiastically complied with the requirements he had previously considered nonsense.

Management by Objectives

The internal auditor's involvement in MBO programs has not been dealt with extensively in the literature. Certainly, there are aspects of the program that can be a part of the auditor's routine examinations. For example, internal auditors traditionally audit the timeliness, accuracy, and usefulness of management reports. And information to managers that helps the managers exercise self-control under an MBO program is little different.

Also, in any audit of an operation, activity, or department, the internal auditor is keenly interested in the objectives that have been established so that he can determine whether they are congruent with those of the enterprise and whether reports of accomplishment are fairly stated and are not merely self-serving declarations.

But the comprehensive audit of an MBO system is probably a rarity. Functioning MBO systems that have top management support are most likely under close executive surveillance. Hence executive management may not see the need for an internal audit of them. Yet many MBO programs fail, and management may want to know why. Also, as audit committees of boards of directors learn to make use of the internal auditor's ability to analyze and appraise, they too may ask questions about ongoing MBO programs.

For those reasons, internal auditors should be prepared to embark on audits of all or part of an MBO program. As in any other management-oriented audit, the internal auditor should understand the objectives of such a program. Among the objectives are these:

- ◻ To provide a means of defining the results that executive managers can expect from operating managers.
- ◻ To assist managers in improving performance.
- ◻ To reward managers fairly for the results they achieve.
- ◻ To improve communication between the various management levels in the enterprise.
- ◻ To provide managers with the means of setting their own goals and controlling their own jobs.
- ◻ To develop managers for higher jobs and to have an objective means of determining when the managers are ready for those jobs.

To achieve the objectives, certain methods should be developed, and there would seem to be no reason why the internal auditor could not evaluate the adequacy and effectiveness of those methods. Here are some of the questions an internal auditor can ask about the system of devising and carrying out an MBO program listed under the four functions of management:

Planning

- How has top management demonstrated its support for the MBO program?
- Do MBO standards take into account certain basic premises such as:
  What is the company's business?
  What should it be?
  Should the company seek growth through internal expansion or through acquisition?
  Should the company take additional risks to stimulate growth?
  Should some product lines be abandoned?
  Should other product lines be acquired or developed?
- Are the objectives clear, specific, and measurable?
- Are the objectives attainable by some stretching?
- Is the range of objectives broad enough to include innovation, labor relations, and improvement of subordinates?
- Do the objectives take into account the organization's responsibility to society?
- To what extent do subordinates contribute to the formulation of objectives? Is participation genuine or just a manipulating device? How do operating managers regard it?
- Are the objectives within the resources of the organization?
- What provision is made to see that all those responsible for meeting objectives understand the objectives?
- Do the objectives seek to anticipate the unexpected? Do they have "what-if's" built into them?
- What evidence is there that all concerned are committed to the objectives?
- Do the objectives merely define the normal responsibilities of the job—being solely a statement of functions and responsibilities—or do they go beyond them to establish mind-stretching goals?

Organizing

- Are objectives properly placed within the organizational structure?
- How is the work delegated to meet the objectives?

□ Is there a clear distinction between staff and line responsibilities with respect to the objectives? Is there a distinct line between the doers and the advisers?

□ Which functions of the organization are not covered by objectives?

□ Does each person responsible for meeting objectives understand to whom he or she reports—is there unity of command?

□ Do the objectives relate to many small jobs that do not force people to extend themselves?

Directing

□ Is there a free flow of information up and down the line?

□ How are policies relating to the objectives defined and interpreted?

□ Are standards set as straitjackets or as a means of showing when objectives have been met?

□ Does the system provide for good communication and liaison between departments to meet mutual objectives?

□ Do people find superiors approachable for changes in objectives when premises change significantly?

□ Are mistakes treated as crimes or as opportunities to learn?

□ Are managers provided with training plans to help in their development?

□ Are the training plans, or courses, relevant and useful?

□ Is the information gained from training courses put to use in terms of setting and meeting objectives?

□ Are rewards to managers fair in terms of their performance in meeting objectives?

Controlling

□ Do managers receive information on how well or how poorly they are moving toward their objectives?

□ Is the information adequate in terms of timeliness, relevance, simplicity, and usefulness?

□ Is the management information system that produces the data adequate, and is it functioning effectively?

□ Is the information excessive? Does it inundate the manager? Could it be made more useful through better summaries?

□ Is the information too expensive in relation to the benefits obtained?

□ Do the budgets related to the objectives seem reasonable? Are they excessive in terms of the importance of the objectives, or do they provide insufficient resources?

□ How are the performance and the potentials of managers judged? Are there periodic reviews? What do the managers themselves think of the reviews?

Obviously, any comprehensive review of an MBO program would present some difficulties to an internal audit staff. But with support from executive management or from the board of directors and with a knowledge of the standards to use in measuring the success or failure of the program, internal auditors could make a signal contribution to the MBO effort.

Some of the answers to the questions just listed may be difficult to support by reference to documentation, but it is well for the auditor to remember that the term "auditor" comes from the Latin *audire*, "to listen." Asking the right questions of managers and subordinates, listening patiently and sympathetically, and evaluating the answers intelligently can produce useful results. First, the very asking of a question can start the hearer thinking along lines of improving the program. Second, the appraisal of a large number of responses can sometimes provide overwhelming evidence of defects in the system.

For example, if all the subordinates of one executive declare that they have difficulty in meshing their objectives with company objectives and in understanding the basic premises for those objectives, there would seem to be a pretty serious problem in that MBO system. The problem is underscored if all the subordinates of another executive demonstrate that the company objectives and premises are abundantly clear to them. Obviously, one of the executives has not communicated adequately. Also, if 50 percent of the managers questioned complain that the information they are receiving to help them control themselves is late and useless, certainly the situation cries for improvement.

Auditors who understand their profession are always on the lookout for indicators that point to poor systems. Here are some indicators that relate to MBO programs:

□ A history of objectives made but never met.

□ An absence of understanding on the part of operating managers about the philosophy of an MBO system.

□ Fuzzy or nonexistent goal-setting guidelines. If corporate goals are unrealistic, unclear, or inconsistent, the operating managers will have difficulty adjusting their own goals to company goals.

□ Goals that are not made measurable. A manager should be able to know when his own goals and those of his subordinates have been met. And that knowledge should come from objective sources, not subjective impressions.

□ Goals that are all short-run—never more than a year. That tends to produce management by drive rather than management by objectives.

□ Using objectives as a punitive rather than a constructive force.

It could well be that MBO programs that failed might have survived and been successful if subjected to a competent, management-oriented internal audit.

The Board of Directors

Relations with Internal Auditors

The internal auditor's involvement with the board of directors is most often through the audit committee of the board. That involvement is getting more prevalent as both the external and internal auditors educate audit committees about the importance of a competent, objective internal audit function as a means of information and control.

Audit committees themselves are beginning to see the need. A 1974 editorial in *Business Week* pointed out that the SEC is now saying that anyone who was in a position to know what was going on in a corporation and could have done something about it would be held liable along with those who actually committed the offense. Accordingly, in the Penn Central case, the SEC included as defendants three outside directors of the company. Many directors are feeling their responsibility keenly. Former U.S. Supreme Court Justice Arthur Goldberg is a case in point. His resignation from TWA's board of directors was prompted by his feeling that he was unable to fulfill his "legal and public" obligations as a member of the board. One of his proposals had been to engage an independent staff of technical specialists to assist outside members of the board.

Maturing audit committees, according to the Mautz and Neumann study, are giving more and more attention to the internal audit function.[19] In some cases, internal audit groups are organized as a result of such attention. In most cases, however, the result has been the upgrading of personnel and responsibilities. In effect, that is what Justice Goldberg was recommending: some means of obtaining objective, professionally developed information on what is going on within the corporation.

Certainly, the audit committee can expect objective professional opinions from the external auditors on financial statements, but the review of internal controls and operating procedures is the full job of internal auditors. The internal auditors are intimately involved with the controls. They therefore have a great deal to offer an audit committee in appraising the company's operations. Thus, as audit committees mature, they have promoted the improved status and effectiveness of the internal audit function.

Obviously, for the internal audit department to provide assistance to audit committees, the internal auditors will require a high degree of independence. That independence will be in direct relation to the status of the director of internal auditing in the enterprise and the charter the director is given by both management and the board. That is made clear in the proposed Standards for the Professional Practice of Internal Auditing, which was approved by the Board of Directors of the Institute of Internal Auditors in June 1978. (See Appendix B.) The pertinent portions of Section 100, Independence, of the Standards are as follows:

110 Organizational Status

The organizational status of the internal auditing department should be sufficient to permit the accomplishment of its audit responsibilities.

.01 Internal auditors should have the support of management and of the board of directors so that they can gain the cooperation of auditees and perform their work free from interference.

.1 The director of the internal auditing department should be responsible to an individual in the organization with sufficient authority to promote independence and to ensure broad audit coverage, adequate consideration of audit reports, and appropriate action on audit recommendations.

.2 The director should have direct communication with the board. Regular communication with the board helps assure independence and provides a means for the board and the director to keep each other informed on matters of mutual interest.

.3 Independence is enhanced when the board concurs in the appointment or removal of the director of the internal auditing department.

.4 The purpose, authority, and responsibility of the internal auditing department should be defined in a formal written document (charter). The director should seek approval of the charter by management as well as acceptance by the board. The charter should (*a*) establish the department's position within the organization; (*b*) authorize access to records, personnel, and physical properties relevant to the performance of audits; and (*c*) define the scope of internal auditing activities.

.5 The director of internal auditing should submit annually to management for approval and to the board for its information a summary of the department's audit work schedule, staffing plan, and financial budget. The director should also submit all significant interim changes for approval and information. Audit work schedules, staffing plans, and financial budgets should inform management and the board of the scope of internal auditing work and of any limitations placed on the scope.

.6 The director of internal auditing should submit activity reports to management and to the board annually or more frequently as necessary. Activity reports should highlight significant audit findings and recommendations and should inform management and the board of any significant deviations from approved audit work schedules, staffing plans, and financial budgets, and the reasons for them.

Internal auditors in different environments report organizationally to different levels within the enterprise. Some report directly to the board of directors. That is particularly true in the case of financial institutions. Others report to the head of the accounting function and have no dealings with the board.

In general, however, as indicated by the Institute's Standards, the desideratum is a "solid line" relation with an executive high enough in the management hierarchy to insure independence of the activities to be audited and a "dotted line" relation with the board of directors through the audit committee.

Because the solid-line–dotted-line relations can place some constraints on auditors, the Mautz and Neumann study disclosed that, where audit committees existed, provision was often made for the nonofficer members of the board to meet independently with the internal auditors. The reason is not hard to understand. With the eyes of the SEC upon them, boards of directors do not want to be caught by unpleasant surprises. They need a clear line of communication with the group within the organization that is professional and objective and has a clear right of access to all assets, records, and personnel in the organization.

Where the audit scope has not been constrained, a competent internal audit staff should have a broader and more intimate knowledge of operations and control systems than any other group in the organization. Such a staff can be a great comfort to an audit committee. As stories of computer fraud become more common, audit committees are asking increasingly pointed questions about the adequacy of controls. The liability for material losses may well become the board's liability.

The responsibility for developing and maintaining systems of control to deter fraudulent practices is placed squarely upon the shoulders of management; it cannot be evaded. Management has line authority over its operations; it must therefore be accountable for whatever occurs within its operations. It is axiomatic that responsibility carries with it accountability. Certainly, management will look to the internal auditor for assistance, but it cannot thrust full responsibility for the prevention and detection of fraud upon the internal auditor.

As we pointed out in Chapter 1, neither the internal auditor nor any other control agency in the organization can be an insurer against fraud. To expect that would be as unrealistic as expecting the legal department in a company to insure it against the filing of law suits and to guarantee that any suits filed against the company will be success- . fully defended. Yet the internal auditor must accept certain responsibilities with respect to fraud, and they are spelled out in the "Standards for the Professional Practice of Internal Auditing," as follows:

280 **Due Professional Care**

Internal auditors should exercise due professional care in performing internal audits.

.01 Due professional care calls for the application of the care and skill expected of a reasonably prudent and competent internal auditor in the same or similar circumstances. Professional care should, therefore, be appropriate to the complexities of the audit being performed. In exercising due professional care, internal auditors should be alert to the possibility of intentional wrongdoing, errors and omissions, inefficiency, waste, ineffectiveness, and conflicts of interest. They should also be alert to those conditions and activities where irregularities are most likely to occur. In addition, they should identify inadequate controls and recommend improvement to promote compliance with acceptable procedures and practices.

.02 Due care implies reasonable care and competence, not infallibility or extraordinary performance. Due care requires the auditor to conduct examinations and verifications to a reasonable extent, but does not require detailed audits of all transactions. Accordingly, the internal auditor cannot give absolute assurance that noncompliance or irregularities do not exist. Nevertheless, the possibility of material irregularities or noncompliance should be considered whenever the internal auditor undertakes an internal auditing assignment.

.03 When an internal auditor suspects wrongdoing, the appropriate authorities within the organization should be informed. The internal auditor may recommend whatever investigation is considered necessary in the circumstances. Thereafter, the auditor should follow up to see that the internal auditing department's responsibilities have been met.

It should be pointed out that section 280.03 calls upon the internal auditor, when he suspects wrongdoing, to notify "appropriate authorities within the organization." And the Introduction to the Standards specifically states that the "organization . . . [includes] . . . management and the board of directors." Thus the internal auditor is not restricted to members of management in reporting suspicions.

This, then, raises a significant point: How should the internal auditor deal with management fraud? The specter of management fraud is pervasive, and the sins of the managers will be visited upon members of the board of directors. It is incumbent upon members of the board and upon internal auditors to be thoroughly aware of the many faces and methods of management fraud and how they can be protected against. That is the purpose of the next section.

Nature of Management Fraud

Management fraud is not necessarily synonymous with fraud as defined by the courts. Management fraud, as considered here, embraces the deceptions managers practice to benefit themselves in any way, not solely by lining their pockets. In many cases management fraud is practiced just to make a manager look good—to make it appear that his unit, division, or company has met established goals when in fact it has not.

Management fraud is often practiced successfully because of the fiduciary status managers have in the organization. By reason of their position, managers command respect; their motives are rarely questioned by the external auditors; and their explanations are usually accepted.

In decentralized organizations particularly, division presidents, vice presidents, and general managers have almost complete authority. Corporate executives judge them on the basis of reported performance, and the reports can be made to tell stories that do not accord with the facts. Similarly, presidents of corporations can deceive the board of directors by concealing material facts, by duping the external auditors, and by either restricting the scope of internal auditors or dispensing with the internal audit function altogether.

Management fraud masquerades in a great many disguises. It has been found in overstatements of inventory, acceptance of inferior goods in collusion with suppliers, delays of key expenditures to show a healthy financial position, overstatements of receivables, records of fictitious sales, and understatements of liabilities. Here is one example, related to the author by a group of consultants who specialize in unearthing management fraud.[20]

> A conglomerate, with about $1 billion in sales, arranged to divest itself of a profit center engaged in distributing rolls of sheet metal. The company acquiring the profit center asked for and received a certified statement of inventory on hand. The conglomerate's external auditors certified the statement, which reported $14 million of sheet stock.
>
> But the external auditors had been duped. Actually, there had been a huge inventory shortage. The accounting department manager had taken the inventory, had determined the exact amount of shortage, and had known how much of the records to falsify. His people had prepared inventory tags and delivered them to the external auditors. The auditors had verified the amount of the stock shown on those tags and had then deposited them in a box in the conference room they used during the audit. The manager added spurious tags to the box at night. Because there was little time to prepare the large number of tags needed to "build up" the inventory, some of them were made to show rolls of sheet stock weighing as much as 50,000 pounds. He also substituted new inventory reconciliation lists to tie in to the total tags, both valid and spurious.
>
> When the sale of the division was consummated, the buyer took its own inventory and found it short by about $6 million. Understandably incensed, the buyer rescinded the sale. After the conglomerate took back the profit center, its chief executive officer sent for the consultants.
>
> In their preliminary survey, these investigators converted $14 million of sheet stock into cubic feet. Then they compared that volume with the available space in the warehouse. They found that it could not have possibly held that volume of sheet; it was far too small. To confirm the lack of reasonableness of the inventory taking, the consultants scanned the inventory tags and found those with weights of up to 50,000 pounds. They then went to the warehouse and examined the forklift trucks employed to move the rolls of sheet stock. Not one of the trucks could possibly lift over 3,000 pounds. Rolls of stock, therefore, could not exceed 3,000 pounds.
>
> The consultants verified purchases of the material reported in inventory and found that purchase orders supported an inventory of about 30 mil-

lion pounds. Yet the reported inventory totaled about 50 million pounds. Obviously, the records had been falsified. Armed with these clues, the consultants started interrogating people and soon obtained a confession from the accounting manager.

He had puffed the value of the inventory to show exceptional performance. He felt compelled to do so in order to meet forecasts by a wildly optimistic profit center general manager. The consultants' findings resulted in a settlement of nearly $1 million from the external auditing firm, because its auditors failed to detect the spurious tags, and a claim of over $10 million under the fidelity bond.

Why Management Fraud Occurs

Managers are pushed into fraud by forces that can be external or internal. The pressures may come from superiors who set impossible goals. Since the goals cannot be met fairly, some managers falsify records and reports to make it appear that they have achieved them. Other managers may have an itch to outperform all others, to exceed past performance, to be given a coveted promotion, or to gain a better bonus. And if their reach exceeds their grasp, they resort to deception. Some of the reasons behind management fraud are as follows:

□ Managers may make rash statements that paint them into a corner. A president may forecast unrealistically high profits to financial analysts. To make the forecast come true, the president may demand distortions in the financial statements that are made to sound plausible to the external auditors and are kept from the board of directors.

□ Autonomous divisions may distort facts to hold off divestment. Their reports may show glowing performance not supported by the facts.

□ Incompetent managers may deceive in order to survive. Good managers keep abreast of change; poor ones may have to distort reported facts to give the appearance of good performance.

□ Managers may distort performance reports to receive larger bonuses. When the size of a reward is based on the size of reported numbers, managers may succumb to temptation if they feel they can escape detection.

□ Ambition may force managers to show superior short-range performance with no concern for long-range growth. Good current returns may be shown by curtailing needed research, reducing maintenance of plant and equipment, and replacing good, well-paid people with poorly paid hacks. But over the long term, the business may be ruined.

□ Unscrupulous managers may serve conflicting interest, as when a president of a company owns a supplier organization from which he requires his buyers to purchase goods at inflated costs.

Each of those reasons exists in abundance in the business world, but like an ever-present virus, they multiply to cause serious illness when the body's guards are down. Corporate illness strikes when superiors do not insist on good business practices, do not know what is going on, and fail to see that reports are independently reviewed.

What to Do When Management Fraud Occurs

When management fraud is revealed, executive managers or boards of directors may take swift and drastic steps. The internal auditor who is called in to help determine the reasons for and the extent of the depredations should counsel against precipitant action. He should point out that the board must regard the matter as a business problem, not a legal one. For example:

□ Key personnel should not be dismissed before the problem is solved. First, there may be innocents among the guilty. Second, with the principals gone, it would be all the more difficult for investigators to obtain answers to their questions.

□ Losses should be kept to a minimum so that the corporation can assure the bonding company that all appropriate steps were taken to prevent extension of losses and to mitigate damages.

□ The corporation must look at the broader picture and not focus completely on the deception. It must be concerned with the organization's loss of credibility, with premiums on new fidelity insurance, and with the impact on new insurance coverage. Besides, the corporation should be able to point out to the insurance company that steps are being taken to see that there will be no recurrences.

□ The corporation should be concerned with disruption to its business. When troops of auditors and investigators descend on a profit center, the effect may be devastating. An executive should be assigned to coordinate the efforts of all groups involved in the investigation. The groups would likely include:

□ External auditors to perform so-called heavy reviews of financial reports.

□ Internal auditors to analyze operating records and support in-house investigators or investigative consultants.

□ Legal counsel to make sure of disclosures at appropriate times, to evaluate legal aspects of recoveries under any fidelity bonds, and to recommend legal action against the culpable parties.

□ Investigative consultants to interrogate witnesses and to advise internal auditors which avenues to explore and what information to obtain and analyze.

Symptoms of Management Fraud

Internal auditors must expand the scope of their concern to protect the enterprise, to the extent they can, from the results of management fraud. They should be aware of the indicators of management fraud and know where to focus their attention when it occurs. When reasonable suspicions are aroused, they should report them to corporate executives if the fraud involves subordinates or to the audit committee of the board if the fraud involves senior management. Here are some of the indicators:

- *Consistently late reports.* Fraudulent reports are often delayed so that the deceiver will know which data should be manipulated.
- *Managers who regularly assume subordinates' duties.* The managers may be carrying out detailed work to hide their own depredations.
- *Noncompliance with corporate directives and procedures.* One financial officer of a subsidiary postponed the installation of a standard cost system because he wanted to hide his serious cost problems.
- *Managers dealing in matters outside the scope of the profit center.* One division manager acted as a broker on products outside his division's assigned responsibilities. He needed the cash to hide other manipulations.
- *Payments to creditors supported by copies instead of originals.* In one company the mixture of originals and duplicates hid duplicate payments and kickbacks. The artful mixture fooled the external auditors. The company employed no internal auditors.
- *Negative debit memos.* At one profit center, credit memos were generated by the computer. When the financial officer wished to write off a credit memo, he issued a negative debit memo. The external auditors were dutifully provided with all the credit memos. They were not made aware of the debit memos. There was no internal audit organization.

The control of management fraud begins with an environment and control system created by the top people in the enterprise: senior management and the board of directors. The control system should include a qualified internal auditing organization with a broad charter and a comprehensive audit program. In a proper environment, competent internal auditors can take steps to see that appropriate systems of control have been installed and to alert senior management and the board whenever the controls are not adequate or are not functioning as intended. Internal auditors should be concerned with the following matters:

- Established standards, both budgetary and statistical, and the investigation and reporting of all significant deviations.
- The use of quantitative and analytical techniques (times series analyses, regression and correlation analyses, and random sampling) to highlight aberrant behavior.
- Comparison of industry norms against company performance.
- Identification of critical process indicators: melt loss in smelting, death loss in feed lots, rework in manufacturing and assembly, and gross profit tests in buy-sell or retail operations.
- Analysis of operations that look too good as well as performance that does not meet standards.

Internal auditors will have to educate audit committees of the board on the protection the committees can obtain from competent internal audit service. It is a sad commentary that many members of boards of directors have little inkling of what the modern internal auditor can accomplish in the evaluation of control systems and the appraisal of the company performance. Many internal auditing departments have developed sophisticated programs to educate audit committees about their accomplishments and their potentials. They have enlisted the aid of the external auditors to help in the education process. Many successful audit committees have matured as a result of the team effort by the board, the internal auditors, and the external auditors.

The aroused interest in the internal auditing function will have significant benefits and will also carry heavier responsibilities. For the external auditor, a strong internal audit function will permit increased reliance on the systems of internal control—their adequacy and effectiveness. For audit committees the internal audit function will create a new window to the organization's operations to provide the committee with current information on the company's systems and problems and to offer it a source of special studies whenever needed. For the internal auditors the relationship will permit a broadened audit scope and opportunities for improved service to the organization, both management and the board.

But with the opportunities will come weightier obligations. Internal auditors will have to rise to the occasion. They will have to develop their understanding of the management process and their ability to make meaningful analyses in all areas of the organization and to provide management-oriented recommendations to improve operations and profitability. The internal auditing profession as a whole will have to elevate the quality of its practitioners by promoting special courses and programs in the universities that will turn out modern internal auditors who will be equipped to take their places as respected problem-solving partners to those who guide the destinies of their organizations.

CONCLUSION

Controlling is not a discrete function of management. It is directly related to the planning function, because nothing can be intelligently controlled until the objectives of the operation to be controlled are understood. And determining objectives is a planning function. That concept is significant for both managers and internal auditors. The guide recently published by Arthur Andersen & Co. underscores the relation in terms of internal accounting control.

Management by objectives is a control concept that has always had great promise. It is often improperly implemented, however, because those who seek to install it in an organization forget that the original concept was "management by objectives and self-control." The concept implies that those whose work is to be controlled should participate in setting the objectives and be given the means needed to control themselves. Although internal auditors have not often been involved in comprehensive audits of MBO programs, there is no reason that they cannot successfully carry them out.

Boards of directors have been placed under mounting pressure by the courts, the SEC, and the New York Stock Exchange to install audit committees made up of outside directors. Those pressures have created an increased awareness of the assistance internal auditors can give the boards of directors. To provide management-oriented assistance, however, the status of many internal auditors in organizations will have to be elevated and the scope of the audits broadened. As primary monitors of the organization's internal control systems, the internal auditors will be relied upon more and more by both the external auditors and the audit committees of boards of directors.

Although his responsibility for the prevention and detection of fraud is limited to due professional care, the internal auditor can be useful to executive management and to the board by being alert to the symptoms of fraud—both employee and management fraud—and by assisting professional investigators in determining the extent of any fraud that has been detected.

The sharpened focus on internal auditing is providing greater opportunities for internal audit staffs, but it is also placing greater responsibilities upon the staffs and heightening the demands for professionalism in the internal auditing function.

References

1. L. B. Sawyer, "The Anatomy of Control," *The Internal Auditor,* Spring 1964, pp. 16, 17.
2. "Performance Measurement—A Report to the House of Commons by the President of the Treasury Board," D.S.S. Publishing Centre, C.G.P.B. Building, Hull, Quebec, November 1977, p. 64.
3. Harold Koontz and Cyril O'Donnell, *Essentials of Management* (New York: McGraw-Hill, 1974), p. 362.
4. G. R. Terry, *Principles of Management* (Homewood, Ill.: Irwin, 1972), p. 559.
5. Koontz and O'Donnell, op. cit., p. 377.
6. R. J. Burke, "Methods of Resolving Superior-Subordinate Conflict: The Constructive Use of Subordinate Differences and Disagreements," *Organizational Behavior and Human Performance,* Vol. 5, No. 4, pp. 400–403.
7. Peter Drucker, *The Practice of Management* (New York: Harper & Row, 1954).
8. Peter Drucker, *Management: Tasks, Responsibilities, Practices* (New York: Harper & Row, 1974), pp. 430, 440.
9. J. G. Longenecker, *Principles of Management and Organizational Behavior* (Columbus, Ohio: Merrill, 1964), p. 527.
10. Drucker, *Management: Tasks,* p. 628.
11. R. L. Colegrove, "The Functions and Responsibilities of the Corporate Audit Committee," *The Internal Auditor,* June 1976, p. 17.
12. "Working Papers," The Institute of Internal Auditors, Vol. 1, No. 2, pp. 1, 3.
13. R. K. Mautz and F. L. Neumann, "Corporate Audit Committees: Policies and Practices," copyrighted by Ernst and Ernst, 1977, and issued in cooperation with The Institute of Internal Auditors, Inc.
14. G. R. Corey, "Some New Comments on the Directors' Audit Committee and the Audit Function," *The Internal Auditor,* October 1977, pp. 25, 26.
15. Mautz and Newmann, op. cit., pp. 68, 69.
16. "Statement of Responsibilities of Internal Auditor," The Institute of Internal Auditors, Inc., 1971.
17. Sawyer, op. cit., pp. 13, 18, 19.

18. L. B. Sawyer, "Internal Control—The Internal Auditor's Open Sesame," *The Internal Auditor,* January-February 1970, pp. 36, 43.
19. Mautz and Neumann, op. cit., p. 90.
20. Insight Services, Inc., Encino, Cal.
21. L. B. Sawyer, A. A. Murphy, and M. R. Crossley, "Management Fraud— the Insidious Specter," *The Internal Auditor,* April 1979.

Appendix A

Statement of Responsibilities of Internal Auditors

NATURE

Internal auditing is an independent appraisal activity within an organization for the review of operations as a service to management. It is a managerial control which functions by measuring and evaluating the effectiveness of other controls.

OBJECTIVE AND SCOPE

The objective of internal auditing is to assist all members of management in the effective discharge of their responsibilities by furnishing them with analyses, appraisals, recommendations and pertinent comments concerning the activities reviewed. Internal auditors are concerned with any phase of business activity in which they may be of service to management. This involves going beyond the accounting and financial records to obtain a full understanding of

Reprinted by permission of The Institute of Internal Auditors, Inc., 249 Maitland Ave., Altamonte Springs, Florida 32701.

the operations under review.   The attainment of this overall objective involves such activities as:

- Reviewing and appraising the soundness, adequacy, and application of accounting, financial, and other operating controls, and promoting effective control at reasonable cost
- Ascertaining the extent of compliance with established policies, plans, and procedures
- Ascertaining the extent to which company assets are accounted for and safeguarded from losses of all kinds
- Ascertaining the reliability of management data developed within the organization
- Appraising the quality of performance in carrying out assigned responsibilities
- Recommending operating improvements

RESPONSIBILITY AND AUTHORITY

The responsibilities of internal auditing in the organization should be clearly established by management policy.   The related authority should provide the internal auditor full access to all of the organization's records, properties, and personnel relevant to the subject under review.   The internal auditor should be free to review and appraise policies, plans, procedures, and records.

The internal auditor's responsibilities should be:

- To inform and advise management, and to discharge this responsibility in a manner that is consistent with the Code of Ethics of The Institute of Internal Auditors
- To coordinate internal audit activities with others so as to best achieve the audit objectives and the objectives of the organization

In performing their functions, internal auditors have no direct responsibilities for nor authority over any of the activities reviewed.   Therefore, the internal audit review and appraisal does not in any way relieve other persons in the organization of the responsibilities assigned to them.

INDEPENDENCE

Independence is essential to the effectiveness of internal auditing.   This independence is obtained primarily through organizational status and objectivity:

- The organizational status of the internal auditing function and the support accorded to it by management are major determinants of its range and value.   The head of the internal auditing function, therefore, should be responsible to an officer whose authority is sufficient to assure both a broad range of audit coverage and the adequate consideration of and effective action on the audit findings and recommendations.

□ Objectivity is essential to the audit function. Therefore, internal auditors should not develop and install procedures, prepare records, or engage in any other activity which they would normally review and appraise and which could reasonably be construed to compromise the independence of the internal auditor. The internal auditor's objectivity need not be adversely affected, however, by determining and recommending standards of control to be applied in the development of the systems and procedures being reviewed.

The Statement of Responsibilities of Internal Auditors was originally issued by the Institute of Internal Auditors in 1947. The continuing development of the profession has resulted in three revisions: 1957, 1971, and 1976. The current statement embodies the concepts previously established and includes such changes as are deemed advisable in light of the present status of the profession.

Appendix B

Standards for the Professional Practice of Internal Auditing

INTRODUCTION

Internal auditing is an independent appraisal function established within an organization to examine and evaluate its activities as a service to the organization. The objective of internal auditing is to assist members of the organization in the effective discharge of their responsibilities. To this end, internal auditing furnishes them with analyses, appraisals, recommendations, counsel, and information concerning the activities reviewed.

The members of the organization assisted by internal auditing include those in management and the board of directors. Internal auditors owe a responsibility to both, providing them with information about the adequacy and effectiveness of the organization's system of internal control and the quality of performance. The information furnished to each may differ in format and detail, depending upon the requirements and requests of management and the board.

The internal auditing department is an integral part of the organization and functions under the policies established by management and the board. The statement of purpose, authority, and responsibility (charter) for the internal auditing department, approved by management and accepted by the board, should be consistent with these *Standards for the Professional Practice of Internal Auditing.*

The charter should make clear the purposes of the internal auditing department, specify the unrestricted scope of its work, and declare that auditors are to have no authority or responsibility for the activities they audit.

Throughout the world internal auditing is performed in diverse environments and within organizations which vary in purpose, size, and structure. In addition, the laws and customs within various countries differ from one another. These differences may affect the practice of internal auditing in each environment. The implementation of these *Standards,* therefore, will be governed by the environment in which the internal auditing department carries out its assigned responsibilities. But compliance with the concepts enunciated by these *Standards* is essential before the responsibilities of internal auditors can be met.

"Independence," as used in these *Standards,* requires clarification. Internal auditors must be independent of the activities they audit. Such independence permits internal auditors to perform their work freely and objectively. Without independence, the desired results of internal auditing cannot be realized.

In setting these *Standards,* the following developments were considered:

1. Boards of directors are being held increasingly accountable for the adequacy and effectiveness of their organizations' systems of internal control and quality of performance.
2. Members of management are demonstrating increased acceptance of internal auditing as a means of supplying objective analyses, appraisals, recommendations, counsel, and information on the organization's controls and performance.
3. External auditors are using the results of internal audits to complement their own work where the internal auditors have provided suitable evidence of independence and adequate, professional audit work.

In the light of such developments, the purposes of these *Standards* are to:

1. Impart an understanding of the role and responsibilities of internal auditing to all levels of management, boards of directors, public bodies, external auditors, and related professional organizations
2. Establish the basis for the guidance and measurement of internal auditing performance
3. Improve the practice of internal auditing

The *Standards* differentiate among the varied responsibilities of the organization, the internal auditing department, the director of internal auditing, and internal auditors.

The five general *Standards* are expressed in italicized statements in upper case. Following each of these general *Standards* are specific standards expressed in italicized statements in lower case. Accompanying each specific standard are guidelines describing suitable means of meeting that standard. The *Standards* encompass:

1. The independence of the internal auditing department from the activities audited and the objectivity of internal auditors
2. The proficiency of internal auditors and the professional care they should exercise
3. The scope of internal auditing work
4. The performance of internal auditing assignments
5. The management of the internal auditing department

The *Standards* and the accompanying guidelines employ three terms which have been given specific meanings. These are as follows:

□ The term *board* includes boards of directors, audit committees of such boards, heads of agencies or legislative bodies to whom internal auditors report, boards of governors or trustees of nonprofit organizations, and any other designated governing bodies of organizations.
□ The terms *director of internal auditing* and *director* identify the top position in an internal auditing department.
□ The term *internal auditing department* includes any unit or activity within an organization which performs internal auditing functions.

100 INDEPENDENCE

INTERNAL AUDITORS SHOULD BE INDEPENDENT OF THE ACTIVITIES THEY AUDIT.

.01 Internal auditors are independent when they can carry out their work freely and objectively. Independence permits internal auditors to render the impartial and unbiased judgments essential to the proper conduct of audits. It is achieved through organizational status and objectivity.

110 Organizational Status

The organizational status of the internal auditing department should be sufficient to permit the accomplishment of its audit responsibilities.
.01 Internal auditors should have the support of management and of the board of directors so that they can gain the cooperation of auditees and perform their work free from interference.
　.1 The director of the internal auditing department should be responsible to an individual in the organization with sufficient authority to promote independence and to ensure broad audit cover-

age, adequate consideration of audit reports, and appropriate action on audit recommendations.

.2 The director should have direct communication with the board. Regular communication with the board helps assure independence and provides a means for the board and the director to keep each other informed on matters of mutual interest.

.3 Independence is enhanced when the board concurs in the appointment or removal of the director of the internal auditing department.

.4 The purpose, authority, and responsibility of the internal auditing department should be defined in a formal written document (charter). The director should seek approval of the charter by management as well as acceptance by the board. The charter should (a) establish the department's position within the organization; (b) authorize access to records, personnel, and physical properties relevant to the performance of audits; and (c) define the scope of internal auditing activities.

.5 The director of internal auditing should submit annually to management for approval and to the board for its information a summary of the department's audit work schedule, staffing plan, and financial budget. The director should also submit all significant interim changes for approval and information. Audit work schedules, staffing plans, and financial budgets should inform management and the board of the scope of internal auditing work and of any limitations placed on that scope.

.6 The director of internal auditing should submit activity reports to management and to the board annually or more frequently as necessary. Activity reports should highlight significant audit findings and recommendations and should inform management and the board of any significant deviations from approved audit work schedules, staffing plans, and financial budgets, and the reasons for them.

120 Objectivity

Internal auditors should be objective in performing audits.

.01 Objectivity is an independent mental attitude which internal auditors should maintain in performing audits. Internal auditors are not to subordinate their judgment on audit matters to that of others.

.02 Objectivity requires internal auditors to perform audits in such a manner that they have an honest belief in their work product and that no significant quality compromises are made. Internal auditors are not to be placed in situations in which they feel unable to make objective professional judgments.

.1 Staff assignments should be made so that potential and actual conflicts of interest and bias are avoided. The director should periodically obtain from the audit staff information concerning potential conflicts of interest and bias.

.2 Internal auditors should report to the director any situation in which a conflict of interest or bias is present or may reasonably be inferred. The director should then reassign such auditors.

.3 Staff assignments of internal auditors should be rotated periodically whenever it is practicable to do so.

.4 Internal auditors should not assume operating responsibilities. But if on occasion management directs internal auditors to perform nonaudit work, it should be understood that they are not functioning as internal auditors. Moreover, objectivity is presumed to be impaired when internal auditors audit any activity for which they had authority or responsibility. This impairment should be considered when reporting audit results.

.5 Persons transferred to or temporarily engaged by the internal auditing department should not be assigned to audit those activities they previously performed until a reasonable period of time has elapsed. Such assignments are presumed to impair objectivity and should be considered when supervising the audit work and reporting audit results.

.6 The results of internal auditing work should be reviewed before the related audit report is released to provide reasonable assurance that the work was performed objectively.

.03 The internal auditor's objectivity is not adversely affected when the auditor recommends standards of control for systems or reviews procedures before they are implemented. Designing, installing, and operating systems are not audit functions. Also, the drafting of procedures for systems is not an audit function. Performing such activities is presumed to impair audit objectivity.

200 PROFESSIONAL PROFICIENCY

INTERNAL AUDITS SHOULD BE PERFORMED WITH PROFICIENCY AND DUE PROFESSIONAL CARE.

.01 Professional proficiency is the responsibility of the internal auditing department and each internal auditor. The department should assign to each audit those persons who collectively possess the necessary knowledge, skills, and disciplines to conduct the audit properly.

The Internal Auditing Department

210 Staffing

The internal auditing department should provide assurance that the technical proficiency and educational background of internal auditors are appropriate for the audits to be performed.

.01 The director of internal auditing should establish suitable criteria of education and experience for filling internal auditing positions, giving due consideration to scope of work and level of responsibility.

.02 Reasonable assurance should be obtained as to each prospective auditor's qualifications and proficiency.

220   Knowledge, Skills, and Disciplines

The internal auditing department should possess or should obtain the knowledge, skills, and disciplines needed to carry out its audit responsibilities.

.01 The internal auditing staff should collectively possess the knowledge and skills essential to the practice of the profession within the organization. These attributes include proficiency in applying internal auditing standards, procedures, and techniques.

.02 The internal auditing department should have employees or use consultants who are qualified in such disciplines as accounting, economics, finance, statistics, electronic data processing, engineering, taxation, and law as needed to meet audit responsibilites. Each member of the department, however, need not be qualified in all of these disciplines.

230   Supervision

The internal auditing department should provide assurance that internal audits are properly supervised.

.01 The director of internal auditing is responsible for providing appropriate audit supervision. Supervision is a continuing process, beginning with planning and ending with the conclusion of the audit assignment.

.02 Supervision includes:

.1 Providing suitable instructions to subordinates at the outset of the audit and approving the audit program

.2 Seeing that the approved audit program is carried out unless deviations are both justified and authorized

.3 Determining that audit working papers adequately support the audit findings, conclusions, and reports

.4 Making sure that audit reports are accurate, objective, clear, concise, constructive, and timely

.5 Determining that audit objectives are being met

.03 Appropriate evidence of supervision should be documented and retained.

.04 The extent of supervision required will depend on the proficiency of the internal auditors and the difficulty of the audit assignment.

.05 All internal auditing assignments, whether performed by or for the internal auditing department, remain the responsibility of its director.

The Internal Auditor

240   Compliance with Standards of Conduct

Internal auditors should comply with professional standards of conduct.

.01 The *Code of Ethics* of The Institute of Internal Auditors sets forth

standards of conduct and provides a basis for enforcement among its members. The *Code* calls for high standards of honesty, objectivity, diligence, and loyalty to which internal auditors should conform.

250 Knowledge, Skills, and Disciplines

> *Internal auditors should possess the knowledge, skills, and disciplines essential to the performance of internal audits.*

.01 Each internal auditor should possess certain knowledge and skills as follows:

.1 Proficiency in applying internal auditing standards, procedures, and techniques is required in performing internal audits. Proficiency means the ability to apply knowledge to situations likely to be encountered and to deal with them without extensive recourse to technical research and assistance.

.2 Proficiency in accounting principles and techniques is required of auditors who work extensively with financial records and reports.

.3 An understanding of management principles is required to recognize and evaluate the materiality and significance of deviations from good business practice. An understanding means the ability to apply broad knowledge to situations likely to be encountered, to recognize significant deviations, and to be able to carry out the research necessary to arrive at reasonable solutions.

.4 An appreciation is required of the fundamentals of such subjects as accounting, economics, commercial law, taxation, finance, quantitative methods, and computerized information systems. An appreciation means the ability to recognize the existence of problems or potential problems and to determine the further research to be undertaken or the assistance to be obtained.

260 Human Relations and Communications

> *Internal auditors should be skilled in dealing with people and in communicating effectively.*

.01 Internal auditors should understand human relations and maintain satisfactory relationships with auditees.

.02 Internal auditors should be skilled in oral and written communications so that they can clearly and effectively convey such matters as audit objectives, evaluations, conclusions, and recommendations.

270 Continuing Education

> *Internal auditors should maintain their technical competence through continuing education.*

.01 Internal auditors are responsible for continuing their education in order to maintain their proficiency. They should keep informed about improvements and current developments in internal auditing standards, procedures, and techniques. Continuing education may be ob-

tained through membership and participation in professional societies; attendance at conferences, seminars, college courses, and in-house training programs; and participation in research projects.

280 Due Professional Care

Internal Auditors should exercise due professional care in performing internal audits.

.01 Due professional care calls for the application of the care and skill expected of a reasonably prudent and competent internal auditor in the same or similar circumstances. Professional care should, therefore, be appropriate to the complexities of the audit being performed. In exercising due professional care, internal auditors should be alert to the possibility of intentional wrongdoing, errors and omissions, inefficiency, waste, ineffectiveness, and conflicts of interest. They should also be alert to those conditions and activities where irregularities are most likely to occur. In addition, they should identify inadequate controls and recommend improvements to promote compliance with acceptable procedures and practices.

.02 Due care implies reasonable care and competence, not infallibility or extraordinary performance. Due care requires the auditor to conduct examinations and verifications to a reasonable extent, but does not require detailed audits of all transactions. Accordingly, the internal auditor cannot give absolute assurance that noncompliance or irregularities do not exist. Nevertheless, the possibility of material irregularities or noncompliance should be considered whenever the internal auditor undertakes an internal auditing assignment.

.03 When an internal auditor suspects wrongdoing, the appropriate authorities within the organization should be informed. The internal auditor may recommend whatever investigation is considered necessary in the circumstances. Thereafter, the auditor should follow up to see that the internal auditing department's responsibilities have been met.

.04 Exercising due professional care means using reasonable audit skill and judgment in performing the audit. To this end, the internal auditor should consider:

   .1 The extent of audit work needed to achieve audit objectives

   .2 The relative materiality or significance of matters to which audit procedures are applied

   .3 The adequacy and effectiveness of internal controls

   .4 The cost of auditing in relation to potential benefits

.05 Due professional care includes evaluating established operating standards and determining whether those standards are acceptable and are being met. When such standards are vague, authoritative interpretations should be sought. If internal auditors are required to interpret or select operating standards, they should seek agreement with auditees as to the standards needed to measure operating performance.

300 SCOPE OF WORK

*THE SCOPE OF THE INTERNAL AUDIT SHOULD ENCOMPASS
THE EXAMINATION AND EVALUATION OF THE ADEQUACY
AND EFFECTIVENESS OF THE ORGANIZATION'S SYSTEM OF
INTERNAL CONTROL AND THE QUALITY OF PERFORMANCE
IN CARRYING OUT ASSIGNED RESPONSIBILITIES.*

.01 The scope of internal auditing work, as specified in this standard, encompasses what audit work should be performed. It is recognized, however, that management and the board of directors provide general direction as to the scope of work and the activities to be audited.

.02 The purpose of the review for adequacy of the system of internal control is to ascertain whether the system established provides reasonable assurance that the organization's objectives and goals will be met efficiently and economically.

.03 The purpose of the review for effectiveness of the system of internal control is to ascertain whether the system is functioning as intended.

.04 The purpose of the review for quality of performance is to ascertain whether the organization's objectives and goals have been achieved.

.05 The primary objectives of internal control are to ensure:

.1 The reliability and integrity of information

.2 Compliance with policies, plans, procedures, laws, and regulations

.3 The safeguarding of assets

.4 The economical and efficient use of resources

.5 The accomplishment of established objectives and goals for operations or programs

310 Reliability and Integrity of Information

Internal auditors should review the reliability and integrity of financial and operating information and the means used to identify, measure, classify, and report such information.

.01 Information systems provide data for decision making, control, and compliance with external requirements. Therefore, internal auditors should examine information systems and, as appropriate, ascertain whether:

.1 Financial and operating records and reports contain accurate, reliable, timely, complete, and useful information.

.2 Controls over record keeping and reporting are adequate and effective.

320 Compliance with Policies, Plans, Procedures, Laws and Regulations

Internal auditors should review the systems established to ensure compliance with those policies, plans, procedures, laws, and regulations which could

have a significant impact on operations and reports, and should determine whether the organization is in compliance.

.01 Management is responsible for establishing the systems designed to ensure compliance with such requirements as policies, plans, procedures, and applicable laws and regulations. Internal auditors are responsible for determining whether the systems are adequate and effective and whether the activities audited are complying with the appropriate requirements.

330 Safeguarding of Assets

Internal auditors should review the means of safeguarding assets and, as appropriate, verify the existence of such assets.

.01 Internal auditors should review the means used to safeguard assets from various types of losses such as those resulting from theft, fire, improper or illegal activities, and exposure to the elements.

.02 Internal auditors, when verifying the existence of assets, should use appropriate audit procedures.

340 Economical and Efficient Use of Resources

Internal auditors should appraise the economy and efficiency with which resources are employed.

.01 Management is responsible for setting operating standards to measure an activity's economical and efficient use of resources. Internal auditors are responsible for determining whether:

.1 Operating standards have been established for measuring economy and efficiency.

.2 Established operating standards are understood and are being met.

.3 Deviations from operating standards are indentified, analyzed, and communicated to those responsible for corrective action.

.4 Corrective action has been taken.

.02 Audits related to the economical and efficient use of resources should identify such conditions as:

.1 Underutilized facilities

.2 Nonproductive work

.3 Procedures which are not cost justified

.4 Overstaffing or understaffing

350 Accomplishment of Established Objectives and Goals for Operations or Programs

Internal auditors should review operations or programs to ascertain whether results are consistent with established objectives and goals and whether the operations or programs are being carried out as planned.

.01 Management is responsible for establishing operating or program objectives and goals, developing and implementing control procedures, and accomplishing desired operating or program results. Internal auditors should ascertain whether such objectives and goals conform with those of the organization and whether they are being met.

.02 Internal auditors can provide assistance to managers who are developing objectives, goals, and systems by determining whether the underlying assumptions are appropriate; whether accurate, current, and relevant information is being used; and whether suitable controls have been incorporated into the operations or programs.

400 PERFORMANCE OF AUDIT WORK

AUDIT WORK SHOULD INCLUDE PLANNING THE AUDIT, EXAMINING AND EVALUATING INFORMATION, COMMUNICATING RESULTS, AND FOLLOWING UP.

.01 The internal auditor is responsible for planning and conducting the audit assignment, subject to supervisory review and approval.

410 Planning the Audit

Internal auditors should plan each audit.

.01 Planning should be documented and should include:

.1 Establishing audit objectives and scope of work

.2 Obtaining background information about the activities to be audited

.3 Determining the resources necessary to perform the audit

.4 Communicating with all who need to know about the audit

.5 Performing, as appropriate, an on-site survey to become familiar with the activities and controls to be audited, to identify areas for audit emphasis, and to invite auditee comments and suggestions

.6 Writing the audit program

.7 Determining how, when, and to whom audit results will be communicated

.8 Obtaining approval of the audit work plan

420 Examining and Evaluating Information

Internal auditors should collect, analyze, interpret, and document information to support audit results.

.01 The process of examining and evaluating information is as follows:

.1 Information should be collected on all matters related to the audit objectives and scope of work.

.2 Information should be sufficient, competent, relevant, and useful to provide a sound basis for audit findings and recommendations.

  ☐ *Sufficient* information is factual, adequate, and convincing so that a prudent, informed person would reach the same conclusions as the auditor.

□ *Competent* information is reliable and the best attainable through the use of appropriate audit techniques.

□ *Relevant* information supports audit findings and recommendations and is consistent with the objectives for the audit.

□ *Useful* information helps the organization meet its goals.

.3 Audit procedures, including the testing and sampling techniques employed, should be selected in advance, where practicable, and expanded or altered if circumstances warrant.

.4 The process of collecting, analyzing, interpreting, and documenting information should be supervised to provide reasonable assurance that the auditor's objectivity is maintained and that audit goals are met.

.5 Working papers that document the audit should be prepared by the auditor and reviewed by management of the internal auditing department. These papers should record the information obtained and the analyses made and should support the bases for the findings and recommendations to be reported.

430 Communicating Results

Internal auditors should report the results of their audit work.

.1 A signed, written report should be issued after the audit examination is completed.   Interim reports may be written or oral and may be transmitted formally or informally.

.2 The internal auditor should discuss conclusions and recommendations at appropriate levels of management before issuing final written reports.

.3 Reports should be objective, clear, concise, constructive, and timely.

.4 Reports should present the purpose, scope, and results of the audit; and, where appropriate, reports should contain an expression of the auditor's opinion.

.5 Reports may include recommendations for potential improvements and acknowledge satisfactory performance and corrective action.

.6 The auditee's views about audit conclusions or recommendations may be included in the audit report.

.7 The director of internal auditing or designee should review and approve the final audit report before issuance and should decide to whom the report will be distributed.

440 Following Up

Internal auditors should follow up to ascertain that appropriate action is taken on reported audit findings.

.01 Internal auditing should determine that corrective action was taken and is achieving the desired results, or that management or the board has assumed the risk of not taking corrective action on reported findings.

500 MANAGEMENT OF THE INTERNAL AUDITING DEPARTMENT

THE DIRECTOR OF INTERNAL AUDITING SHOULD PROPERLY MANAGE THE INTERNAL AUDITING DEPARTMENT.

.01 The director of internal auditing is responsible for properly managing the department so that:
  .1 Audit work fulfills the general purposes and responsibilities approved by management and accepted by the board.
  .2 Resources of the internal auditing department are efficiently and effectively employed.
  .3 Audit work conforms to the *Standards for the Professional Practice of Internal Auditing.*

510 Purpose, Authority, and Responsibility

The director of internal auditing should have a statement of purpose, authority, and responsibility for the internal auditing department.
.01 The director of internal auditing is responsible for seeking the approval of management and the acceptance by the board of a formal written document (charter) for the internal auditing department.

520 Planning

The director of internal auditing should establish plans to carry out the responsibilities of the internal auditing department.
.01 These plans should be consistent with the internal auditing department's charter and with the goals of the organization.
.02 The planning process involves establishing:
  .1 Goals
  .2 Audit work schedules
  .3 Staffing plans and financial budgets
  .4 Activity reports
.03 The goals of the internal auditing department should be capable of being accomplished within specified operating plans and budgets and, to the extent possible, should be measurable. They should be accompanied by measurement criteria and targeted dates of accomplishment.
.04 *Audit work schedules* should include (a) what activities are to be audited; (b) when they will be audited; and (c) the estimated time required, taking into account the scope of the audit work planned and the nature

and extent of audit work performed by others. Matters to be considered in establishing audit work schedule priorities should include (a) the date and results of the last audit; (b) financial exposure; (c) potential loss and risk; (d) requests by management; (e) major changes in operations, programs, systems, and controls; (f) opportunities to achieve operating benefits; and (g) changes to and capabilities of the audit staff. The work schedules should be sufficiently flexible to cover unanticipated demands on the internal auditing department.

.05 Staffing plans and financial budgets, including the number of auditors and the knowledge, skills, and disciplines required to perform their work, should be determined from audit work schedules, administrative activities, education and training requirements, and audit research and development efforts.

.06 Activity reports should be submitted periodically to management and to the board. These reports should compare (a) performance with the department's goals and audit work schedules and (b) expenditures with financial budgets. They should explain the reasons for major variances and indicate any action taken or needed.

530   Policies and Procedures

The director of internal auditing should provide written policies and procedures to guide the audit staff.

.01   The form and content of written policies and procedures should be appropriate to the size and structure of the internal auditing department and the complexity of its work. Formal administrative and technical audit manuals may not be needed by all internal auditing departments. A small internal auditing department may be managed informally. Its audit staff may be directed and controlled through daily, close supervision and written memoranda. In a large internal auditing department, more formal and comprehensive policies and procedures are essential to guide the audit staff in the consistent compliance with the department's standards of performance.

540   Personnel Management and Development

The director of internal auditing should establish a program for selecting and developing the human resources of the internal auditing department.

.01   The program should provide for:

.1 Developing written job descriptions for each level of the audit staff
.2 Selecting qualified and competent individuals
.3 Training and providing continuing educational opportunities for each internal auditor
.4 Appraising each internal auditor's performance at least annually
.5 Providing counsel to internal auditors on their performance and professional development

550 External Auditors

The director of internal auditing should coordinate internal and external audit efforts.

.01 The internal and external audit work should be coordinated to ensure adequate audit coverage and to minimize duplicate efforts.

.02 Coordination of audit efforts involves:

.1 Periodic meetings to discuss matters of mutual interest

.2 Access to each other's audit programs and working papers

.3 Exchange of audit reports and management letters

.4 Common understanding of audit techniques, methods, and terminology

560 Quality Assurance

The director of internal auditing should establish and maintain a quality assurance program to evaluate the operations of the internal auditing department.

.01 The purpose of this program is to provide reasonable assurance that audit work conforms with these Standards, the internal auditing department's charter, and other applicable standards. A quality assurance program should include the following elements:

.1 Supervision

.2 Internal reviews

.3 External reviews

.02 *Supervision* of the work of the internal auditors should be carried out continually to assure conformance with internal auditing standards, departmental policies, and audit programs.

.03 *Internal reviews* should be performed periodically by members of the internal auditing staff to appraise the quality of the audit work performed. These reviews should be performed in the same manner as any other internal audit.

.04 *External reviews* of the internal auditing department should be performed to appraise the quality of the department's operations. These reviews should be performed by qualified persons who are independent of the organization and who do not have either a real or an apparent conflict of interest. Such reviews should be conducted at least once every three years. On completion of the review, a formal, written report should be issued. The report should express an opinion as to the department's compliance with the *Standards for the Professional Practice of Internal Auditing* and, as appropriate, should include recommendations for improvement.

Index